Maternal a

Cont   *...challenges*

Edited by

Victoria Hall Moran and Fiona Dykes

QUAY
BOOKS

A division of MA Healthcare Ltd

Note

Health care practice and knowledge are constantly changing and developing as new research and treatments, changes in procedures, drugs and equipment become available.

The author and publishers have, as far as is possible, taken care to confirm that the information complies with the latest standards of practice and legislation.

Quay Books Division, MA Healthcare Ltd, St Jude's Church, Dulwich Road, London SE24 0PB

British Library Cataloguing-in-Publication Data
A catalogue record is available for this book

© MA Healthcare Limited 2006

ISBN 1 85642 285 2

Printed by Gutenberg Press Ltd, Gudja Road, Tarxien, Malta

Contents

Contents

Contributors

Susan Battersby
Senior Lecturer, University of Sheffield
I am a midwife employed as a Lecturer in Midwifery at the University of Sheffield. My areas of particular interest are infant feeding and sociology. I have had a special interest in breastfeeding for many years and am currently reading for a PhD, focusing upon conflicting paradigms within breastfeeding. I was the founder of the Sheffield Infant Feeding Initiative in 1989 and I am still an active member of the Sheffield Breastfeeding Forum. I have been the key researcher in the evaluation of four breastfeeding peer support programmes, three of which were funded by the Department of Health.

Fiona Dykes
Reader in Maternal and Infant Health, University of Central Lancashire
I lead the Maternal and Infant Nutrition and Nurture Unit (MAINN) at the University of Central Lancashire, Preston. My research in this field focuses upon the social, political and economic influences upon infant feeding practices from a global perspective. I have a particular interest in the infant feeding experiences of women within socially excluded settings. I have worked on WHO and UNICEF projects and have conducted research funded by the Government Department of Health and the National Institute for Health and Clinical Excellence (NICE).

Victoria Hall Moran
Senior Lecturer, University of Central Lancashire
I am a nutritional physiologist in the Maternal and Infant Nutrition and Nurture Unit (MAINN). My research has focused on evaluating the knowledge, attitudes and skills of health practitioners and voluntary supporters in supporting breastfeeding women, particularly those belonging to socially excluded communities. I teach on a range of infant and young child feeding modules. I am the founder and a Senior Editor of the international and interdisciplinary journal *Maternal and Child Nutrition* (Blackwell Publishing).

Darren Hart
Research Midwife, St Thomas' Hospital, London
As a nurse and midwife I have always been interested in research and have had the opportunity to be involved in a study at St Thomas' Hospital for the past four years. I am currently conducting a randomised controlled trial monitoring the effects of eating and drinking during labour. Through this investigation I intend to discover the physiological effects of women eating and drinking in labour. I am also conducting a study which examines the views of women who have eaten or not eaten during their labour. More recently, I have been involved in the implementation of the NHS-wide learning and development tool.

Sally Inch
Infant feeding specialist, Oxford Radcliffe NHS Trust
I am a midwife, employed since 1997 as the infant feeding specialist, UNICEF UK Baby Friendly Initiative, and Human Milk Bank co-ordinator for the Oxford Radcliffe NHS Trust. I run a drop-in breastfeeding clinic at the John Radcliffe Maternity hospital. I assisted the three midwife-led units in the Oxford Radcliffe Trust to obtain the WHO/UNICEF Global Baby Friendly Hospital Initiative award in 2000. For the last 20 years I have written widely on aspects of birth and (particularly) breastfeeding, and was both a contributor to and editor of *Successful Breastfeeding*, the RCM Handbook now in its third edition and published in 11 languages. During 2001–2003, I worked with the University of Coventry on the Department of Health-funded multi-centred randomised controlled trial – *the Best Start Breastfeeding Project*.

Mavis Kirkham
Professor of Midwifery, University of Sheffield
I have conducted clinical midwifery and midwifery research since 1971. My clinical commitments include shifts in a rural birth centre and a few home births each year. My research is mainly within WICH (Women's Informed Childbearing and Health) Research Group, where I am currently supervising research on the childbearing experiences of groups of women who experience social exclusion and vulnerability. We are also completing a series of research projects on staff retention in NHS midwifery. I have a close research link with Doncaster which has included involvement with Breastfriends since the project started.

Gill Rapley
Deputy Programme Director, UNICEF UK Baby Friendly Initiative
I am currently responsible for the development and delivery of the education programmes offered throughout the UK by the UNICEF UK Baby Friendly Initiative. My background includes health visiting and midwifery, as well as voluntary breastfeeding counselling. I have longstanding interests both in supporting breastfeeding and in infant development. My studies for a Masters degree

enabled me to combine these two interests in a piece of research into the way babies are introduced to solid foods.

Magda Sachs
Breastfeeding Supporter
I am a Breastfeeding Supporter with The Breastfeeding Network (BfN) and have recently completed my PhD, an ethnographic study of the effects of routine weighing on breastfeeding women, at University of Central Lancashire, Preston. I received my BA from King's College, Cambridge. In 1986 my first child was born. I then trained as a volunteer breastfeeding supporter, and have continued in this work to the present. I spent seven years as a tutor, training others as volunteer supporters. I lecture on a variety of breastfeeding issues. My particular interest in HIV and infant feeding dates from 1999. Since 2000, I have been a member of AnotherLook, a group devoted to discussion and debate on this issue.

Angela Sherridan
Community breastfeeding co-ordinator
I am a community breastfeeding co-ordinator at Barnsley Primary Care Trust and prior to that I was an Infant Feeding Co-ordinator and Midwife at Doncaster and Bassetlaw NHS Foundation Hospital Trust. I worked as a project co-ordinator for the Breastfriends Doncaster Project for over four years. I thoroughly enjoyed working with the mothers involved in the project and learnt a great deal from their experiences and have continued to develop peer support groups in my present role. I am currently completing an MPhil at The University of Sheffield, exploring mothers' reflections upon working as volunteers in their community supporting other mothers to breastfeed.

Mary Smale
Breastfeeding Counsellor and Tutor
I have worked as a National Childbirth Trust volunteer with breastfeeding women for around 30 years using counselling skills, offering information and support for decision-making. I have facilitated training for voluntary NCT workers, health professionals and, increasingly, peer supporters, using a person-centred model. This integrates sound information from research and women's own lives with an awareness of the power of personal, vicarious and cultural experiences for those being helped and for their helpers. I am interested in learning from women how they manage significant others, including health professionals, to achieve the breastfeeding experience they want.

Alison Spiro
Health Visitor and Breastfeeding Counsellor
I trained as an NCT Breastfeeding Counsellor 26 years ago and then became a tutor, training counsellors both locally and nationally, and I still work as a volunteer NCT counsellor. I have worked as a Health Visitor in the London Borough of Harrow for 20 years and have audited breastfeeding rates and trained NHS staff locally and nationally. I have been interested in why women in the UK find it difficult to sustain this natural way of feeding their children, and this led me to conduct research for a PhD, using anthropological methods, in an attempt to gain greater understanding about the cultural origins and motivations for breastfeeding.

Daniella Thornton
Breastfeeding peer supporter and trainer
I was a breastfed baby myself and chose to breastfeed my three children. I got involved with Breastfriends in 2000 and worked as a volunteer for four years. During this time I worked as a peer supporter. I also trained to go into schools to talk about breastfeeding and trained to become a peer support trainer. In June 2004, I started work as Breastfriends New Generation Co-ordinator for Doncaster & Bassetlaw NHS Foundation Trust. My role is to support teenagers in their choice to breastfeed and to train teenagers up to the age of 20 to become peer supporters.

Nutrition and nurture: introducing the challenges

Victoria Hall Moran and Fiona Dykes

Promoting and supporting optimal maternal and infant nutrition is a major international health issue across the globe. Traditionally, maternal and infant nutrition was viewed as the biochemical transfer of nutrients from mother to child. While this biomedical understanding is crucial, there is a growing need to understand and address the political, socio-cultural and economic influences upon eating, feeding and nutrition. It is being increasingly recognised that despite the international agenda, maternal eating and infant feeding practices relate substantially to local cultural norms and constraints. This book utilises a socio-biological perspective; that is, a perspective that recognises complex interactions between political, socio-cultural and biological factors in food and health. It illuminates some of the many challenges and considerable controversies inherent in the field.

The diversity within this book reflects the vast pool of expertise involved in compiling the book. The contributors to this book represent the disciplines of anthropology, breastfeeding peer support, health visiting, midwifery, nursing, nutritional physiology and voluntary accredited breastfeeding supporters and counsellors from the Breastfeeding Network and the National Childbirth Trust. It has been an enormous pleasure to collaborate with so many experienced and passionate practitioners within the field of maternal and infant nutrition and nurture.

In Chapter 1, the editors, Fiona Dykes and Victoria Hall Moran, explore the complex and synergistic relationships and interactions between socio-economic and physiological factors in relation to notions of transmitted nutritional deprivation from mother to child. To illustrate the socio-biological perspective we use as our starting point Barker's hypothesis on fetal origins of disease and transmitted nutritional deprivation. We outline the political economy of health perspective that supports us in balancing Barker's arguments with a sociological perspective. We discuss Barker's biologically-focused series of arguments in the light of growing understandings related to sociological influences upon health and well-being. In order to bring together the issues associated with the relationship between sociological factors, *in utero* environment and later health, we discuss three areas. Firstly, we explore the relationship between transmitted nutritional deprivation and low birth weight. Secondly, we discuss the relationship between low birth weight and later health, taking coronary heart disease as a key example. Finally, we consider some of the implications of this debate for health professionals working in the field of maternal and infant health.

In Chapter 2, Victoria Hall Moran discusses issues of nutrition during pregnancy, with particular reference to adolescent pregnancy. A socio-biological perspective is used to evaluate the multiple influencing factors that each play a role in the eating behaviour and subsequent nutritional status of the pregnant adolescent. Theoretical models to help understand adolescent behaviour and identify the ways in which adolescents can be supported to make dietary changes are discussed. The latest research regarding nutrition in adolescents is evaluated, revealing that, although improvements appear to have been made in recent years, adolescents' nutritional intakes still fall considerably below current dietary recommendations. This has particularly negative implications for adolescents who become pregnant. Socio-economic differences in nutrient intake and nutritional status among this population are explored, identifying those of low socio-economic status to be at particular risk of poor nutrition. Victoria discusses the influences on pregnant adolescents' food choices, together with suggestions for achieving significant and sustainable improvements in this vulnerable population.

In Chapter 3, Darren Hart discusses the controversial topic of eating and drinking during labour, assessing both the benefits and the risks. Darren places the topic in an historical context, enabling us to understand the origin of policies on nutrition in labour in maternity units today. Although maternity unit policies appear to have become more liberal in recent years and most endorse a risk selection process, there remains varied opinion as to what constitutes 'risk' for eating and drinking in labour. Darren suggests that the positive changes have come about, in part, due to the rise in midwifery-led care and the collaborative efforts of health professionals and service users in campaigning against the aggressive management policies that govern normal labour in modern maternity units.

In Chapter 4, Sally Inch explores the history of infant feeding practices, and documents the rise and fall of the popularity of breastfeeding as the preferred way to feed an infant. Sally discusses the composition of breast milk and the impact of maternal diet and combines the discussion of biological data with socio-economic influences. A discussion of breast milk substitutes follows, describing the problems with the manufacture, use and delivery of breast milk substitutes, and why attempts to imitate the substances in breast milk fail. Issues related to milk banks as an alternative substitute for mothers' own milk are discussed. Sally argues that infant feeding decisions appear to be heavily constrained by social circumstances, with formula (or mixed) feeding being the cultural norm. Thus, any changes to the socially accepted norm within a community will happen slowly at best, and then only when the appropriate support infrastructures are put in place and sustained.

In Chapter 5, Magda Sachs explores the controversies and global challenges that relate to infant feeding in HIV+ women. She commences with a review of the international literature on HIV transmission through breast milk and explores the implications of exclusive versus partial breastfeeding in comparison to no breastfeeding with regard to transmission risk. Magda then explores the international policy recommendations and associated counselling issues. Finally, she focuses specifically upon the complex ethical, legal, policy and practice issues in the UK with regard to screening, diagnosis, prevention and treatment. The chapter highlights the ways in which HIV has challenged breastfeeding as an activity and illuminated the low cultural value of breastfeeding in the West and the ways in which people are ready to abandon breastfeeding in the face of uncertainty.

In Chapter 6, Sue Battersby focuses upon the development of societal attitudes towards breastfeeding in general and more specifically attitude formation in midwives. Sue commences by defining attitudes and then exploring ways in which attitudes to breastfeeding and infant feeding develop. She illuminates some of the influences upon cultural perceptions of the human breast. Sue then explores, in depth, the development of midwives' attitudes to infant feeding practices and the role of personal experiences in that development. Finally, Sue presents a synopsis of a workbook developed at Sheffield University that enables midwives to explore and deconstruct their own attitudes towards infant feeding.

In Chapter 7, Alison Spiro presents her anthropological work with Hindu and Jain Gujarati women living in Harrow, England. She firstly discusses attitudes to breastfeeding and decision-making which takes place within the context of family life and through close interaction and consultation with kin and close friends. Alison highlights the ways in which relationships between other close female kin and the baby begin the network of interdependency that constitutes Gujarati kinship. This contrasts with the supervaluation of the mother–baby bond in western societies and the way in which independence rather than interdependence is aspired to. She then focuses upon the embodiment of breastfeeding, highlighting the ways in which western notions regarding the body fundamentally differ from those of Gujarati women. Finally, Alison examines the groups' religious beliefs and associated rituals related to infant feeding.

In Chapter 8, Mavis Kirkham, Angela Sherridan, Daniella Thornton and Mary Smale describe the story of the development of a breastfeeding peer support project in a socially deprived town in the north of England. They commence with a description of the origins of 'Breastfriends Doncaster' and then proceed to describe the training programme that they developed and delivered, based on principles of person-centred counselling approaches advocated and utilised within the National Childbirth Trust. The comprehensive evaluation programme, part funded by the government Department of Health (DH), is described. Mavis and the team then discuss the subsequent development, again with DH funding, of a schools education programme utilising the Breastfriends. The ways in which the project has been subsequently sustained and developed are discussed and finally the team present their reflections upon the project.

In Chapter 9, Gill Rapley discusses the phenomenon of baby-led weaning. She begins by discussing how the recommendations for the introduction of complementary foods have changed over the last decade. The concept of developmental readiness, i.e. letting the infant indicate his or her readiness for solid foods, is central to the argument. Baby-led, as opposed to carer-led, weaning could have potential implications for later health and well-being and could also help prevent feeding and eating disorders. Gill argues that infants are fully equipped to follow a path to family meals, without fuss and at the right time, which will enhance both their development and their nutrition.

In Chapter 10, Fiona Dykes and Victoria Hall Moran argue that any understanding of maternal and infant nutrition needs to take account of the embodied, emotional and social nature of eating and feeding, the ways in which women negotiate these in a range of cultural contexts and the macropolitical influences upon women in relation to their dietary and infant feeding practices. We commence with an overview of the development of some of the specific disciplinary perspectives within the field; the biomedical, social constructionist and political economic perspectives. We then advocate a positive move to disrupt disciplinary boundaries that have, in many cases, persisted with regard to maternal and infant nutrition, eating and feeding. We summarise the ways in which the chapters have illustrated the synergies between perspectives to produce new ways of seeing within the field of maternal and infant nutrition and nurture. We then discuss ways of integrating perspectives and emphasise the need for practitioners in the field to become highly reflexive and to recognise the need for a strategic, political approach to the field. We argue that a socio-biological synthesis of perspectives has both informed and indeed emerged from this book.

Since the ultimate goal of maternal and child nutrition is the optimal health and development for both mother and child, it is helpful to envisage the topic in the context of a Life Course Health Development framework. This is a conceptual approach to understanding the interrelating adverse and beneficial factors that influence health and development, thereby enabling an integrated implementation and assessment of related research and policy (Halfon and Hochstein, 2002; Aggett and Hall Moran, 2005). Drawing on research from the fields of public health, medicine, human development and social sciences, the Life Course Health Development framework shows that:

- Health is a consequence of multiple determinants operating in nested genetic, biological, behavioural, social and economic contexts that change as a person develops.
- Health development is an adaptive process composed of multiple transactions between these contexts and the bio-behavioural regulatory systems that define human functions.
- Different health trajectories are the product of cumulative risk and protective factors and other influences that are programmed into bio-behavioural regulatory systems during critical and sensitive periods.
- The timing and sequence of biological, psychological, cultural and historical events and experiences influence the health and development of both individuals and populations (Halfon and Hochstein, 2002, p. 433).

This framework, therefore, allows us to understand how nutritional risk factors, protective factors and early life experiences affect an individual's long-term well-being. With an improved understanding of health development, it may be possible to manipulate early risk factors and protective factors and help us shift our emphasis from managing the outcomes of these factors to the promotion of earlier, more effective preventative strategies and interventions focused on maximising optimal health and development. The chapters in this book, by drawing together socio-political, economic, cultural, physiological and psychological aspects of maternal and infant nutrition, eating and feeding, support us in applying the Life Course Health Development framework to this area of health.

References

Aggett, P. and Hall Moran, V. (2005) Editorial. *Maternal and Child Nutrition*, **1**(1), 1.

Halfon, N. and Hochstein, M. (2002) Life Course Health Development: an integrated framework for developing health, policy, and research. *The Millbank Quarterly*, **80**(3), 433–79.

CHAPTER I

Transmitted nutritional deprivation from mother to child

A socio-biological perspective

Fiona Dykes and Victoria Hall Moran

Introduction

In this chapter, we explore the complex and synergistic relationships and interactions between socio-economic and physiological factors in relation to notions of transmitted nutritional deprivation from mother to child. To illustrate the socio-biological perspective, we use as our starting point Barker's hypothesis on fetal origins of disease and transmitted nutritional deprivation (Barker, 1992, 1994). We outline the political economy of health perspective that supports us in balancing Barker's arguments with a sociological perspective. We discuss Barker's biologically focused series of arguments in the light of growing understandings related to sociological influences upon health and well-being. In order to bring together the issues related to the relationship between sociological factors, *in utero* environment and later health we discuss three areas. Firstly, we explore the relationship between transmitted nutritional deprivation and low birth weight. Secondly, we discuss the relationship between low birth weight and later health, taking coronary heart disease as a key example. Finally, we consider some of the implications of this debate for health professionals working in the field of maternal and infant health.

The fetal origins of adult disease hypothesis

Barker (1992, 1994) proposed the fetal origins of adult disease hypothesis. He argued that inadequate nutrition, health and development in young females, whilst *in utero* and subsequently, is the origin of high death rates from coronary heart disease (CHD) in the next generation. This nutritional deprivation, he argued, jeopardises women's reproductive capacity, thereby prejudicing their ability to appropriately nourish their babies *in utero*. He asserts that the fetus who is undernourished *in utero* adapts by undergoing physiological and metabolic changes which provide for survival. These changes can lead to a significantly higher risk of developing CHD in later life. This work has been subsequently developed further, leading to the conclusion by proponents of Barker's hypothesis that low birth weight related to reduced intra-uterine growth increases rates of CHD and type 2 diabetes in later life (Osmond *et al.*, 1993; Law and Shiell, 1996; Eriksson *et al.*, 1999; Gillman and Rich-Edwards, 2000).

The initial evidence for these assumptions developed from medical geographical and historical data. Mapping of CHD showed that its incidence was twice as high in poorer areas in England and Wales and among low income groups, for example northern industrial towns and the poorer rural areas in the north and west. A direct geographical parallel existed between CHD deaths during the 1960s to 1970s and past infant death rates in the 1920s, expressed as standardised mortality rates (Barker and Osmond, 1986, 1992a).

Barker (1994) noted that other common diseases which had the same geographical parallel were chronic bronchitis, stomach cancer and chronic rheumatic heart disease. This might be expected because they are related to poor social conditions. However, as their rates declined as the 20th century progressed, CHD rates increased. The close geographical paralleling between past infant mortality and current CHD induced mortality appeared to suggest that detrimental environmental influences *in utero* and in infancy, related to poor living standards, directly raised the risk of CHD.

CHD is claimed to be a disease of 'affluence', but it appears to be a disease that is more prevalent in lower socio-economic occupational groups in affluent societies (Wilkinson, 1996). Barker (1994) and Cade *et al.* (1992) claim that adult lifestyle factors alone are less important and reliable predictors of CHD than previously thought. They argue that it does not seem to follow that past infant mortality correlates with adult lifestyle factors associated with CHD, because smoking, known to be a risk factor for CHD, is highly correlated with lung cancer and the geographical distribution of lung cancer is very different from that of past infant mortality.

Barker (1994) draws upon other supporting studies, for example that of Rose (1964) who noted that the siblings of individuals with CHD were twice as likely to have a stillbirth or infant mortality than a control group of adults who did not have a sibling with the disease. This, Barker argues, makes a case for a weaker stock having increased susceptibility to this disease. Barker (1994) also claims support from the well known study by Marmot *et al.* (1984) which demonstrated that employees of short stature, claimed by Barker to be a mark of a poorer *in utero* environment, were more likely to die from CHD.

Barker (1994) cites the work of Woolfe (1947) who studied approximately 1 million deaths from CHD, demonstrating that there was a high association with neonatal mortality rather than post neonatal mortality earlier in the century, suggesting *in utero* influences. He noted a strong relationship between neonatal mortality and the percentage of unemployed men in England and Wales and attributed this to the influence of poverty upon maternal nutrition.

Osmond *et al.* (1992) and Barker (1994) utilised studies of migrants and English people who have moved to a different area to claim that it is the birth place rather than the place where the person moved to that has more influence over disease rates, although they do acknowledge that it is difficult to know how much of this data is confounded by the different characteristics of those who move compared with those who do not.

From these studies, Barker (1994) concludes that the research focus into CHD should be shifted to *in utero* environments. He proposes a hypothesis of programming of the fetus by *in utero* nutrition. He examines evidence from numerous animal studies that show that lowering of the calorie and/or protein intake of the mother in pregnancy impairs *in utero* growth and that the time in the gestation when the dietary deficiency occurs influences the type of growth impairment. This is a concept of 'sensitive' or 'critical' periods. He proposes several mechanisms by which *in utero* under-nutrition may influence growth and subsequent health: by altering gene expression; reducing cell numbers; creating imbalance between cell types; altering organ structure and functioning; and influencing of hormonal patterns.

Barker (1994) draws upon available evidence to elucidate the effects of uterine under-nutrition upon the fetus and subsequent health. In early pregnancy, the fetus undergoes development and differentiation, while the pattern changes to one of rapid growth in mid- to late pregnancy. Thus under-nutrition early in pregnancy and/or throughout the pregnancy appears to retard embryonic growth, leading to permanent down-regulation of growth generally, i.e. weight, length and head circumference. This proportionate (symmetrical) smallness then appears to be set following the birth with a limited ability to stray from the set tracking pattern displayed on the centile charts. This, Barker argues, is a biological protection to enable the individual to survive on a restricted diet. Under-nutrition which occurs in mid-pregnancy appears to influence interactions between the fetus and the placenta, resulting in a baby who is thin and has a small head circumference at birth. There is a 'catch up' in weight during the first year of life. On the other hand, under-nutrition which starts in later pregnancy results in a disproportionate (asymmetrical) growth retardation. It seems that blood and nutrients are diverted to the brain (brain sparing) at the expense of the abdominal organs and trunk size. Length may also be compromised, resulting in shortness for age. The liver is growing rapidly and is particularly vulnerable at this time. As a result, impaired liver development, blood clotting and cholesterol metabolism may be jeopardised and the blood pressure (BP) elevated. Cholesterol levels are raised from childhood into adulthood in asymmetrical low birth weight (LBW) individuals. Raised clotting factors associated with later CHD may be found in individuals who showed asymmetrical LBW. Weight remains reduced at one year of life. Under-nutrition *in utero* also influences placental and fetal growth hormones and insulin, leading to permanent changes in metabolism and growth patterns.

To add to the evidence, Barker draws upon epidemiological studies (Barker *et al.*, 1989; Barker, 1994). These examined archives from the early 19th century on males from Hertfordshire and showed a statistically significant association between birth weight and deaths due to CHD. Follow-up studies reveal a similar relationship in women (Osmond *et al.*, 1993).

Similar studies in Sheffield demonstrated that low ponderal index, i.e. low weight to length ratio (thinness) and/or low head circumference, led to increased CHD (Barker, 1994). Osmond *et al.* (1993) claim that due to a more rapid growth potential males are more vulnerable to CHD. Barker (1994) also notes that a high placental weight:birthweight ratio is significant in predicting CHD. The placenta appears to attempt to compensate for under-nutrition by enlarging.

Studies in Sheffield and Preston by Barker *et al.* (1990) and Barker (1994) are claimed to show clear evidence that adult raised BP is related to LBW babies. Elevated BP is a marker for potential CHD, as is high serum cholesterol. After controlling for birth weight and current body size, weight gain in infancy was not a factor, suggesting *in utero* growth as being important. The association between LBW and high BP were independent of later alcohol consumption and body mass. Large placental size to birth weight was a risk factor for elevated BP.

Barker (1994) claims that in support of his hypothesis of transmitted nutritional deprivation are studies that demonstrate that women who have LBW babies are more likely to have been LBW themselves, and likewise their mothers before that, i.e. there is a multigenerational effect (Ounsted and Scott, 1986; Emanuel *et al.*, 1992; Leff *et al.*, 1992; Wang *et al.*, 1995). Barker interprets this evidence as indicative of a maternal regulated growth constraint set in motion when the mother herself was *in utero*, which outweighs simple genetic determination of size by the mother's own size. This is described by Elliot and O'Reilly (1995, p. 14) as the 'intergenerational cycle of growth failure'.

Barker (1994) supports the deduction by Gluckman *et al.* (1990) from embryo transfer research that growth *in utero* is primarily controlled by the *in utero* environment, i.e. maternal and placental factors, secondarily by maternal genes, and to a lesser extent by fetal genes. The father's genes, he argues, appear to come in to play once the baby is born.

Barker (1994) uses the evidence from the Dutch hunger war (Stein and Susser, 1975; Lumey, 1992), to substantiate this argument. The work of Lumey (1992) demonstrated that mothers on starvation diets during the third trimester of pregnancy had reduced birth weight babies, but it was the mothers exposed to famine during their own early and mid *in utero* life who had babies of lower birth weight than mothers not exposed. This, Barker (1994) argues, demonstrates that there is clearly more involved than a simple lack of *in utero* transmission of nutrients. It points to transmitted impairment in the maternal physiology whereby the actual transferability of nutrients across the placenta (placental perfusion) is inadequate. The difficulty in separating maternal nutrition during pregnancy from placental perfusion is acknowledged by Barker (1994). The evidence from the Dutch hunger war is confusing, however, as mothers who were not exposed to *in utero* famine also had reduced birth weight babies (Lumey, 1992).

Barker (1994) claims that what emerges is that it is a woman's nutrition throughout life, including in her own *in utero* experience, that is more important in controlling the growth of her baby than nutrition during pregnancy. It is not, however, made clear as to what extent *in utero* and subsequent nutrition act independently (e.g. good *in utero* nutrition but poor subsequently or vice versa). He acknowledges that diet in pregnancy and its influence on birth weight is confounded by the interaction between the effects of diet and maternal physiology and metabolism.

Barker and Osmond (1992b) and Barker (1994) attempt to explore the social context of poor growth and subsequent growth by returning to a geographical and historical examination of three adjacent Lancashire towns; Burnley, Nelson and Colne. There were higher mortality rates in Burnley and Colne than in Nelson, which they attribute to differences in the health and physique of the mothers, Burnley and Colne women suffering from transmitted disadvantages of urban employment in the mills. Nelson women were largely rural migrants, were sturdier, healthier and more likely to breastfeed, and had better housing and sanitation. It is therefore argued that social class and income did not appear to be influential as they were similar in all three towns.

Ultimately Barker (1994) recommends that considerable importance should be attached to nutrition of young girls and women in order to protect the health of future generations. We now critique the above by incorporating a sociological perspective, in combination with some more recent arguments that challenge and/or expand upon the original Barker hypothesis. Firstly, it is important to emphasise that LBW (i.e. birth weight of 2.5 kg or below) may stem from intrauterine growth retardation leading to a small for gestational age baby (SGA) and/or preterm birth. As Kramer (1987) highlights, LBW stemming from compromised *in utero* growth retardation may have a different aetiology from LBW related to prematurity. As Wilcox (2001) argues, this adds enormous complexity to any analysis of the evidence, as SGA and prematurity are often considered together under the general 'umbrella' of low birth weight.

The developmental origins of adult disease

There has been growing recognition that early life events that might have long-term consequences span a broader period than just fetal life and consequently there is an increasing consensus that early life environmental factors must be incorporated into our understanding of the genesis of later health and disease (Gluckman *et al.*, 2005a). Support for the developmental origins of adult disease comes from an increasing understanding that environmental factors can have permanent effects on the organism through both developmental plasticity and teratogenic disruption of development, and that biological trade-offs between processes occur during the lifespan (e.g. rapid early growth is associated with reduced longevity).

The nature of these long-lasting responses to the environment may depend on when in development an environmental cue acts and how extreme the stressor is. Bateson *et al.* (2004) proposed that an extreme cue is likely to induce a developmental disruption, whereas a milder cue could lead to some other form of adaptive response, having either immediate consequences or predictive value. Gluckman *et al.* (2005b), however, argue that developmental disruption would be a flawed strategy in evolutionary terms and thus is unlikely to form the basis of the developmental origins of disease hypothesis. Rather, Gluckman *et al.* (2005b) suggest that later disease risk is dependent on the degree of match/mismatch between the environment predicted during the plastic (developmental) phase and the actual post-plastic (mature) phase environment. The greater the degree of mismatch between the predicted and actual mature environments, the greater the disturbance in physiology and the greater the risk of disease. Nutrition is a particularly important environmental cue. In particular, the phenomenon of 'maternal constraint' on fetal growth (which implicitly provides an upper limit of postnatal nutritional environment that humans have adapted for but which is now frequently exceeded) increases the risk of a mismatch between fetal and postnatal environment. Postnatally, the environment may not be as bad as predicted because constraint may mask the true state of the environment. Alternatively, if the infant is overfed or if the postnatal environment improves because of migration or better economic circumstances, this too could have the potential to lead to a greater degree of mismatch and, therefore, disease risk.

Gluckman *et al.* (2005a) argue that, while components of the epidemiological analyses have been challenged, there is strong evidence to suggest that developmental factors contribute to the later risk of metabolic disease (including insulin resistance, obesity and heart disease), as well as other conditions, such as osteoporosis, polycystic ovarian disease, chronic obstructive lung disease, cognitive decline, depression and schizophrenia.

A political economy of health perspective

Our critique is underpinned by a political economy of health perspective that focuses upon the relationships between capitalist modes of production, health and illness. These are interpreted in various ways by leading authors in this field (Frankenburg, 1980; Doyal and Pennell, 1981; Gray, 1993; Illich, 1995). Collectively, these authors illustrate the overwhelming contradictions between the goals of improving health and the imperatives of capital accumulation inherent within the capitalist mode of production. Health and health care practices therefore need to be understood in relation to the activities of powerful groups within society and power relationships that stem from them. Taking the food manufacturers as an example, as James (2005, p. 200) asserts:

> We are now in a position where the industries involved in the food chain, whether in agricultural technology, food production, processing, manufacturing or retailing, are all huge players. They are far more powerful than the tobacco industry and in practice have discovered the value of using the same techniques, i.e. obtaining political influence through selective party funding, recruiting pliant nutritionists, scientists and doctors, and employing major public health relations companies to cope with the media. So unsurprisingly, they are able to gain access at short notice to government ministers and indeed to presidents and prime ministers.

The political economy of health perspective, when set alongside the biomedical perspective, creates a shift in thinking towards issues related to unequal access to health care, the social organisation of health care and socio-economic divisions. It allows us to explore the social, political and economic roots of ill health within society and the need for socio-economic reform. This perspective enables us to consider the ways in which, despite growing knowledge of health indicators, we have not alleviated the overwhelming levels of morbidity and mortality occurring across the world (Doyal and Pennell, 1981; Gray, 1993).

Is it transmitted nutritional deprivation that primarily contributes to low birth weight ?

LBW is now recognised as a stable indicator of social inequalities and has remained stable at approximately 7% of all live births in the UK for several decades (Oakley, 1985; MacFarlane *et al.*, 2000). This is cause for considerable concern as LBW appears to be a major contributor to neonatal and infant mortality (Spencer, 2003). There is a clear association between social disadvantage and LBW babies (Olsen and Frische, 1993; Wilcox *et al.*, 1995; Van de Mheen, *et al.* 1998; Hodnett and Fredericks, 2003). However, Barker appears to argue that these effects manifest primarily via physiological or pathological routes after controlling for behavioural differences such as smoking (Barker, 1994; Godfrey *et al.*, 1996). To support this position, studies increasingly use sophisticated and robust methods to adjust for socio-economic factors, such as occupation, income, education, car ownership, smoking, physical activity, diet and childhood socio-economic status (Rich-Edwards *et al.*, 1997; Leon *et al.*, 1998). However, the appropriateness of certain socio-economic status indicators for health inequality remains controversial, particularly for women. It has been shown, for example, that the extent of health inequality in the community is influenced by the measure of social inequality used (Sacker *et al.*, 2000).

The strength of the patho-physiological argument is challenged somewhat by studies which point to the complex and broader socio-economic and culturally related influences on LBW (Olsen and Frische, 1993, Kogan, 1995, Wilcox *et al.*, 1995, Collins *et al.*, 2004, Grjibovski *et al.*, 2004). While evidence for a biologically-based inter-generationally transmitted nutritional deprivation is clear, the contribution of other factors that could affect birth weight needs to be highlighted. Kogan's (1995) categorisation of the causes of LBW into psychosocial, behavioural, environmental and physical factors provides a useful framework for this discussion.

Psychosocial factors

The complex nature of stress and anxiety and their influences upon health always need to be considered. Clear links have been established between maternal stress and anxiety and lower than average birth weight for gestational age (Hedegaard *et al.*, 1996; Zimmer-Gembeck and Helfand, 1996). For example, a recent prospective study carried out in the USA found that women with high psychosocial strain jobs had babies with birth weights 190 g lower than those born to mothers in low strain jobs or unemployed (95% CI = 48 g, 333 g) (Oths *et al.*, 2001). It has been indicated that the influence of maternal anxiety may be one mechanism by which the intrauterine environment contributes to later disease in children (Teixeira *et al.*, 1999).

One fascinating study by Edwards *et al.* (1994) in the USA provides an example of research that challenges arguments based on purely biomedical assumptions regarding transmitted nutritional deprivation. Prospective data was obtained from a longitudinal observational study designed to investigate nutritional, medical, biochemical, psychosocial, socio-economic, lifestyle and environmental factors that influenced pregnancy outcomes in a group of African American women during their pregnancies. This minority ethnic group consti-tuted a socially deprived section of the community. The incidence of LBW fell from 20.6% to 8.3% in women enrolled. This, it is hypothesised, was due, in part, to the participants' increased 'social coping' resulting from feeling sup-ported and indeed cared about by the sensitive researchers during the many face to face contacts and telephone calls (p. 1007S). This research was not intended to be one of introducing a social support intervention.

Edwards *et al.* (1994) argued that the high incidence of LBW was related to psychosocial stresses in this group. These included low income, poverty, high unemployment, poor housing, poor environment (crowded, noisy, polluted, crime ridden), lower quality social and public services, and racism. These stres-sors contributed to a loss of self-esteem and a sense of hopelessness. Edwards *et al.* (1994) found that the size of the social network of the participants was highly correlated with infant gestation and ponderal index. Infant birth weight was significantly positively correlated with self respect, efficacy, and a positive self attitude. The impact of the unintentional intervention in Edward *et al.*'s study demonstrates that when interventions to increase birth weight are tested it is crucial that the control group receive equal additional human contact.

Edwards *et al.* (1994) argue, based on psychoneuroimmunological theory (Geiser, 1989), that social support is related to health status, via behav-ioural, psychological, and biological routes. They hypothesise a complex web of interactions between psycho-social stress, the immune system, the endocrine system and amino acid utilisation and synthesis. Social support, they argue, enhances immuno-competence and reduces levels of cholesterol, adrenaline, noradrenaline and related hypertension. They relate this to the combined influences of release of stress and tension caused by external pres-sures, reduction in unhealthy behaviours and some dietary improvement. One inevitable weakness of the study was a failure to unravel the individual effects of each factor.

Salfield and Durward (1985) highlight similar causes of stress to those described by Edwards in unemployed families in the UK, noting that financial worries and difficulty getting out with small children can lead to depression, con-flict, guilt, tension, malaise, lack of energy and isolation. Fleming *et al.* (1987) demonstrate the clear relationship between chronic stress created by living in overcrowded housing conditions and heightened cardiovascular activity. Rutter and Quine (1990) also hypothesise that being in a low socio-economic group is detrimental to pregnancy outcomes via psycho-social risk factors.

McAnarney and Stevens-Simon (1990) refer to animal experiments and provide a useful analysis of the relationship between maternal stress and LBW. Firstly maternal stress, in addition to suppressing immunity, causes the release of adrenaline and noradrenaline – the fight or flight hormones – which in turn may reduce placental perfusion and lead to fetal growth impairment and/or preterm labour. Secondly, stress-related behaviours, such as smoking, have an indirect and additive effect upon lowering of *in utero* growth and preterm delivery. The same relationship in human studies is supported by the work of others who have demonstrated that low social support and high social stress were significantly related to low birth weight (Mutale *et al.*, 1991; Zimmer-Gembeck and Helfand, 1996; Norbeck *et al.*, 1997; Feldman *et al.*, 2000).

Behavioural factors

Attitudes and behaviour are inevitably influenced by social circumstances, with lower socio-economic status creating a culture in which deprivation, in its broader sense, becomes a lived experience. This situation is summarised by Rutter and Quine (1990, p. 563) who argue that deprivation contributes to an 'increase in negative life events, often with an absence of social support'. This, in turn, leads to emotional problems, including stress, anxiety, lowering of self-esteem and depression. Secondly, deprivation contributes to a reduced level of education and access to information and corresponding attitudes and beliefs that create a sense of helplessness (p. 563):

> The emotional and cognitive effects combine, we suggest, to produce a set of coping strategies which are characterised by learned helplessness and a willingness to take potentially hazardous risks. From coping strategies come behaviours and from behaviours come negative outcomes.

These assertions are supported by a clear relationship between family stress combined with low social support and addictive behaviours such as smoking (McCormick *et al.*, 1990; Sheehan, 1998). Smoking, when considered independently of social factors, is known to increase the risk of LBW (Olsen and Frische, 1993; McCormick *et al.*, 1990; Wilcox *et al.*, 1995; Zaren *et al.*, 1996; Zimmer-Gembeck and Helfand, 1996; Williams and Poulton, 1999). It provides a classic example of a behaviour that has a higher incidence in socially deprived communities and lower socio-economic occupational groups (McCormick *et al.*, 1990; Townsend *et al.*, 1992; Graham, 1996; Sheehan, 1998; Lumley *et al.*, 2004). Continued smoking and high daily consumption during pregnancy shows a strong association with social disadvantage, low income, high parity and being without a partner (Lumley *et al.*, 2004). It is clearly a behaviour that cannot be isolated from social, political and economic factors.

Like smoking, eating is also related to the socio-cultural, political and economic context. Eating behaviour is highly influenced by socio-economic occupational grouping status, with lower socio-economic groups eating a nutritionally inferior diet due to lack of knowledge and motivation and most importantly poverty (Dallison and Lobstein, 1995; Oppenheim and Harker, 1996; Wardle *et al.* 2000; Dowler *et al.*, 2001). Low income families, socially excluded groups and those living in deprived areas consume less fruit and vegetables and higher levels of fat, sugar and salt in their diets than higher social groups (Hunt *et al.*, 2000; Department of Health, 2003a). The recent National Diet and Nutrition Survey of adults aged 19–64 years illustrates that significant socio-economic differences in dietary intake continue to exist in the UK. Adults in households in receipt of benefits had lower intakes of energy, protein, fibre, riboflavin, vitamins B_6, B_{12}, C and E, folate and most minerals and ate fewer portions of fruit and vegetables than those who were not receiving benefits. In addition, women in households receiving benefits had lower intakes of vitamin A, total carotene and vitamin D than those not receiving benefits (Henderson *et al.*, 2003). A number of these macro- and micronutrients are, of course, essential to optimal fetal growth and development and therefore pregnancy outcome, as well as having an independent impact on diet-related disease risk in later life. Eating behaviour is also associated with health-compromising behaviours. For example, Keski-Rahkonen *et al.* (2003) reported that smoking, infrequent exercise, low education level, low family socio-economic status, higher BMI and more frequent alcohol use were associated with missing breakfast. (It is consistently reported that breakfast consumers have superior nutritional profiles and are more likely to meet nutrient intake recommendations than those who miss breakfast; Rampersaud *et al.*, 2005.)

Environmental factors

It is crucial to focus upon the broad environmental issues that influence health care, such as access to health care. It has long been recognised that for health care there is unequal quality of service and unequal uptake in relation to need, according to socio-economic status (Townsend *et al.*, 1992; Braveman and Tarimo, 2002; Kirkham *et al.*, 2002). Indeed, the availability of quality health provision tends to vary inversely with the need of the population served, a pattern described by Townsend *et al.* (1992, p. 277) as the 'Inverse Care Law'. This higher socio-economic occupational group centredness can be very disempowering for women from socially deprived settings (Oakley *et al.*, 1993).

Macintyre *et al.* (1993) categorise key aspects of local environment which tend to deteriorate as the social class of the occupants falls. These include the physical environment (for example air quality), home, work and play environments and socio-cultural features of the neighbourhood, affecting behaviour and reputation of the neighbourhood. These may directly or indirectly raise stress levels, undermine self-esteem and lower general and reproductive health.

Environmental factors may also contribute to the quality of an individual's diet, particularly in low-income populations. Block *et al.* (2004) found that, after taking into account various environmental confounders, fast-food restaurant density was independently correlated with low household income, suggesting that low-income populations have more convenient access to fast food, a factor associated with higher consumption of convenience foods (French *et al.*, 2000). Moreover, studies have suggested that low income households in poor central cities and sparsely populated rural areas often have less access to food stores and face higher prices for food, including fruits and vegetables, compared with other households (Kaufman, 1999; Dowler *et al.*, 2001). Such issues can significantly affect the quality and affordability of food available to low income consumers (Krebs-Smith and Kantor, 2001). The absence of adequate transport and therefore mobility can also be highly problematic for families with young children.

Physical factors

Birth weight is known to vary in accordance with infant sex, maternal age, height, parity and ethnicity (Polednak, 1989; Wilcox and Russell, 1990; Luke, 1994a,b,c; Fraser *et al.*, 1995; Rodriguez *et al.*, 1995; Wilcox *et al.*, 1995; WHO, 1995; Power *et al.*, 1996; Zimmer-Gembeck and Helfand, 1996; Zambrana *et al.*, 1999; Mohsin *et al.*, 2003). It has been found that, after controlling for confounding sociodemographic factors, adolescent mothers were significantly more likely to give birth to LBW babies (Fraser *et al.*, 1995) and infants born to young adolescents (<15 years) were twice as likely to be LBW (Lenders *et al.*, 2000) compared with infants born to older mothers. Power *et al.* (1996) note that LBW is more common in the first baby and thereafter is associated with high parity, itself a marker of low socio-economic grouping. Olsen and Frische (1993), in a large survey of Danish women, noted that women in the lower socio-economic groups were younger, smaller and had a higher pre-pregnancy weight. However, after controlling for these confounders they found a persistent relationship between low birth weight and low socio-economic status.

In summary, as Hytten (1990) asserts, there appears to be a complex package of deprivation and many of its components contribute to a reduced reproductive capacity and a raised incidence of low birth weight. We now move on to discuss the relationship between low birth weight and subsequent CHD.

Associations between low birth weight and coronary heart disease: a sociological perspective

There is ongoing debate as to whether the physical *in utero* and early child-hood conditions or lifelong socio-economic conditions exert the greatest influence upon later health in relation to pathologies such as CHD (Hall Moran and Dykes, 2003). Power *et al.* (1996) summarise the two main arguments. The first, Barker's (1994) predominantly biological explanation, emphasises the physical *in utero* environment as biologically programming an individual for certain pathologies with later environmental influences playing a more limited role.

The second argument referred to by Power (1996) stems from a sociological perspective, hypothesising that it is poor socio-economic conditions which predispose to LBW and although there is likely to be some *in utero* conditioning for later health, it is the continuing poor socio-economic conditions and lowered life chances that are largely responsible for adult disease. This emphasis upon a life cycle of deprivation and ill health is highlighted by Townsend *et al.* (1992). However, the second argument is often marginalised by the first within the bio-medical domain of health research.

Having already discussed Barker's biological explanation, we now focus upon the sociological perspective. There is growing evidence that it is a combination of childhood influences and adult factors which act synergistically to create conditions such as CHD (Ostberg and Vagero, 1991; Elford *et al.*, 1991, 1992; Bartley *et al.*, 1994; Nystrom Peck, 1994). Bartley *et al.* (1994) carried out a longitudinal prospective study on the 1958 birth cohort study and assessed the relationship between a range of indicators of social disadvantage for males at age 7, 11, 16 and 23 and their birth weight. They report a clear linear relationship between lower birth weight and greater socio-economic disadvantage at all stages of childhood and adolescence and state that this must be accounted for in identifying associations with adult diseases. They acknowledge Barker's evidence (1992) for a relationship between LBW and development of CHD, but claim that his assumptions are weakened by the absence of data on socio-economic circumstances during the 40 to 60+ intervening years. They also criticise Barker's claims that the relationship between birth weight and later CHD were unrelated to social class, noting the crudity of the social class measure for determining income and social conditions and recognising that the enormous social mobility of cohorts from the 1970s and 1980s makes social class in adulthood unreliable as an indicator of social class at birth.

Power *et al.* (1996) rigorously extend the analysis of the 1958 cohort, controlling for the known relationship between a mother's high parity related to low social class and the social class of her offspring in early adulthood. They draw the same conclusions; that low birth weight appears to be acting as a marker of a disadvantaged life trajectory and for subsequent socio-economic circumstances. Rahkonen *et al.* (1997) take this perspective one step further. They utilised data from a nationwide Finnish survey on living conditions. They separated economic from social problems during childhood and using logistic regression analysis found that the former was more strongly related to adult health. Social problems during childhood included conflicts, fears and alcohol-related problems in the family. Secondly, they found that socio-economic status during adulthood, measured by levels of education, was more strongly related to adult health than childhood socio-economic status as measured by the father's and the mother's education and living area.

This emphasis upon the economic status of the child's family is highlighted by Wilkinson (1996). He points out that, following the epidemiological transition, the diseases of affluence such as hypertension and CHD and conditions such as obesity became diseases of the 'poor' in affluent societies. Having examined the literature relating to the impact of economic inequality upon society he reported that once a country has risen above a collective threshold level for poverty that it is the extent to which there is economic polarity between rich and poor that influences health, i.e. the more egalitarian the society, the better the nation's health; for example, Sweden and Japan. This reflects the psychosocial impact of relative poverty in any given society; relative poverty being more important than absolute poverty above the mentioned threshold. He suggests that part of the effect of high levels of relative poverty relates to the negative influences upon health stemming from feeling subordinated within society. He notes that the greater the polarisation of wealth and poverty, the bigger the differences in health. Studies by Ben-Schlomo *et al.* (1996) and Kaplan *et al.* (1996) confirm a strong relationship between mortality and deprivation, but further argue that the degree of socio-economic variation (inequality) within an area significantly increases mortality further.

Perceived racism and racial stigma may also have a similarly negative affect through the perceived socio-economic inequality it creates. A recent study has shown that, whilst living in a better area reduces the risk of adverse pregnancy outcomes among African-American women, living in an area in which they are in a racial minority may increase the risk. Using a 1991 cohort of single infants born to African-American women in Chicago, Pickett *et al.* (2005) measured census tract socio-economic status and defined women as having 'positive income incongruity' if they lived in wealthier tracts than the average African-American woman of comparable education and marital status. They examined whether or not the effect of positive income incongruity differed according to whether or not African-American women lived in predominantly black or mixed tracts. Positive income incongruity among women living in predominantly black census tracts was associated with a lower risk of LBW and preterm delivery. In contrast, positive income incongruity among the women living in mixed tracts was not associated with these adverse birth outcomes. The expected benefits of positive income incongruity in mixed areas seemed to be offset, suggesting that the positive effects of a better socio-economic context may be countered for minority women by the adverse effects of racism or racial stigma.

Wilkinson (1996) also claims that the degree of social cohesion and social support within a community, which often coincides with egalitarian societies, appears to be a potent influence upon health. He asserts that anthropological literature demonstrates that collectivism, sharing and reciprocity have been the cultural norms, globally, for most of human existence, until the outset of market economies and consumerism which brought with them individualism and inequality and concomitant health risks.

There are clearly complex socio-biological issues related to social hierarchies and their effects upon development of CHD. Marmot *et al.* (1984, 1996) illustrate that the social hierarchy (pecking order) effect can be seen even in the absence of poverty. Utilising much-cited civil servant data they demonstrate a steep inverse relationship between grade and heart disease rates. In a more recent study, Armstrong *et al.* (2003) observed an inverse association between CHD mortality and occupational structure among blue collar and white collar workers; mortality was approximately twice that observed among blue collar than white collar workers. This, as argued by Nystrom Peck (1994), appears to point to psychosocial differences between upper and lower grades rather than to a straightforward biological programming demonstrated by differing heights purported by Barker (1994). The fact that this effect is seen even between grades at the higher end of the organisation means that individual factors known to be associated with CHD and also social class, such as smoking, obesity, short stature, inactivity and a high fat diet, are unlikely to completely account for this effect. Indeed, Marmot (1996) claims that such factors account for less than 50% of cases of CHD.

Syme (1996) and Brunner (1996) support Marmot's assertions and hypothesise that for each 'rung' down on the social ladder, there is a reduced opportunity for control over events. Brunner, for example, suggests that this limiting of autonomy translates via a psychoendocrine pathway to poor health. To further elaborate upon the differences in CHD according to social rank, Tarlov (1996, p. 84) suggests a model described as the 'sociobiological translation', whereby the cause of CHD commences in childhood and continues throughout life. This, he suggests, involves chronic dissonance between social expectation and social reality, which in turn contributes to progressive pathological changes and CHD. The body of knowledge that points to the relationship between socio-economic inequalities and lowered health that is not related specifically to absolute poverty (Blane *et al.*, 1996; Wilkinson, 1992, 1996, 1997; Braveman and Tarimo, 2002), we feel, holds enormous promise for understanding the socio-biological factors contributing to CHD.

In conclusion, it seems to be problematic to endeavour to separate the biological argument from the sociological. It is equally inappropriate to focus upon one perspective to the exclusion of the other. The influences upon diseases such as coronary heart disease appear to reflect a complex and only partially understood socio-biological phenomenon that is likely to relate to a synergistic interaction between *in utero* environment *and* life cycle events and reactions to them. We now consider the implications of our conclusions for policy and practice.

Implications for policy and practice

Nutritional interventions

When considering Barker's hypothesis, nutritional supplementation for the pregnant woman might seem to offer one 'solution' to improve fetal growth when it appears to be impaired. However, a recent systematic review of the literature to assess the effects of maternal nutrient administration for suspected fetal growth impairment on fetal growth and perinatal outcome revealed that no difference was detected in the number of small for gestational age infants whose mothers had received nutrients compared to those who did not (Say *et al.*, 2003). The reviewers concluded that there was not enough evidence to evaluate the use of nutrient therapy for suspected impaired fetal growth and that further research was needed.

Although improved diet and supplementation may have a key role to play, this cannot be achieved without taking sufficient account of the social and motivational barriers to behaviour modification. Advocating nutritional intervention for the pregnant woman as a means of increasing birth weight is hugely problematic when a culture of poverty exists (Dowler *et al.*, 2001). Hickey *et al.* (1995), having established a clear relationship between low pregnancy weight gain and poor scores on several psychosocial constructs, argue that efforts to simply manipulate pregnancy weight gain through dietary interventions will meet with variable success until underlying psychosocial variables are further delineated.

Given the intergenerational implications of diet, a much longer-term strategy for dietary improvement for all appears to be the way forward. The UK government has introduced a number of initiatives over the last five years aimed at improving diet, particularly amongst poorer groups in society. The initiatives aim to promote 'healthier' food choices to reflect World Health Organization guidelines (WHO, 1990), i.e. higher consumption of fruit and vegetables and lower consumption of foods high in saturated fat, sugar and salt (Department of Health, 2003b, 2004a). The NHS Plan highlighted diet and nutrition as key areas for action, and introduced the *5 a day* programme, as part of a government drive to address problems in disadvantaged areas of the country (Department of Health, 2000). The *5 a day* programme aims to increase consumption of fruit and vegetables by improving access to and availability of them through targeted action, and improving attitudes and awareness of the health benefits of increased consumption (Department of Health, 2003b). The programme incorporates five main strands: the National School Fruit Scheme (entitling every child aged 4–6 years in England to a free piece of fruit or vegetable each school day); local *5 a day* community initiatives (to facilitate access to fruit and vegetables specifically to families on low incomes); a communications programme (which aims to provide clear and consistent messages about the *5 a day* initiative using the *5 a day* logo); working with the food industry (e.g. producers, caterers and retailers to improve access to and availability of fruit and vegetables); and working with national and local partners (e.g. government, health, education and consumer groups) (Department of Health, 2002, 2003b). A reformed Welfare Food Scheme (renamed *Healthy Start*) has introduced vouchers for fresh produce and milk for low income families (Department of Health, 2004b). Other schemes aimed at improving nutrition for people living in disadvantaged areas include Single Regeneration Budget programmes, Sure Start initiatives, Healthy Living Centres, school breakfast clubs and neighbourhood renewal projects (Department of Health, 2004a). Many interventions are designed to be implemented in partnership with local communities, including food co-operatives, community cafes and 'cook and eat' projects (Attree, in press).

Although these targeted initiatives have a key role to play in improving nutrient intake, this goal cannot be achieved without taking sufficient account of the socio-economic and motivational barriers to behaviour modification. Relatively little is known about what might motivate people to eat a more healthful diet, despite evidence to suggest that socio-economic factors could account for the greatest variability in, for example, fruit and vegetable consumption (Ling and Horwath, 2001). Barriers may be material or they may be more abstract, relating to psychology, identity and the general political culture (Leather, 1997). Common barriers are cost in time and money, effort to prepare, difficulty in changing habits, preference for other foods, lack of availability, concern for pesticides, support of family and friends, shopping practicalities and, in the context of fruit and vegetable consumption, lack of awareness of what constitutes sufficient amounts to be consumed (Anderson *et al.*, 1998; Ling and Horwath, 2001). The government policies do little to address all these barriers and are therefore likely to meet with limited success. Indeed, the latest Family

Food – Expenditure and Food Survey 2003–2004, revealed that the quantity of fruit and vegetables purchased in the UK *fell* by 1.6% in 2003–04 compared to 2002–03 (DEFRA, 2005). Although this change was not statistically significant, the findings are far from encouraging.

Leather (1997) claims that the current 'hands off' role of the UK government, which rules out interventions in what are seen as 'market' operation, is a further barrier to increased intake. Political unwillingness to intervene confounds attempts to build a co-ordinated base for marketing and promoting fruit and vegetables. Leather acknowledges that it is very difficult to structure or restrain food choices without the accusation that this impinges on people's freedom. However, the assumption that, if choice is left to the market, it is 'free' ignores the fact that powerful forces operate to constrain and mould these choices. Food consumption is the result of a complex interaction of forces as diverse as how foods are marketed and promoted, where they are sold and at what price, whether we know what to do with them, and the images they conjure up for us. For example, just because a child is given a piece of fruit at school, there is no guarantee that they will eat it. They are just as likely, perhaps more so, to eat the packet of crisps that was given to them by their parents or that they purchased from the tuck shop. A consequence of the hands-off role of the government is that health education and food industry messages are allowed to co-exist in stark contradiction to one another. Globally, food manufacturers are a powerful force and can afford to spend billions on advertising their products. There is no commitment from the government either to limit the amount of money that can be spent on advertising these foods, or to match their spending by advertising healthier eating options. Leather (1997) suggests that the absence of such a policy signals the lack of importance given to nutrition and denies a forum of sufficient stature where the implementation of policies to overcome the barriers to improved nutrition can take place.

Smoking cessation

Culturally appropriate smoking cessation strategies offered to women during pregnancy support a change in smoking habits (Dolan-Mullen, 1999; Lumley *et al.*, 2004) and contribute towards reducing LBW (Lumley *et al.*, 2004). However, as Spencer (2003) asserts, behaviours such as smoking are often firmly established long before a woman becomes pregnant and are difficult to modify in the short-term period of a pregnancy. As stated above, smoking is also strongly associated with social deprivation and associated stressful living conditions and under these circumstances cessation may be extremely difficult, and indeed may create more psycho-social stress (Graham and Blackburn, 1998; Lumley *et al.*, 2004). As with nutrition, smoking cessation needs to take place on a broad population base, to impact upon both women at the pre-pregnant and pregnant stage and adults throughout their lives. This provides a two-fold influence upon reducing CHD, through influencing *in utero* conditions and health throughout the life span. The socio-political issues are summarised by Lumley *et al.* (2004, p. 8):

> Given the clear difficulties which most women still smoking at the first antenatal visit have in stopping smoking, midwives, general practitioners, and obstetricians need to support strategies for smoking control in the whole community so as to reduce the initiation of smoking by young people: action to prevent sales of tobacco products to young people, prohibition of smoking in all public places, increases in tobacco taxation, workplace smoking cessation programs and banning tobacco sponsorship of prestigious sporting and cultural events.

And from a political economic perspective (p. 8):

> Given the strong association between social inequality and continued smoking by pregnant women, and bearing in mind the contribution of smoking to the global burden of disease in developed market economies, midwives, general practitioners and obstetricians need to support strategies in the wider community to reduce social inequalities.

Social support

Social support is variously defined by those advocating it, making analysis of its impact extremely complex. Sarafino (1994, p. 395) provides a comprehensive definition whereby social support includes:

- Emotional support – 'The expression of empathy, caring, and concern toward the person.'
- Esteem support – 'Positive regard for the person, encouragement and agreement with the individual's ideas or feelings.'
- Informational support – 'Giving advice, directions, suggestions, or feedback about how the person is doing.'
- Instrumental support – 'Direct assistance' of a tangible and practical nature.
- Network support – 'Provides a feeling of membership in a group of people who share interests and social activities.'

It appears that a focused strategy of social support, targeted towards socially excluded communities, has potential to exert greater influence upon health status via a combination of socio-biological and behavioural routes (Mutale *et al.*, 1991; Zimmer-Gembeck and Helfand, 1996; Norbeck *et al.*, 1997; Feldman *et al.*, 2000). However, the evidence for social support interventions is highly varied and much disputed. Hodnett and Fredericks (2003) conducted a systematic review of 16 randomised controlled trials that provided additional support during at-risk pregnancy by either a professional or specially trained lay person and compared it to standard antenatal care. There was no significant effect upon low birth weight or preterm birth. However, they do acknowledge (p. 6) that 'abilities to identify women who are at high risk of preterm or low birth weight babies are seriously limited'. Secondly, the ways in which social support was defined and operationalised were enormously varied. In addition, as Ball (2004) highlights, it would have been unethical to withhold standard antenatal care, which varies enormously from one maternity service to another within and across countries. This inevitably limits generalisability.

Studies not included in the review by Hodnett and Fredericks (2003) because they did not employ a RCT (for example Edwards *et al.* (1994) referred to above) led to a much larger effect of social support on birth weight. This effect may relate to the types of support employed and by whom. Zimmer-Gembeck and Helfand (1996) conducted a retrospective observational study and demonstrated that receiving over 45 minutes of psychosocial services reduced the odds of low birth weight by approximately one half in low income women from a range of ethnic groups, including African American and Latina and white women. Psychosocial services included (p. 190):

> Assessments of mental illness, emotional problems, abuse and violence, homelessness, financial difficulties, substance abuse, etc., and actions taken to alleviate these problems.

This illustrates the effectiveness of a very specific approach to providing social support for those identified as needing it.

The long-term effects of a social support intervention during pregnancy were illustrated by Oakley *et al.* (1990), who carried out a randomised controlled trial providing social support for socially deprived pregnant women. This resulted in a small but non-significant increase in birth weight, reduced needs for intervention, and significantly improved physical health of mothers and babies and maternal psychosocial well-being. In one year and seven year follow-ups to this study, they demonstrated continuing and significant differences in the physical and psychological health of the mothers and in the developmental health of the children (Oakley, 1992; Oakley *et al.*, 1996).

If we look at social support in the light of Barker's hypothesis related to intergenerational nutritional deprivation, while we definitely should acknowledge its importance, it would seem that there needs to be a much broader and long-term approach, not simply commencing during a pregnancy. This point is made by Hodnett and Fredericks (2003) who state (p. 5):

> While the theoretical rationale for links between social support, stress, and health is strong, it may be that social support (regardless of quality and quantity) is not sufficiently powerful to improve the outcomes of the pregnancy during which it is provided. [...] Given the immense social deprivation experienced by most of the women in these trials, it would be surprising if social support could have such an immediate and powerful effect.

Infant feeding

Clearly, the method of infant feeding and nutrition cannot influence the *in utero* experience. However, nutrition in infancy does have an impact upon patterns of growth and adult health (Law, 2005; Stein *et al.*, 2005). Breastfeeding may therefore be crucial in terms of its damage limitation potential with regard to the subsequent development of CHD. Breastfeeding may also have a transmitted intergenerational effect in that it provides optimum nutrition to babies, many of whom later become mothers. After controlling for confounding variables, breastfed babies have a lower risk of hypertension (Singhal *et al.*, 2001; Martin *et al.*, 2004), hypercholesterolaemia (Owen *et al.*, 2002), obesity (von Kries, 1999; Armstrong and Reilly, 2002; Thorsdottir *et al.*, 2003) and CHD (Fall *et al.*, 1992; Ravelli *et al.*, 2000; Das, 2003). Singhal and Lucas (2004) argue that this may relate, in part, to breastfed infants growing more slowly (Ong *et al.*, 2002) thus reducing the risks of growth acceleration, which may be problematic especially for babies who have experienced *in utero* growth compromise. Eriksson (2005), however, disputes arguments that 'catch-up' growth in infancy may be detrimental, although he emphasises that accelerated growth as childhood progresses is indeed associated with increased obesity and coronary heart disease risk in later life.

A second key route to reducing the risk of CHD and its predisposing factors involves the delay of solids (Wilson *et al.*, 1998). Indeed, WHO now recommends exclusive breastfeeding for at least six months (WHO/UNICEF, 2003). However, infant feeding practices across the globe are closely connected with socio-cultural, political and economic factors (Dykes, 2002, 2005a).

Breastfeeding rates vary enormously between socio-economic groups and this in itself is a key aspect of the cycle of nutritional deprivation. In the UK there are striking differences between the breastfeeding initiation and continuation rates related to socio-economic factors. Eighty-five per cent of women in higher socio-economic occupational groups commenced breastfeeding in 2000 compared with 59% of women in lower socio-economic occupations, utilising the ONS National Statistics Socio-Economic Classification NS-SEC (Hamlyn *et al.*, 2002). Addressing this differential clearly requires co-ordinated international, national and local strategies to protect, promote and support breastfeeding (WHO, 1990). Currently, particular emphasis is being placed upon breastfeeding peer support projects that reach into local communities and empower women to support each other with skill and confidence in the art of breastfeeding (Dykes, 2003, 2005b).

Social policy implications

While the value of interventions such as the provision of specific social support 'packages' in pregnancy and in other specific situations should not be disregarded, they cannot in themselves make a fundamental impact upon *in utero* well-being and long-term health. They do not address the depth of influence of cultural, socio-economic and environmental determinants upon health. What seems to emerge from the literature related to individuals' lived experiences relates to the sense of feeling valued and indeed being cared about (or not) by significant others, health professionals, organisations and society in general. Social inequality, both absolute and relative, whether at a societal or organisational level, appears to be a key trigger to lowered health and well-being. Therefore we need a comprehensive, local, national and indeed international review of co-ordinated community wide social programmes to reduce social inequalities.

In a summary of social policy issues related to low birth weight, Spencer (2003) argues that, from a biopsychosocial perspective, a long-term strategy to reduce levels of poverty in children is likely to improve physical growth, cognitive development and psychosocial well-being. He highlights the practices of the Scandinavian countries with their redistribution policies to improve the living standards of the poorest members of society. They also provide adequate social security combined with flexible parenting-friendly employment policies, a very high standard of affordable day care and associated pre-school education. It is interesting to note that these countries also have some of the highest exclusive breastfeeding rates in the western countries. These relate, in part, to excellent maternity rights, pay and workplace flexibility, ensured through effective statutory processes (Gerrard, 2001; Galtry, 2003).

A redistribution of wealth in western countries, while appearing to be the way forward, requires enormous commitment from governments. This would have to include a radical review and reconfiguration of the role of multinational corporations in determining the economic climate of a given country. However, given the current power of these corporations to influence governments within capitalist economies and government reluctance to disrupt the status quo, there are formidable barriers to such endeavours. As Grant (1995, p. 43) states:

> Bringing about fundamental change, in the face of the political and economic vested interest that circumscribe the freedom of action of all political leaderships, is a challenging task.

Conclusion

We argue for continued exploration and recognition of the complex interaction between socio-economic and physiological factors and the ways in which they influence *in utero* well-being and health outcomes. The mechanisms that underlie the associations between birth weight and later disease are clearly complex and extensive. We highlight some of the potentially contributory and confounding factors that still require consideration in the design of further studies in this area. It is suggested that a balance should be maintained between a sociological perspective that focuses on behavioural and societal influences and the biological perspective focusing on the fetal origins of adult disease. Ultimately, however, we argue that it is the broader political economic issues related to the enormous material disparities within western countries such as the UK that need to be addressed. Only when we reach a more egalitarian situation with dramatic reductions in the current high levels of absolute *and* relative poverty and associated powerlessness and marginalisation will there be a major impact upon birth weight and later health.

References

Anderson, A. S., Cox, D. N., McKellar S., Reynolds, J., Lean, M. E. and Mela, D. J. (1998) Take Five, a nutrition education intervention to increase fruit and vegetable intakes: impact on attitudes towards dietary change. *British Journal of Nutrition*, **80**(2), 133–40.

Armstrong, J. and Reilly, J. J. (2002) Breastfeeding and lowering the risk of childhood obesity. *Lancet*, **359**, 2003–04.

Armstrong, D. L., Strogatz, D., Barnett, E. and Wang, R. (2003) Joint effects of social class and community occupational structure on coronary mortality among black men and white men, upstate New York, 1988–92. *Journal of Epidemiology & Community Health*, **57**(5), 373–8.

Attree, P. (in press) A critical analysis of UK public health policies in relation to diet and nutrition in low-income households. *Maternal and Child Nutrition*.

Ball, L. (2004) Low birth weight: exploring an enigma of failure. *British Journal of Midwifery*, **12**, 374–9.

Barker, D. J. P. (ed.) (1992) *Fetal and Infant Origins of Adult Disease*. British Medical Journal, London.

Barker, D. J. P. (1994) *Mothers, Babies and Disease in Later Life*. British Medical Journal, London.

Barker, D. J. P. and Osmond, C. (1986) Infant mortality, childhood nutrition, and ischaemic heart disease in England and Wales. *Lancet*, **i**, 1077–88.

Barker, D. J. P. and Osmond, C. (1992a) Infant mortality, childhood nutrition, and ischaemic heart disease in England and Wales. In *Fetal and Infant Origins of Adult Disease* (ed. D. J. P. Barker), pp. 23–37. British Medical Journal, London.

Barker, D. J. P. and Osmond, C. (1992b) Inequalities in health in Britain: specific explanations in three Lancashire towns. In *Fetal and Infant Origins of Adult Disease* (ed. D. J. P. Barker), pp. 68–78. British Medical Journal, London.

Barker, D. J. P., Winter, P. D., Osmond, C., Margetts, B. and Simmonds, S. J. (1989) Weight in infancy and death from ischaemic heart disease. *Lancet*, **2**, 577–80.

Barker, D. J. P., Winter, P. D., Osmond, C. and Simmonds, S. J. (1990) Fetal and placental size and risk of hypertension in adult life. *British Medical Journal*, **301**, 259–62.

Bartley, M. (1994) Unemployment and ill heath: understanding the relationship. *Journal of Epidemiology and Community Health*, **48**, 333–7.

Bartley, M., Power, C., Blane, D., Davey Smith, G. and Shipley, M. (1994) Birth weight and later socioeconomic disadvantage: evidence from the 1958 British cohort study. *British Medical Journal*, **309**, 1457–9.

Bateson, P., Barker, D., Clutton-Brock, T., Deb, D., D'Udine, B., Foley, R. A., Gluckman, P., Godfrey, K., Kirkwood, T., Mirazon Lahr, M., McNamara, J., Metcalfe, N. B., Monaghan, P., Spencer, H. G. and Sultan, S. E. (2004) Developmental plasticity and human health. *Nature*, **430**, 419–21.

Ben-Schlomo, Y., White, I. R. and Marmot, M. (1996) Does the variation in the socioeconomic characteristics of an area affect mortality? *British Medical Journal*, **312**, 1013–14.

Blane, D., Brunner, E. and Wilkinson, R. (eds.) (1996) *Health and Social Organization, Towards a Health Policy for the 21st Century*. Routledge, London.

Block, J. P., Scribner, R. A. and DeSalvo, K. B. (2004) Fast food, race/ethnicity, and income: a geographic analysis. *American Journal of Preventive Medicine*, **27**(3), 211–17.

Braveman, P. and Tarimo, E. (2002) Social inequalities in health within countries: not only an issue for affluent nations. *Social Science & Medicine*, **54**, 1621–35.

Brunner, E. (1996) The social and biological basis of cardiovascular disease in office workers. In: *Health and Social Organization, Towards a Health Policy for the 21st Century* (eds. D. Blane, E. Brunner and R. Wilkinson), pp. 272–302. Routledge, London.

Cade, J. E., Barker, D. J. P., Margetts, B. M. and Morris, J. A. (1992) Diet and inequalities in health in three English towns. In *Fetal and Infant Origins of Adult Disease* (ed. D. J. P. Barker), pp. 93–102. British Medical Journal, London.

Collins, J. W. Jr, David, R. J., Handler, A., Wall, S. and Andes, S. (2004) Very low birthweight in African American infants: the role of maternal exposure to interpersonal racial discrimination. *American Journal of Public Health*, **94**(12), 2132–8.

Das, U. N. (2003) A perinatal strategy to prevent coronary heart disease. *Nutrition*, **19**, 1022–7.

Dallison, J. and Lobstein, T. (1995) *Poor Expectations, Poverty and Undernourishment in Pregnancy*. NCH Action for Children and The Maternity Alliance, London.

Department of Health (2000) *NHS Plan*. Department of Health, London.

Department of Health (2002) *The National School Fruit Scheme*. Department of Health, London.

Department of Health (2003a) *Health Survey for England*. The Stationery Office, London.

Department of Health (2003b) *A local 5 A DAY initiative: increasing fruit and vegetable consumption – improving health. Booklet 1*. Department of Health, London.

Department of Health (2004a) *Choosing Health: Choosing a Better Diet*. Department of Health, London.

Department of Health (2004b) *Healthy Start*. Department of Health, London.

Department for Environment, Food and Rural Affairs (DEFRA) (2005) *Family Food in 2003–04. A National Statistics Publication by Defra*. The Stationery Office, London.

Dolan-Mullen, P. (1999) Maternal smoking during pregnancy and evidence based interventions to promote cessation. *Primary Care*, **26**, 577–89.

Dowler, E., Turner, S. and Dobson, B. (2001) *Poverty Bites: Food Health and Poor Families*. Child Poverty Action Group, London.

Doyal, L. and Pennell, I. (1981) *The Political Economy of Health*. Pluto Press, London.

Dykes, F. (2002) Western marketing and medicine: construction of an insufficient milk syndrome. *Health Care for Women International*, **23**, 492–502.

Dykes, F. (2003) *Infant Feeding Initiative: A Report Evaluating the Breastfeeding Practice Projects 1999–2002*. Department of Health, London.

Dykes, F. (2005a) 'Supply' and 'Demand': breastfeeding as labour. *Social Science & Medicine*, **60**(10), 2283–93.

Dykes, F. (2005b) Government funded breastfeeding peer support projects: implications for practice. *Maternal & Child Nutrition*, **1**(1), 21–31.

Edwards, C., Cole, O. J., Oyemade, U. J., Knight, E. M., Johnson, A. A., Westney, O. E., Laryea, H., West, W., Jones, S. and Westney, L. S. (1994) Maternal stress and pregnancy outcomes in a prenatal clinic population. *Journal of Nutrition*, **124**, 1006S–1021S.

Elford, J., Whincup, P. and Shaper, A. G. (1991) Early life experience and adult cardiovascular disease: longitudinal and case-control studies. *International Journal of Epidemiology*, **20**, 833–44.

Elford, J., Shaper, A. G. and Whincup, P. (1992) Early life experience and cardiovascular disease-ecological studies. *Journal of Epidemiology and Community Health*, **46**, 1–11.

Elliot, V. and O'Reilly, F. (1995) Maternal nutrition and health. A summary of research on birthweight. *Mothers and Children*, **14**, 14–17.

Emanuel, I., Haroulla, F. E. A. and Evans, S. J. W. (1992) Intergenerational studies of human birth weight from the 1958 birth cohort. 1. Evidence for a multigenerational effect. *British Journal of Obstetrics and Gynaecology*, **99**, 67–74.

Eriksson, J. G., Forsen, T., Tuomilehto, J., Winter, P. D., Osmond, C. and Barker, D. J. P. (1999) Catch-up growth in childhood and death from coronary heart disease: longitudinal study. *British Medical Journal*, **323**, 1273–6.

Eriksson, J. G. (2005) Early growth and adult health outcomes – lessons learned from the Helsinki Birth Cohort Study. *Maternal & Child Nutrition*, **1**(3), 149–54.

Fall, C. H. D., Barker, D. J. P., Osmond, C., Winter, P. D., Clark, P. M. S. and Hales, C. N. (1992) Relation of infant feeding to adult serum cholesterol concentration and death from ischaemic heart disease. *British Medical Journal*, **304**, 801–5.

Feldman, P. J., Dunkel-Schetter, C., Sandman, C. A. and Wadhwa, P. D. (2000) Maternal social support predicts birth weight and fetal growth in human pregnancy. *Psychosomatic Medicine*, **62**, 715–25.

Fleming, I., Baum, A., Davidson, L., Rectanus, E. and McArdle, S. (1987) Chronic stress as a factor in physiologic reactivity to challenge. *Health Psychology*, **6**, 221–37.

Frankenberg, R. (1980) Medical anthropology and development: a theoretical perspective. *Social Science and Medicine*, **14B**, 197–207.

Fraser, A. M., Brockett, J. E. and Ward, R. H. (1995) Association of young maternal age with adverse reproductive outcomes. *New England Journal of Medicine*, **332**, 1113–17.

French, S., Harnack, L. and Jeffery, R. (2000) Fast food restaurant use among women in the Pound of Prevention study: dietary, behavioral and demographic correlates. *International Journal of Obesity*, **24**, 1353–9.

Galtry, J. (2003) The impact on breastfeeding of labour market policy and practice in Ireland, Sweden and the USA. *Social Science and Medicine*, **57**, 167–77.

Geiser, D. S. (1989) Psychosocial influences on human immunity. *Clinical Psychology Review*, **9**, 689–715.

Gerrard, A. (2001) Breast-feeding in Norway: where did they go right? *British Journal of Midwifery*, **9**, 294–300.

Gillman, M. W. and Rich-Edwards, J. W. (2000) The fetal origins of adult disease: from sceptic to convert. *Pediatric and Perinatal Epidemiology*, **14**, 192–4.

Gluckman, P., Breier, B. H., Oliver, J., Harding, J. and Bassett, N. (1990) Fetal growth in late gestation – a constrained pattern of growth. *Acta Paediatrica Scandinavica*, **S367**, 105–10.

Gluckman, P. D., Hanson, M. A., Morton, S. M. B. and Pinal, C. S. (2005a) Life-long echoes – a critical analysis of the developmental origins of adult disease model. *Biology of the Neonate*, **87**, 127–39.

Gluckman, P. D., Hanson, M. A. and Pinal, C. S. (2005b) The developmental origins of adult disease. *Maternal and Child Nutrition*, **1**(3), 130–41.

Godfrey, K., Robinson, S., Barker, D. J. P., Osmond, C. and Cox, V. (1996) Maternal nutrition in early and late pregnancy in relation to placental and fetal growth. *British Medical Journal*, **312**, 410–14.

Graham, H. (1996) Smoking prevalence among women in the European community, 1950 to 1990. *Social Science & Medicine*, **43**, 243–54.

Graham, H. and Blackburn, C. (1998) The socio-economic patterning of health and smoking behaviour among mothers with young children on income support. *Sociology of Health and Illness*, **20**, 215–40.

Grant, J. (1995) *The State of the World's Children UNICEF*. Oxford University Press, New York.

Gray, A. (ed.) (1993) *World Health And Disease*. Open University Press, Buckingham.

Grjibovski, A., Bygren, L. O., Svartbo, B. and Magnus, P. (2004) Housing conditions, perceived stress, smoking, and alcohol: determinants of fetal growth in Northwest Russia. *Acta Obstetricia et Gynecologica Scandinavica*, **83**(12), 1159–66.

Hall Moran, V. and Dykes, F. (2003) Disadvantaged at birth or by life? An analysis of the relationship between socio-economic factors, in-utero environment and later health. (Abstracts issue from second world congress on fetal origins of adult disease). *Pediatric Research*, **53**, 43A.

Hamlyn, B., Brooker, S., Oleinikova, K. and Wands, S. (2002) *Infant Feeding 2000*. The Stationery Office, London.

Hedegaard, M., Henriksen, T. B., Secher, N. J., Hatch, M. C. and Sabroe, S. (1996) Do stressful life events affect the duration of gestation and risk of preterm delivery? *Epidemiology*, **7**(4), 339–45.

Henderson, L., Gregory, J. and Swan, G. (2003) *The National Diet and Nutrition Survey: Adults aged 19 to 64 years*. The Stationery Office, London.

Hickey, C. A., Cliver, S. P., Goldenberg, R. L., McNeal, S. F. and Hoffman, H. J. (1995) Relationship of psychosocial status to low prenatal weight gain among non obese black and white women delivering at term. *Obstetrics & Gynaecology*, **86**, 177–83.

Hodnett, E. D. and Fredericks, S. (2003) Support during pregnancy for women at increased risk of low birth weight babies. *The Cochrane Database of Systematic Reviews*, Issue 3. Art. No.: CD000198. DOI: 10.1002/14651858. CD000198.

Hunt, C. T., Nichols, P. N. and Pryer, J. A. (2000) Who complied with the national fruit and vegetable population goals? Findings from the dietary and nutritional survey of British adults. *European Journal of Public Health*, **10**, 178–84.

Hytten, F. (1990) Nutritional requirements in pregnancy: what happens if they are not met? *Midwifery*, **6**, 140–5.

Illich, I. (1995) *Limits to Medicine. Medical Nemesis: The Expropriation of Health*, 2nd edn. Marion Boyars Publishers, London.

James, W. P. T. (2005) The policy challenge of coexisting undernutrition and nutrition-related chronic diseases. *Maternal & Child Nutrition*, **1**(3), 197–203.

Kaufman, P. K. (1999) Rural poor have less access to supermarkets and large grocery stores. *Rural Development Perspective*, **13**, 19–25.

Kaplan, G. A., Pamuk, E. R., Lynch, J. W., Cohen, R. D. and Balfour, J. L. (1996) Inequality in income and mortality in the United States: analysis mortality and potential pathways. *British Medical Journal*, **312**, 999–1003.

Keski-Rahkonen, A., Kaprio, J., Rissanen, A., Virkkunen, M. and Rose, R. J. (2003) Breakfast skipping and health-compromising behaviors in adolescents and adults. *European Journal of Clinical Nutrition*, **57**(7), 842–53.

Kirkham, M., Stapleton, H., Curtis, P. and Thomas, G. (2002) The inverse care law in antenatal midwifery care. *British Journal of Midwifery*, **10**, 509–13.

Kogan, M. (1995) Social causes of low birth weight. *Journal of the Royal Society of Medicine*, **88**, 611–15.

Kramer, M. (1987) Determinants of low birth weight: methodological assessment and meta-analysis. *Bulletin of the World Health Organization*, **65**, 663–737.

Krebs-Smith, S. M. and Kantor, L. S. (2001) Choose a variety of fruits and vegetables daily: understanding the complexities. *Journal of Nutrition*, **131**(2S-1), 487S–501S.

Law, C. M. and Shiell, A. W. (1996) Is blood pressure inversely related to birth weight? The strength of evidence from a systematic review of the literature. *Journal of Hypertension*, **14**, 935–41.

Law, C. (2005) Early growth and chronic disease; a public health overview. *Maternal & Child Nutrition*, **1**(3), 169–76.

Leather, S. (1997) Reaching the recommendations: what are the barriers? In: *At Least Five a Day: Strategies to Increase Vegetable and Fruit Consumption*, National Heart Forum. The Stationery Office, London.

Leff, M., Orleans, M., Haverkamp, A. D., Baron, A. E., Alderman, B. W. and Freedman, W. L. (1992) The association between maternal low birthweight (LBW) and infant low birthweight in a racially mixed population. *Paediatric & Perinatal Epidemiology*, **6**, 51–61.

Lenders, C. M., McElrath, T. F. and Scholl, T. O. (2000) Nutrition in adolescent pregnancy. *Current Opinion in Pediatrics*, **12**, 291–6.

Leon, D. A., Lithell, H., Vagero, D., Koupilova, I., Mohsen, R., Berglund, L., Lithell, U.-B. and McKeigue, P. M. (1998) Reduced fetal growth rate and increased risk of death from ischaemic heart disease: cohort study of 15000 Swedish men and women born 1915–29. *British Medical Journal*, **317**, 241–5.

Ling, A. M. C. and Horwath, C. (2001) Perceived benefits and barriers of increased fruit and vegetable consumption: validation of a decisional balance scale. *Journal of Nutrition Education*, **33**, 257–65.

Luke, B. (1994a) Nutritional influences on Fetal Growth, *Clinical Obstetrics and Gynaecology*, **37**(3), 538–49.

Luke, B. (1994b) Maternal-fetal nutrition. *Clinical Obstetrics and Gynaecology*, **37**, 93–109.

Luke, B. (1994c) Nutrition during pregnancy. *Current Opinion in Obstetrics and Gynaecology*, **6**, 402–7.

Lumey, L. H. (1992) Decreased birthweights in infants after maternal *in utero* exposure to the Dutch famine of 1944–45. *Paediatric and Perinatal Epidemiology*, **6**, 240–53.

Lumley, J., Oliver, S. and Waters, E. (2004) Interventions for promoting smoking cessation during pregnancy (Cochrane Review). In: The *Cochrane Library, Issue 3*: John Wiley & Sons, Chichester.

Marmot, M. G., Shipley, M. J. and Rose, G. (1984) Inequalities in death – specific explanations of a general pattern? *The Lancet*, **1**, 1003–6.

Marmot, M. (1996) The social pattern of health and disease. In: *Health and Social Organization, Towards a Health Policy for the 21st Century* (eds. D. Blane, E. Brunner and R. Wilkinson), pp. 42–70. Routledge, London.

Martin, R. M., Ness, A. R., Gunnell, D., Emmett, P. and Davey Smith, G. (2004) Does breast-feeding in infancy lower blood pressure in childhood? The Avon longitudinal study of parents and children. *Circulation*, **109**, 1259–66.

MacFarlane, A., Mugford, M., Henderson, J., Furtado, A., Stevens, J. and Dunn, A. (2000) *Birth Counts. Statistics of Pregnancy and Childbirth*. The Stationery Office, London.

Macintyre, S., Maciver, S. and Soomans, A. (1993) Area, class and health: should we be focusing on places or people? *Journal of Social Policy*, **22**, 213–34.

McAnarney, E. R. and Stevens-Simon, C. (1990) Maternal psychological stress/ depression and low birth weight: is there a relationship? *American Journal of Diseases in Children*, **144**, 789–92.

McCormick, M. C., Brooks-Gunn, J., Shorter, T., Holmes, J. H., Wallace, C. Y. and Heagarty, M. C. (1990) Factors associated with smoking in low-income pregnant women: Relationship to birthweight, stressful life events, social support, health behaviours and mental distress. *Journal of Clinical Epidemiology*, **43**(4), 441–8.

Mohsin, M., Wong, F., Bauman, A. and Bai, J. (2003) Maternal and neonatal factors influencing premature birth and low birth weight in Australia. *Journal of Biosocial Science*, **35**, 161–74.

Mutale, T., Creed, F., Maresh, M. and Hunt, L. (1991) Life events and low birthweight-analysis by infants preterm and small for gestational age. *British Journal of Obstetrics & Gynaecology*, **98**, 166–72.

Norbeck, J. S., DeJoseph, J. F. and Smith, R. T. (1997) A randomized trial of an empirically-derived social suppot intervention to prevent low birthweight among African American women. *Social Science & Medicine*, **43**, 947–54.

Nystrom Peck, M. (1994) The Importance of childhood socio-economic group for adult health. *Social Science & Medicine*, **39**, 553–62.

Oakley, A. (1985) Social support in pregnancy. The 'soft' way to increase birth weight? *Social Science & Medicine*, **21**, 1259–68.

Oakley, A., Rajan, L. and Grant, A. (1990) Social support and pregnancy outcome (1990) Social support and pregnancy outcome. *British Journal of Obstetrics and Gynaecology*, **97**, 155–62.

Oakley, A. (1992) Social Support in Pregnancy: Methodology and Findings of a 1-year follow-up study. *Journal of Reproductive and Infant Psychology*, **1**, 219–31.

Oakley, A., Rigby, A. S. and Hickey, D. (1993) Women and children last? Class, health and the role of the maternal and child health services. *European Journal of Public Health*, **3**, 220–6.

Oakley, A., Hickey, D. and Rajan, L. (1996) Social support in pregnancy: does it have long-term effects? *Journal of Reproductive and Infant Psychology*, **14**, 7–22.

Olsen, J. and Frische, G. (1993) Social differences in reproductive health. *Scandinavian Journal of Social Medicine*, **21**, 90–7.

Ong, K. K. L., Preece, M. A., Emmett, P. M., Ahmed, M. L. and Dunger, D. B. (2002) Size at birth and early childhood growth in relation to maternal smoking, parity and infant breast-feeding: longitudinal birth cohort study and analysis. *Pediatric Research*, **52**, 863–7.

Oppenheim, C. and Harker, L. (1996) *Poverty, the Facts*. Child Poverty Action Group, London.

Osmond, C., Barker, D. J. P. and Slattery, J. M. (1992) Risk of death from cardiovascular disease and chronic bronchitis determined by place of birth in England and Wales. In *Fetal and Infant Origins of Adult Disease* (ed. D. J. P. Barker), pp. 79–95. British Medical Journal, London.

Osmond, C., Barker, D. J. P., Winter, P. D., Fall, C. H. D. and Simmonds, S. J. (1993) Early growth and death from cardiovascular disease in women. *British Medical Journal*, **307**, 1519–24.

Ostberg, V. and Vagero, D. (1991) Socio-economic differences in mortality among children. Do they persist into adulthood? *Social Science & Medicine*, **32**, 403–10.

Oths, K. S., Dunn, L. L. and Palmer, N. S. (2001). A prospective study of psychosocial job strain and birth outcomes. *Epidemiology*, **12**(6), 744–6.

Ounsted, M. and Scott, A. (1986) Transmission through the female line of a mechanism constraining human fetal growth. *Annals of Human Biology*, **13**, 143–51.

Owen, C. G., Whincup, P. H., Odoki, K., Gilg, J. A. and Cook, D. G. (2002) Infant feeding and blood cholesterol: a study in adolescents and a systematic review. *Pediatrics*, **110**, 597–608.

Pickett, K. E., Collins, J. W. Jr, Masi, C. M. and Wilkinson, R. G. (2005) The effects of racial density and income incongruity on pregnancy outcomes. *Social Science & Medicine*. **60**(10), 2229–38.

Polednak, A. P. (1989) *Racial and Ethnic Differences in Disease*. Oxford University Press, Oxford.

Power, C., Bartley, M., Davey Smith, G. and Blane, D. (1996) Transmission of social and biological risk across the life course. In: *Health and Social Organization, Towards a Health Policy for the 21st Century* (eds. D. Blane, E. Brunner and R. Wilkinson), pp. 188–203. Routledge, London.

Rahkonen, O., Lahelma, E. and Huuhka, M. (1997) Past or present? Childhood living conditions and current socioeconomic status as determinants of adult health. *Social Science & Medicine*, **44**, 327–36.

Rampersaud, G. C., Pereira, M. A., Girard, B. L., Adams, J. and Metzl, J. D. (2005) Breakfast habits, nutritional status, body weight, and academic performance in children and adolescents. *Journal of the American Dietetic Association*, **105**, 743–60.

Ravelli, A. C., van der Meulen, J. H., Osmond, C., Barker, D. J. and Blecker, O. P. (2000) Infant feeding and adult glucose tolerance, lipid profile, blood pressure, and obesity. *Archives of Diseases in Childhood*, **82**, 248–52.

Rich-Edwards, J. W., Stampfer, M. J., Mason, J. E., Rosner, B., Hankinson, S. E., Colditz, G. A., Hennekens, C. H. and Willet, W. C. (1997) Birth weight and risk of cardiovascular disease in a cohort of women followed up since 1976. *British Medical Journal*, **315**, 396–400.

Rodriguez, C., Redigor, E. and Guitierrez-Fisac, J. L. (1995) Low birth weight in Spain associated with sociodemographic factors. *Journal of Epidemiology & Community Health*, **49**, 38–42.

Rose, G. (1964) Familial patterns in ischaemic heart disease. *British Journal of Preventive Social Medicine*, **18**, 75–80.

Rose, G. (1985) Sick individuals and sick populations. *International Journal of Epidemiology*, **14**, 32–8.

Rutter, D. R. and Quine, L. (1990) Inequalities in pregnancy outcome: a review of psychological and behavioural mediators. *Social Science & Medicine*, **30**, 553–68.

Sacker, A., Firth, D., Fitzpatrick, R., Lynch, K. and Bartley, M. (2000) Comparing health inequality in men and women: prospective study of mortality 1986–96. *British Medical Journal*, **320**(7245), 1303–130.

Salfield, A. and Durward, L. (1985) 'Coping, but only just' – families' experiences of pregnancy and childbearing on the dole. In: *Born Unequal* (ed. L. Durward), pp. 4–20. Maternity Alliance, London.

Say, L., Gulmezoglu, A. M. and Hofmeyr, G. J. (2003) Maternal nutrient supplementation for suspected impaired fetal growth. *The Cochrane Database of Systematic Reviews*, Issue 1. Art. No.: CD000148. DOI: 10.1002/14651858. CD000148.

Sarafino, E. P. (1994) *Health Psychology: Biopsychosocial Interactions.* Wiley & Sons, New York.

Sheehan, T. J. (1998) Stress and low birth weight: a structural modelling approach using real life stressors. *Social Science & Medicine*, **47**, 1503–12.

Singhal, A., Cole, T. J. and Lucas, A. (2001) Early nutrition in preterm infants and later blood pressure: two cohorts after randomised trials. *Lancet*, **357**, 413–19.

Singhal, A. and Lucas, A. (2004) Early origins of cardiovascular disease: is there a unifying hypothesis? *Lancet*, **262**, 1642–5.

Spencer, N. (2003) *Weighing the Evidence: How is Birthweight Determined?* Radcliffe Medical Press, Oxfordshire.

Stein, Z. and Susser, M. (1975) The Dutch Famine, 1944–45, and the Reproductive Process. 1. Effects on Six Indices at Birth. *Pediatric Research*, **9**, 70–6.

Stein, A. D., Thompson, A. M. and Waters, A. (2005) Childhood growth and chronic disease: evidence from countries undergoing the nutrition transition. *Maternal & Child Nutrition*, **1**(3), 177–84.

Syme, S. L. (1996) To prevent disease. The need for a new approach. In: *Health and Social Organization, Towards a Health Policy for the 21st Century* (eds. D. Blane, E. Brunner and R. Wilkinson), pp. 21–31. Routledge, London.

Tarlov, A. R. (1996) Social determinants of health: the sociobiological translation. In: *Health and Social Organization, Towards a Health Policy for the 21st Century* (eds. D. Blane, E. Brunner and R. Wilkinson), pp. 71–93. Routledge, London.

Teixeira, J. M. A., Fisk, N. M. and Glover, V. (1999) Association between maternal anxiety in pregnancy and increased uterine artery resistance index: cohort based study. *British Medical Journal*, **318**, 153–7.

Thorsdottir, I., Gunnarsdottir, I. and Palsson, G. I. (2003) Association of birth weight and breast-feeding with coronary heart disease risk factors at the age of 6 years. *Nutrition, Metabolism & Cardiac Diseases*, **13**, 267–72.

Townsend, P., Davidson, N. and Whitehead, M. (1992) *Inequalities in Health.* Penguin, London.

Van de Mheen, H., Stronks, K. Looman, C. W. and Mackenbach, J. P. (1998) Role of childhood health in the explanation of socio-economic inequalities in early adult health. *Journal of Epidemiology and Community Health*, **52**(1), 15–19.

von Kries, R., Koletzo, B., Sauerwald, T., von Mutius, E., Barnert, D., Grunert, V. and von Voss, H. (1999) Breastfeeding and obesity: a cross-sectional study. *British Medical Journal*, **319**, 147–50.

Wang, X., Zuckerman, B., Coffman, G. A. and Corwin, M. J. (1995) Familial aggregation of low birth weight babies among whites and blacks in the United States. *New England Journal of Medicine*, **333**, 1744–99.

Wardle, J., Parmenter, K. and Waller, J. (2000) Nutrition knowledge and food intake. *Appetite*, **34**(3), 269–75.

WHO (1990) *Diet, Nutrition, and the Prevention of Chronic Diseases*. WHO, Geneva.

WHO (1995) Maternal anthropometry and pregnancy outcomes. *Bulletin of World Health Organization*, **73**, S1–98.

WHO/UNICEF (2003) *Global Strategy for Infant and Young Child Feeding*. WHO, Geneva.

Wilcox, A. and Russell, I. (1990) Why small black infants have a lower mortality rate than small white infants: the case for population-specific standards for birth weight. *Journal of Pediatrics*, **116**(1), 7–10.

Wilcox, A. J. (2001) On the importance – and unimportance – of birthweight. *International Journal of Epidemiology*, **30**, 1233–41.

Wilcox, M. A., Smith, S. J., Johnson, I. R., Maynard, P. V. and Chilvers, C. E. (1995) The effect of social deprivation on birthweight, excluding physiological and pathological effects. *British Journal of Obstetrics & Gynaecology*, **102**, 918–24.

Williams, S. and Poulton, R. (1999) Twins and maternal smoking: ordeals for the fetal origins hypothesis? A cohort study. *British Medical Journal*, **318**, 1–5.

Wilkinson, R. (1992) Income distribution and life expectancy. *British Medical Journal*, **304**, 165–8.

Wilkinson, R. (1996) *Unhealthy societies: the afflictions of inequality*. Routledge, London.

Wilkinson, R. (1997) Socioeconomic determinants of health. Health inequalities: Relative or absolute material standards? *British Medical Journal*, **314**, 591–5.

Wilson, A., Forsyth, S., Greene, S., Irvine, L., Hau, C. and Howie, P. (1998) Relation of infant diet to childhood health: seven year follow up of cohort of children in Dundee infant feeding study. *British Medical Journal*, **316**, 21–5.

Woolfe, B. (1947) Studies on infant mortality: part II, social aetiology of stillbirths and infant deaths in county boroughs of England and Wales. *British Journal of Social Medicine*, **1**, 73–125.

Zambrana, R. E., Dunkel-Schetter, C., Collins, N. L. and Scrimshaw, S. C. (1999) Mediators of ethnic-associated differences in infant birth weight. *Journal of Urban Health*, **76**, 102–16.

Zaren, B., Lindmark, G. and Gebre-Mehdin, M. (1996) Maternal smoking and body composition of the newborn. *Acta Paediatrica*, **85**, 213–19.

Zimmer-Gembeck, M. J. and Helfand, M. (1996) Low birthweight in a public prenatal care program: behavioural and psychosocial risk factors and psychosocial intervention. *Social Science & Medicine*, **43**, 187–97.

CHAPTER 2

Nutrition during adolescent pregnancy

A biopsychosocial perspective

Victoria Hall Moran

Introduction

Teenage pregnancy is one of the major public health challenges in the UK. In the most up-to-date and comprehensive surveys of teenage birth rates in the industrialised world, it was reported that, in 1998, the UK had the highest teenage birth rate in Europe. Rates of teenage births (the number of births per 1000 women aged 15–19 years) in the UK were five times those of the Netherlands, three times those of France, and twice those of Germany (UNICEF, 2001). Although there has been a fall in the under 18 and under 16 conception rates in England since 1998 (9.8% and 9.9% respectively) (ONS, 2005), teenage pregnancy rates remain high.

The latest teenage pregnancy statistics for England and Wales from the Office of National Statistics revealed that in 2003, the conception rate was 8.0 per 1000 adolescents in those aged 13–15 years ($n = 23,845$). In adolescents aged 15–17 years, the conception rate was 42.3 per 1000 ($n = 42,183$) (ONS, 2005). In Scotland in 2003, there were 657 pregnancies in adolescents aged 13–15 years (rate of 7.0 per 1000 adolescents) and 7899 in adolescents aged 16–19 years (rate of 63.3 per 1000 adolescents) (ISD Online, 2003). Conception data is not available for Northern Ireland, due to the lack of complete data on the number of women having abortions, which are legal only in Northern Ireland in exceptional circumstances. In 2003 there were 1,484 births in adolescents under the age of 20 years, a rate of 22.9 per 1,000. This rate has fallen by 10.5% since 2000 when the rate was 25.6 per 1,000 (General Register Office, 2004).

Teenage pregnancy has been associated with a number of negative outcomes for the infants and children of teenage mothers. These outcomes have been summarised by the NHS Centre for Reviews and Dissemination (1997). Negative impacts on the infant's health include an increased risk of lower than average birth weight; infant mortality; some congenital anomalies; sudden infant death syndrome; prematurity; hospitalisation due to accidental injuries; experiencing abuse; and of becoming pregnant when they are teenagers themselves (NHS Centre for Reviews and Dissemination 1997). Recent data confirm that children born to teenage mothers have the highest infant mortality rate of 7.9 per 1000 live births. This contrasts with a rate of 4.3 per 1000 live births in women aged 30–34 years (the lowest risk group) (ONS, 2004). Children of teenage parents are also at an increased risk of negative socio-economic outcomes. For example, children of teenage mothers tend to display developmental delays in the pre-school years, and are at an increased risk of living in poverty and poor housing conditions and of suffering from poor nutrition (NHS Centre for Reviews and Dissemination, 1997).

Teenage pregnancy is also associated with adverse outcomes for the adolescent herself and may result in significant public costs (Burt, 1986). It is estimated that the cost to the NHS alone of pregnancy among under-18 year olds is over £63 million per year (Teenage Pregnancy Strategy Evaluation Team, 2003). Negative health outcomes include hypertension, anaemia, placental abruption, obstetric complications, depression and isolation. An adolescent mother is also more likely to drop out of education early, have reduced employment opportunities, have an increased reliance on state welfare, live in poor housing and experience poor nutrition (NHS Centre for Reviews and Dissemination, 1997). It is clear, therefore, that compared to older women, becoming pregnant during adolescence is consistently associated with increased risks of poor social, economic and health outcomes for both mother and child.

There is evidence to suggest that the poor outcomes of teenage pregnancy are largely attributable to sociodemographic factors associated with pregnancy among teenagers, rather than the mother's age *per se* (Smith and Pell, 2001). For example, teenage mothers are more likely than older mothers to come from unskilled manual backgrounds or live in areas with higher social deprivation; have mothers who were teenage mothers themselves; be of Caribbean, Pakistani or Bangladeshi origin; have low self-esteem; and have low educational achievement (Teenage Pregnancy Unit, 2004). Teenage mothers are also more likely than older mothers to smoke during pregnancy. In the latest Infant Feeding Survey (Hamlyn *et al.*, 2002), 39% of mothers aged less than 20 years reported smoking during pregnancy, compared with 29% of mothers aged 20–24 years and 19% of mothers aged 25–29 years. Most of the variables listed above are risk factors for poor birth outcomes in their own right.

Indeed, it is argued that the biological risk associated with young maternal age has been exaggerated due to inadequate control of such sociodemographic factors in research (Anderson *et al.*, 2000). Well-controlled studies have shown that, even when mothers are under 15 years old, young age alone is not associated with adverse perinatal outcomes (Berenson *et al.*, 1997). Instead, maternal and infant well-being should always be considered within a broader biopsychosocial context.

The importance of maternal nutrition for the achievement of maternal and infant well-being is well documented. This chapter will begin with a discussion of the role of maternal nutrition in pregnancy, describing the specific nutrient needs of pregnancy. The chapter will also examine the interaction between nutrient needs and the physiological, metabolic and endocrinologic changes that occur in pregnancy. Nutrient requirements will be discussed with reference to their impact on maternal and fetal well-being and birth outcome.

Adolescence is a critical period during which lifetime habits are established (Cavadini *et al.*, 2000) and, as adolescents are particularly susceptible to certain risk behaviours, including unhealthy eating, the impact that their eating behaviour has on both their short- and long-term nutritional status is considerable. The chapter will discuss the eating behaviours and barriers to healthy eating in the adolescent population, with particular reference to surveys that have been conducted in the UK. 'Adolescence' can be described as the transitional stage of development between childhood and adulthood. *Stedman's Medical Dictionary* defines an adolescent as 'a young person who has undergone puberty but who has not reached full maturity; a teenager' (2004). Adolescence is a cultural and social phenomenon and therefore its endpoints are not easily defined. For reasons of clarity, throughout this chapter the terms adolescent and teenager are used interchangeably to refer to the ages 13–19 years (unless otherwise stated).

The chapter will build upon this evidence to discuss the specific nutritional needs of the pregnant adolescent, and to examine the factors that influence her eating behaviours. As biochemical data relating to the nutrient status of pregnant adolescents is scarce, a critical evaluation of the current research describing nutrient intakes of pregnant adolescents will be conducted. Particular attention will be made to the only nutritional survey that has been conducted with pregnant adolescents in the UK (the 'Good Enough to Eat' survey; Burchett and Seely, 2003).

Maternal nutrition

During pregnancy, maternal body composition, metabolism and physiological system functioning change to accommodate the growing fetus. During this period, the maternal diet must provide sufficient nutrients to meet this increased demand and to ensure maternal well-being and the birth of a healthy, thriving infant.

Maternal nutrient intake and nutritional status are known to influence birth outcome. It should be remembered, however, that birth outcome is influenced by an array of interrelated factors, including: sociodemographic factors (e.g. age, parity, ethnic background and socio-economic status); nutritional factors (e.g. pre-pregnancy weight and BMI, height, lean body mass and body fat); genetics; health and illness (e.g. diabetes, hypertension, chronic disease, systemic or genital tract infections); environmental factors (e.g. geography, climate); behavioural factors (e.g. stress, anxiety and drug, alcohol and cigarette use); and adequacy of prenatal care (Institute of Medicine, 1990).

It has been reported that the short-term health outcomes of inadequate maternal nutritional status include pregnancy and birth complications, poor postpartum nutritional status, poor lactational performance, and increased mortality in mothers and compromised fetal growth, increased risk of preterm births, spontaneous abortion, congenital abnormalities and morbidity and mortality in the infant (IOM, 1990).

Impaired intrauterine growth and development may also 'program' the fetus for cardiovascular, metabolic, or endocrine disease in adult life (the fetal origins of adult disease hypothesis) (Barker and Osmond, 1986). Epidemiological associations have been found to exist between lower birth size and a greater risk of death in later life from cardiovascular disease (Barker and Osmond, 1986) and Type 2 diabetes mellitus (Ravelli *et al.*, 1998). However, using fetal growth as a marker for an adverse intrauterine environment is imprecise, as not all foetuses exposed to an abnormal fetal environment have altered growth, and not all altered fetal growth is a function of the responses to environmental stimuli (Harding, 2001). More recent work has suggested that adult disease risk has developmental origins, i.e. the concept that certain adult diseases come about as a consequence of the fetal response to its environment, rather than indicating a causal role for birth size. Thus the current working model is one whereby early life events, acting through the processes of developmental plasticity (i.e. the ability of the fetus to respond to environmental cues by choosing a trajectory of development that often has adaptive advantage), alter the development of the organism to such an extent that it affects its capacity to cope with the environment of adult life and therefore influences disease risk. Experimental data suggest that the period in which these early life events influence lifelong consequences can extend from conception (and possibly preconception) to infancy, depending on the organ system involved (Gluckman *et al.*, 2005).

Physiological changes in pregnancy

Physiological and anatomical alterations develop in many organ systems during the course of pregnancy. The cardiovascular, respiratory, gastrointestinal and renal systems all adapt under pregnancy conditions. Early changes are due, in part, to the metabolic demands brought on by the fetus, placenta and uterus and, in part, to the increasing levels of pregnancy hormones, particularly those of progesterone and oestrogen. Later changes, starting in mid-pregnancy, are anatomical in nature and are caused by mechanical pressure from the expanding uterus. These alterations create unique requirements for the nutritional needs of the pregnant woman.

A detailed discussion of the physiological adaptations to pregnancy can be found elsewhere (e.g. Stables and Rankin, 2004). This chapter will focus on the important pregnancy-induced endocrinological and metabolic alterations relevant to nutrition.

Endocrine and metabolic changes in pregnancy

In non-pregnant women, endocrinologic control is classically mediated by central nervous system perceptions of the body's environment. Hypothalamic signals are sent to the anterior pituitary, whose secretions regulate metabolic rate (via the pituitary–thyroid axis), growth rate (via the pituitary–growth hormone IGF-I axis) and reproductive function (via the anterior pituitary–ovarian axis), and protects against stress (via the anterior pituitary–adrenocortical axis).

In the normal pregnant woman, the hypothalamic–pituitary control of maternal target endocrine glands is supplanted by the feto-placental unit. In general, pituitary trophic hormones are suppressed while target organ hormone secretion is increased. For example, placental thyroid-stimulating hormone, corticotrophin-releasing hormone and growth hormone secretion suppresses the pituitary secretion of thyrotrophins, adrenocorticotrophins and growth hormone respectively. Reproductive function is also controlled by the feto-placental unit. Pituitary follicle stimulating hormone (FSH) and luteinising hormone (LH) secretion is suppressed by secretion of oestrogen and progesterone from the placenta. In the first trimester, oestrogen and progesterone are secreted by the corpus luteum under the stimulation of human chorionic-gonadotrophin (hCG) originating in the placenta. In mid- to late-gestation the hormone secretion occurs directly from the placenta.

These maternal hormone adaptations influence the deposition of maternal nutrients to favour fetal growth in a number of ways. Adaptations of maternal calcium metabolism enhance calcium absorption, storage and diversion to the fetus. Calcium absorption, transport and accretion of calcium in maternal bone are enhanced in the mother in the first two trimesters. From 30 weeks gestation, calcium reabsorption from bone is significantly increased, which likely serves the need of the growing fetus for calcium and bone mineralisation. This calcium mobilisation has been shown to accompany a 2.5× increase in parathyroid hormone levels in the third trimester of pregnancy, the likely trigger for this change (Kumar *et al.*, 1979).

Similarly, the mother is able to store increased supplies of energy in adipose tissue in the first two trimesters and divert them to the fetus in the third trimester. Maternal adipose tissue storage is largely complete by the end of the second trimester and then ceases or declines in the third trimester, due largely to the exponential growth of the fetus (Knopp, 1997). Additional maternal nutrients are acquired principally due to an increase in food intake (of approximately 250–300 kCal per day). Maternal appetite is stimulated to achieve this increase, probably as a result of the increased progesterone levels in pregnancy. High oestrogen levels are thought to enhance insulin sensitivity (Barrett-Connor and Laakso, 1990), which may lead to an enhancement of maternal adipose tissue storage. The mechanism by which the mother ceases to store extra energy as fat, diverting it for fetal growth, is via insulin resistance. This mechanism is mediated by the hormones progesterone, placental lactogen, prolactin, cortisol, T3 (a thyroid hormone) and growth hormone, all of which are elevated in pregnancy. Each of these agents induces insulin resistance, enhances lipolysis, mobilises fat and reduces the utilisation of glucose. The mobilisation of fatty acids serves as an alternative source of energy for contracting muscle, sparing glucose for maternal brain function and the increasing energy expenditure of the growing fetus. In the pregnant diabetic, this process is exacerbated and transport of glucose to the fetus is excessive due to hyperglycaemia in the mother. The fetus responds by laying down excessive amounts of fat by increasing its own secretion of insulin, leading to an increased risk of macrosomia.

Other circulating nutrients, including amino acids, free fatty acids and various lipoprotein species, also serve as direct sources of energy and essential nutrients for cell growth in the fetus as well as potential regulators of endocrine steroidogenesis and polypeptide hormone secretion. As yet, many of these are *in vitro* observations and have yet to be tested *in vivo* (Knopp, 1997).

Nutrient requirements during pregnancy

Requirements increase for several nutrients during pregnancy. Compared with US recommendations, the UK recommendations for nutrient increments during pregnancy are modest. The following section will discuss only the nutrients for which the UK Department of Health (Department of Health, 1991a) has indicated an increased need during pregnancy or those that have been shown to play an important role in maternal and fetal well-being.

Energy cost of pregnancy

The energy cost of pregnancy comprises a combination of factors; namely the energy cost of increased tissue mass (consisting of the products of conception – the fetus, placenta, amniotic fluid; and hypertrophy of several maternal tissues – the uterus, breasts, blood, fat stores, extracelluar extravascular fluid), and concomitant changes in basal metabolic rate (BMR), (the maintenance costs of the increased tissue mass during pregnancy) (Prentice *et al.*, 1996). Estimations of the energy costs of pregnancy can vary widely. This can be illustrated by comparing pregnant women living in diverse environments. Durnin (1987) estimated the energy cost of pregnancy to range from 78 MJ for women living in the Gambia to 286 MJ for those living in the Netherlands. Whereas women in developed countries had increased BMRs compatible with increased total energy expenditure, women in developing countries appeared to display a *reduction* in energy expenditure during pregnancy. This appears to imply an adaptive response to adverse environmental conditions of unreliable food supplies. However, wide variations in energy expenditure have also been shown to occur between individuals living in comparable environments. In a study of eight healthy European pregnant women, Prentice *et al.* (1989) reported that approximately 50% were energy profligate, whilst the remaining 50% were energy sparing. Thus it appears that maternal metabolic adaptation to pregnancy is highly variable, making recommendations for energy intake extremely contentious.

Expert committees differ in their assessment of the need for extra energy intake in pregnancy. European recommendations are that pregnant women should increase their daily energy intake by 0.75 MJ (approximately 180 kCal) throughout pregnancy (EC Scientific Committee for Food Report, 1993), the US recommendation for healthy, active individuals is an additional 340 kCal/day during the second trimester and an extra 450 kCal/day during the third trimester of pregnancy (IOM, 2005), and the UK and World Health Organization (WHO) dietary reference values (DRVs)[1] recommend that pregnant women increase their energy intake by an additional 200 kCal/day during the last trimester of pregnancy only (FAO/WHO/UNU, 1985; Department of Health, 1991a).

---

1 DRVs are benchmark intakes of energy and nutrients – they can be used for guidance, but should not be seen as exact recommendations. They show the amount of energy or an individual nutrient that a group of people of a certain age range (and sometimes sex) needs for good health. DRV is a general term used to cover EAR, RNI and LRNI (see footnotes 2, 3 and 4).

Protein

The UK DRVs recommend that pregnant women increase their protein intake by 6 g/day throughout pregnancy (Department of Health, 1991a). This recommendation is based on the protein requirement for tissue formation of the growing fetus. During pregnancy, approximately 925 g of protein are retained, with the rate of protein retention increasing throughout the course of pregnancy (Garza and Rasmussen, 2000).

Maternal protein intake at the onset of pregnancy has been found to correlate well with pregnancy outcome, particularly with the size of the infant at birth (Wynn and Wynn, 1988). In animal studies, maternal protein deprivation before conception has been associated with reduced birth weight, over-compensatory growth post-weaning, increased systolic blood pressure and disproportionate growth of specific organs. These effects may be mediated by a mildly hyperglycaemic maternal environment and consequent reduction in insulin levels together with reduced essential amino acid levels (Coad, 2003). Generally though, human populations that have a ready access to food consume more protein than the recommended daily allowance amount (Garza and Rasmussen, 2000).

Carbohydrate

Although there are no specific DRVs for carbohydrate intake during pregnancy in the UK, research has found that the type of carbohydrate eaten during pregnancy influences maternal fat deposition and retention and infant birth weight (Clapp, 2002). Clapp (1998) found that women who consumed a high-glycaemic diet demonstrated an increased glucose and insulin response throughout pregnancy, whilst those on a low-glycaemic diet experienced no increase in their glucose response and a blunted insulin response. The women who consumed the high glycaemic diet also experienced excessive weight gain and delivered infants with larger birth weights (>800 g above mean weight) and had larger placentas than the low glycaemic group (Clapp, 1997).

Therefore it appears that a significant portion of the variance in maternal fat deposition and infant birth weight may be related to differences in maternal dietary carbohydrate, which alters circulating maternal glucose and insulin levels. Dietary carbohydrates that elevate postprandial glucose levels in pregnancy markedly increase feto-placental growth rate. Thus, the increased availability of high-glycaemic carbohydrate sources in Western industrialised societies may explain the gradual increase in birth weight that has occurred over the last 50 years (Clapp, 2002).

Fatty acids

There are no DRVs set for fats or fatty acid intake in pregnant women in the UK. However, essential fatty acids are vital to the development of the membranes and brain of the fetus. During the third trimester, there is a growth spurt in the human brain, with a large increase in the cerebral content of achidonic acid (AA) and docosahexaenoic acid (DHA). Haggarty and colleagues (1997) have shown that the uptake of long chain polyunsaturated fatty acids (PUFAs) by the fetus depends on maternal dietary supply, and maternal long chain PUFA status during pregnancy is critical for the long chain PUFA status in the newborn.

Maternal consumption of fats and fatty acids has been implicated in the aetiology of pre-eclampsia (Scholl *et al.*, 2005). Pre-eclampsia is an important cause of preterm delivery, fetal growth restriction, and maternal and infant mortality. Whilst the exact cause(s) remain unknown, a current theory holds that, in pre-eclampsia, there is an imbalance between prooxidant production and antioxidant defences (oxidative stress) (Roberts and Hubel, 2004; Scholl *et al.*, 2005). It has been found that increased intakes of fat, PUFAs and specific PUFAs (i.e. linolenic and linoleic acid) are associated with higher isoprostane levels (a specific marker for oxidative damage to lipids from endogenous lipid peroxidation), and higher isoprostane excretion has been associated with a five-fold increase in the risk of pre-eclampsia (Scholl *et al.*, 2005). Thus it has been suggested that diets high in polyunsaturates could contribute to the oxidative stress associated with pre-eclampsia (Turpeinen *et al.*, 1998).

Vitamins

Vitamin A

The UK Department of Health recommends that pregnant women increase their vitamin A intake by an additional 100 µg retinol equivalent/day (Department of Health, 1991a). Vitamin A has a critical role in normal vision, cell differentiation and proliferation and maintenance of epithelial cell integrity. Although rare in the UK, clinical vitamin A deficiency is one of the most prevalent deficiencies in developing countries. In western countries, intakes of retinol and its precursors usually meet baseline needs and the additional requirements imposed by pregnancy (Garza and Rasmussen, 2000). It has been shown, however, that vitamin A deficiency may be problematic at subclinical, as well as clinical, levels in pregnant women. Recent research carried out in India demonstrated that, after adjusting for confounding factors, subclinical vitamin A deficiency (defined as a serum retinol level of <200 µg/L) in the third trimester was associated with an increased risk of preterm delivery and maternal anaemia. As vitamin A is essential for the absorption and utilisation of non-haem iron, it is possible that the low retinol levels had a possible contributory role in limiting iron utilisation and aggravating pregnancy anaemia (Radhika *et al.*, 2002). Subclinical vitamin A deficiencies seem to be rare in the UK, although recent survey data indicates that women aged 19–64 years have adequate plasma retinol values, despite 9% having vitamin A intakes which were below the lower reference nutrient intake (LRNI)[2] of 250 µg/day (Henderson *et al.*, 2003).

High intakes of vitamin A from dietary supplements around the time of conception have been associated with congenital abnormalities (Hathcock *et al.*, 1990). The UK Department of Health advises against the consumption of high-dose vitamin A supplements, liver and liver products in pregnancy as these may contain hazardous levels of vitamin A (Department of Health, 1991b).

Vitamin D

The UK DRVs for vitamin D state that pregnant women should consume an additional 10 µg/day vitamin D from a non-pregnant DRV of 0 (it is assumed that non-pregnant women obtain sufficient vitamin D from sunlight alone) (Department of Health, 1991a). Maternal vitamin D status during pregnancy has been linked to maternal osteomalacia and reduced birth weight, hypocalcaemia and tetany in the infant (Cockburn *et al.*, 1980). Risk factors for vitamin D deficiency are low sun exposure, dark skin and living in northern latitudes. In a cohort study of 744 pregnant nulliparous women in the UK, vitamin D intakes were far below the reference nutrient intake (RNI)[3] of 10 µg for the majority of women in the study (the median intake was 2.4 µg from food and supplement sources) (Matthews and Neil, 1998). Matthews and Neil (1998) suggest that the current UK RNI is unlikely to be achievable without supplementation.

Vitamin D toxicity can cause hypercalcaemia in women. In animal studies, high vitamin D intakes have been associated with neonatal aortic malformations, although there is no clear evidence that this also occurs in humans (Garza and Rasmussen, 2000).

2 The lower reference nutrient intake (LRNI) is the amount of a nutrient that is enough for a small number of people in a group with the smallest needs. Most people will need more than this.
3 The reference nutrient intake (RNI) is the amount of a nutrient that is enough for only the small number of people who have low requirements (2.5%).The majority need more.

Vitamin E

The basis for the increased DRV for vitamin E during pregnancy (an additional 2 mg/day; Department of Health, 1991a) is grounded in the general expectation that higher vitamin E levels are required to promote fetal growth (Garza and Rasmussen, 2000). Premature infants may be particularly susceptible to vitamin E deficiency, as the majority of vitamin E transfer from mother to fetus is thought to occur in the last trimester. Inadequate vitamin E status in preterm infants has been associated with bronchopulmonary dysplasia, retinopathy and intraventricular haemorrhage. Vitamin E deficiency is rarely seen in healthy adults and the consequences of deficiency on mothers during pregnancy have not been described in humans; research has possibly been impeded by the low observance of overt vitamin E deficiency (Garza and Rasmussen, 2000; Rumbold and Crowther, 2005a).

Vitamin K

A deficiency of vitamin K in the newborn is associated with haemorrhagic disease of the newborn and, as the available evidence suggests that babies are born with inadequate stores of vitamin K, it is recommended that all infants are administered with vitamin K soon after birth (Autret-Leca and Jonville-Bera, 2001).

The current UK DRV for vitamin K intake in pregnancy is the same as for non-pregnant women (i.e. 1 µg/kg body weight; Department of Health, 1991a). There is limited research regarding the influence of maternal vitamin K supplementation during pregnancy on neonatal outcome. A systematic review found that administration of vitamin K to women prior to very preterm birth was not shown to significantly prevent periventricular haemorrhages in preterm infants (Crowther and Henderson-Smart, 2001). There is some evidence, however, to suggest that for infants of mothers who are being treated with drugs that are known to inhibit vitamin K activity (e.g. anticonvulsant drugs), antenatal maternal prophylaxis could prevent early vitamin K deficiency bleeding (Autret-Leca and Jonville-Bera, 2001).

Vitamin C

Recommended intakes of vitamin C during pregnancy are increased to reflect falling ascorbic acid concentrations in maternal plasma (an additional 10 mg/day is recommended; Department of Health, 1991a). This is probably due to the normal expansion of blood volume and relatively high levels of vitamin C uptake by the fetus (Garza and Rasmussen, 2000). Intake of vitamin C during pregnancy has been associated with birth weight and risk of preterm delivery.

In a prospective cohort study of 693 pregnant women in the UK, Matthews *et al.* (1999) found that vitamin C intake independently predicted birth weight. Each 1 mg increase in vitamin C intake was significantly associated with a 50.8 g (95% CI, 4.6, 97.0 g) increase in birth weight. They did not find an association between birth weight with any other macro- or micronutrient.

Siega-Riz *et al.* (2003) examined vitamin C intake preconceptionally and during the second trimester of pregnancy in 2064 women in the USA. They found that women who had total vitamin C intakes of <24 mg preconception-ally had twice the risk of preterm delivery because of premature rupture of the membranes (relative risk, 2.2; 95% CI, 1.1, 4.5). This risk was attenuated slightly for second-trimester intake (relative risk, 1.7; 95% CI, 0.8, 3.5). The elevated risk of preterm premature rupture of the membranes was greatest for women with a low vitamin C intake during both time periods and for women who also smoked (Siega-Riz *et al.*, 2003). This finding is consistent with studies that have reported associations between leukocyte (Casanueva *et al.*, 1991) and amniotic (Barrett *et al.*, 1994) levels of vitamin C and premature rupture of the membranes.

Since low vitamin C intakes are associated with poor birth outcomes, it may seem reasonable to advise women to take vitamin C supplements during pregnancy. However, as vitamin C is actively transported across the placenta during pregnancy, supplementation could result in higher than normal vitamin C levels in the developing fetus. At present, there is limited evidence to assure the long- or short-term safety of vitamin C supplementation for mother and child. A recent systematic review of vitamin C supplementation in pregnancy concluded that, although it appeared that a low vitamin C intake was associated with complications in pregnancy, such as pre-eclampsia, anaemia and low birth weight (LBW), there was insufficient evidence to determine whether supplementing women with vitamin C during pregnancy prevents neonatal mortality or LBW. Whilst vitamin C supplementation appeared to be associated with a decreased risk of pre-eclampsia, it was also associated with a moderate *increase* in the risk of preterm birth, although the authors acknowledge that more research is needed (Rumbold and Crowther, 2005b).

Thiamin

The UK DRVs for thiamin recommend that pregnant women consume an additional 0.1 mg/day for the last trimester of pregnancy (Department of Health, 1991a). Marked thiamin deficiency has been associated with severe cardiac depression in pregnant women, which may lead to congestive heart failure in their newborns. When populations at risk of thiamin deficiency are supplemented, reductions in stillbirths, maternal and perinatal mortality and toxaemia have been demonstrated (Garza and Rasmussen, 2000).

Riboflavin

It is recommended that pregnant women increase their riboflavin intake by an additional 0.3 mg/day (Department of Health, 1991a). Nutritional deficits in riboflavin have been described in pregnant women in developing and industrialised countries (Bates *et al.*, 1981; Wacker *et al.*, 2000). Maternal riboflavin status appears to decrease as pregnancy approaches term, possibly due to an increased uptake by the fetus (Bates *et al.*, 1981; Wacker *et al.*, 2000). The importance of riboflavin in pregnancy is underlined by the fact that placenta formation depends on a reproductive-specific riboflavin carrier protein (Natraj *et al.*, 1988). Severe riboflavin deficiency may prevent conception and moderate deficiency has been associated with fetal malformation and intrauterine death (Heller *et al.*, 1974). Pregnant women with inadequate riboflavin status have been shown to be at increased risk of developing pre-eclampsia (28.8%) compared to non-deficient women (7.8%, $p < 0.001$), even when controlled for parity, maternal age and weight, and gestational age (Wacker *et al.*, 2000).

Folic acid

Folate is the generic name of a number of naturally occurring analogues that are essential to diet. Folic acid is the synthetic form of the vitamin, which is metabolised as the other forms of folate, but is more stable and biologically effective. Folate has two important biological roles: it is a cofactor for *de novo* synthesis of purine and thymidine required for DNA and RNA synthesis; and it is required for the transfer of methyl groups in the amino acid methylation cycle and the recycling of homocysteine back to methionine. As folate has a key role in DNA/RNA synthesis, any decrease in the rate of cell division resulting from a depletion in serum folate levels could be an important factor in the development of neural tube defects (NTDs) were it to occur at a critical stage of neural tube formation. The precise cause and the exact mechanism by which folic acid protects against NTD remain unknown (Coad, 2003).

The UK has one of the highest rates of NTDs in the world, affecting 1–2 per 1000 pregnancies (MRC Vitamin Study Research Group, 1991). There is a weight of evidence that suggests that supplementing mothers with folic acid can prevent the initial occurrence (Czeizel and Duda, 1992) as well as the reoccurrence (MRC Vitamin Study Research Group, 1991) of neural tube defects in infants. There is an inverse dose–response relationship between folate status and risk of NTDs (Wald, 2004). This knowledge has led governments around the world to recommend folic acid supplementation for women of childbearing age, particularly those considering pregnancy (Buttriss, 2004). Crucially, folic acid needs to be taken periconceptionally, as once a pregnancy is confirmed it may be too late for the folic acid to be protective (Wald, 2004). Since 1992, the UK Department of Health has advised women to take a daily folic acid supplement (400 µg/d) prior to conception and during the first 12 weeks of pregnancy. This is in addition to ensuring their diet is rich in foods providing folates and folic acid (Department of Health, 1992). It is estimated that consumption of 400 µg /d of folic acid could reduce the incidence of NTDs by 36% (Wald, 2004).

There is evidence of growing awareness of the benefits of folic acid supplementation amongst mothers. In the UK survey of infant feeding and antenatal care, Hamlyn *et al.* (2002) reported that 92% of mothers knew that increasing their intake of folic acid in early pregnancy could be beneficial, compared with 75% in 1995. Eighty-nine per cent of all mothers questioned in the survey reported that they had increased their intake of folic acid in early pregnancy, although there is no data on whether they took this action prior to conception or once pregnancy was detected. There was little difference in folic acid knowledge between social groups, with 98% of mothers in higher socio-economic groups being aware, compared with 93% of those in lower socio-economic groups (Hamlyn *et al.*, 2002).

Despite this increased awareness, dietary surveys of pregnant women reveal that folate intakes are below the RNIs. In a cohort study of 744 pregnant nulliparous women in the UK, total folate intakes from food and supplements was below the RNI (median intake of 261 µg) (Matthews and Neil, 1998). However, the women included in this study were between 9 and 20 weeks gestation, and therefore may have stopped taking folic acid supplements prior to taking part in the study.

Minerals

United Kingdom DRVs do not specify incremental intakes of any minerals during pregnancy, although there are recommendations for increased intakes of many minerals during lactation (Department of Health, 1991a). In contrast, in the United States, the recommended dietary allowances (RDAs) for most minerals are increased during both pregnancy and lactation (IOM, 1997). The following section will discuss those minerals that are known to be of particular importance during pregnancy.

Iron

During pregnancy, iron is required for the formation of new fetal tissue and haematopoiesis in both the mother and fetus. Iron deficiency is a common cause of maternal anaemia, which is a problem in both developing and industrialised countries, where maternal iron stores at the beginning of pregnancy are often low (Fernadez-Ballart and Murphy, 2001). A cohort study of 744 pregnant nulliparous women in the UK reported that iron intakes fell short of the DRVs (median daily intake of 10.7 mg from food and supplement sources compared to the UK DRV for females aged 15–50 years of 14.8 mg/day) (Matthews and Neil, 1998). Women in lower socio-economic groups, adolescents and multiparous women are at the highest risk of iron deficiency (Garza and Rasmussen, 2000). As a consequence of women's low iron status in pregnancy, the routine iron supplementation of pregnant women is common practice. This is despite the fact that there have been no trials conducted to establish if there is any benefit to iron supplementation during pregnancy to prevent iron deficiency anaemia and thus reduce adverse pregnancy outcomes (Yip, 2000); as iron supplementation is common practice in most countries, it is unethical to withhold iron assigned to a control group. The efficacy of iron supplementation in correcting iron deficiency anaemia has, however, been shown under research conditions (Yip, 2000).

Severe anaemia, described by WHO as haemoglobin (Hb) concentrations of less than 70 g/L (DeMaeyer, 1989), puts both mother and infant at risk, mainly of hypoxia and heart failure (Yip, 2000). The evidence for effects of mild to moderate anaemia on adverse outcomes is less certain. A well-controlled study by Zhou *et al.* conducted in Shanghai (1998) reported that the risk of preterm delivery was increased 1.6 times for women with Hb concentrations of 100–109 g/L; a 2.6-fold increase was seen in Hb concentrations of 90–99 g/L; and a 3.7-fold increase in risk was demonstrated for Hb concentrations of 60–89 g/L.

Overall, the association between moderate anaemia and poor perinatal outcomes has only been found through epidemiological studies and the available evidence cannot establish this relationship as causal (Yip, 2000). Indeed, anaemia, unless very severe, may not be a direct cause of poor pregnancy outcomes. Some studies have found an association between anaemia and adverse pregnancy outcomes, whereas other studies have not (Rush, 2000). It is possible that a common factor could cause both anaemia and poor birth outcomes.

There is limited research on the effect of anaemia on maternal morbidity and mortality, particularly in developed countries. Recent research has associated iron deficiency anaemia with increased maternal mortality and morbidity, including increased fatigue, deceased work capacity, reduced resistance to cold, poor tolerance to heavy blood loss and increased risk of urinary tract infections (Hercberg *et al.*, 2000).

The normal newborn's body iron concentration is approximately 50% greater than in the normal adult, and therefore term infants have significant iron reserves. Except for infants of the most iron-deficient women, iron stores are similar in those with iron-sufficient and iron-deficient mothers, suggesting that fetal iron needs are met at the expense of maternal stores (Garza and Rasmussen, 2000).

Calcium

Calcium is needed for the development of the fetal skeleton. The majority of the newborn's calcium content is deposited in the last trimester of pregnancy and is derived from the maternal skeleton, rather than from dietary sources. The mother's ability to absorb calcium increases during pregnancy, although the mechanisms responsible for this enhanced absorption are not well understood (Garza and Rasmussen, 2000).

There have been a number of studies of the effect of calcium supplementation on pregnancy-induced hypertension and pre-eclampsia. A meta-analysis of 14 randomised controlled trials found that calcium supplementation during pregnancy reduced systolic blood pressure by 5.40 mmHg and diastolic blood pressure by 3.44 mmHg, and reduced the incidence of pre-eclampsia in pregnant women (Bucher *et al.*, 1996). However, the subsequent large multi-centre Trial of Calcium for Pre-eclampsia Prevention yielded conflicting results. The trial found that calcium supplementation did not affect systolic or diastolic blood pressures; nor did it influence the rate of pre-eclampsia, pregnancy-associated hypertension or perinatal outcome (including preterm delivery, intrauterine growth restriction (IUGR) and perinatal death) (Levine *et al.*, 1997). This trial was conducted in a low-risk population of American pregnant women, whose dietary calcium intakes are generally relatively high (Wright, 2000). It may be that calcium supplementation is only beneficial for women who are at high risk of gestational hypertension and/or in communities with low dietary calcium intake (Hofmeyer *et al.*, 2003).

It is possible that other trace elements, possibly in association with calcium, have a role in the development of pre-eclampsia. Kumru *et al.* (2003) found that women with pre-eclampsia had lower serum levels of calcium (10% lower), zinc (43% lower) and copper (68% lower) than healthy pregnant women. The numbers in this study were small, however, consisting of 30 pre-eclamptic and 30 healthy pregnant women, and further large scale studies are required to corroborate these findings.

There is also evidence to suggest that calcium supplementation during pregnancy is associated with lower systolic blood pressure in childhood, particularly in overweight children (Belizan *et al.*, 1997). These findings could reflect a long-term programming of blood pressure *in utero* by calcium supplementation in the mother.

Zinc

Zinc is an essential micronutrient that participates in carbohydrate and protein metabolism, nucleic acid synthesis, and other vital functions. Recent research has associated zinc deficiency with an increased rate of pregnancy and delivery complications in women and an increased incidence in infants of morbidity, e.g. rickets, atopic dermatitis and anaemia. Furthermore, zinc deficiency at birth was associated with a reduced rate of linear growth and delayed psychomotor development in children in their first year of life (Scheplyagina, 2005).

There is also some evidence to suggest that zinc supplementation reduces pregnancy-induced hypertension, but overall studies have been inconsistent (Rush, 2000). In Gibson's review of seven zinc supplementation studies of pregnant women, only one reported a reduced incidence of pregnancy-induced hypertension (Gibson, 1994). However, these studies suffered from methodological weaknesses and small sample sizes, and more large scale well-controlled studies are required.

Iodine

Iodine deficiency (ID) during pregnancy has important repercussions for both the mother and fetus. Iodine is required for the synthesis of thyroid hormones and a deficiency results in relative hypothyroxinaemia (through the thyroid stimulating hormone feedback mechanisms), thus leading to enhanced thyroidal stimulation and goitrogenesis in both mother and fetus. Since thyroid hormones are crucial for brain development during both fetal and early postnatal life, any impairment in hormone availability during critical periods of brain development may induce irreversible brain damage (i.e. endemic cretinism) (Glinoer, 2004).

National iodine supplementation programs have been in place in countries such as the USA, Japan and a limited number of European regions for many years, although mild to moderate ID is still present in such countries (Glinoer, 2004). For example, a study in the US found that almost 7% had iodine excretion levels below 50 µg/L (which constitutes moderate ID in pregnancy) (Dunn, 1998). The recent UK National Diet and Nutrition Surveys revealed that low iodine intakes were common in young women (12% of women aged 19–24 years (Henderson *et al.*, 2003) and 10% of adolescents aged 15–18 years (Gregory *et al.*, 2000) had average daily intakes of iodine below the LRNI of 70 µg), which could translate into a deficient iodine status in a significant proportion of women of childbearing age. This situation may need to be addressed by the medical community and public health authorities in order to prevent the negative health outcomes of ID in future generations.

The influence of good maternal nutrition on both maternal and infant well-being seems clear. Protein is needed for healthy function of all cells, certain PUFAs are needed for healthy brain, nerve and heart development, and vitamins and minerals are used in growth, repair and the regulation of body processes. The growing fetus receives nutrients from either maternal dietary intake or the mother's own body stores. If the mother has a history of poor nutrition these nutrient stores will already be low, affecting the ability of the fetus to sustain adequate access to the nutrients needed. If the mother's diet during pregnancy is also nutrient-deficient, this will further increase the risk of inadequate nutrition for the growing fetus. Inadequate nutrition *in utero* has both short-term and lifelong health implications for the infant.

It should be remembered, however, that, as well as nutritional factors, there are multiple factors that influence maternal and infant outcome, including sociodemographic, genetic, environmental and behavioural factors and health and illness (Garza and Rasmussen, 2000). Such biopsychosocial factors include losses or malabsorption of nutrients associated with disease, lack of knowledge about adequate prenatal nutrition, dietary taboos associated with pregnancy, poor antenatal care, heavy physical work, smoking and parity. Maternal and infant well-being should always be considered within this broader context.

Adolescent nutrition

Adolescence is a time of physiological, psychological and social development. It is one of the most dynamic and complex transitions in the lifespan. During puberty, teenagers gain 50% of their adult weight, 50% of their skeletal mass and 20% of their adult height. In females, puberty results in twice as much body fat deposition as males (Wahl, 1999). The changes that occur during adolescence can have a direct consequence on eating behaviours and nutritional health. Total nutrient needs are higher in adolescence than at any other time in the lifespan (Story *et al.*, 2002). Nutritional surveys have shown that the highest prevalence of nutritional deficiencies occurs in adolescence, with most commonly noted deficiencies in calcium, iron, riboflavin, thiamin and vitamins A and C (Wahl, 1999).

Inadequate intake of nutrients during adolescence can potentially affect growth and delay sexual maturity (Story, 1992), as well as having an impact on major health problems such as atherosclerosis, hypertension and birth of LBW infants (Malcom *et al.*, 1997; Lenders *et al.*, 2000). More immediate effects of poor nutrition during adolescence include iron deficiency, eating disorders, obesity, under-nutrition and dental caries (Story, 1992). The increased physical activity of adolescents places intense demands on the body, whilst at the same time it has been reported that approximately 60% of female adolescents claim to be trying to lose weight (Wahl, 1999).

Furthermore, dietary habits acquired during adolescence have the potential to enhance or undermine health throughout life. For example, high fat intake during adolescence and into adulthood is associated with an increased risk of heart disease, and low calcium intake during adolescence is associated with low bone density and an increased risk of osteoporosis in later life (Lytle, 2002).

Conceptual framework for understanding adolescent eating behaviour

Conceptual theories are useful in helping to understand and explain the dynamics of health behaviours, the processes for changing behaviours and the effects of external influences on such behaviours (Story *et al.*, 2002). Unhealthy eating has been described a 'risk behaviour' in the adolescent population (Irwin *et al.*, 1997). It is helpful to evaluate the nature of risk behaviour in order to understand why adolescents behave this way.

Risk behaviours often associated with adolescents include unhealthy eating, dangerous driving, alcohol and drug use, sexual behaviour and injury-related behaviours. In a recent survey of 1516 teenagers aged 14–15 years in the UK, 23% reported that they smoked, 35% had been drunk in the previous three months, 64% considered they ate unhealthily and 39% took little exercise (Walker *et al.*, 2002). Risk behaviours have a developmental trajectory; typically they increase in prevalence over the adolescent years, with rates peaking in late adolescence and declining in young adulthood (Irwin *et al.*, 1997). These potentially health-damaging behaviours, established during adolescence, often have lasting deleterious effects throughout life. Negative health outcomes of risk-taking behaviours include sexually transmitted diseases, unplanned pregnancy, failure at school, habituation, premature cardiovascular disease, hypertension, obesity and its associated medical sequelae, physical and psychological disability and death (Irwin *et al.*, 1997).

Risk-taking behaviours have been defined by Irwin *et al.* (1997, p. 2):

Risk-taking behaviours can be distinguished from developmentally appropriate exploratory behaviour by their potentially serious, long-term, and negative consequences. Whereas adolescence exploratory behaviour in a safe or positive context enhances competence and confidence, risk-taking behaviours jeopardise health and well-being. Some risk-taking behaviours are defined by their adolescent age of onset. For example, sexual activity, certain eating behaviours, driving a car, drinking alcohol, or leaving home may be considered risk-taking behaviours at age 13, but may not be at age 21. Some behaviours are risky regardless of age such as unhealthy eating behaviours, promiscuous sexual behaviour, cocaine use, or driving under the influence of alcohol.

It is difficult to attribute an absolute reason why adolescents are at increased risk of risky behaviour, together with the associated negative nutritional outcomes. As with all health problems, there is a complex relationship between the individual and a variety of biopsychosocial and environmental factors that are associated with an increased likelihood of engaging in risky behaviours.

Theories of risk-taking behaviours

There are a number of theoretical models that can be used to help understand the initiation and trajectory of risk-taking behaviours. These theories may be useful in understanding why adolescents take 'risky' decisions and may enable us to develop more effective help promoting programmes for them.

Dispositionally-based theories view risk-taking behaviours as deviant. It is hypothesised that traits such as low self-esteem, depression, inadequate social skills, impulsivity characteristic of attention deficit disorder, or a general propensity for unconventionality lead to this deviancy. Whilst there is evidence that each of these factors is associated with risky behaviours under a specific condition, there is also evidence to contradict it. For example, poor self-esteem appears to be associated with a number of risky behaviours. However, it has been shown that risk-taking itself can raise self-esteem, or that certain risky behaviours, such as sexual behaviour, are associated with a higher level of self-esteem (Irwin *et al.*, 1997).

Theories of sensation-seeking state that individuals differ in terms of their underlying needs for stimulation (or sensation or thrill-seeking), which underlies much of risk-taking behaviour. Sensation seekers are willing to take risks for the sake of increases in stimulation and arousal. There is evidence to suggest that these traits may be protective if the environmental context is supportive (Irwin *et al.*, 1997).

The ecological perspective considers risk-taking within the social and environmental context. These theories propose that contextual factors, such as economic status, cultural background and general social environment provide social norms, models, opportunities and reinforcements for adolescent participation in risky behaviours. The social world of the adolescent consists of proximal and distal influences. Proximal contexts include those aspects of the environment that the adolescent comes most into contact with, such as family members, peers and social institutions such as schools or churches. Distal contexts include the community, the mass media and social policies. Many of the conceptual models of risk-taking can be overlaid into this general ecological model (Irwin *et al.*, 1997).

Biological models of risk-taking behaviour, as described by Irwin *et al.* (1997), consider the role of genetic factors, neuroendocrine processes, including hormonal influences, and the timing of pubertal events. Genetic predisposition has been implied in adolescent alcohol abuse (Cloninger, 1997) and it has been suggested that genetic factors may contribute about half the variance underlying certain eating disorders (Crisp, 1995). Neuroendocrine factors are viewed as the aetiological agent of some sensation-seeking theories. Examples include the effect of testosterone levels on sexual intercourse and other risky behaviours in males. Biological factors may have an indirect effect on risk-taking behaviours. For example, puberty is associated with rapid and significant changes in body shape, size and appearance. These physiological differences may be associated with differences in how the social environment responds to the adolescent, including different expectations for behaviour. Research has shown an association between pubertal onset and changes in family interactions (Steinberg, 1981), parental feelings (Cohen *et al.*, 1986) and peer expectations (Savin-Williams, 1979).

The biopsychosocial model of risk-taking behaviour (Irwin and Millstein, 1986) recognises the importance of direct and interactive effects of multiple factors. The model integrates biological (i.e. pubertal timing, hormonal effects and genetic predisposition) and psychological aspects of development (i.e. self-esteem, sensation-seeking and cognitive state) with the social environment (i.e. the influence of peers, parents and school). In addition, the model has a developmental perspective, viewing risk-taking within the context of the developmental changes of adolescence (Irwin *et al.*, 1997).

As it is a multitude of interactive factors that influence not only the nutrition of adolescent mothers, but also the occurrence of teenage pregnancy and the development of eating habits during adolescence, the biopsychosocial model of risk-taking behaviour is perhaps the most useful in this context. According to this model, biological, psychological and social or environmental variables, mediated by perceptions of risk and peer-group characteristics, could predict adolescent risk-taking. This model may be useful in understanding pregnant adolescents' behaviour and in doing so aiding the development of suitable nutrition programmes for this population.

Interrelationship between risk behaviours

There is evidence to suggest that involvement in one type of risk behaviour increases the likelihood of becoming involved in other risk behaviours. Risk-taking behaviours cluster and interact with one another. For example, research has shown that adolescents who have sexual intercourse also engage in other risk behaviours, such as smoking, drug and alcohol use (Mott and Haurin, 1988). Even when sociodemographic variables (such as race, religion, parental education, family structure and personality) are controlled for, the association remains. Other research has shown that adolescents who have sexual intercourse are less likely to aspire to advanced education and less likely to report being very religious (Miller and Simon, 1974). There has been limited research that focuses specifically on the covariance of eating behaviours and other risk behaviours. A study of 36,284 adolescents found that, after controlling for sociodemographic and personal variables, male and female adolescents who engaged in health-promoting behaviours were less likely to have unhealthy eating behaviours, while those engaging in risk-taking behaviours were more likely to have unhealthy eating behaviours (Neumark-Sztainer *et al.*, 1997). A US study of schoolchildren found that students in the 8th grade who reported making less healthy food choices had lower physical activity patterns and were more likely to smoke cigarettes, and that these behaviours persisted until the 12th grade (Lytle *et al.*, 1995). It has also been reported that adolescents who have sex, drink and smoke are more likely to eat high-salt, high-fat and high-sugar foods (Irwin *et al.*, 1997). While several explanations for this clustering of behaviours have been proposed (Story *et al.*, 2002), the most frequently cited and tested explanation is that these behaviours cluster because they share a common aetiology; i.e. they are each a manifestation of a general predisposition towards unconventionality (Elliot, 1994).

It seems clear that eating behaviours are related to other behaviours often displayed in adolescents and should not be viewed in isolation. Adolescents who engage in a wide range of health-compromising behaviours may be particularly at risk of unhealthy eating. The interactive relationship between risk behaviours impacts on how health education for adolescents should be structured and delivered. It suggests that health education efforts should address a lifestyle approach, rather than specific individual health behaviours. Thus, health education should promote healthy lifestyles through health-enhancing curricula and personal, behavioural and environmental conditions conducive to healthful behaviours (Lytle and Roski, 1997). This will empower adolescents with a sense of personal responsibility, decision-making skills and a clear understanding of the benefits of making healthy lifestyle decisions. Furthermore, it may be possible to identify high-risk adolescents and target and tailor health promotion programs to them.

Adolescent eating practices

Adolescents' nutritional status can be affected by specific aspects of the adolescent lifestyle. It has been reported that adolescents frequently miss meals and eat away from home, and that convenience and fast foods, which tend to be high in saturated fat and total fat, cholesterol and sodium, are popular choices among this population (Lifshitz *et al.*, 1993).

Breakfast is an important component of a healthy diet and has been shown to have a positive impact on adolescents' health and well-being. Missing breakfast, however, is highly prevalent in children and adolescents, with cited incidences ranging from 12–34% (Rampersaud *et al.*, 2005). Pregnant adolescents also regularly miss breakfast. The UK 'Good Enough to Eat' survey of pregnant adolescents revealed that 50% of participants claimed to miss breakfast at least once a week. The most common reasons given for missing meals were insufficient money, lack of hunger and lack of time (Burchett and Seeley, 2003). A recent review summarised the results of 47 studies examining the association of breakfast consumption with nutritional adequacy, body weight and academic performance in children and adolescents (Rampersaud *et al.*, 2005). Although the quality of breakfast was variable within and between studies reviewed, those who reported eating breakfast on a consistent basis tended to have superior nutritional profiles; they consumed more calories and were less likely to be overweight than non-breakfast eaters. Missing breakfast was found to be typically more prevalent in females, children from lower socio-economic backgrounds, older children and adolescents. A number of studies have found that breakfast-skipping behaviour was associated with other risk behaviours, such as smoking, sexual behaviour in females, frequent alcohol use, behavioural disinhibition and missing school (e.g. Barker *et al.*, 2000; Kleinman *et al.*, 2002; Keski-Rahkonen *et al.*, 2003; Sjoberg *et al.*, 2003).

Snacking is a common phenomenon among adolescents, with up to 90% of teenagers reporting eating between meals (Bigler-Doughten and Jenkins, 1987). Results from a US student health survey revealed that 39% of adolescents reported eating nutritious snacks, including fruit, vegetables, juice, milk or cheese. The remaining 61% described consuming 'junk foods' such as fizzy drinks, chips, confectionary and cake (Portnoy and Christenson, 1989). Snacking may fulfil an important role in an adolescent's diet. A US nationwide dietary survey revealed that snacks provided up to a third of adolescents' daily energy intake, as well as providing significant amounts of calcium, magnesium and vitamin C (US Department of Health, 1989). Indeed, reduced snacking, missing meals, or restriction to very low-calorie snacks can result in poor weight gain and growth (Lifshitz and Moses, 1989). Wisely chosen snacks, therefore, appear to be a potential asset to an adolescent's diet (Lifshitz *et al.*, 1993).

The diet of adolescents in the UK

Compared with the abundance of US literature on the topic, there is very little research that has been carried out to describe the eating habits of adolescents in the UK. The most significant publication available to date is the National Diet and Nutrition Survey (NDNS) of young people aged 4–18 years (Gregory *et al.*, 2000), which is a cross-sectional survey of the dietary habits and nutritional status of children and adolescents in the UK. It is the largest and most comprehensive survey ever undertaken of the diet and nutritional status of young people in the UK. The NDNS programme was established in 1992 by the Ministry of Agriculture, Fisheries and Food (MAFF) and the Department of Health. The survey informs the Government's White Paper, 'Saving Lives: Our Healthier Nation', a Government action plan aimed at tackling poor health, particularly for those who are worst off in society, which sets out key areas and targets for improving the health of children and young people, in which diet plays a key role (Department of Health, 1999).

The programme assesses nutritional status and dietary biomarkers, using blood and urine samples, and relates these to dietary, physiological and social data. It is therefore able to monitor the food and nutrient intakes, source of nutrients and nutritional status of a nationally representative sample of children and adolescents in the UK. Fieldwork was conducted over a twelve-month period to take account of seasonality in both eating behaviour and also in the nutrient content of foods (e.g. full fat milk). The data collection methods included a seven-day weighed intake dietary record, anthropometric measurements, urine and blood samples and interviews. In total, 1701 young people (64% of those approached) completed all parts of the survey. The survey did not specify whether any participants were pregnant, although the NDNS for adults specifically excluded those who were pregnant or breastfeeding on the grounds that 'the diet and physiology of pregnant or breastfeeding women is likely to be so different from those of other similarly aged women as to possibly distort the results' (Henderson *et al.*, 2003, p. 6).

Findings of the survey

The findings of the survey have been summarised elsewhere (Smithers *et al.*, 2000). In this chapter, only the key findings relating to females, particularly those of reproductive age, will be discussed. Where possible, energy and nutrient intakes will be compared with the UK Dietary Reference Values for this age group (Department of Health, 1991a). Particular note will be taken of how nutrient intake and nutrient status change with age. Finally, the sociodemographic influences on nutrient intake and status will be discussed.

Energy intake

There was an increase in mean energy intake in female adolescents with increasing age, from 5.87 MJ (4–6 year olds) to 7.03 MJ (11–14 year olds, $p < 0.01$), but then no further increase for those aged 15–18 years (6.82 MJ). Mean energy intakes were below estimated average requirements (EARs)[4] for each age group. Apart from those aged 15–18 years, mean energy intakes were at least 83% of the appropriate EAR. For 15–18 year olds, intake was only 77% of the EAR. This was likely to be due, in part, to under-reporting of food consumption, which was a phenomenon identified in the feasibility study for the survey, particularly in the oldest age group (Smithers *et al.*, 2000). There was no association between low energy intake and smoking status or dieting behaviour.

Macronutrient intake

Mean daily protein intakes for females increased from 44.5 g/d for those aged 4–6 years to 54.8 g/d for those aged 15–18 years ($p < 0.01$). Average protein intakes were in excess of the RNI, particularly in the younger age groups.

The mean intake for total carbohydrate was broadly comparable for all age groups. On average, total carbohydrate provided 51.1% of food energy intake. This is comparable to the UK DRV of 50% of food energy when alcohol is excluded (expressed as a population average) (Department of Health, 1991a).

The average percentage of food energy from total fat was close to the DRVs for adults (expressed as population averages) for each age group (between 35.9% and 36.1% compared to the DRV of 35% – excluding alcohol). There are no separate recommendations for young people. The mean percentage of food energy derived from saturated fatty acids (SFAs) was 14.3% (higher that the adult population average of 11%), and declined significantly with age ($p < 0.01$), i.e. from 15.3% 4–6 year-olds to 13.8% in 15–18 year-olds. The mean percentage of food energy derived from trans fatty acids was 1.3% – below the adult recommendation of 2%. The mean value for monounsaturated fatty acids (MFAs) was 11.8%, again below the adult recommendation of 13% of food energy as a population average. The mean percentage contribution to food energy intakes from total cis polyunsaturated fatty acids (PUFAs) (cis n-3 and cis n-6) was 6.1%, close to the DRV of 6.5%.

There are no DRVs set for cholesterol. However, in its Report on Nutritional Aspects of Cardiovascular Disease, the Committee on Medical Aspects

---

4 The EAR is an estimate of the average requirement for energy or a nutrient – approximately 50% of a group of people will require less, and 50% will require more. For a group of people receiving adequate amounts, the range of intakes will vary around the EAR.

of Food and Nutrition Policy (COMA) recommended that average daily population intakes of cholesterol should not rise above 245 mg (Department of Health, 1994). The mean daily intake of cholesterol in females was below this at 169 mg.

Micronutrient intake

With the exception of vitamin A, the mean daily intakes of all vitamins from food sources (i.e. excluding dietary supplements) were well above the RNIs (see Figure 2.1). The mean daily intake of vitamin A from food sources was 487 μg (retinol equivalents). The mean vitamin A intake tended to increase with age, from 449 μg (4–6 years) to 545 μg (15–18 years, which represented 91% of the RNI).

Furthermore, in those aged 11–14 years and 15–18 years, 20% and 12% respectively had average daily intakes of vitamin A below the lower reference nutrient intake (LRNI). Low intakes of riboflavin were also seen in a proportion of older adolescents. Overall, the mean daily riboflavin intake was 136% of the RNI, but decreased with age (15–18 year olds had intakes that were 118% of the RNI). Importantly, a large proportion of females had intakes that fell below the LRNI (22% aged 11–14 years and 21% aged 15–18 years).

Other possible causes for concern in older adolescents were vitamin B_6 and folate intake. The overall mean intake of vitamin B_6 was approximately 150% of the RNI for each age group. However, 5% of 15–18 year olds had intakes below the LRNI.

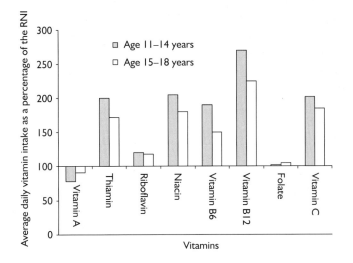

Figure 2.1 Average daily intake of vitamins as a percentage of Reference Nutrient Intake (RNI) of females aged 11–14 years and 15–18 years.

The average intake of folate from food sources was 194 µ/day in females aged 4–18 years, somewhat less than the mean intake of 250 µg/day in women aged 19–64 years (Henderson *et al.*, 2003). Whilst the average intake in young females was 123% of the RNI, between 3 and 4% of those aged 11 to 18 years had an average daily folate intake below the LRNI, i.e. less than 100 µg/day. This is compared with 2% of women aged 19–64 years who had intake below the LRNI (Henderson *et al.*, 2003). When supplements were taken into account, intake was 210 µg/day and 215 µg/day in adolescents aged 11–14 and 15–18 years respectively. The proportions of those with intakes under the LRNI did not alter.

In the younger age groups (4–10 years), mean intakes of minerals (with the exception of zinc) were above or close to the RNI and the proportions with intakes below the LRNI were small. For the older age groups (11–18 years), however, mineral intakes were often below the RNI. Average intakes of zinc, potassium, magnesium, calcium, iron, iodine and copper were all below the RNI in older females (see Figure 2.2). Thus, intakes of these minerals declined markedly with age. For example, average daily iron intake declined from 119% of the RNI in those aged 4–6 years to 58% in those aged 15–18 years and calcium intakes fell from 146% to 82% of the RNI with increasing age. By the age of 15–18 years, intakes of magnesium, potassium and copper had declined to 64%, 62% and 80% of the RNI respectively.

A significant proportion of females had intakes below the LRNI for zinc, potassium, magnesium, calcium and iron. For zinc, less than one in three 11–14 year olds and one in ten 15–18 year olds had intakes below the LRNI. One in

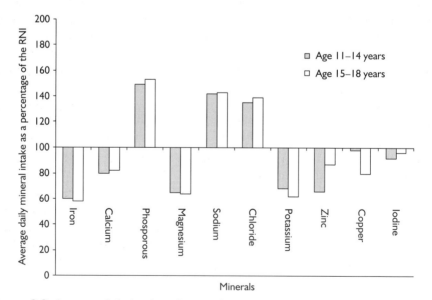

Figure 2.2 Average daily intake of minerals as a percentage of Reference Nutrient Intake (RNI) of females aged 11–14 years and 15–18 years.

five aged 11–14 years and more than one in three aged 15–18 years had intakes of potassium below the LRNI. For magnesium, 51–53% of 11–18 year olds had intakes below the LRNI. For calcium, 25% of 11–14 year olds and 19% of 15–18 year olds had intakes below the LRNI. 45%–50% of those aged 11–18 year old had mean iron intakes from food sources that were less than the LRNI.

Young people who took dietary supplements tended to have higher intakes of vitamins from food sources than non-supplement users, suggesting a greater overall sense of nutritional awareness in this group. Intakes of vitamins A and C were increased by supplement use by 5–10%, but the proportions with intakes below the LRNI were unaffected. Supplements contributed significantly to iron and zinc intakes, but again did not affect intakes below the LRNIs (Smithers *et al.*, 2000).

Nutritional status

Nutritional status was measured by analysis of blood and plasma. There was little evidence of any age group being at high risk of poor status for vitamin A, vitamin B_{12}, vitamin E, magnesium, selenium, zinc or copper. There was some evidence, however, for poor vitamin D, folate, riboflavin, vitamin B_6 and iron status in some individuals.

Indicators of iron status were of particular concern. Eight per cent of those aged 4–6 years had blood haemoglobin levels below 11.0 g/L, which is the WHO limit defining anaemia for children aged six months to six years. The haemoglobin levels for older children and adolescents are more difficult to interpret due to the lack of appropriate reference standards. Serum ferritin levels (which give an indication of the level of iron stores) were below the normal range for adults for 14% of females overall (ranging from 9% of the youngest to 27% of the oldest age group).

Of adolescents aged 15–18 years: 95% had biochemical values normally considered to indicate riboflavin deficiency (i.e. an erythrocyte glutathione reductase activation coefficient (EGRAC) above 1.30); 8% had biochemical evidence of vitamin B_6 (pyridoxine) deficiency (i.e. an erythrocyte aspartate aminotransferase activation coefficient (EAATAC) of over 2.00); 10% had evidence of vitamin D deficiency (plasma 25-hydroxy vitamin D of less than 25 nmol/l); and 39% had red cell folate levels (a measure of long-term folate status) considered to indicate marginal status (i.e. less than 425 nmol/l). As with the nutrient intake data, there was evidence of nutritional status declining (particularly with regards to riboflavin, vitamin D and folate) as age increased.

Implications of the findings for adolescent pregnancy

A number of the nutrients described above are recognised to be important for fetal growth and development during pregnancy. Although signs of overt deficiency are now rare in the UK, it appears that suboptimal nutrient intake and status is relatively common (Buttriss, 2000).

Eleven per cent of females aged 11–14 years and 10% of those aged 15–18 years showed biochemical evidence of vitamin D deficiency (this figure had increased with age, from only 2% of children aged 4–6 years demonstrating vitamin D deficiency). There is no RNI for vitamin D for young people aged over four years as it has been assumed that children get sufficient sunshine exposure, by playing outside for example, for their skin to synthesise sufficient amounts of vitamin D (Buttriss, 2000). Mean intakes of vitamin D from food, however, were low (2.1 µg/day for all females). This intake compares unfavourably with the RNI for children under four years of 10 µg/day (Buttriss, 2000). These findings are similar to the NDNS of adults, which reported that approximately 15% of respondents aged 19–64 years had low vitamin D status, with low status being more common in the younger age groups (Henderson *et al.*, 2003). Vitamin D deficiency in pregnancy has been associated with reduced birth weight and neonatal hypocalcaemia and tetany (Garza and Rasmussen, 2000). As vitamin D is essential for calcium absorption, poor vitamin D status also has implications for adolescents, who are still growing themselves. Poor vitamin D status, combined with the poor calcium intake reported in this age group (calcium intake was 82% of the RNI in the NDNS), may enhance their risk of low bone density. Most bone mineral deposition occurs during adolescence, with up to 50% of bone mass being acquired during this period of development (Buttriss, 2000). Peak bone mass in the spine and proximal femur, for example, is reached at the age of 16 years (Albertson *et al.*, 1997). Variations in calcium intake during adolescence may account for as much as 5–10% of adult peak bone mass, which can cause a 50% greater risk of hip fracture in later life (Wahl, 1999).

As the growing fetus obtains its calcium requirements from the maternal skeleton, this problem could be further compounded in pregnant adolescents, suggesting that this population may be particularly at risk of bone fragility in later life. It has also been shown that calcium supplementation during pregnancy is associated with a reduced risk of gestational hypertension, preterm delivery and possibly pre-eclampsia (Repke and Villar, 1991), emphasising the importance of adequate calcium intake during pregnancy. Authors of the NDNS also revealed that mean vitamin D status in young Asian people were well under half that of Caucasians in the survey (as reported by Buttriss, 2000), suggesting even greater potential problems within this particular sector of the population. Furthermore, as human milk concentrations of vitamin D are closely linked to maternal vitamin D status, the exclusively breastfed infants of such adolescents may be at risk of vitamin D deficiency if maternal vitamin D intake is limited (Garza and Rasmussen, 2000).

According to Department of Health recommendations, pregnant women do not need to consume more calcium than non-pregnant women (Department of Health, 1991a). There are no special recommendations for pregnant adolescents in the UK. US recommendations state that pregnant adolescents should consume 1300 mg calcium per day (IOM, 1997). Others have argued that the calcium intake recommendations should reflect the varying needs of the fetus during pregnancy, i.e. 1000 mg/day during the first two trimesters and 2000 mg/day during the last trimester to meet fetal skeletal demands, with enough remaining to maintain a positive calcium balance in the pregnant woman's bones (Winick, 1989). The average calcium intake reported in the NDNS for adolescents aged 15–18 years was 653 mg/day, well below these recommendations. In this oldest age group, 15% reported not drinking milk, a major source of calcium in the British diet according to the National Food Survey (Ministry of Agriculture, Fisheries and Food (MAFF), 1999), providing up to 40% of calcium intake.

Although no more that 1% of any age group had red cell folate levels representing severe folate deficiency (<230 nmol/l), the NDNS revealed that 39% of adolescents aged 15–18 years had red cell folate levels considered to be an indication of marginal status. Intake data in this age group revealed that the average folate intake from food and supplement sources was 215 µg/day (4% had an average daily folate intake below the LRNI). Whilst the majority had folate intakes above the RNI of 200 µg/day, this average intake does not meet the increased requirements of pregnancy. Since 1992, the UK Department of Health has advised women who could become pregnant to take a daily folic acid supplement of 400 µg/d, in addition to ensuring that their diet is rich in foods providing folates and folic acid (Department of Health, 1992). Insufficient intake of folate in the early stages of pregnancy is linked to increased risk of neural tube defects in infants. Folate deficiency during pregnancy has also been linked to megaloblastic anaemia, high rates of spontaneous abortion, toxaemia, intrauterine growth retardation, premature delivery and antepartum haemorrhage (Garza and Rasmussen, 2000). The findings of the NDNS of young people reflect those of the recent NDNS of adults, which found that 86% of women aged 19–24 years, 92% aged 25–34 years and 84% aged 35–49 years had intake of folate from all sources (including supplements) of less than 400 µg/day (Henderson *et al.*, 2003). It appears, therefore, that the use of folic acid supplements is far from being widespread. There is no folic acid fortification programme in the UK (unlike other countries), due to concerns about masking vitamin B_{12} deficiency. This policy may need to be readdressed, however, in light of these recent findings.

Of adolescents aged 15–18 years, 95% had biochemical values normally considered to indicate riboflavin deficiency and 21% had riboflavin intakes that fell below the LRNI. Most dietary riboflavin occurs as the coenzymes flavin mononucleotide (FMN) and flavin adenine dinucleotide (FAD), which are involved in oxidation–reduction reactions in a number of metabolic pathways and affect cellular respiration. Riboflavin coenzymes are required in the metabolism of other nutrients, such as tryptophan and folic acid, and in the absorption of iron (Thurnham *et al.*, 2000). It has been suggested that, due to the increased energy demand during adolescence, more riboflavin, thiamin and niacin are necessary to facilitate the release of energy from carbohydrates (Lifshitz *et al.*, 1993). Because of the importance of riboflavin in metabolism, particularly folate metabolism, and due to the increased demand for riboflavin in adolescence, any deficiency occurring in adolescent pregnancy may have serious implications on birth outcome.

Biochemical evidence of vitamin B_6 deficiency was seen in 8% of adolescents aged 15–18 years and 5% had vitamin B_6 intakes below the LRNI. This reflects the findings of the NDNS of adults, in which 5% of women aged 19–24 years were also shown to have an intake of vitamin B_6 below the LRNI (Henderson *et al.*, 2003). The increased protein needs during pregnancy and the role of pyridoxal phosphate and pyridoxamine phosphate as coenzymes of transamination and other products of protein metabolism may increase the requirements of this vitamin during pregnancy. There is, however, limited direct evidence to support this hypothesis at present (Garza and Rasmussen, 2000). Inadequate maternal vitamin B_6 status has been associated with toxaemia, low birth weight and poor general conditions of infants at birth (IOM, 1990).

NDNS data revealed that in adolescents aged 15–18 years, mean daily intake of total iron from food and supplement sources was 8.7 mg, 58% of the RNI, and 50% had mean iron intakes from food sources that were less than the LRNI. Biochemical data revealed that 27% had serum ferritin levels below the normal range for adults. Even when iron supplements were taken into account, the proportions remained similar. These findings are similar to those of the NDNS of adults, which reported that 42% aged 18–24 years and 41% of women aged 25–34 years had total dietary iron intakes below the LRNI (Henderson *et al.* 2003).

Iron requirements during pregnancy total approximately 800–900 mg (Garza and Rasmussen, 2000). The UK dietary reference values for iron during pregnancy are the same as in non-pregnant women (14.8 mg/day; Department of Health, 1991a), although the US RDA for pregnancy is more than twice that at 30 mg/day (IOM, 1997). The NDNS data compare unfavourably with these recommendations. Iron is needed for the rapid expansion of maternal blood volume and the deposition of iron in fetal tissues. Reduced oxygen-carrying capacity of the maternal blood can cause poor oxygenation in the fetus (Reifsnider and Gill, 2000). It has previously been reported that iron deficiency is common in adolescence, especially among older adolescent females, lower socio-economic groups and pregnant adolescents (Looker *et al.*, 1987). Adolescents who consume vegetarian diets are also at risk. Iron deficiency during

adolescence is partly related to rapid growth. The sharp increases in
mass, blood volume and red cell mass increase iron needs for myo
muscle and haemoglobin in blood (Lifshitz *et al.*, 1993). Iron-deficien
mia is fairly common during adolescence and peak incidence occurs at   ₉
years in females (Wahl, 1999).

Another important nutrient in pregnancy is zinc. Although there was little
evidence of a biochemical deficiency of zinc in females in the NDNS, data suggested that intake was insufficient for all age groups of females. Overall mean
daily intake of zinc was 5.7 mg, 77% of the RNI, and was below the RNI for
all age groups. One in ten of those aged 15–18 years had a zinc intake below
the LRNI. By the age of 19–24 years, the proportion of women whose zinc
intake fell below the LRNI was one in 20 (Henderson *et al.*, 2003). Therefore it
appears that adolescents are particularly at risk of a deficient zinc intake. Zinc
is crucial for tissue growth and zinc deficiency can cause poor fetal growth.
There is no increment on the UK RNI for zinc intake during pregnancy (which
remains at the non-pregnant level of 7.0 mg/day) (Department of Health, 1991a).
It has previously been reported that zinc deficiency is common in pregnancy, as
zinc is found in the same foods as iron and calcium (meat and dairy products),
which are often also deficient in pregnant women (Reifsnider and Gill, 2000).
In adolescents, additional zinc is required during puberty for normal growth and
sexual maturation (Wahl, 1999).

Socio-economic differences in nutrient intake and nutritional status

There appeared to be differences in the quality of diet between socio-economic
groups in the NDNS. Indicators of socio-economic status such as parents' receipt
of benefits, household income and social class showed that young females in
households of lower socio-economic status had lower intakes of energy, protein
and carbohydrates. Although there was a general pattern for young people in
manual classes to have more poor mean daily intakes of vitamins than those in
non-manual households, there were few statistically significant differences and
most disappeared when differences in energy intake were taken into account.
An exception to this was vitamin C, for which intakes remained markedly lower
in those of lower socio-economic status. Females from lower socio-economic
groups had lower calcium, phosphorus and iodine intakes and also tended to
have lower biochemical status of vitamins and minerals such as vitamin C,
vitamin D, β-carotene, retinol and iron. However, in general the associations
were statistically weak, which may be due in part to the relatively small sample
size of some of the subgroups analysed. Nevertheless, these results do suggest
that females from lower socio-economic backgrounds may have poorer nutrient
intakes and status than those from higher socio-economic backgrounds. Some

of these nutrients (particularly iron, calcium and vitamin D) have particular importance in helping to maintain a healthy adolescent pregnancy and ensure positive maternal and infant outcomes. This suggests that pregnant adolescents from lower socio-economic backgrounds may be at increased risk of nutrient deficiency and associated negative birth outcomes.

Secular trends in adolescent nutrition

Data from the USA suggests that adolescent food choices have changed somewhat over time (Cavadini *et al.*, 2000). Comparing food intake trends from 1965 to 1996, Cavadini and colleagues reported a decrease in the total energy intake, as did the proportion of energy derived from total fat (39% to 32%) and saturated fat (15% to 12%). Although rising steadily over the thirty-year period, intakes of iron and folate continued to be below recommendations in females. The authors expressed some concern about the falling calcium intakes observed over the study period, due to a decrease in the consumption of dairy products. Mean calcium intakes by adolescents in the USA, however, were still much higher than adolescent intakes in the UK, as described in the NDNS for young people (960 mg/day for males and females in the USA versus 784 mg/day for males and 652 mg/day for females in the UK). The number of servings of fruit and vegetables had risen over the period under study (from an average of 2.7 in 1965 to 3.3 portions in 1996), but remained below the recommended five portions per day.

There is very little information regarding secular trends in adolescent nutrition in the UK. In the past 20 years in the UK, two national surveys of the diet of school-aged children have been conducted (Department of Health, 1989; Gregory *et al.*, 2000). However, there do not appear to be any in-depth comparisons carried out on these data. Buttriss (2002) compared the macronutrient component of these surveys and found that, over recent years, there has been a reduction in energy intake and fat intake as a percentage of energy, with a corresponding increase in the proportion of energy derived from protein and carbohydrate in both males and females. Data collected in 1983 (Department of Health, 1989) showed that fat intake in females aged 14–15 years was 82.2 g/day (38.7% energy from fat), which reduced to 65.0 g/day (36.1% energy from fat) in females of the same age by 1997 (Gregory *et al.*, 2000).

These findings are similar to a study of the dietary intakes of adolescents in Northern Ireland (aged 12–15 years) over a ten-year period (1990–2000) (Ward *et al.*, 2002). It was shown that, whilst overall mean energy intake had increased by 3%, there was a significant decrease in the percentage of energy derived from total fat, saturated fat, monounsaturated fat and polyunsaturated fat and a significant increase in the overall percentage of energy derived from carbohydrates and total sugars. Overall, adolescent diets in 2000 were closer to the recommended intakes for fat (Department of Health, 1991a) than the diets of adolescents in 1990. Fruit and vegetable consumption, however, remained low (three portions per day) and sugar intake remained high. The authors conclude that, despite some improvement in recent years, adolescent diets remain poor (Ward *et al.*, 2002).

Thus there is some evidence that, in Western counties, the proportion of energy derived from fat, and in particular saturated fat, has declined over recent years. The more recent records of average fat intake of young people have been reported to be more in line with recommended intakes (Buttriss, 2002; Ward, 2002). There still appears to be some cause for concern, however, particularly with regard to inadequate fruit and vegetable consumption, a relatively high sugar intake and possible deficient intakes of iron, calcium and folate – all-important nutrients for a healthy pregnancy.

Barriers to healthy eating behaviour in adolescents

Health education theories suggest that health behaviours are influenced in part by the perceived benefits of and barriers to a specified action (Ajzen, 1991). Barriers that limit healthier eating among adolescents can be described within four basic areas: individual factors, environmental barriers, other risk behaviours and policy (Adams, 1997).

Individual barriers to healthy eating include attitudes and perceptions about food types, a lack of sense of urgency about personal health, and limitations on time, cost, taste, filling power, appearance, choice, availability and convenience (Neumark-Sztainer *et al.*, 1999; Morrissey *et al.*, 2002; O'Dea, 2003). There is some indication that adolescents can identify healthy foods, yet lack the ability to apply that knowledge when selecting and preparing foods (Adams, 1997).

Environmental factors include influence of the family and cultural factors, peers and the health care system. The pattern of eating has changed over the last few decades, with families not regularly eating together as much as they once did and many adolescents being responsible for the purchasing and preparation of their own food. This, combined with inadequate skills in food selection and preparation, can serve as a major barrier to healthy eating. Other issues that could also create barriers for adolescents include cultural conflicts (traditional versus modern foods) and the amount of parental guidance and supervision that is available to reinforce the healthy eating message. Peer influences can serve to represent unhealthy eating as socially acceptable, and thereby reinforce unhealthy eating habits (Morrissey *et al.*, 2002). Similarly, structural barriers can passively reinforce the social acceptability of poor eating habits. These include factors such as easy access to unhealthy food choices at school and shops and widespread advertising of unhealthy foods, such as snacks and confectionery, which is often directly aimed at children and adolescents (Adams, 1997).

Other interrelated behavioural factors may also act as barriers to healthy eating in adolescents. The covariance of risk factors has been discussed earlier. Briefly, it appears that risk-taking behaviours cluster and interact with one another. For example, adolescents who eat unhealthily may be also more likely to engage in other risky behaviours, such as early sexual behaviour, drinking alcohol and taking drugs. Thus it is this complement of risk behaviours that need to be addressed, rather than the problem of poor nutrition in isolation.

Government policy can also act as a barrier to healthier nutrition. The case of folic acid can be used as an example of this. Since 1992 the UK Department of Health has recommended that women who are trying to conceive should consume an extra 400 µg of folic acid per day until the twelfth week of pregnancy, in addition to normal dietary intake, for the prevention of neural tube defects (Department of Health, 1992). Since it is difficult with a normal diet to achieve an intake of naturally occurring folates equivalent to 600 µg/day of folate, supplementation of folic acid is advised. However, it has been reported that, whilst there is an increase in awareness of the benefits of supplementation amongst women, a significant proportion do not take folic acid, even among those who plan their pregnancies (Sillender, 2000). In order to combat this problem, it has been suggested that the UK government should enforce a programme of mandatory folic acid fortification.

At present, fortification of food products with folic acid in the UK is solely on a voluntary basis. The Government's former advisory committee, COMA, reviewed the role of folic acid in the prevention of disease and concluded that a more widespread fortification programme was needed (Department of Health, 2000). COMA estimated that its recommendation to fortify flour with folic acid at 240 µg/100 g of flour could reduce the risk of NTD-affected births by 41% without resulting in unacceptably high intakes in any group of the population. This would prevent a significant number of annual NTD-affected births: 38 out of a total of 93 in England and Wales; 30 out of 74 in Scotland; and 6 out of 14 in Northern Ireland (FSA, 2002a). The level of fortification was calculated based upon intake patterns of different groups in the population to limit excessive intake by any group. On 9 May 2002, however, the UK Food Standards Agency Board decided against mandatory folic acid fortification. It concluded that further evidence on the impact of folic acid supplementation on older people needed to be considered (FSA, 2002b) as high doses of folic acid (>1 mg/day) can mask the symptoms of vitamin B_{12} deficiency, a condition that may ultimately cause nervous system damage.

Folic acid has been compulsorily added to flour in the United States since 1998 at a concentration of 140 µg per 100 g of flour (Kloeblen and Batish, 1999). It has been reported that the fortification programme was followed by a 19% reduction in NTD birth prevalence (Honein *et al.*, 2001), although the authors do admit that factors other than fortification may have contributed to this decline. It remains possible, however, that the continued reluctance of the UK government to enforce a programme of mandatory folic acid fortification may be having an adverse effect on the number of infants born with NTDs in the UK.

Adolescence is a time of physiological, psychological and social development and is one of the most dynamic and complex transitions in the lifespan. Adolescents are at increased risk of risky behaviours, such as unhealthy eating practices, and understanding the interrelation of these behaviours can help us to tailor interventions to suit this particular population. The UK NDNS has revealed that adolescents' nutrient intakes are particularly low in vitamin A, folate, vitamin B_6, riboflavin and most minerals. Biochemical markers of nutrient status suggested that a significant proportion of adolescent females of reproductive age had low levels of vitamin D, folate, riboflavin, vitamin B_6 and iron. Many of these nutrients are vital to the well-being of both mother and fetus in pregnancy.

Although there have been improvements over time in adolescent eating behaviour, they are modest in the main and far more needs to be achieved to ensure optimal nutrition. Overcoming the barriers to better adolescent nutrition requires multidisciplinary collaborations of adolescent health care providers, academics, professional organisations, policy makers, industry (in an ethical and non-compromising way) and service users. Key tasks should be to define healthy eating for adolescents realistically; simplify and clarify the healthy eating message; reframe the message to fit adolescent audiences; promote skill-based interventions to accompany the message; and strengthen environmental support for nutrition. Only then can adolescent nutrition, and adolescent nutrition in pregnancy, be significantly and sustainably optimised.

Adolescent nutrition during pregnancy

Pregnancy may be a risk factor for poor nutrition during adolescence, just as adolescence may be a risk factor for poor nutrition during pregnancy. Infants born to young adolescents (<15 years) are twice as likely to be LBW and three times as likely not to survive the neonatal period compared with infants born to older mothers (Lenders *et al.*, 2000). Rates of spontaneous miscarriage and of very preterm birth (<32 weeks) are highest in those aged 13–15 years (Olausson *et al.*, 1999). They also have an increased risk of giving birth to preterm or small-for-gestational-age infants (Scholl *et al.*, 1994; Story and Alton, 1995). Young adolescent mothers are at higher risk of maternal complications than older mothers, e.g. abnormally high maternal weight gains, pregnancy-induced hypertension, pre-eclampsia, anaemia and renal disease (Hediger *et al.*, 1990;

Story and Alton, 1995; Lenders *et al.*, 2000; Umans and Lindheimer, 2001). Pregnant adolescents are also more likely to enter prenatal care late and less likely to obtain an adequate quantity of care compared to adults (Stevens-Simon *et al.*, 1992). Lactational performance of adolescent mothers has been shown to differ from that of adult women, with adolescents producing 37–54% less milk postpartum than adults ($p < 0.05$) (Motil *et al.*, 1997). Whilst adolescents and adults differed with regards to lactational behaviour, Motil *et al.* argued that this was not the sole reason for the observed differences in milk production. Instead, they contend that the explanation for the difference was likely to be multifactorial, encompassing both behavioural and biologic factors (Motil *et al.*, 1997).

The cause of adverse pregnancy outcome in the adolescent is the subject of much debate. Some attribute the poor outcomes to various factors associated with being young, e.g. poor socio-economic status, lifestyle and adequacy of prenatal care. For example, Casanueva and colleagues (1991) investigated the effect of late prenatal care on nutritional status of 163 pregnant adolescents aged 11–17 years (mean age 15 ± 1) and found that late prenatal care (accessed when ≥25 weeks pregnant) was associated with increased risk of maternal anaemia (57% compared to 20% of adolescents accessing prenatal care before 25 weeks), iron deficiency and zinc deficiency. Research has shown, however, that the association between poor fetal and maternal outcomes persists even after sociodemographic factors are controlled for (Fraser *et al.*, 1995).

Other researchers have attributed the poor pregnancy outcomes of adolescent mothers to an independent factor related to some aspect of the woman's physiology, such as gynaecologic immaturity, competition for nutrients, or the growth and nutritional status of the mother (King, 2003). A plausible explanation for the negative effect of young gynaecological age on pregnancy outcome is the competition for nutrients between the mother and fetus. The competition for nutrients hypothesis was first proposed by Naeye (1981). Further support for the hypothesis was provided by a study conducted in Peru that reported that infants born to young, growing mothers were smaller than those born to adult women (Frisancho *et al.*, 1983). In more recent research, Scholl *et al.* (1990, 1994) reported that many pregnant adolescents continue to grow during gestation, as assessed by measuring knee height length, and that these adolescents give birth to smaller infants (about 155 g less) despite a tendency to gain more weight during pregnancy and retain more weight postpartum than non-growing adolescents. This is in contrast to adults, where generally an increased weight gain during pregnancy is associated with larger birth weights (King, 2003). In their subsequent research, Scholl *et al.* (2000) found that growing teenagers have a surge in maternal leptin concentrations during the last trimester, which may reduce the rate of maternal fat breakdown during late pregnancy and thereby increase the mother's use of glucose for energy. This would result in less energy being available for fetal growth. Therefore it looks possible, therefore, that the pregnant teenager partitions metabolic fuels to enable more energy to become available for maternal growth (and therefore higher maternal fat gains) at the expense of that available for fetal growth (resulting in lower birth weights).

Dietary intake of pregnant adolescents

A number of studies have compared the nutrient intakes of pregnant adolescents and pregnant adults. In separate studies carried out in American and Australia, it has been reported that pregnant teenagers have similar intakes of nutrients to pregnant adults (Giddens *et al.*, 2000; Job and Capra, 1995).

Giddens *et al.* (2000) examined the dietary intake of 59 pregnant adolescents (mean age 16.9 ± 1.3) and 97 pregnant adults (mean age 25.6 ± 5.0) in the second and third trimesters in the USA. They used two seven-day records – the first at 19–21 weeks and the second at 29–31 weeks gestation. They found that both adolescents and adults had intakes deficient in energy, iron, zinc, calcium, magnesium, folate and vitamins D and E. Total daily intakes for energy and eleven nutrients were significantly higher in adolescent compared with adult diets, due to a higher energy intake in teenagers and therefore a greater intake in nutrient-dense foods. These results may not be generalisable to other adolescent populations, however, as the study participants were prescribed multivitamin/mineral supplements and consequently reported a high use of nutrient supplementation. As all participants were participating in a trial for calcium supplementation, it is not unreasonable to suggest that the participants were generally more compliant to supplement intake than non-participating adolescents. Indeed, previous studies have reported that pregnant adolescents reported limited use of supplements (Skinner and Carruth, 1991). Giddens' study failed to examine dietary differences between supplement users and non-users, and this therefore could be a significant confounding factor.

In Australia, Job and Capra (1995) compared the nutrient intakes of 35 pregnant teenagers (mean age 17 years) and 25 pregnant adults (mean age 26 years) (standard deviations not given). A 24-hour recall method was used, together with a food frequency questionnaire (FFQ) to help validate the results. Pregnant teenagers were interviewed on between one and three occasions (with the initial intention to interview once during each trimester, although the researchers found that this was not always possible). Many of the pregnant adults were recruited later in pregnancy and so were interviewed on one occasion only. In a similar way to the Giddens *et al.* study (2000), Job and colleagues found that pregnant teenagers were at comparable nutritional risk to pregnant adults. Both adolescents and adults had diets low in energy, iron and zinc. The pregnant adults, however, had a higher calcium intake than the pregnant teenagers. The study was limited by the small sample size and the introduction of potential sampling bias due to the way in which adolescents were referred to the study (i.e. not by random allocation).

Both studies suffered from limitations that may restrict the usefulness of their findings. Neither study evaluated biochemical indicators for nutrient status nor conducted follow-up studies to assess infant morbidity. There are limitations of the 24-hour recall method used by Job *et al.*, including the reliance on participants' memory and their ability to estimate portion sizes leading to differential misclassification between those with good memories and those with poor memories. Compared with records of food consumption, 24-hour recall methods typically overestimate consumption. This has been shown to be the case for vegetables, energy and energy-yielding nutrients (Nelson and Bingham, 1997). For other nutrients, under-reporting of intakes may occur (e.g. under-reporting of alcohol intake). In addition, the 24-hour recall method is not indicative of an individual's overall diet, as recording may not take place on a 'typical' day. Individuals do not consume the same food from day to day and therefore substantial errors may be introduced when assessing a single day's diet. Furthermore, if participants are notified in advance of the procedure, they may choose to alter their habits (Nelson and Bingham, 1997).

Job and Capra (1995) reported that 'teenagers were generally single and supported by their families' (p. 79). The living circumstances of the adolescents in the Giddens *et al.* study were not clarified. It is likely that the diets of pregnant teenagers who are supported by their families are dissimilar from those who are not supported. A recent UK nutritional survey of pregnant adolescents (Burchett and Seely, 2003) found that a third of their participants (*n* = 15/46) did not live with family (or foster parents). Most of these adolescents (*n* = 12/15) had incomes of £45 or less per week and 13 (of 15) found it hard to manage on the money they received. Only two (who were living with partners) said that they managed without much or with no difficulty. Burchett and Seely (2003) also reported that money had a considerable effect on the food choices and eating behaviours of many participants. Three-quarters (approximately 35) of the participants missed meals and a quarter (approximately 12) said that this was because they did not have enough money.

In both studies (Job and Capra, 1995; Giddens *et al.*, 2000), the mean age of pregnant adolescents was approximately 17 years. By the age of 17, the females' sexual, biological, physiological and skeletal development is said to be complete, whether the teenager matures early or late (McGanity *et al.*, 1954). Therefore, as growth is complete it is not unreasonable to suggest that the energy and nutrient intake of this older teenage group would be similar to that of adults. A more striking difference may be more likely to be seen if a younger teenage group had been studied, whose nutritional requirements are needed to sustain their own growth, as well as the growth of their fetus. Studies that group all ages of teenagers together should be interpreted with care.

Victor

A study by Endres *et al.* (1987) took into account the influe
economic class on the nutritional intake patterns of pregnant ado'
US study compared the energy, nutrient and food intake patterns o₁ ₁ᴗ..
pregnant adolescents, i.e. 15–18 years old (*n* = 526), and low-income older
pregnant women, i.e. over 35 years old (*n* = 63). No data was provided on the
average age of the adolescents participating in the study, and therefore it is possible that the majority were older adolescents (i.e. >17 years). A 24-hour recall
protocol was used to assess nutrient intake. All participants were enrolled in the
Special Supplementary Food Program for Women and Children (WIC), which
provides food, nutrition education and medical care for low-income pregnant
women. The food supplements provide as much as 1300 kCal energy and 46 g
protein per day, providing a substantial percentage of the RDAs for energy and
several nutrients. Additional foods are required to meet the total energy and
nutrient allowances. Despite this, energy values for both groups were found
to be below recommended levels and neither group gained the recommended
amount of weight. Pregnant adolescents had significantly higher mean dietary
energy intakes but lower vitamin D, phosphorus and calcium intakes compared
with older pregnant women. The study may have been confounded by the fact
that 50% of the adults had been diagnosed as obese prior to pregnancy. Certainly the lack of weight gain in the adult group may be explained by this, as
most recommendations state that overweight pregnant women can safely gain
less weight during pregnancy (Endres *et al.*, 1987). A subsequent US study
comparing the weight gains of 136 pregnant adolescents (mean age 15.9 ±
0.9) and 193 pregnant young adults (mean age 21.7 ± 2.0) found that the mean
total maternal weight gains were similar for both groups, at about 14.9–16.1 kg
(Johnston and Kandell, 1992); amounts that are consistent with US guidelines
(IOM, 1990). The participants in Johnston and Kandell's study, however, were
all 'middle-class to upper-class' (p. 1515) who had access to private health care
– a significant factor that limits the generalisability of the results.

Other studies undertaken in the United States and its territories have reported
that pregnant adolescents have inadequate intakes of iron (Loris *et al.*, 1985;
Overturf *et al.*, 1992; Skinner *et al.*, 1992; Dunn *et al.*, 1994; Pobocik *et al.*,
2003), folate (Skinner *et al.*, 1992; Dunn *et al.*, 1994; Pobocik *et al.*, 2003),
magnesium (Skinner *et al.*, 1992; Dunn *et al.*, 1994; Pobocik *et al.*, 2003), calcium and vitamin E (Pobocik *et al.*, 2003), zinc (Overturf *et al.*, 1992; Skinner
et al., 1992), vitamin A (Overturf *et al.*, 1992; Dunn *et al.*, 1994), vitamin D and
vitamin B$_6$ (Skinner *et al.*, 1992) and fibre (Dunn *et al.*, 1994). When considering these data, however, it must be remembered that US dietary intake recommendations during pregnancy are much higher than UK recommendations and
therefore an 'inadequate' intake in the US may not be considered so in the UK.
Furthermore, many of the studies listed above suffer from methodological limitations (small sample numbers, limitations with the data collection tool etc.),
and should therefore be interpreted with caution.

It seems that only two UK studies, both carried out in England, have been conducted that examine the relationship of nutrient intakes in pregnancy to age. Matthews *et al.* (2000) conducted a cohort study of 774 nulliparous women in Portsmouth. The Maternity Alliance, in association with The Food Commission, conducted a survey of the diets of pregnant adolescents in seven locations in England (Burchett and Seely, 2003).

In Mathews and colleagues' study (2000), 774 women completed seven-day food diaries and provided details of supplement use. Nutrient intakes were compared between three age groups (<24 years, 24–27 years and >28 years). Age was strongly and significantly associated with the intake of most nutrients (with the exception of carbohydrate, vitamin E and vitamin D), i.e. as age increased so did maternal intake of most nutrients. This association was independent of other maternal factors, such as education, smoking status and socio-economic status. Increasing age was also associated with higher supplement intake (with the exception of folic acid, iron, zinc and carotenoid supplementation). The authors attributed these differences to both the greater total food intakes of older women and the higher nutrient densities of their diets and they provide two possible explanations for these trends. The first is that the diets of young people may be different from those of older people, e.g. young people tend to eat less fresh fruit and vegetables than older people (Henderson *et al.*, 2003). Secondly, women whose first pregnancy is delayed may differ from younger women of equivalent education and socio-economic status in a variety of health-related activities, e.g. they are more likely to have planned their pregnancy and therefore may be more motivated to change to a 'healthier diet' (Mathews *et al.*, 2000).

However, this study does not focus specifically on *adolescent* nutrition during pregnancy. Indeed, the authors did not clarify whether adolescents were included at all in the study. Therefore, whilst clearly showing that age may be an important predictor of nutrient intake during pregnancy, it may not be possible to extrapolate the findings to a younger age group. Furthermore, the results were based on maternal nutrient intake in women in Portsmouth, 90% of who were between 14 and 17 weeks pregnant. This is a particularly narrow window that may not represent the eating habits of women during either early or late pregnancy. Previous studies have reported that it is early maternal nutrition that is particularly important when considering birth outcome, such as low birth weight (Doyle *et al.*, 1992). Indeed, programmes of nutritional intervention both preconceptually and during the first trimester with low-income women in the USA, have shown a reduction in the incidence of LBW (Scholl *et al.*, 1997). Portsmouth is an area with a relatively low level of socio-economic deprivation and social classes IIIM, IV and V were under-represented when compared with those in the nationally representative NDNS (Doyle and Crawford, 2000). These findings, therefore, may not be generalisable to other areas of the UK, nor to younger pregnant adolescents.

The 'Good Enough to Eat' survey

The Maternity Alliance, in association with The Food Commission, conducted a study of the diets of pregnant adolescents in seven locations around England (Burchett and Seely, 2003). Interviews were conducted with 46 nulliparous pregnant adolescents under the age of 18 years and covered topics such as perceptions of what constitutes healthy eating and what the barriers are to achieving it, the dietary changes made since becoming pregnant, how food choices were made and what influenced eating behaviours. Diets were assessed using a food frequency questionnaire and 24-hour recall. Biochemical indicators of nutritional status were not assessed. Adolescents were aged between 14 and 17 years, the majority (91%) being 16 or 17 years. Twenty-seven (59%) were 7–9 months pregnant, 18 (39%) were 4–6 months pregnant and 1 (2%) was 1–3 months pregnant at the time of the study. The majority of participants were white ($n = 35$, 76%) and 65% ($n = 30$) were living with family at home. Nearly half received a training allowance (usually £40–50 per week) and a fifth received welfare benefits. Of those living with family or partners ($n = 35$), half of their families/partners were in receipt of benefits. Incomes ranged from £0 ($n = 8$) to £100 ($n = 2$) per week, but the majority ($n = 22$, 48%) received £31–50 per week.

Key findings

Many adolescents appeared to consume dairy products on a regular basis. The most commonly consumed food in the 24-hour recall was milk ($n = 40$, 87%), with teenagers reporting drinking, on average, 2–3 portions per day. In the FFQ, slightly less ($n = 35$) reported consuming milk at least once a day. Cheese and yoghurt were reported to be consumed by 15 and 3 adolescents respectively in the 24-hour recall. When a subgroup of participants were analysed for calcium intake, however, 42% ($n = 5/12$) had intakes that were considered inadequate (<800 mg/day), three of whom were considered to have seriously inadequate intakes (<480 mg/day). Pregnant adolescents, especially those who have not yet reached their peak adult height and peak bone mass, may be particularly vulnerable to calcium insufficiency during pregnancy (Scholl *et al.*, 1994). Inadequate calcium intake, particularly during growth, is known to be an important determinant of bone mineralisation and therefore bone density in the growing adolescent (Matkovic, 1992) and has been associated with increased risk of osteoporosis in later life (Weaver, 2000). Maternal calcium intake may also have an effect on fetal skeletal development. In a well-controlled study, Chang *et al.* (2003) found that diary intake had a significant positive effect on fetal femur growth in their sample of 1120 pregnant African American adolescents (mean age 15.9 ± 17 years). A dose–response relationship was demonstrated between amount of dairy intake and femur length, i.e. fetal femur length was longest in those consuming more than three servings per day, less when two to three portions per day were consumed and lowest in those consuming less than two servings per day. These results suggest that consumption of less than two servings of dairy products (estimated at <600 mg Ca/day) per day may negatively affect fetal bone development in the foetuses of adolescents by limiting the amount of calcium provided to the fetus. Such findings may have serious implications for the adolescents in the 'Good Enough to Eat' survey (Burchett and Seely, 2003).

In the 'Good Enough to Eat' survey, only two adolescents had eaten the recommended five portions of fruit and vegetables, a fifth had eaten none at all. This is reflected in the findings of the NDNS of 4–18 year olds, which showed that young people in the UK ate on average less than half the recommended five portions of fruit and vegetables a day, with one in five eating no fruit and vegetables at all (Gregory *et al.*, 2000). Fish consumption was low, and none of the women ate oily fish. Only two adolescents reported drinking alcohol. Forty of the adolescents had eaten more than five portions of foods that were high in salt, fat and/or sugar.

A sample of twelve 24-hour recalls were analysed to provide more information on their nutritional composition. Based on current recommendations, many did not consume enough energy ($n = 8$) or fibre ($n = 9$). Five adolescents had energy intakes that could be considered to be seriously inadequate (<1700 kCal). Despite this, the percentage of energy derived from total fat, saturated fat and sugar was in excess of recommended intakes for many adolescents ($n = 6$, 10 and 9 respectively). High sugar intake among pregnant adolescents has previously been associated with increased risk of small-for-gestational-age infants (Lenders *et al.*, 1997).

None of the 12 adolescents met all of their micronutrient requirements, as defined by the UK DRVs (Department of Health, 1991). Again, this reflects the findings of the NDNS survey, which showed that a significant proportion of adolescents had intakes and blood levels below the LRNI for nutrients important to pregnancy, such as vitamin A, zinc, iron and calcium (Gregory *et al.*, 2000). Inadequate intakes were most common for vitamin A ($n = 10$), folic acid ($n = 9$), iron ($n = 9$) and magnesium ($n = 8$). Vitamin A is required for fetal growth, particularly in the third trimester, and a deficiency during pregnancy has been associated with increased intrauterine growth restriction, premature birth and lower birth weight (Shah and Rajalakshmi, 1984). Of the nine (75%) adolescents who had inadequate intakes of folic acid (<300 mg/day), two had seriously inadequate intakes (<200 mg/day). Gadowsky *et al.* (1995) reviewed the literature and found that reports of the prevalence of folate deficiency among non-pregnant adolescents are varied, ranging from 3–48%. Deficiencies in folate, particularly in the periconceptional period, have been associated with congenital malformations. Since most adolescents do not plan their pregnancies, few are likely to supplement with folic acid in this period. In their study, Gadowsky and colleagues (1995) found that adolescents who consumed a prenatal folic acid supplement at least once a week had a low prevalence of suboptimal folate status. This suggests that regular folic acid supplementation has the potential to improve the biochemical folate status of pregnant adolescents, and perhaps health promotion efforts to increase folic acid uptake in young people of reproductive age should be targeted more specifically at this group.

Inadequate iron intake, particularly when combined with low vitamin C intake (half of the participants in the survey ($n = 6$) also had inadequate vitamin C intakes), may lead to anaemia. Indeed, 26% ($n = 12/46$) of the entire sample reported suffering from anaemia. Of the nine (75%) adolescents who were considered to have an inadequate intake of iron (<18.8 mg/day), two had a seriously inadequate intake (<8 mg/day). This finding compared well to that of a study of 58 pregnant adolescents in Canada, which found that 13 (22%) had anaemia and 45 (78%) had depleted iron stores (Gadowsky *et al.*, 1995). Adolescent pregnancy puts increased demands on maternal iron stores, particular if stores are already low. Previous research has revealed a high prevalence of anaemia in low-income pregnant adolescents (Schneck *et al.*, 1990). Low iron status in the pregnant adolescent has been associated with a greater risk of LBW, prematurity and perinatal mortality (Ward, 2000).

There are a number of limitations to the survey that limit the usefulness of its findings. Nutrient status and preconceptual nutrient intake were not considered and the survey included only one participant who was in the first trimester, thus providing severely limited information about nutrition before and in the early stages of pregnancy. The sample was small, particularly with regard to the nutrient intake data, and open to sampling bias since participants were not randomised to the study. The survey used 24-hour recall methods, the limitations of which have been discussed earlier. Indeed, when asked, only three-fifths of participants said that what they ate in the 24-hour recall was typical of what they normally ate. The remainder thought that factors such as illness or unusual activities prevented usual eating patterns. Thus it seems likely that the survey has failed to describe pregnant adolescents 'typical' nutrient intake.

Influences on pregnant adolescents' food choices

Financial constraints have been found to have an important influence on pregnant adolescents' food choices, particularly those living away from family (Burchett and Seeley, 2003). As money ran out, pregnant adolescents consumed more 'cheap fillers' and had less variety and less fresh produce. Burchett and Seeley (2003) estimated that the minimum amount a pregnant woman needs to spend on food is £20.25 per week, which would be sufficient to purchase a 'modest but adequate' diet. This assumes that the adolescent has local access to a wide range of foods at average prices and that she is knowledgeable about what constitutes a nutritionally adequate diet. The survey reported, however, that most adolescents who shopped and cooked for themselves were not able to afford this amount. The amount of benefits they could claim ranged from £32.90 per week (for 16–17-year-olds living at home, available, under most circumstances, from 29 weeks gestation only) to £43.25 per week (for 16–17-year-olds who are estranged from their family and all 18–24-year-olds). Women aged over 25 years are entitled to benefits of £54.65 per week. Despite having comparable living costs, this constitutes £11.40 per week more than pregnant 16–17 year olds who live away from home. For a pregnant 16–17-year-old living away from home claiming £43.25 per week, the estimated cost of eating a healthy diet represents almost half her income. Burchett and Seeley (2003) concluded that this was not sufficient for adolescents to survive on, with teenagers often running out of food before their next payment and resorting to buying less healthy 'cheap filler' foods and borrowing money.

These findings are similar to those of the UK NDNSs of adults and young people. The NDNS of adults showed that women living on benefits ate fewer portions of fruit and vegetables compared with those living in non-benefit households (1.9 portions compared to 3.1 portions a day) (Henderson *et al.*, 2003). In the NDNS of young people aged 4–18 years, those from households in receipt of benefits were more likely to consume whole milk, table sugar and sugar confectionary compared with those not receiving benefits. They also consumed significantly less protein, total carbohydrate, total sugars, non-starch polysaccharides, vitamin C and biotin (Gregory *et al.*, 2000).

In the 'Good Enough to Eat' survey (Burchett and Seely, 2003), the influence of the family on food choices and eating behaviours was particularly strong for pregnant adolescents. For over half of the teenagers interviewed, family members shopped and cooked for them. As a consequence, adolescents were unlikely to have been in full control of their food choices. Family influence was often positive, encouraging healthy eating and providing meals if the teenager was not living at home. In some cases, however, dependence on the family meant that they ate the same as the rest of the family, which may have been less healthy than they would have wished.

Improving pregnant adolescents' diets

The nutritional challenges that face the pregnant adolescent are unique. The increased nutrient demands of pregnancy, together with the increased nutrient demands of the still-growing adolescent, may generate competition for nutrients between mother and fetus. Although relatively limited, the current research seems to suggest that pregnant adolescents' diets are suboptimal. The most common dietary deficits appear to be energy, iron, zinc, calcium, folate, zinc and magnesium. Many pregnant adolescents do not consume the recommended amount of fruit and vegetables and may consume too much salt, saturated fat, and sugar.

A 'one size fits all' approach has not been shown to be particularly effective in modifying food choice in the general population. In a review of the factors that influence food choice, Buttriss and colleagues (2004) suggested that tailored approaches for different cultural settings should be a key consideration. For example, peer-led interventions have been shown to be successful for adolescents and 'hard to reach' groups (e.g. Fitzgibbon *et al.*, 1996). Hands on practical interventions, such as cook and eat classes, have been shown to appeal to low-income groups (e.g. Weaver *et al.*, 1999). For sustainability of positive changes, Buttriss *et al.* (2004) emphasise the need for message reinforcement.

An important factor that should be considered when developing appropriate and effective strategies to promote healthy eating in pregnant adolescents is the heterogeneity of the group. Factors affecting food choices vary considerably, depending on the individual's particular circumstances. Family and peers are likely to have a strong influence on the eating habits of most pregnant adolescents. Poverty is a significant factor that limits the ability of the pregnant adolescent to eat a healthy diet, even in those who aspire to it.

As many adolescents do not plan pregnancy, the issue of periconceptional nutrition is problematic. A UK survey of 674 adolescents (aged 14–15 years) on their perceptions of what constitutes a healthy pregnancy revealed that 70% of respondents thought that the optimum time to initiate changes in what a woman eats and drinks to ensure a healthy pregnancy was when pregnancy had been confirmed (Edwards *et al.*, 1997). This suggests that the benefits of preconceptual nutrition are not well understood by this population. The preceding small associated pilot study also revealed that, whilst most adolescents thought that vitamin supplements were 'good for the baby', few thought that folic acid tablets were beneficial, suggesting that participants did not recognise folic acid as a vitamin (Parker, 1998). A further complication is that many teenagers may be unaware of their pregnancy or may not have accessed services in their first trimester, so providing the appropriate support to these individuals may be difficult.

Growth, adolescent eating behaviours and psychosocial factors must be considered when recommendations are made for the optimal nutritional care for this vulnerable population. The multiple psychosocial and economic stressors of prospective adolescent mothers often interfere with their ability to follow recommendations regarding nutrient intake. Effective interventions will need to go beyond education alone in order to tackle these barriers. For example, financial issues and food poverty are significant barriers, particularly for those adolescents who live away from family. Therefore initiatives and policies that aim to improve the financial circumstances or limit the effects of food poverty on pregnant adolescents could be much more effective in improving diets than any other intervention (Burchett and Seely, 2003).

At present there are very few projects that aim to improve pregnant adolescents' nutrition in the UK. The few that have been conducted have been subjected to short-term funding and have not been formally evaluated (e.g. the Waltham Forest Young Parents' Project in London and the breakfast club for school-age mothers in Leeds, which have been briefly described by Burchett and Seely (2003)). Without proper evaluation it is impossible to provide evidence of their effectiveness, or otherwise, thus making progress in this area problematic. It is clear that more research in this area is urgently needed. Research should seek to further clarify the barriers to dietary improvements in pregnant adolescents. This information could then inform the development of effective nutritional programs that are targeted to suit this particularly vulnerable population.

Conclusion

Teenage pregnancy is one of the major public health challenges in the UK. Each year in the UK, over 75,000 adolescents under 20 years of age conceive. Although teenage pregnancy rates appear to be falling, rates are still much higher than in most other countries. Teenage pregnancy has been associated with a number of negative outcomes for the infants and children of teenage mothers, such as infant mortality and morbidity, maternal morbidity and negative impacts on various socio-economic outcomes.

Nutrition in adolescent pregnancy must be viewed within a biopsychosocial context, since it has consistently been shown that there are multiple influencing factors that play a role in the eating behaviour and subsequent nutritional status of the pregnant adolescent. Eating behaviours are likely to be related to other, often 'risky', behaviours displayed in adolescents and should not be viewed in isolation. Achieving dietary change in this particularly vulnerable section of the population, many of whom are from disadvantaged backgrounds (Social Exclusion Unit, 1999), presents a major public health challenge. Biopsychosocial factors often experienced by such groups, including low levels of disposable income, unemployment, poor housing, sub-optimal mental and physical health and limited access to a wide variety of reasonably priced foods, all contribute to difficulties tackling behavioural change (Symon and Wriden, 2003). These factors in turn lead to increasing health inequalities (Acheson, 1998).

Extremely limited research has been conducted in the field of adolescent nutrition during pregnancy in the UK. In the single, most relevant study conducted in the UK, Burchett and Seely (2003) found that inadequate nutrient intakes were found to be most common for vitamin A, folic acid, iron and magnesium. Many did not consume enough energy or fibre and several had energy intakes that could be considered to be seriously inadequate (<1700 kCal). Several consumed too much fat, particularly saturated fat, and sugar. However, as this part of the study was based on only 12 adolescents, the findings must be interpreted with care. However, they do reflect, in part, the findings of the much larger nationally representative NDNS of young people, which reported that adolescent females had particularly poor intakes of calcium, iron, zinc, folate, vitamin D, riboflavin and vitamin B_6. Although the data from the NDNS was extracted from non-pregnant young females, the statistics are worrying, as many of these nutrients are essential to a healthy pregnancy. It would be much more useful, of course, if the NDNS included pregnant women and adolescents as discrete groups in future surveys.

Given the multiple factors that have the potential to influence nutrient intake in pregnant adolescents, interventions should perhaps use a lifestyle approach, rather than focusing specifically on eating behaviours. However, since very little work has been conducted in this area, it is first necessary to conduct further exploratory work. Resources could be wasted if essential information, such as the information regarding the feasibility of conducting a particular intervention, is not evaluated first. A recent study in Dundee confirmed that compliance among pregnant teenagers invited to attend a nutrition education intervention programme was very poor – only 16 of 120 invitees attended (Wrieden and Symon, 2003). There are numerous barriers to optimal nutrition in adolescent pregnancy, and any intervention should consider these carefully.

Overcoming the barriers in order to achieve improved nutrition in pregnancy among adolescents requires multidisciplinary collaborations of adolescent health care providers, academics, professional organisations, policy makers, industry and service users. Certainly, more needs to be done at a policy level, both with regard to enabling adolescents to be able to afford good nutrition and in modifying the nutrition message that adolescents receive. For example, the UK government could ensure that there is consistency in the food and nutrition message in schools, to include the curriculum, food provision in the canteen, vending machine policies, breakfast clubs, snacking and lunchbox policies, and so on. Only once this is achieved can adolescent nutrition, and adolescent nutrition in pregnancy, be significantly and sustainably optimised.

References

Acheson, D. [chairman] (1998) *Independent Inquiry into Inequalities in Health.* HMSO, London.

Adams, L. B. (1997) An overview of adolescent eating behavior barriers to implementing dietary guidelines. *Annals of the New York Academy of Sciences*, **817**, 36–48.

Ajzen, I. (1991) The theory of planned behaviour. *Organizational Behaviour and Human Decision Processes*, **50**, 179–211.

Albertson, A. M., Tobelmann, R. C. and Marquart, L. (1997) Estimated dietary calcium intake and food sources for adolescent females: 1980–92. *Journal of Adolescent Health*, **20**, 20–6.

Anderson, N. E., Smiley, D. V., Flick, L. H. and Lewis, C. Y. (2000) Missouri Rural Adolescent Pregnancy Project (MORAPP). *Public Health Nursing*, **17**, 355–62.

Autret-Leca, E. and Jonville-Bera, A. P. (2001) Vitamin K in neonates: how to administer, when and to whom. *Paediatric Drugs*, **3**, 1–8.

Barker, D. J. P. and Osmond, C. (1986) Infant mortality, childhood nutrition, and ischaemic heart disease in England and Wales. *Lancet*, **i**, 1077–88.

Barker, M., Robinson, S., Wilman, C. and Barker, D. J. P. (2000) Behaviour, body composition and diet in adolescent girls. *Appetite*, **35**, 161–70.

Barrett, B. M., Sowell, A., Gunter, E. and Wang, M. (1994) Potential role of ascorbic acid and 36-carotene in the prevention of preterm rupture of fetal membranes. *International Journal of Vitamin Nutrition Research*, **64**, 192–7.

Barrett-Connor, E. and Laakso, M. (1990) Ischemic heart disease risk in postmenopausal women: effects of estrogens use on glucose and insulin levels. *Arteriosclerosis*, **10**, 531–4.

Bates, C. J., Prentice, A. M., Paul, A. A., Sutcliffe, B. A., Watkinson, M. and Whitehead, R. G. (1981) Riboflavin status in Gambian pregnant and lactating women and its implications for Recommended Dietary Allowances. *American Journal of Clinical Nutrition*, **34**, 928–35.

Belizan, J. M., Villar, J., Bergel, E., del Pino, A., Di Fulvio, S., Galliano, S. V. and Kattan, C. (1997) Long term effect of calcium supplementation during pregnancy on the blood pressure of offspring: follow up of a randomised controlled trial. *British Medical Journal*, **315**, 281–5.

Berenson, A. B., Wiemann, C. M. and McCombs, S. L. (1997) Adverse perinatal outcomes in young adolescents. *Journal of Reproductive Medicine*, **42**, 559–64.

Bigler-Doughten, S. and Jenkins, R. M. (1987) Adolescent snacks: nutrient density and nutritional contribution ton total intake. *Journal of the American Dietetic Association*, **87**, 1678–9.

Bucher, H. C., Guyatt, H. C., Cook, R. J., Hatala, R., Cook, D. J., Lang, J. D. and, H.unt D (1996) Effect of calcium supplementation on pregnancy-induced hypertension and preeclampsia: a meta-analysis of randomised controlled trails. *Journal of the American Medical Association*, **275**, 1113–17.

Burchett, H. and Seeley, A. (2003) *Good Enough to Eat? The Diet of Pregnant Teenagers*. Maternity Alliance/Food Commission, London.

Burt, M. R. (1986) Estimating the public costs of teenage childbearing. *Family Planning Perspectives*, **18**, 221–6.

Buttriss, J. (2000) Diet and nutritional status of 4–18-year-olds: public health implications. *Nutrition Bulletin*, **25**, 209–17.

Buttriss, J. (2002) Nutrition, health and schoolchildren. *Nutrition Bulletin* **27**, 275–316.

Buttriss, J. (2004) Strategies to increase folate/folic acid intake in women: an overview. *Nutrition Bulletin*, **29**, 234–44.

Buttriss, J., Stanner, S., McKevith, B., Nugent, A. P., Kelly, C., Phillips, F. and Theobald, H. E. (2004) Successful ways to modify food choice: lessons from the literature. *Nutrition Bulletin*, **29**, 333–43.

Casanueva, E., Magana, L., Pfeffer, F. and Baez, A. (1991) Incidence of premature rupture of membranes in pregnant women with low leukocyte levels of vitamin C. *European Journal of Clinical Nutrition*, **45**, 401–5.

Cavadini, C., Siega-Riz, A. M. and Popkin, B. M. (2000) US adolescent food intake trends from 1965 to 1996. *Archives of Disease in Childhood*, **83**, 18–24.

Chang, S.-C., O'Brien, K. O., Nathanson, M. S., Caulfield, L. E., Mancini, J. and Witter, F. R. (2003) Fetal femur length is influenced by maternal dairy intake in pregnant African American adolescents. *American Journal of Clinical Nutrition*, **77**, 1248–54.

Clapp, J. F. (1997) Diet, exercise and feto-placental growth. *Archives of Gynecology and Obstetrics*, **261**, 101–7.

Clapp, J. F. (1998) The effect of dietary carbohydrate on the glucose and insulin response to mixed caloric intake and exercise in both nonpregnant and pregnant women. *Diabetes Care*, **21**, B107–B112.

Clapp, J. F. (2002) Maternal carbohydrate intake and pregnancy outcome. *Proceedings of the Nutrition Society*, **61**, 45–50.

Cloninger, C. R. (1997) Neurogenetic adaptive mechanisms in alcoholism. *Science*, **236**, 410–16.

Coad, J. (2003) Pre- and periconceptual nutrition. In: *Nutrition in Early Life* (eds J. B. Morgan and J. W. T. Dickerson). Wiley, Chichester, pp. 39–71.

Cockburn, F., Belton, N. R., Purvis, J. R., Giles, M. M., Brown, J. K., Turner, T. L., Wilkinson, E. M., Forfar, J. O., Barrie, W. J. M., McKay, G. S. and Pocock, S. J. (1980) Maternal vitamin D intake and mineral metabolism in mothers and their new-born infants. *British Medical Journal*, **218**, 11–14.

Cohen, M., Adler, N. E., Beck, A., Irwin, C. E. (1986) Parental reactions to the onset of adolescence. *Journal of Adolescent Health Care*, **7**, 101–6.

Crisp, A. H. (1995) The dyslipophobias: a view of the psychopathologies involved and the hazards of constructing anorexia nervosa and bulimia nervosa as 'eating disorders'. *Proceedings of the Nutrition Society*, **54**, 701–9.

Crowther, C. A. and Henderson-Smart, D. J. (2001) Vitamin K prior to preterm birth for preventing neonatal periventricular haemorrhage. *The Cochrane Database of Systematic Reviews* 2001, Issue 1. Art. No.: CD000229. DOI: 10.1002/14651858.CD000229.

Czeizel, A. E. and Dudas, I. (1992) Prevention of first occurrence of neural-tube defects by periconceptional vitamin supplementation. *New England Journal of Medicine*, **327**, 1832–5.

Department of Health (1989) Report on Health and Social Subjects: 36. *The Diets of British Schoolchildren*. HMSO, London.

Department of Health (1991a) Report on Health and Social Subjects: 41. *Dietary Reference Values for Food energy and Nutrition for the United Kingdom*. HMSO, London.

Department of Health (1991b) *Folic Acid in the Prevention of Neural Tube Defects*. Letter from Chief Medical and Nursing Officers. PL/CMO (91)11, PL/CNO (91)6. London, 12 August 1991.

Department of Health (1992) *Folic Acid and the Prevention of Neural Tube Defects*. Report from an expert advisory panel. HMSO, London.

Department of Health (1994) Report on Health and Social Subjects: 46. *Nutritional Aspects of Cardiovascular disease*. HMSO, London.

Department of Health (1999) *Saving Lives, Our Healthier Nation*. The Stationery Office, London.

Department of Health (2000). Folic acid and the prevention of disease. *Report of the Committee on Medical Aspects of Food and Nutrition Policy*. The Stationery Office, London.

DeMaeyer, E. M. (1989) *Preventing and controlling iron deficiency anemia through primary health care*. WHO, Geneva.

Doyle, W., Wynn, A. H. A., Crawford, M. A. and Wynn, S. W. (1992) Nutritional counselling and supplementation in the second and third trimester of pregnancy, a study in a London population. *Journal of Nutrition and Medicine*, **3**, 249–56.

Doyle, W. and Crawford, M. (2000). Letter to editor. *British Medical Journal*, **320**, 941.

Dunn, C., Kolasa, K., Dunn, P. C. and Ogle, M. B. (1994) Dietary intake of pregnant adolescents in a rural southern community. *Journal of the American Dietetic Association*, **94**, 1040–1.

Dunn, J. T. (1998) What is happening to our iodine? [editorial] *Journal of Clinical Endocrinology and Metabolism*, **83**, 3398–400.

Durnin, J. V. G. A. (1987) Energy requirements of pregnancy. An integration of the longitudinal data from the five-country study. *The Lancet*, **ii**, 1131–3.

EC Scientific Committee for Food Report (1993) *Nutrient and energy intakes for the European Community (31st series)*. Directorate-General Industry, Luxembourg.

Edwards, G., Stainisstreet, M. and Boyes, E. (1997) Adolescents' ideas about the health of the fetus. *Midwifery*, **13**, 17–23.

Elliot, D. S. (1994) Health-enhancing and health-compromising life-styles. In: *Promoting the Health of Adolescents: New Directions for the Twenty-First Century* (eds. S. G. Millstein, A. C. Peteresen and E. O. Nightingale). Oxford University Press, Oxford.

Endres, J. M., Poll-Odenwalk, K., Sawicki, M. and Welch, P. (1987) Older pregnant women and adolescents: nutrition data after enrolment in WIC. *Journal of the American Dietetic Association*, **87**, 1011–19.

FAO/WHO/UNU (1985) *Energy and protein requirements. Report of a joint FAO/WHO/UNU expert consultation*. Technical Report Series 724. WHO, Geneva.

Fernandez-Ballart, J. and Murphy, M. M. (2001) Preventative nutritional supplementation throughout the reproductive life cycle. *Public Health Nutrition*, **4**, 1363–6.

Fitzgibbon, M. L., Stolley, M. R., Avellone, M. E., Sugerman, S. and Chavez, N. (1996) Involving parents in cancer risk reduction: a program for Hispanic American families. *Health Psychology*, **15**, 413–22.

Food Standards Agency (FSA) (2002a) Food Standards Agency and UK Health Departments encourage debate on fortification of flour with folic acid. http://www.food.gov.uk/news/pressreleases/2002/mar/flourfolic/ [Accessed 20 August 2005].

Food Standards Agency (FSA) (2002b) Board reaches conclusion on folic acid. http://www.food.gov.uk/news/newsarchive/2002/may/62488 [Accessed 12 August 2005].

Fraser, A. M., Brokert, J. E. and Ward, R. H. (1995) Association of young maternal age with adverse reproductive outcomes. *New England Journal of Medicine*, **332**, 1113–17.

Frisancho, A. R., Matos, J. and Flegel, P. (1983) Maternal nutritional status and adolescent pregnancy outcome. *American Journal of Clinical Nutrition*, **38**, 739–46.

Gadowsky, S. L., Gale, K., Wolfe, S. A., Jory, J., Gibson, R., O'Connor, D. L. (1995) Biochemical folate, B_{12} and iron status of a group of pregnant adolescents accessed through the public health system in Southern Ontario. *Journal of Adolescent Health*, **16**, 465–74.

Garza, C. and Rasmussen, K. M. (2000) Pregnancy and lactation. In: *Human Nutrition and Dietetics*, 10th edn (eds. J. S. Garrow, W. P. T. James and A. Ralph). Churchill Livingstone, Edinburgh, pp. 437–48.

General Register Office (Northern Ireland) (2004) Registrar General Annual Report 2003 Stationery Office, Belfast.

Gibson, R. (1994) Zinc nutrition in developing countries. *Nutrition Research Reviews*, **7**, 151–73.

Giddens, J. B., Krug, S. K., Tsang, R. C., Guo, S., Miodovnik, M. and Prada, J. A. (2000) Pregnant adolescent and adult women have similarly low intakes of selected nutrients. *Journal of the American Dietetic Association*, **100**, 1334–40.

Glinoer, D. (2004) The regulation of thyroid function during normal pregnancy: importance of the iodine nutrition status. *Best Practice and Research Clinical Endocrinology and Metabolism*, **18**, 133–52.

Gluckman, P. D., Hanson, M. A. and Pinal, C. (2005) The developmental origins of adult disease. *Maternal and Child Nutrition*, **1**, 130–41.

Gregory, J., Lowe, S., Bates, C., Prentice, A., Jackson, L., Smithers, G., Wenlock, R. and Farron, M. (2000) Report of the Diet and Nutrition Survey volume 1, *National Diet and Nutrition Survey: Young People Aged 4 to 18 Years*. The Stationery Office, London.

Haggarty, P., Page, K., Abramovich, D. R., Ashton, J. and Brown, D. (1997) Long-chain polyunsaturated fatty acid transport across the perfused human placenta. *Placenta*, **18**, 635–42.

Hamlyn, B., Brooker, S., Oleinikova, K. and Wands, S. (2002) *Infant Feeding 2000*. The Stationery Office, London.

Harding, J. E. (2001) The nutritional basis of the fetal origins of adult disease. *International Journal of Epidemiology*, **30**, 15–23.

Hathcock, J. N., Hattan, D. G., Jenkins, M. Y., McDinald, J. T., Sundaresan, P. R. and Wilkening, V. L. (1990) Evaluation of vitamin A toxicity. *American Journal of Clinical Nutrition*, **52**, 183–202.

Hediger, M. L., Scholl, T. O., Ances, I. G., Belsky, D. H. and Salmon, R. W. (1990) Rate and amount of weight gain during adolescent pregnancy: associations with maternal weight-for-height and birth weight. *American Journal of Clinical Nutrition*, **52**, 793–800.

Heller, S., Salkeld, R. M. and Korner, W. F. (1974) Riboflavin status in pregnancy. *American Journal of Clinical Nutrition*, **27**, 1225–30.

Henderson, J., Irving, K., Gregory, J. *et al.* (2003) *The National Diet and Nutrition Survey: Adults Aged 19–64 Years, Volume 3: Vitamin and Mineral Intakes and Urinary Analyte.* The Stationery Office, London

Hercberg, S., Galan, P., Preziosi, P. and Aissa, M. (2000) Consequences of iron deficiency in pregnant women: current issues. *Clinical Drug Investigation*, **19**(Suppl.), 1–7.

Hofmeyr, G. J., Roodt, A., Atallah, A. N. and Duley, L. (2003) Calcium supplementation to prevent pre-eclampsia – a systematic review. *South African Medical Journal*, **93**, 224–8.

Honein, M. A., Paulozzi, L. J., Mathews, T. J., Erickson, J. D. and Wong, L. C. (2001) Impact of folic acid fortification of the US food supply on the occurrence of neural tube defects. *Journal of the American Medical Association*, **285**, 2981–8.

Institute of Medicine (IOM) (1990) *Nutrition During Pregnancy.* National Academy Press, Washington DC.

Institute of Medicine (IOM) (1997) *Dietary Reference Intakes: Calcium, Phosphorus, Magnesium, Vitamin D and Fluoride.* National Academy Press, Washington DC.

Institute of Medicine (IOM) (2005) *Dietary Reference Intakes for Energy, Carbohydrate, Fiber, Fat, Fatty Acids, Cholesterol, Protein, and Amino Acids (Macronutrients).* National Academy Press, Washington DC.

Irwin, C. E. and Millstein, S. G. (1986) Biopsychosocial correlates of risk-taking behaviors during adolescence. Can physicians intervene? *Journal of Adolescent Health Care*, **7**(Suppl), 82S–96S.

Irwin, C. E., Igra, V., Eyre, S. and Millstein, S. (1997) Risk-taking behavior in adolescents: the paradigm. *Annals of the New York Academy of Sciences*, **817**, 1–35.

ISD Online (Information and Statistics Division NHS Scotland) (2003) http://www.isdscotland.org/isd/info3.jsp?pContentID=2070&p_applic=CCC&p_service=Content.show& [Accessed 8 August 2005].

Job, J. and Capra, S. (1995) Nutritional assessment of pregnant teenagers attending a metropolitan, public, maternity hospital in Brisbane 1. Nutrient intakes. *Australian Journal of Nutrition and Dietetics*, **52**(2), 7682.

Johnston, C. S. and Kandell, L. A. (1992) Prepregnancy weight and rate of maternal weight gain in adolescents and young adults. *Journal of the American Dietetic Association*, **92**, 1515–17.

Keski-Rahkonen, A., Kaprio, J., Rissanen, A., Virkkunen, M. and Rose, R. J. (2003) Breakfast skipping and health-compromising behaviors in adolescents and adults. *European Journal of Clinical Nutrition*, **57**, 842–53.

King, J. C. (2003) The risk of maternal nutritional depletion and poor outcomes increases in early or closely spaced pregnancies. *Journal of Nutrition*, **133**, 1732S–1736S.

Kleinman, R. E., Hall, S., Green, H., Korzec-Ramirez, D., Patton, K., Pagano, M. E. and Murphy, J. M. (2002) Diet, breakfast and academic performance in children. *Annals of Nutrition and Metabolism*, **46**(suppl. 1), 899–907.

Kloeblen, A. M. and Batish, S. S. (1999) Understanding the intention to permanently follow a high folate diet among a sample of low-income pregnant women according to the Health Belief Model. *Health Education Research*, **14**, 327–38.

Knopp, R. H. (1997) Hormone-mediated changes in nutrient metabolism in pregnancy: a physiological basis for normal fetal development. *New York Academy of Sciences*, **817**, 259–71.

Kumar, R., Cohen, W. R., Solva, P. and Epstein, F. H. (1979) Elevated 1,25-dihydroxyvitamin D plasma levels in normal human pregnancy and lactation. *Journal of Clinical Investigation*, **63**, 342–4.

Kumru, S., Aydin, S., Simsek, M., Sahin, K., Yaman, M. and Ay, G. (2003) Comparison of serum copper, zinc, calcium, and magnesium levels in preeclamptic and healthy pregnant women. *Biological Trace Element Research*, **94**, 105–12.

Lenders, C. M., Hedinger, M. L., Scholl, T. O., Khoo, C.-S., Slap, G. B. and Stallings, V. A. (1997) Gestational age and infant size at birth are associated with dietary sugar intake among pregnant adolescents. *Journal of Nutrition*, **127**, 1113–17.

Lenders, C. M., McElrath, T. F. and Scholl, T. O. (2000) Nutrition in adolescent pregnancy. *Current Opinion in Pediatrics*, **12**, 291–6.

Levine, R. J., Hauth, J. C., Curet, L. B., Sibai, B. M., Catalano, P. M., Morris, C. D., DerSimonian, E., Esterlitz, J. R., Raymond, E. G., Bild, D. E., Clemens, J. D. and Cutler, J. A. (1997) Trail of calcium to prevent preeclampsia. *New England Journal of Medicine*, **337**, 69–76.

Lifshitz, F. and Moses, N. (1989) Growth failure. A complication of dietary treatment of hypercholesterolemia. *American Journal of Diseases in Childhood*, **143**, 537–42.

Lifshitz, F. and Tarim, O. and Smith, M. M. (1993) Nutrition in adolescence. *Adolescent Endocrinology*, **22**, 673–83.

Looker, A. C., Sempos, C. T., Johnson, C. L. and Yetley, E. A. (1987) Comparison of dietary intakes and iron status of vitamin-mineral supplement users and nonusers aged 1 to 19 years. *American Journal of Clinical Nutrition*, **46**, 655–72.

Loris, P., Dewey, K. G. and Poirier-Brode, K. (1985) Weight gain and dietary intake of pregnant teenagers. *Journal of the American Dietetic Association*, **85**, 1296–305.

Lytle, L., Kelder, S., Perry, C. and Klepp, K. (1995) Covariance of adolescent health behaviours: the class of 1989 study. *Health Education Research: Theory & Practice*, **19**, 133–46.

Lytle, L. A. and Roski, J. (1997) Unhealthy eating and other risk-taking behavior: are they related? *Annals of the New York Academy of Sciences*, **817**, 49–65.

Lytle, L. A. (2002) Nutritional issues for adolescents. *Journal of the American Dietetic Association*, **102**(Suppl), S8–12.

Malcom, G. T., Oalmann, M. C. and Strong, J. P. (1997) Risk factors for atherosclerosis in young subjects: the PDAY Study. *Annals of the New York Academy of Sciences*, **817**, 179–88.

Matkovic, V. (1992) Calcium and peak bone mass. *Journal of Internal Medicine*, **231**, 151–60.

Matthews, F. and Neil, H. A. W. (1998) Nutrient intakes during pregnancy in a cohort of nulliparous women. *Journal of Human Nutrition and Dietetics*, **11**, 151–61.

Matthews, F., Yudkin, P. and Neil, A. (1999) Influence of maternal nutrition on outcome of pregnancy: prospective cohort study. *British Medical Journal*, **319**, 339–43.

Matthews, F., Yudkin, P., Smith, R. F. and Neil, A. (2000) Nutrient intakes during pregnancy: the influence of smoking and age. *Journal of Epidemiology and Community Health*, **54**, 17–23.

McGanity, W. J., Cannon, R. O. and Bridgforth, E. B. (1954) The Vanderbilt cooperative study of maternal and infant nutrition VI. Relationship of obstetric performance to nutrition. *American Journal of Obstetrics and Gynecology*, **67**, 501–27.

Miller, P. Y. and Simon, W. (1974) Adolescent sexual behaviour: context and change. *Social Problems*, **22**, 58–76.

Ministry of Agriculture, Fisheries and Food (MAFF) (1999) *National Food Survey 1998*. MAFF, London.

Morrissey, M., McKinley, M. C., Lowis, C., Robson, P. J., Moran, A. and Livingstone, M. B. E. (2002) Adolescents talking about food and health: a focus group approach. *Proceedings of the Nutrition Society*, **61**, 88A.

Motil, K. J., Kertz, B. and Thotathuchery, M. (1997) Lactational performance of adolescent mothers shows preliminary differences from that of adult women. *Journal of Adolescent Health*, **20**, 442–9.

Mott, E. L. and Haurin, R. J. (1988) Linkages between sexual activity and alcohol and drug use among American adolescents. *Family Planning Perspectives*, **20**, 108–28.

MRC Vitamin Study Research Group (1991) Prevention of neural tube defects: results of the Medical Research Council Vitamin Study. *The Lancet*, **338**, 131–7.

Naeye, R. L. (1981) Teenage and pre-teenaged pregnancies: consequences of the fetal-maternal competition for nutrients. *Pediatrics*, **67**, 146–59.

Natraj, U., George, S. and Kadam, P. (1988) Isolation and partial characterization of human riboflavin carrier protein and the estimation of its level during human pregnancy. *Journal of Reproductive Immunology*, **13**, 1–7.

Nelson, M. and Bingham, S. A. (1997) Assessment of food consumption and nutrient intake. In: *Design Concepts in Nutritional Epidemiology*, 2nd edn (eds. B. M. Margetts and M. Nelson). Oxford University Press, Oxford.

Neumark-Sztainer, D., Story, M., Toporoff, E., Himes, J. H., Resnick, M. D. and Blum, R. W. (1997) Covariations of eating behaviors with other health-related behaviors among adolescents. *Journal of Adolescent Health*, **20**, 450–8.

Neumark-Sztainer, D., Story, M., Perry, C. and Casey, M. A. (1999) Factors influencing food choices of adolescents: Findings from focus group discussions with adolescents. *Journal of the American Dietetic Association*, **99**, 929–37.

NHS Centre for Reviews and Dissemination (1997) *Preventing and Reducing the Adverse Effects of Unintended Teenage Pregnancies*. NHS Centre for Reviews and Dissemination, University of York.

O'Dea, J. A. (2003) Why do kids eat healthful food? Perceived benefits of and barriers to healthful eating and physical activity among children and adolescents. *Journal of the American Dietetic Association*, **103**, 497–501.

Office for National Statistics (2004) *Health Statistics Quarterly, Winter 2004*. The Stationery Office, London.

Office for National Statistics (2005) *Teenage Conception Statistics for England 1998–2003*. http://www.dfes.gov.uk/teenagepregnancy/ [Accessed 5 August 2005].

Olausson, P. O., Cnattingius, S. and Haglund, B. (1999) Teenage pregnancies and risk of late fetal death and infant mortality. *British Journal of Obstetrics and Gynaecology*, **106**, 116–21.

Overturf, C. M., Smith, A. M., Engelbert-Fenton, K. A., Elster, A. B. and Geiger, C. J. (1992) Potential role of energy and nutrient intakes in decreasing the incidence of genitourinary tract infections in pregnant adolescents. *Journal of the American Dietetic Association*, **92**, 1513–15.

Parker, T. (1998) Vitamins and pregnancy: teenagers' beliefs. *The Practising Midwife*, **1**, 23–4.

Pobocik, R. S., Benavente, J. C., Boudreau, N. S. and Spore, C. L. (2003) Pregnant adolescents in Guam consume diets low in calcium and other micronutrients. *Journal of the American Dietetic Association*, **103**, 611–14.

Portnoy, B. and Christenson, G. M. (1989) Cancer knowledge and related practices: results from the National Adolescent Student Health Survey. *Journal of School Health*, **59**, 218.

Prentice, A. M., Goldberg, G. R., Davies, H. L., Murgatroyd, P. R. and Scott, W. (1989) Energy sparing adaptations in human pregnancy assessed by whole body calorimetry. *British Journal of Nutrition*, **62**(1), 5–22.

Prentice, A. M., Spaaij, C. J. K., Goldberg, G. R., Poppitt, S. D., van Raaij, J. M. A., Swann, D. and Black, A. E. (1996) Energy requirements of pregnant and lactating women. *American Journal of Clinical Nutrition*, **50**(Suppl. 1), S82–S111.

Radhika, M. S., Bhaskaram, P., Balakrishna, N., Ramalakshmi, B. A., Devi, S. and Siva Kumar, B. (2002) Effects of vitamin A deficiency during pregnancy on maternal and child health. *British Journal of Obstetrics and Gynaecology*, **109**, 689–93.

Rampersaud, G. C., Pereira, M. A., Girard, B. L., Adams, J. Metzl, J. D. (2005) Breakfast habits, nutritional status, body weight, and academic performance in children and adolescents. *Journal of the American Dietetic Association*, **105**, 743–60.

Ravelli, A. C., van der Meulen, J. H., Michels, R. P., Osmond, C., Barker, D. J., Hales, C. N. and Bleker, O. P. (1998) Glucose tolerance in adults after prenatal exposure to famine. *Lancet*, **351**, 173–7.

Reifsnider, E. and Gill, S. L. (2000) Nutrition for the childbearing years. *Journal of Obstetric, Gynecologic, & Neonatal Nursing*, **29**, 43–55.

Repke, J. T. and Villar, J. (1991) Pregnancy-induced hypertension and low birth weight: the role of calcium. *American Journal of Clinical Nutrition*, **54**, 237S–241S.

Roberts, J. M. and Hubel, C. A. (2004) Oxidative stress in preeclampsia. *American Journal of Obstetrics and Gynecology*, **190**, 1177–8.

Rumbold, A. and Crowther, C. A. (2005a) Vitamin E supplementation in pregnancy. *The Cochrane Database of Systematic Reviews*, Issue 2. Art. No.: CD004069. DOI: 10.1002/14651858.CD004069.pub2.

Rumbold, A. and Crowther, C. A. (2005b) Vitamin C supplementation in pregnancy. *The Cochrane Database of Systematic Reviews*, Issue 1. Art. No.: CD004072. DOI: 10.1002/14651858.CD004072.pub2.

Rush, D. (2000) Nutrition and maternal mortality in the developing world. *American Journal of Clinical Nutrition*, **72**, 212S–240S.

Savin-Williams, R. (1979) Dominance hierarchies in groups of early adolescents. *Child Development*, **50**, 923–35.

Scheplyagina, L. A. (2005) Impact of the mother's zinc deficiency on the women's and newborn's health status. *Journal of Trace Elements in Medicine and Biology*, **19**, 25–35.

Schneck, M. E., Sideras, K. S., Fox, R. A. and Dupuis, L. (1990) Low income pregnant adolescents and their infants: dietary findings and health outcomes. *Journal of the American Dietetic Association*, **90**, 555–8.

Scholl, T. O., Hediger, M. L. and Ances, I. G. (1990) Maternal growth during pregnancy and decreased birth weight. *American Journal of Clinical Nutrition*, **51**, 790–3.

Scholl, T. O., Hediger, M. L., Schall, J. I., Khoo, C. S. and Fischer, R. L. (1994) Maternal growth during pregnancy and competition for nutrients. *American Journal of Clinical Nutrition*, **60**, 183–8.

Scholl, T. O., Hediger, M. L., Benich, A., Schall, J. I., Woolcott, K. S. and Fruger, P. M. (1997) Use of prenatal supplements: influence on the outcome of pregnancy. *American Journal of Epidemiology*, **146**, 134–41.

Scholl, T. O., Stein, T. P. and Smith, W. K. (2000) Leptin and maternal growth during adolescent pregnancy. *American Journal of Clinical Nutrition*, **72**, 1542–7.

Scholl, T. O., Leskiw, M., Chen, X., Sims, M. and Stein, T. P. (2005) Oxidative stress, diet, and the etiology of preeclampsia. *American Journal of Clinical Nutrition*, **81**, 1390–6.

Shah, R. S. and Rajalakshmi, R. (1984) Vitamin A status in the newborn in relation to gestational care, body weight and maternal nutritional status. *American Journal of Clinical Nutrition*, **40**, 794–800.

Siega-Riz, A. M., Promislow, J. H. E., Savitz, D. A., Thorp, J. M. and McDonald, T. (2003) Vitamin C intake and the risk of preterm delivery. *American Journal of Obstetrics and Gynecology*, **189**, 519–25.

Sillender, M. (2000) Continuing low uptake of periconceptional folate warrants increased food fortification. *Journal of Human Nutrition and Dietetics*, **13**, 425–31.

Sjoberg, A., Hallberg, L., Hoglund, D. and Hulthen, L. (2003) Meal patter, food choice, nutrient intake and lifestyle factors in The Goteborg Adolescence Study. *European Journal of Clinical Nutrition*, **57**, 1569–78.

Skinner, J. D. and Carruth, B. R. (1991) Dietary quality of pregnant and non-pregnant adolescents. *Journal of the American Dietetic Association*, **91**, 718–20.

Skinner, J. D., Carruth, B. R., Pope, J., Varner, L. and Goldberg, D. (1992) Food and nutrient intake of white, pregnant adolescents. *Journal of the American Dietetic Association*, **912**, 1127–9.

Smith, G. C. S. and Pell, J. P. (2001) Teenage pregnancy and risk of adverse perinatal outcomes associated with first and second births: population based retrospective cohort study. *British Medical Journal*, **323**, 476–9.

Smithers, G., Gregory, J. R., Bates, C. J., Prentice, A., Jackson, L. V. and Wenlock, R. (2000) The National Diet and Nutrition Survey: young people aged 4–18 years. *Nutrition Bulletin*, **25**, 105–11.

Social Exclusion Unit (1999) *Teenage Pregnancy: Report by the Social Exclusion Unit*. HMSO, London.

Stables, D. and Rankin, J. (eds.) (2004) *Physiology in Childbearing, With Anatomy and Related Biosciences*, 2nd edn. Baillière Tindall, Edinburgh.

Stedman's Medical Dictionary, 2nd edn (2004) Houghton Mifflin Company, Wilmington, MA.

Steinberg, L. (1981) Transformation in family relations at puberty. *Developmental Psychology*, **17**, 833–40.

Stevens-Simon, C., Fullar, S. and McAnarney, E. R. (1992) Tangible differences between adolescent-oriented and adult-oriented prenatal care. *Journal of Adolescent Health*, **13**, 298–302.

Story, M. (1992) Nutritional requirements during adolescence. In: *Textbook of Adolescent Medicine* (eds. E. R. McAnarney, R. E. Kreipe, D. E. Orr and G. D. Comerci). WB Saunders, Philadelphia, pp. 75–84.

Story, M. and Alton, I. (1995) Nutrition issues and adolescent pregnancy. *Nutrition Today*, **30**, 142–51.

Story, M., Neumark-Sztainer, D. and French, S. (2002) Individual and environmental influences on adolescent eating behaviors. *Journal of the American Dietetic Association*, **102**(Suppl.): S40–S51.

Symon, A. G. and Wrieden, W. L. (2003) A qualitative study of pregnant teenagers' perceptions of the acceptability of a nutritional education intervention. *Midwifery*, **19**, 140–7.

Teenage Pregnancy Strategy Evaluation Team (2003) *Annual Report Synthesis 2002*. Teenage Pregnancy Unit, London.

Teenage Pregnancy Unit (2004) *Teenage Pregnancy: An Overview of the Research Evidence*. Health Development Agency, London.

Thurnham, D. I., Bender, D. A., Scott, J. and Halsted, C. H. (2000) Water-soluble vitamins. In: *Human Nutrition and Dietetics*, 10th edn (eds. J. S. Garrow, W. P. T. James and A. Ralph). Churchill Livingstone, Edinburgh, pp. 249–87.

Turpeinen, A. M., Basu, S. and Mutanen, M. (1998) A high linoleic acid diet increases oxidative stress in vivo and affects nitric oxide metabolism in humans. *Leukot Essent Fatty Acids*, **59**, 229–33.

Umans, J. G. and Lindheimer, M. D. (2001) Antihypertensive therapy in pregnancy. *Current Hypertension Reports*, **3**, 392–9.

UNICEF (2001) *A League Table of Teenage Births in Rich Nations*. Innocenti Report Card No 3, UNICEF Innocenti Research Centre, Florence. http://www.unicef-icdc.org/publications/index.html [Accessed 6 July 2005].

US Department Health Human Services (1989) *The National Adolescent Student Health survey: A report of the Health of America's Youth*. Third Party, Oakland.

Wacker, J., Fruhauf, J., Schulz, M., Chiwora, F. M., Volz, J. and Becker, K. (2000) Riboflavin deficiency and preeclampsia. *Obstetrics and Gynecology*, **96**, 38–44.

Wahl, R. (1999) Nutrition in the adolescent. *Pediatric Annals*, **28**, 107–11.

Wald, N. J. (2004) Folic acid and the prevention of neural tube defects. *New England Journal of Medicine*, **35**, 101–3.

Walker, Z., Townsend, J., Oakley, L., Donovan, C., Smith, H., Hurst, Z., Bell, J. and Marshall, S. (2002) Health promotion for adolescents in primary care: Randomised controlled trial. *British Medical Journal*, **326**, 524–9.

Ward, B. (2000) Sandwell report in note 31. In: *Poverty in Plenty: A Human Development Report for the UK* (ed. J. Seymour). Earthscan, London.

Ward, O. A., Robson, P. J., Cran, G. W. and Boreham, C. A. G. (2002) Energy and macronutrient intakes reported by adolescents in Northern Ireland: comparison of 1990 and 2000 data. *Proceedings of the Nutrition Society*, **61**, 83A.

Weaver, M., Poehlitz, M. and Hutchinson, S. (1999) 5 a day for low-income families: evaluation of an advertising campaign and cooking events. *Journal of Nutrition Education*, **31**, 161–9.

Weaver, C. M. (2000) The growing years and prevention of osteoporosis in later life. *Proceedings of the Nutrition Society*, **59**, 303–6.

Winick, M. (1989) The role of early nutrition in subsequent development and optimal future health. *Bulletin of the New York Academy of Medicine*, **65**, 1020–5.

Wrieden, W. L. and Symon, A. (2003) The development and pilot evaluation of a nutrition education intervention programme for teenage women (food for life). *Journal of Human Nutrition and Dietetics*, **16**, 67–71.

Wright, C. M. (2000) Letter to editor. http://adc.bmjjournals.com/cgi/eletters/83/1/18 [Accessed 22/08/05].

Wynn, A. and Wynn, M. (1988) Nutrition around conception and the prevention of low birthweight. *Nutrition and Health*, **6**, 37–52.

Yip, R. (2000) Significance of an abnormally low or high hemoglobin concentration during pregnancy: special considerations of iron nutrition. *American Journal of Clinical Nutrition*, **72**(Suppl.), 272S–279S.

Zhuo, L. M., Yang, W. W., Hua, J. Z., Deng, C. Q., Tao, X. and Stolzfus, R. J. (1998) Relation of hemoglobin measured at different times in pregnancy to preterm birth and low birth weight in Shanghai, China. *American Journal of Epidemiology*, **148**, 998–1006.

CHAPTER 3

Eating and drinking during labour

Darren Hart

Introduction

Eating and drinking are necessary and natural processes that provide nutrition – a requirement of the body to maintain homeostasis. If regular energy sustenance were withheld we would die within a matter of weeks. In pregnancy it is acknowledged that metabolic changes occur that are essential for the development and growth of the fetus. These adaptations are marked with increased insulin sensitivity, increased blood volume, and the need for the woman to create vital energy reserves in the form of adipose tissue. It seems clear, therefore, that women should be provided with sound dietary advice at this physiologically demanding time. This can be said not only for pregnancy but also birth, when energy expenditure is expected to be at its maxim.

Nutrition requirement during labour and birth has been a subject of controversy for many years. Before modern hospitals provided a structured maternity service, women ate and drank as they wished under the guidance of their carer. Since awareness of the anaesthetic risks for labouring women was highlighted in the mid-1940s, few practitioners have agreed on the best approach that promotes safety, as well as fulfilling the nutritional requirements of the woman and her fetus. It is therefore impossible to consider the benefits of nutrition during labour without also assessing the risks.

The risks for women eating and drinking during labour are predominantly associated with pulmonary aspiration of gastric contents during emergency caesarean section, when all practitioners are working in potentially rushed and stressed situations. The same risks are not evident in women prepared for elective caesarean section under regional or general anaesthetic and who have received aspiration prophylaxis (Department of Health, 1957–2001). 'Nil by mouth' policies were introduced more than 50 years ago in an attempt to reduce the chances of pulmonary aspiration in relation to the administration of general anaesthesia.

In modern maternity units, there now exists a huge variation in both practice and policies regarding eating and drinking during labour. These discrepancies have come about due to the lack of evidence to support such guidelines and the belief by many clinicians, particularly midwives, that starving in labour is intrinsically wrong. In addition, many midwives, supported by increasingly influential user groups in maternity services, encourage eating and drinking in labour because of the theoretical metabolic and psychological benefits. There is limited evidence, however, to support all viewpoints.

Aggressive dietary management aimed at reducing the risks associated with the aspiration condition is not adopted in all parts of the world (Champion and McCormick, 2001). There appears to be little documentation regarding specific dietary recommendations for labouring women because many cultures continue to support birth at home. The woman's cultural background will inevitably influence practices regarding eating and drinking in labour. These range from prolonged starvation to carefully considered and intense dietary programmes. Maternal mortality associated with pulmonary aspiration is currently unreported in many developing countries.

Pulmonary aspiration is now so rare in the developed world that it is an impossible endpoint to investigate, even by large multi-centre clinical trials. Yet if eating in labour is related to this serious complication, its rarity may well justify the risk of a more liberal approach to caloric intake in normal labouring women. Given the enormous number of women involved, this more liberal approach could be scientifically justified if an important benefit associated with oral intake could be proven.

An historical perspective of maternity care and eating and drinking in labour

In the latter part of the 1800s, maternal mortality in hospitals was up to ten times higher than at home – labour-related sepsis, toxaemia and haemorrhage being the main causes of death (Loudon, 2000). The introduction and development of anti-sepsis contributed significantly to reversing this trend. The move to hospital births in the first half of the 20th century in the USA, and somewhat later in the UK, permitted the easier implementation of organised, medically orientated maternity care. This inevitably meant a greater number of obstetric interventions, in turn leading to an increased requirement for general anaesthesia. However, the US and UK had among the highest rates of maternal mortality in the developed world. This has been attributed to excessive obstetric intervention by hospital practitioners in the US, and in the UK by general practitioners administering general anaesthesia for instrumental deliveries in the home (Loudon, 2000). Scandinavian obstetricians, practising in countries with much lower incidences of maternal death, were shocked at the 'indulgent' practices of their American counterparts.

At that time there appeared to be no reason to prevent labouring women from eating and drinking. Medical texts advised professionals to encourage women to eat and drink as much as could be tolerated (DeLee, 1918). It was assumed that not feeding a labouring woman would result in weakness, delayed labour and serious postpartum haemorrhage. Changing social circumstances were also influencing health care practices. Women were voraciously lobbying for more rights, greater advocacy and an equal representation. At this time maternity units noticed a sharp increase in women's demands for reductions in the pain experienced in childbirth. Clinicians experimenting with such analgesics endeavoured to accommodate this increase in demand.

A more dramatic decline in maternal mortality was evident in the decade leading up to the Second World War. Key factors that influenced mortality rates were the introduction of penicillin, blood transfusions and use of ergometrine, along with improved treatment of pre-eclampsia and safer caesarean section procedures (Loudon, 2000). By the late 1930s, hospitals were providing organised maternity care for women in many parts of the developed world. The dilemma was that maternal mortality was not reducing in the manner that had initially been predicted (O'Sullivan *et al.*, 2000). All aspects of care provision were in need of scrutiny. In the 1940s, Mendelson, an obstetrician, played a key role in establishing policies in an attempt to help reduce maternal mortality for labouring women in America. Over a 13-year period, Mendelson examined the records of 44,016 pregnant women in a New York hospital and found 66 cases of aspiration of stomach contents into the lungs during obstetric anaesthesia (Mendelson, 1946). An important consideration was that, at this time, general anaesthesia meant inhalation of ether and was frequently administered by a new and inexperienced practitioner. Mendelson was the first investigator to highlight the potentially serious consequences of gastric aspiration (Mendelson, 1946). He was also the first to distinguish the different reactions caused by the aspiration of solids or liquids from the stomach. It is often overlooked that only two women in his study actually aspirated solids; both died either from obstructive asphyxia or due to the development of a bronchial obstruction. The remaining women aspirated acidic gastric fluid into the lung and all developed a non-fatal asthmatic-like illness, eventually named 'Mendelson's syndrome' (Mendelson, 1946).

Mendelson went on to conduct further experiments on rabbits, attempting to determine the causes of this gastric fluid effect. There were no deaths due to inhalation of neutral liquids, the deaths only occurred when the aspirated fluid contained hydrochloric acid. After extensive animal experiments, he concluded that delayed gastric emptying during labour was the primary cause of gastric aspiration and this resulted in an intrinsic increase in acidity. The acidic pH had a direct bearing on the severity of the condition. Mendelson's syndrome, now also known as 'acid aspiration syndrome' or 'aspiration pneumonitis', is one of three factors consistently associated with maternal death related to obstetric general anaesthesia, along with emergency operations and difficult tracheal intubations (Department of Health, 1957–2001). The problem is that these three can occur at the same time. Mendelson's recommendation for clinical practice was that *all* women abstain from food during labour, that the woman's stomach should be emptied prior to general anaesthesia and that antacids should be prescribed during labour (Mendelson, 1946). He also advocated increasing the use of local anaesthesia, as well as the need to ensure competent anaesthetic procedures were upheld. Hospitals in the United States were quick to respond to this advice and adopted this approach for the next 40 years. The United Kingdom was initially less inspired by these suggestions. However, the introduction of the national Confidential Enquiry triennial reports (Department of Health, 1957–2001) into maternal deaths produced the evidence that supported the need for a change in practice. The resultant effect was to impose antacid regimes and strict nil by mouth dictates on women that laboured in hospital.

The decline in maternal mortality from pulmonary aspiration

The true reason for the decline in maternal deaths over the last 50+ years (as shown in Figure 3.1) is difficult to ascertain, but it is understandable that any new evidence supporting practice associated with this reduction would be eagerly accepted. From the 1940s, strategies to reduce gastric volume and increase pH were introduced, as the evidence at that time suggested that the physical consistency of the aspirate intake was an important cause of this potentially lethal complication (Mendelson, 1946). Obstetric anaesthetic practices were being developed in the 1950s that were reducing fatal risks for women. Tracheal intubation almost certainly played a significant part in reducing the incidence of pulmonary aspiration in obstetrics. However, its use today is always in association with a rapid sequence induction of anaesthesia (RSI). In this procedure, the woman is pre-oxygenated for three minutes and a broncho-relaxant administered. Pressure is then applied to the cricoid cartilage with the thumb and forefinger in order to prevent regurgitation of the stomach contents.

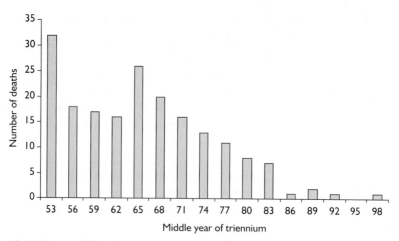

Figure 3.1 Maternal deaths related to pulmonary aspiration (DH CEMDI reports 1957–2001).

While pressure is being applied, the anaesthetist intubates thc person. Because of varying degrees of success with this procedure, the universal use of this technique in every term pregnant woman, both elective and emergency, could be questioned (Hawthorne *et al.*, 1996).

After the initial decline in anaesthesia-related deaths, the late 1950s and early 1960s saw an increase in mortality, at which time failed or misplaced intubation was recognised to be a significant complication of general anaesthesia within the pregnant population. In these situations, extensive manipulation of the airway in the course of a difficult intubation was frequently associated with aspiration. Understandably, under these circumstances anaesthetists preferred a starved patient. Unfortunately, even modern obstetric practice has a significant incidence of failed intubation, reported to be as high as 1 in 250 cases (Hawthorne *et al.*, 1996).

Perhaps the most significant change in practice that has reduced the risk of pulmonary aspiration has been the dramatic reduction in the use of general anaesthesia for caesarean section (O'Sullivan *et al.*, 2000). Caesarean section rates have escalated in the last 20 years, however, meaning that the overall number of general anaesthetic (GA) procedures has not significantly reduced. In the UK, the National Sentinel Caesarean Section Audit showed that 1 in 29 women were unconscious during childbirth (Thomas and Paranjothy, 2001). The audit found that the overall caesarean section rate had risen to 21.5%. As general anaesthesia was used for 9.5% of the elective and 22.8% of the emergency cases (*n* = 10,923 and 18,534 respectively) it can be calculated that 5,244 (3.5%) of the 3-month cohort of 150,139 women must have delivered under GA (Bewley and O'Sullivan, 2003). Therefore a reduction in the use of GA cannot be the only explanation for the remarkable reduction in deaths from aspiration. Improved training in obstetric anaesthesia with better understanding of the risks associated with GAs could have contributed to the overall decline. Since

Mendelson's recommendations, pharmaceutical products have been developed in an attempt to reduce the acidic environment of the stomach, as through X-ray studies it became clear that the risks of aspiration for women increased when they had a critical pH of <2.5. Acid antagonists were then routinely introduced based on the assumption that reduced acid base would have a direct impact on mortality. The evidence that H_2 antagonists reduce morbidity and mortality has not been conclusively demonstrated (O'Sullivan *et al.*, 2000).

Gastric function in pregnancy and labour

Gastro-oesophageal reflux frequently occurs in pregnancy. Studies of oesophageal pH have demonstrated increased levels of gastric acidity, even in asymptomatic women (Hey *et al.*, 1977; Van Thiel *et al.*, 1977). This can be attributed to both an increase in intra-gastric pressure and a fall in lower oesophageal sphincter pressure, probably as a result of the relaxing effects of progesterone (Van Thiel *et al.*, 1976). Opioids and some anaesthetic agents can further compound these effects (Holdsworth, 1978). There have been a number of studies using various techniques to measure gastric motility; some of which today would not be acceptable for ethical reasons. Pregnancy is not known to significantly alter the rate of gastric emptying (La Salvia and Steffen, 1950; O'Sullivan *et al.*, 1987; Carp *et al.*, 1992; Sandar *et al.*, 1992; Chiloiro *et al.*, 2001). However, studies have shown that once labour begins the stomach is less efficient at emptying physiologically (Hirsheimer *et al.*, 1938; La Salvia and Steffen, 1950; Davison *et al.*, 1970; Nimmo *et al.*, 1977; Wright *et al.*, 1992; Ewah *et al.*, 1993; Kelly *et al.*, 1997). This has significant implications for women that may need an anaesthetic in labour. If the rate of motility slows and the woman has eaten, the volume of the stomach's contents will increase, which in turn means that she will aspirate larger quantities of partially digested food. Physical exertion and stress are also known to further compound matters by redirecting as much as 70% of blood flow away from the gastrointestinal tract to other more demanding tissues of the body (Konturek *et al.*, 1973; Van Nieuwenhoven *et al.*, 1999).

Studies using absorption of paracetamol, which is not absorbed within the stomach but rapidly so by the small intestine, have been widely used to measure gastric emptying (Heading *et al.*, 1973; Nimmo *et al.*, 1975; Nimmo *et al.*, 1977; Macfie *et al.*, 1991; Wright *et al.*, 1992; Wong *et al.*, 2002). Unfortunately, this technique is principally related to the gastric emptying of liquids and the evaluation of solids and semi-solids has proved more difficult. Findings from these studies must therefore be interpreted with a degree of caution.

Bolus doses of epidural and intrathecal opioids are also known to further delay gastric emptying (Wright *et al.*, 1992; Ewah *et al.*, 1993; Kelly *et al.*,

1997). Two studies have evaluated the effect of epidural infusions of low-dose local anaesthetics (LA) with opioids on gastric emptying during labour (Zimmerman *et al.*, 1996; Porter *et al.*, 1997). In one study, women received 90 µg fentanyl (50 µg bolus + 2 hour epidural infusion @ 20 µg/hr), resulting in no significant delay in gastric emptying (Zimmerman *et al.*, 1996). In the other study, two groups of women were assessed. One group was infused with 75 µg fentanyl whilst the other group received 100–125 µg (Porter *et al.*, 1997). In both groups, further epidural LA + fentanyl was infused during the study period. The study reported a delay in gastric emptying in those women who had received greater than 100 µg fentanyl. Although low dose epidurals appear to demonstrate a reduced delay in gastric emptying when compared to the administration of systemic opioids during labour, there is a delay nonetheless. It would therefore be wrong to assume that there is no risk associated with pulmonary aspiration for those women who receive an epidural during labour, particularly as the studies concerned noted that the biggest delays occurred primarily in women who had been in labour for a significant length of time, where there is a greater likelihood of intervention.

The stomach's acidic environment can be dramatically altered if the rate of gastrointestinal motility slows significantly, such that there will be an overproduction of digestive acids. Eating and drinking further compounds this effect, leading to greater gastric secretions and increases the acidity of the woman's stomach contents, bringing it close to a pH of 2.5. If the pH of stomach contents is below 2.5, or gastric secretions are greater than 25 cc, women are at a higher risk of aspiration. Teabeaut (1952) studied varying pH and risk of aspiration and identified a critical pH of >2.4 associated with a reduced risk. This was reinforced by Bannister and Sattilaro's (1962) work, stating a pH of 2.5 as being critical. Further trials discovered that the volume of stomach contents was less significant than the acidity (James *et al.*, 1984; Broach and Newton, 1988). These studies all found that a low volume with high acidity was associated with a higher risk than a high volume with a buffered low acidity. It is now generally accepted that there is an equilibrium of risk, such that smaller volumes are required if the pH is lower. Therefore, it can be interpreted that fluids are less risky than small amounts of food, which cause increased secretion of gastric acids.

Eating in labour

The labouring woman has often been compared to an athlete performing strenuous activities. This is because, like labouring women, athletes also have a delayed gastric emptying time, faster absorption of oral glucose, increased stroke volumes and increased cardiac output (Sleutel and Golden, 1999). The main concern when comparing the two has been that an athlete is always persuaded to increase both their solid and fluid intake, whilst the labouring woman, although under similar stresses, is prohibited from doing the same.

Many midwives and doctors argue that starvation in labour is both physiologically and psychologically detrimental for women (Champion and McCormick, 2001). The contention is that labour and birth indisputably require a large calorific expenditure and that food and drink must be made available to support the great physical demands. The resultant effect of withholding calorie-laden food and drink may be to impair the progress of labour by starving vital organs of essential resources. As the woman becomes exhausted and the uterus is unable to function, the outcome can be transformed from a healthy normal birth to a delayed distressing instrumental delivery (Yiannouzis and Parnell, 1992; Newton and Champion, 1997).

The British Nutrition Foundation suggests that a sedentary pregnant woman requires approximately 90 kCal/hr in the last three months of pregnancy. It is also estimated that a labouring woman may require up to 121 kCal/hr once in established labour (BNF, 2003). It has been demonstrated that an oral intake rate of 47 kCal/hr will prevent the production of plasma ketones and non-esterified fatty acids in labouring women (Kubli *et al.*, 2002). This would equate to approximately 150 ml/hr if provided as an isotonic sports drink. However, as discovered by Kubli *et al.* (2002), women found it difficult to tolerate more than 750 ml of fluid once in active labour. These quantities would, in principle, prevent ketosis for between 5 and 7 hours, which would not sustain a labouring primiparous woman who could be expected to labour for twice this time. Evidence has suggested that women are unable to tolerate the expected calories needed to support them in established labour (Chern-Hughes, 1999; Kubli *et al.*, 2002). This would suggest that, on the whole, women are able to fight off the theoretical compromising effects of ketosis by usefully utilising glucose reserves stored in the last trimester of pregnancy. This suggests that ketosis, for most women, does not have the detrimental physiological effects that has been hypothesised by many.

There is some disparity between the recommendations of food types that can be safely consumed during labour and what women will actually eat and drink. Isotonic sports drinks can be absorbed efficiently by the gut and provide sufficient calories to abolish ketosis in the short-term (Kubli *et al.*, 2002). Dieticians advise liquid/semi-liquid, high-carbohydrate, low-fat and low-residue nutritional sustenance for labouring women (Newton and Champion, 1997). These should be consumed at a neutral temperature, as chilled or hot foods slow the rate of gastric absorption.

Although these recommendations are frequently supported in hospital policies, women will often consume what is most convenient. This has often meant drinking chilled 'artificially sweetened' carbonated drinks and eating high fat foods, such as cakes and chocolate. These are products readily available from onsite shops and dispensaries. If women are free to choose what to eat and drink during labour, it is unlikely that safety will be their primary concern. Information based on current knowledge of risks and benefits should be provided for those women able to eat during labour, taking into consideration culture, preference and availability. This has to be a responsibility of the health care providers during the antenatal period, as well as at the time of birth. Information, if any, offered to many women remains inconsistent (Scheepers *et al.*, 2001). Women have been shown to have greater satisfaction of their labour experience when they are provided with information during the antenatal period (Scheepers *et al.*, 2001). So often women arrive on the ward shocked to discover that their maternity unit does not support eating and drinking in labour!

Hospitals may well have oral intake policies that support risk selection criteria, such that as the risk of operative delivery increases so the likelihood of being able to eat and drink decreases. The problems highlighted in the last national protocol survey were that units have different definitions of what constitutes a labouring woman at risk (Hart *et al.*, 2003). The discretion and confidence of the practitioner will also influence the degree to which the policy is applied. If they perceive the risk to be real they will support the guidance; if not then they may well go their own way. Why is there the potential for this inconsistent approach to oral intake policies? The answer may lie in the diverse interpretation of the limited available evidence that supports practice.

Risks associated with eating during labour

The odds of dying from aspiration during childbirth from 1979 to 1990 have been reported as 0.67 per million women in the US (Hawkins *et al.*, 1998). This is an extremely rare occurrence, especially when compared with the odds of being struck by lightning each year in the US, which was 1.67 per million in 1998 (Sleutel and Golden, 1999). Since 1990, there have been more than 10 million births in the UK, with four maternal deaths related to pulmonary aspiration (Department of Health, 1990–2001). Two of these women had not started labour before developing the complication. If mortality rates remain the same, the real risk for women dying of pulmonary aspiration during labour can be estimated at approximately 1 in 5 million, using data provided by the Confidential Enquiries. Indeed, O'Sullivan *et al.* (2000) speculates that the majority of anaesthetists trained today have never encountered acid aspiration during the induction of anaesthesia. Even if aspiration did occur, it is likely that facilities in modern intensive care units would ensure better outcomes than those experienced in Mendelson's day. However, many stalwarts continue to argue that, although gastric aspiration is now rare, it still has the potential to claim lives.

The ultimate aim of restricting oral intake during labour is the reduction of the risks associated with inhalation of gastric contents. Although starving policies result in a reduced mean stomach volume (Roberts and Shirley, 1976), particulate matter may still be present in the stomach for up to 12 hours after eating (Carp *et al.*, 1992). Regurgitation and vomiting can occur at any time during anaesthesia. Obstetricians and anaesthetists believe that it is not possible to predict who will aspirate; therefore decreasing the odds in any way possible is favourable. However, a study conducted in Nottingham by midwives and anaesthetists suggested that there is a method to identify those that are at greater risk of aspiration (Newton and Champion, 1997). They formulated and audited a policy among a convenience sample of 250 women, identifying those who were not at immediate known risk and allowing them to eat and drink a recommended diet. Those who were booked for elective induction and did not require analgesia other than transcutaneous electrical nerve stimulation (TENS) were also permitted to eat and drink as tolerated. If women required an epidural, they were allowed to drink free fluids. If requiring pethidine, only water was allowed; this is based on the understanding that intramuscular narcotics increase gastric emptying time (Nimmo *et al.*, 1975). Those already in established labour who required augmentation or whose labour became complicated in any way, were allowed 'water only' – supported by a regimen of antacids (Newton and Champion, 1997). This was historically the recommended practice for women considered to be at a higher risk of requiring a caesarean section. The audit reported no misinterpretation of the policy. Seventy-one per cent ($n = 39$) of women took the opportunity to eat in hospital when offered, but 249 women ate in the latent phase of labour. Over two-thirds of women, however, opted to drink only water once in established labour, but nearly as many ($n = 167; 66.8\%$) were restricted to fluids because they opted for parentaral or intrathecal analgesia during labour. Although it could be argued that this is a sound approach which most maternity units are willing to adopt; the limited number of births audited could not eliminate the risk potential of Mendelson's syndrome occurring. Furthermore, more than two-thirds of women did not in fact have the choice they believed was being offered, as they chose to have analgesics during their labour; an option for many labouring women today. It would take many more years to evaluate the full effect of locally designed and audited policies.

The effects of withholding food in labour

Maternity units had, until the mid-1980s, adopted starvation policies when managing the care of labouring women. The mechanisms that support homeostasis during a fasted period are well understood. The metabolic consequence of withholding food during labour, on the other hand, remains unclear. Women may adequately adapt to rapid onset of starvation during pregnancy and labour by utilising fat-stored energy reserves accumulated in the last trimester of pregnancy (Anderson, 1998). It comes as no surprise that labour is also associated with an increased energy expenditure resulting in elevated ketone bodies, in particular β-hydroxybutyrate and acetoacetic acid (Scrutton et al., 1999, Kubli et al., 2002). Ketones have been shown to occur rapidly following withdrawal of calories in pregnant women (Metzger et al., 1982). This feature, where the plasma ketone levels are likely to be raised naturally, has been described as 'accelerated starvation syndrome' (Freinkel et al., 1972). When under stress, the body is forced to use fat stored in adipocytes for energy due to a lack of available glucose; this produces free fatty acids and glycerol via lipolysis. This process is initiated by a rise in plasma glucagon and a decrease in plasma insulin. If glucose levels are not replenished, the rate of lipolysis rises and an excess of acetyl coenzyme A is produced. This leads to the formation of ketone bodies. In normal physiological situations, muscle uses these ketones as an alternative fuel, which is understood to have no ill effect. However, this is not the case if excess quantities of ketones are produced. The body is unable to cope with this overproduction and the excess ketones in the blood are eventually excreted in urine (ketonuria). This is known as a state of 'ketosis' (Tortora and Grabowski, 1993). Ketonuria occurs more frequently in pregnant women due to hormonal changes, where progesterone levels increase and there exists a higher rate of fat utilisation (Dumoulin and Foulkes, 1984). It has been found that ketonuria occurs in pregnancy despite normal ketone levels in the blood (Coetzee et al., 1980). As pregnancy progresses, basal levels of glucose fall, suppressing insulin secretion and increasing lipolysis. In later stages, insulin resistance also occurs, further potentiating this process. There is the potential for such reserves to be metabolised at critical times, such as supporting the woman and fetus during labour. Whilst this is certainly true for most smooth muscles, it is not fully understood whether the uterus is able to call upon fatty acids in the same way or whether it can only make use of the limited protected glucose reserves. There is no current knowledge as to whether mild ketonuria is actually harmful to either woman or child.

Studies that have examined the effects of ketosis on pregnant and labouring ewes have shown that these animals suffer fatigue and become lethargic, often accompanied by a loss of appetite (Swartz, 2001). Dumoulin and Foulkes (1984) went as far as reporting a relationship between 'marked ketonuria' and the incidence of prolonged labour; a view supported by little explanation. Ketosis has also been claimed to increase the likelihood of instrumental delivery (Armstrong and Johnston, 2000). However, Paterson *et al.* (1967) have shown that women who fasted in labour had lower levels of ketones in comparison to those who had been starved and rested for 12 hours in preparation for a caesarean section. This may suggest the effective utilisation of ketone bodies during labour.

The placenta may even *use* ketone bodies (Paterson *et al.*, 1967). There is evidence that the placenta contains the enzymes needed to convert acetyl CoA to ketones, and that ketones are used in preference to glucose during ketosis in laboratory experiments (Shambaugh *et al.*, 1977). Suggestions have been made that ketones are able to cross the placenta via passive diffusion. Bencini and Symonds (1972) demonstrated a linear correlation in blood ketone levels in the woman and her baby at birth. This has the potential of reducing fetal activity and well-being if accumulated (Swift, 1991). However, the increase in these acids, including non-esterified fatty acids which increase with starvation, have not been shown to have a negative effect on maternal and fetal acid–base balance (Bencini and Symonds, 1972; Dumoulin and Foulkes, 1984). Animal studies have illustrated the importance of ketones in the development of the fetal brain, liver and lung (Robinson and Williamson, 1980). Ketosis is often associated with metabolic acidosis despite the contradicting evidence mentioned above.

Ketonuria indicates the presence of an excess of ketone bodies, i.e. ketones that are *not* being used. This cannot be ignored, nor can the suggestion that the excess may still be harmful. However, if ketones are useful to labour, then actively encouraging diet during this time might even be detrimental to progress. The impact that ketosis or other effects of starvation has on the progress and outcome of labour remains unclear. The haemodynamic and uterine metabolic adaptations associated with eating/starving are in need of further investigation.

Intravenous hydration in labour – more harm than good?

In the 1960s and 1970s, hospitals throughout the world began administering intravenous dextrose in an attempt to reduce maternal ketosis, traditionally thought to be harmful. This understanding coincided with a more aggressive approach to labour management; so that a long labour was far less tolerated and prolonged exposure to an intense ketotic state rare (O'Driscoll *et al.*, 1969). A number of investigators have evaluated the effect of managed hydration on labour outcome (Romney and Gabel, 1966; Dumoulin and Foulkes, 1984; Garite *et al.*, 2000).

Infusions of normal saline have been shown to reduce maternal ketosis and possibly improve fetal well-being (Morton *et al.*, 1985). Other investigators have demonstrated that infusing a litre of normal saline will reduce uterine contractility, thus prolonging labour (Cheek *et al.*, 1996). However, serious hyponatremia in both the woman and her fetus can result if salt-free intravenous solutions are used. Although maternal pH and lactate levels have not been proven to be altered, fetal blood glucose and umbilical arterial blood pH increase (Morton *et al.*, 1985).

Administration of intravenous glucose infusions have since been abandoned as it has become clear that this causes increased insulin production in the fetus, resulting in adverse effects in the neonate with a risk of fetal acidosis and fetal hyperglycaemia. These symptoms are followed by neonatal hypoglycaemia and jaundice (Romney and Gabel, 1966; Bencini and Symonds, 1972; Tarno-Mordi *et al.*, 1981; Kenepp *et al.*, 1982; Lawrence *et al.*, 1982; Feeney, 1982; Dumoulin and Foulkes, 1984).

Garite *et al.* (2000) conducted a randomised controlled trial comparing the effects of intravenous administration of Ringers lactate solution (125 ml vs. 250 ml h^{-1}) on 195 nulliparous women during labour. The study showed that the incidence of labour lasting more than 12 hours was statistically higher in the 125 ml h^{-1} group (26% vs. 13%; $p = 0.047$). It was also suggested that there was a reduced need for oxytocics in the 250 ml h^{-1} group, although this fell just outside statistical significance (65% vs. 49%; $p = 0.06$). The caesarean section rate was slightly higher in the smaller infusion group, but the trial was inadequately powered to prove significance in this outcome. In today's practice, it would be difficult to support the routine administration of such large volumes of intravenous fluid to a normal pregnant woman.

Intravenous hydration is not without its problems. Women are exposed to the potentials of fluid overload, discomfort, psychological stress and reduced mobility. Encouraging a labouring woman to drink seems more physiological than aggressive interventions aimed at preventing ketosis and the effects of dehydration.

Do labouring women want to eat?

Labour is clearly understood by all to be a stressful, potentially distressing experience. Practices are constantly reviewed in order to facilitate a more relaxing and comfortable experience of labour. When a woman is stressed, she will produce higher levels of catecholamines which have the potential to reduce uterine contractions, thus prolonging labour. During stress, as with exercise, blood is shunted away from the uterus. This can be harmful to the fetus, causing hypoxia, and may result in an increased likelihood of intervention during labour. This leads to a higher incidence of operative delivery, which in turn affects the risk of aspiration of undigested food.

Naturally stimulated labour hormones, as well as therapeutic supplements, are known to impact on the desire to eat. In animal models, centrally administered oxytocin is known to suppress appetite and reduce gastrointestinal function (Antonijevic *et al.*, 1995). If these findings were reflected in humans it would suggest that the production of contraction inducing hormones naturally reduce the aspiration risks associated with general anaesthesia.

Undoubtedly some women want to eat. However, in the struggle to move away from starvation policies has the woman's desire to eat during labour become overemphasised? Armstrong and Johnston (2000) studied 149 women in Scotland, of which 30% indicated that they would have appreciated the opportunity to be able to eat in the early stages of their labour. This was a retrospective study, so the actual figures are likely to be different as it is known from this methodological approach that perceptions of experiences change over time, be it long-term or even short-term (Mann, 2003). There were also a substantial number of women who indicated that they had secretly eaten during early labour. In the elective caesarean setting, this could result in the cancelling of their operation. In an emergency, the staff involved will be given no choice to delay matters and general anaesthesia may be necessary. The implications of this are that anaesthetists may not know what they are dealing with. Armstrong and Johnston (2000) reported no significant differences in terms of labour duration between those that ate or those that did not.

In an observational study of 5,000 women in American hospitals that had no oral restriction policy, it was found that more than two thirds ingested only clear fluids once in established labour (Chern-Hughes, 1999). Women were more likely to consume solids and non-clear fluids at home rather than hospital, and those that laboured longer consumed more. Scheepers *et al.* conducted a retrospective survey in the Netherlands in 2001 which monitored the influence of the caregiver on women's eating behaviour during labour. They discovered that most women were not advised about oral intake for labour and, when left to their own devices, only one third of women would eat when in a hospital environment.

Hospital policies regarding eating and drinking during labour

In the USA, the incidence of pulmonary aspiration is comparable to that of the UK. However, in the USA many hospitals recommend clear fluids/nil by mouth policies in labour, in the belief that this reduces the risks of fatal aspiration for women (Hawkins, 1998). In 1988, less than 2% of units in the USA allowed solid intake, while this figure was almost 33% in England and Wales (Michael *et al.*, 1991). A more recent survey conducted in the USA indicates that little has changed (Hawkins *et al.*, 1998). The Netherlands has a more liberal approach to eating and drinking during labour, although the incidence of aspiration is no greater (Scheepers *et al.*, 2002). This would suggest that there is, indeed, a limited association between dietary intake and pulmonary aspiration.

In a recent survey investigating the existence and nature of oral intake policies in the UK, it was discovered that there had been a complete reversal of approaches towards 'eating and drinking in labour' recommendations (Hart *et al.*, 2003). The number of maternity units that recommended women to eat and drink freely in labour had more than doubled since the last survey of England and Wales in 1989, conducted by Michael *et al.* (1991). Hart *et al.* (2003) reported that 81% of maternity units supported women eating and drinking during labour through their policies, compared to 31% in 1989 (+50%, chi-squared 149.15, $p < 0.00001$). This is of interest because in 2003, only 65% actually had oral intake policies. Fifty-seven per cent endorsed a risk selection process. There was, however, varied opinion as to what constituted risk for eating and drinking. Labouring women were restricted to 'water only' or 'ice chips' in 19% of units (Hart *et al.*, 2003).

The reason for the more liberal approach is likely to be multifactorial. Since the early 1990s there has been a concerted effort at national and local levels to readdress the manner in which maternity care is provided in the UK. In 1993, the Department of Health (UK) in *Changing Childbirth: Report of the Expert Maternity Group* stated:

> Pregnancy is not a pathological process or disease. It is a physiological event which occurs in a very high proportion of women during their lifetimes. The majority of pregnancies end normally and without complication. (Foreword by J. Cumberledge, page II, Department of Health, 1993)

As a result, more women now receive midwifery-led care which provides comprehensive care for most. Furthermore, many midwives campaign against the aggressive management policies that govern normal labour in modern maternity units. They believe that the imposition of 'starvation' policies on the entire population of women for fear of a condition which only affects a few is wrong (Champion and McCormick, 2001). Pregnancy and birthing support groups reinforce the belief of many practitioners that women should be the initiators and decision makers in their own care. As a consequence, the design and implementation of hospital guidelines have become a united responsibility in the maternity unit. The resulting effect has been the relaxation, and in some cases abandonment, of historically strict oral intake dictates that have served as part of the prophylaxis against acid aspiration. This is in light of the fact that maternal mortality due to pulmonary aspiration is now negligible. Although rare, however, acid aspiration still does occur and a degree of caution must be maintained, as there is as yet no evidence to support all women being permitted to eat during labour.

Calories vs. fasting: the impact on labour

There are few well-designed trials available that analyse the impact calorific intake has on labour outcome (Table 3.1). Four randomised controlled trials exist that compare calorific intake with non-calorific intake. Yiannouzis and Parnell (1992) allocated 297 primiparous and multiparous women to either a 'light diet' or 'water only', once in established labour. Outcome measures were labour duration, type of birth, need for augmentation and incidence of vomiting. The length of labour was found to be one hour and thirty-four minutes longer in the eating group (mean range: 1.33–28.78 hr). Those that ate were also more likely to vomit (31/154 vs. 14/143). However, there were no statistical power data provided to support these findings. The trial also reported that many women declined to participate due to the suggestion of an epidural anaesthesia, should a caesarean section be needed at any point. The study ended after five months due to poor recruitment. They also reported that a proportion of midwives involved in the study had decided that feeding women during labour was qualitatively better. Hence, due to the lack of any kind of blinding, the study could not continue further. This trial highlights the complexities and confounding factors involved when conducting research on participants where such diverse opinions are held.

In 1999, Scrutton *et al.* investigated whether a light diet would affect a woman's metabolic profile and increase her residual gastric volume. Labour outcome was also evaluated. The light diet consisted of cereal, milk, toast, bread, semisweet biscuits and low fat cheese. Women were randomised to either a 'light diet' or a 'water-only' group. Women who had received intramuscular pethidine were excluded from the trial. Gastric volumes were measured with real-time ultrasound by the same investigator and power was based on differences in metabolic endpoints, namely plasma β-hydroxybutyrate and non-esterified fatty acids and plasma glucose. Glucose levels were higher in the eating group, while eating prevented the rise in hydroxybutyrate and fatty acids. Perhaps due to the small sample number ($n = 88$), there were no significant differences in other labour endpoints. Women in the eating group, however, did have significantly larger gastric volumes at the time of birth and these women vomited larger vol-

Table 3.1 Randomised controlled trials comparing calorific versus non-calorific intake.

Study	Number recruited	Methods	Participants	Interventions	Outcomes
Yiannouzis and Parnell (1992)	297	Randomisation with sealed envelopes	Multiparae and nulliparae, singleton fetus, cephalic presentation, gestation ≥ 37 weeks, cervical dilatation ≤ 3 cm	Light diet after randomisation versus water only	Duration of labour Mode of delivery Apgar scores Oxytocin requirement Vomiting: incidence
Scrutton et al. (1999)	88	Computer randomisation with sealed envelopes	Multiparae and nulliparae, singleton fetus, cephalic presentation, gestation ≥ 37 weeks, cervical dilatation ≤ 3cm	Light diet after randomisation versus water only	Duration of labour Interventions Mode of delivery Apgar scores Oxytocin requirement Blood gases Vomiting: incidence, volume, gastric volume Metabolic profile in early and late labour – ketones, FFA, glucose, insulin, lactate
Kubli et al. (2002)	60	Computer randomisation with sealed envelopes	Multiparae and nulliparae, singleton fetus, cephalic presentation, gestation ≥ 37 weeks, cervical dilatation ≤ 5 cm	Isotonic drinks (carbohydrate 64 g/L) after randomisation versus water only	Duration of labour Interventions Mode of delivery Apgar scores Oxytocin requirement Blood gases Vomiting: incidence, volume, gastric volume Metabolic profile in early and late labour – ketones, FFA, glucose, insulin, lactate
Scheepers et al. (2002)	200	Double blinding randomisation with sealed envelopes	Nulliparae, singleton fetus, cephalic presentation fetus, gestation ≥ 37 weeks, cervical dilatation 2–4 cm, diabetes	Carbohydrate (126 g/L) drinks after randomisation versus placebo	Duration of labour Mode of delivery Apgar scores Oxytocin requirement Arterial pH Pain medication

umes, which contained a considerable amount of solid residue.

A further study from the same unit randomised 60 women comparing the metabolic effects of 'isotonic sports drinks' to 'water-only' during labour (Kubli *et al.*, 2002). As with the previous trial, the metabolic profile was examined, along with residual gastric volumes and labour outcome. Those receiving sports drinks were encouraged to drink up to half a litre in the first hour and then a similar amount every 3–4 hours. The 'water-only' group had no restrictions. Despite the calorific limitation of the isotonic fluids, it was shown that these drinks prevented the rise in β-hydroxybutyrate and non-esterified fatty acids seen in the starved group. Once again, there was no change in any outcome of labour, but, in contrast to the light diet allowed in the original study, there was no increase in residual gastric volume in the isotonic sport drink group. While this approach may not provide the whole answer, it does at least provide a way of preventing ketosis that might be acceptable to the majority of anaesthetists.

In Holland, Scheepers *et al.* (2002) performed a randomised controlled trial with 200 women who received either carbohydrate solutions or a placebo. Both groups were allowed to drink as desired and the total intake assessed. Food was given on specific demand to either group, although it is not explained why, as this had a potentially confounding effect upon the results. Notably, 80% of the women who participated were deemed to be high risk, many were induced (40%, $n = 80$) and a significant number were post-term pregnancies (22%, $n = 43$). The main outcomes were operative deliveries, labour duration and need for analgesia. They found a three-fold increase in caesarean section in women who received calories (21/101 vs. 7/99, $p = 0.007$). However, in this trial, the caesarean section rate in the placebo group was only 7% compared to the usual rate of 19% for that unit. Further, one would expect that the nulliparous, high-risk population recruited for this study should have had a much higher caesarean section rate. The three-fold increase in caesarean section rate (7% vs. 21%) could therefore be due to a Type 1 statistical error, i.e. hypothesising that a difference exists when it really does not. These trials do not support the concept that eating and drinking shortens the duration of labour and do not support the claim that oral intake decreases the caesarean section rate.

Three of the trials that provided data on the incidence of vomiting suggested that feeding women in labour caused a significant increase in vomiting (Yiannouzis and Parnell, 1992; Scrutton *et al.*, 1999; Kubli *et al.*, 2002). The gastric cross-sectional area and volume of material vomited was greater in women that consumed solids (Scrutton *et al.*, 1999; Kubli *et al.*, 2002). Where fluids only were consumed, there was no increase in gastric cross-sectional area. From the point of view of vomiting, feeding women solid food may increase their discomfort during labour. However, there is no data to suggest that parturients should be routinely denied clear fluids. In the two trials that evaluated metabolic effects, calorific intake significantly reduced ketone levels (Scrutton *et al.*, 1999; Kubli, 2002). There was a similar reduction in non-esterified fatty acids. Increases in plasma glucose were also demonstrated. More substantial increases were seen in women who consumed calorific drinks than those that ate. Calorific intake did not appear to affect the incidence of a low Apgar score (less than 7) at one minute or mean umbilical artery pH. Further, there was no difference in the use of intrapartum oxytocin. Again, eating and drinking do not seem to be an advantage, although it is difficult to draw firm conclusions from these limited sample numbers.

Summary

It is undeniable that the incidence of fatal aspiration pneumonitis, related to general anaesthesia, is extremely low in the developed world. It is unlikely that the low incidence is directly related to a policy of restriction of oral intake during labour, although it may be a factor. Obstetric anaesthetic practices have developed from simple mask-administered ether in the home to advanced rapid sequence techniques in well-supported maternity units. The administration of regional anaesthesia during labour by competent anaesthetists, supported by beneficial H_2 acid antagonists when necessary, has also contributed to ensuring that maternal mortality has remained consistently low throughout the UK in the last 15 years. Equally, the increased liberalisation of eating policies in the UK over the same period has not resulted in an increase in maternal deaths. It should be considered that the incidence of acute or permanent airway injury, due to problematic administration of general anaesthesia, is not known. An audit of non-fatal aspiration, collated from locally stored anaesthetic registers, would provide greater insight into the true incidence of Mendelson's syndrome.

Clear calorific fluids reverse the biochemical markers associated with starvation and provide a degree of maternal comfort. Fluids ingested during labour do not appear to be associated with vomiting, larger gastric volume and lower pH in the same way that solids are. Women are unable to tolerate the required calculated calorific intake requirements during this period. This supports the concept that energy reserves stored in the third trimester are utilised effectively by most women during parturition. Women who wish to eat solid foods during labour should be informed of the known risks and benefits and, while 'nil by mouth' policies may be responsible for unnecessary discomfort, there is very little evidence that they cause other problems. However, because nausea is associated with reduced appetite for many women, it is not right to assume that all women do not want the freedom of choice. The psychological impact of such practices is in need of further investigation. Routine administration of intravenous fluids during labour, intended to reduce the incidence of ketosis and maintain hydration, cannot be supported in view of the potential complications, i.e. neonatal hypogly-caemia, jaundice, systemic infection and maternal discomfort associated with such practice. A key question relating to labour outcome is whether there are significant improvements in women who eat and drink. There is a scarcity of robust controlled data looking specifically at the birth outcome of women that are able to eat and drink during their labour, but there are some randomised control trials that have evaluated other obstetric endpoints. Current available studies suggest there is no change in the length of labour, type of birth or neonatal outcome (fetal blood pH and glucose, Apgar score) when women have fasted during labour compared to those who have fed (Yiannouzis and Parnell, 1992; Scrutton *et al.*, 1999; Kubli, 2002).

The extent to which women are encouraged to eat and drink during labour remains unknown and there is an urgent need to evaluate this in view of current conflicting clinical directives. Maternal mortality and morbidity can then be reviewed in light of these findings to inform future policies, i.e. if Mendelson's syndrome does not increase despite liberal eating practices, then these policies could be supported. Large well-designed trials are urgently required to inform the debate. Qualitative data would provide vital information on what women really want to eat if given the choice. It is often forgotten that it is the anaesthetist who assumes the responsibility of managing anaesthetic requirements in labour when operative delivery appears likely. Local policies relating to nutrition recommendations are influenced by the confidence and competence of these practitioners. Future confidential enquiries will ultimately determine the fatal risks associated with pulmonary aspiration and the design of hospital policies that currently support nutritional intake in labour. Whatever the practice, an informed debate is imperative as interpretation of the available facts is currently based on physiological principles and anecdotal reports.

Acknowledgements

The author wishes to thank Professor Andrew Shennan and Dr Geraldine O'Sullivan at St Thomas' Hospital, London, for their knowledge and support that helped facilitate the contribution of this chapter.

References

Anderson, T. (1998) Is ketosis in labour pathological? *The Practising Midwife*, **1**(9), 22–6.

Antonijevic, I., Leng, G., Luckman, S., Douglas, A., Bicknell, R. J. and Russell, J. A. (1995) Induction of uterine activity with oxytocin in late pregnant rats replicates the expression of *c-fos* in neuroendocrine and brain stem neurons as seen during parturition. *Endocrinol*, **136**(1), 154–63.

Armstrong, T. and Johnston, I. (2000) Which women want food during labour? Results of an audit in a Scottish DGH. *Health Bulletin*, **58**(2), 141–4.

Bannister, W. K. and Sattilaro, A. J. (1962) Vomiting and aspiration during anesthesia. *Anesthesiology*, **23**, 251–64.

Bencini, F. X. and Symonds, E. M. (1972) Ketone bodies in fetal and maternal blood during parturition. *Australia and New Zealans Journal of Obstetrics and Gynaecology*, **12**, 176–8.

Bewley, S. and O'Sullivan, G. (2003) Editorial response to: Caesarean section in Malawi. Prospective study of early maternal and perinatal mortality (Authors: P. Fenton, C. Whitty and F. Reynolds). *British Medical Journal*, **327**, 587.

British Nutrition Foundation (2003) Nutrition requirements. http://www.nutrition.org.uk/.

Broach, J. and Newton, N. (1988) Food and beverages in labor. Part II: The effects of cessation of oral intake during labor. *Birth*, **15**, 88–92.

Carp, H., Jayaram, A. and Stoll, M. (1992) Ultrasound examination of the stomach contents of parturients. *Anesthesia and Analgesia*, **74**, 683–7.

Champion, P. and McCormick, C. (2001) *Eating and Drinking in Labour*. Books for Midwives, Oxford.

Cheek, T. G., Samuels, P., Miller, F. *et al.* (1996) Normal saline iv fluid load decreases uterine activity in active labor. *British Journal of Anaesthesia*, **77**, 632–5.

Chern-Hughes, B. (1999) Oral intake in labor: Trends in midwifery practice. *Journal of Nurse-Midwifery*, **44**(2), 135–8.

Chiloiro, M., Darconza, G., Piccioli, E., De Carne, M., Clemente, C. and Riezzo, G. (2001) Gastric emptying and orocecal transit time in pregnancy. *Journal of Gastroenterology*, **36**(8), 538–43.

Coetzee, E. J., Jackson, W. P. and Berman, P. A. (1980) Ketonuria in pregnancy – with special reference to calorie-restricted food intake in obese diabetics. *Diabetes*, **29**(3), 177–81.

Davison, J. S., Davison, M. C. and Hay, D. M. (1970) Gastric emptying time in late pregnancy and labour. *British Journal of Obstetrics and Gynaecology*, **77**, 37–41.

Department of Health (1957–2001) *Reports on Confidential Enquiries Into Maternal Deaths in England and Wales/United Kingdom*. HMSO, London (16 Triennial Reports).

Department of Health (1993) *Changing Childbirth: Report of the Expert Maternity Group*. HMSO, London.

DeLee, J. (1918) *Obstetrics for Nurses*, 5th edn. W. B. Saunders, Philadelphia (courtesy of British Library).

Dumoulin, J. G. and Foulkes, J. E. B. (1984) Ketonuria during labour. *British Journal of Obstetrics and Gynaecology*, **91**, 97–8.

Ewah, B., Yau, K., King, M., Reynolds, F., Carson, R. and Morgan, B. (1993) Effect of epidural opioids on gastric emptying in labour. *International Journal of Obstetrics and Anesthesia*, **2**, 125–8.

Feeney, J. G. (1982) Water intoxication and oxytocin. *British Medical Journal*, **284**, 243.

Freinkel, N., Metzger, B. and Nitzan, M. (1972) Accelerated starvation and mechanisms for the conservation of maternal nitrogen during pregnancy. *Israel Journal of Medical Sciences*, **8**, 426–39.

Garite, T. J., Weeks, J., Peters-Phair, K., Pattillo, C. and Brewster, W. R. (2000) A randomised controlled trial of the effect of increased intravenous hydration on the course of labor in nulliparous women. *American Journal of Obstetrics and Gynecology*, **183**(6), 1544–8.

Hart, D., Shennan, A. H. and O'Sullivan, G. (2003) To eat or not to eat? A national survey of maternity unit policies regarding oral intake during labour. Abstract. *Research in Midwifery & Perinatal Health Conference*, Birmingham.

Hawkins, J. L., Gibbs, C. P., Martin-Salvaj, G., Orleans, M. and Beaty, B. (1998) Oral intake policies on labour and delivery: a national survey. *Journal of Clinical Anesthesia*, **10**(6), 449–51.

Hawthorne, L., Wilson, R., Lyons, G. and Dresner, M. (1996) Failed intubation revisited: 17 year experience in a teaching maternity unit. *British Journal of Anaesthesia*, **76**(5), 680–4.

Heading, R. C., Nimmo, J., Prescott, L. F. and Tothill, P. (1973) The dependence of paracetamol absorption on the rate of gastric emptying. *British Journal of Pharmacology*, **47**(2), 415–21.

Hey, V. M., Cowley, D. J., Ganguli, P. C., Skinner, L. D., Ostick, D. G. and Sharp, D. S. (1977) Gastro-oesophageal reflux in late pregnancy. *Anaesthesia*, **32**(4), 372–7.

Hirsheimer, A., January, D. A. and Daversa, J. J. (1938) An X-ray study of gastric function during labor. *American Journal of Obstetrics and Gynecology*, **36**, 671–3.

Holdsworth, J. D. (1978) Relationship between stomach contents and analgesia in labour. *British Journal of Anaesthesia*, **50**, 1145–8.

James, C., Modell, J., Gibbs, C., Kuck, E. and Ruiz, B. (1984) Pulmonary aspiration: effects of volume and pH in the rat. *Anaesthesia and Analgesia*, **15**, 213–21.

Kelly, M. C., Carabine, U. A., Hill, D. A. and Mirakhur, R. K. (1997) A comparison of the effect of intrathecal and extradural fentanyl on gastric emptying in labouring women. *Anaesthesia and Analgesia*, **85**, 834–8.

Kenepp, N. B., Kumar, S., Shelley, W. C., Stanley, C. A., Gabbe, S. G. and Gutsche, B. B. (1982) Fetal and neonatal hazards of maternal hydration with 5% dextrose before caesarean section. *Lancet*, **1**(8282), 1150–2.

Konturek, S., Falser, J. and Obtulowicz, W. (1973) Effects of exercise on gastrointestinal secretions. *Applied Physiology*, **34**, 324–8.

Kubli, M., Scrutton, M. J., Seed, P. T. and O'Sullivan, G. (2002) An evaluation of isotonic 'sport drinks' during labor. *Anesthesia and Analgesia*, **94**(2), 404–8.

La Salvia, L. A. and Steffen, E. A. (1950) Delayed gastric emptying time in labor. *American Journal of Obstetrics and Gynecology*, **59**, 1075–81.

Lawrence, G. F., Brown, V. A., Parsons, R. J. and Cooke, I. D. (1982) Feto-maternal consequences of high-dose glucose infusion during labour. *British Journal of Obstetrics and Gynecology*, **89**(1), 27–32.

Loudon, I. (2000) The transformation of maternal mortality. *American Journal of Clinical Nutrition*, **72**, 241–6.

Ludka, L. and Roberts, C. (1993) Eating and drinking in labor. A literature review. *Journal of Nurse-Midwifery*, **38**, 199–207.

Macfie, A. G., Magides, A. D., Richmond, M. N. and Reilly, C. S. (1991) Gastric emptying in pregnancy. *British Journal of Anaesthesia*, **67**, 54–7.

Mann, C. J. (2003) Observational research methods. Research design II: cohort, cross sectional, and case-control studies. *Emergency Medicine Journal*, **20**, 54–60.

Mendelson, C. L. (1946) The aspiration of stomach contents into the lungs during obstetric anesthesia. *American Journal of Obstetrics and Gynecology*, **52**, 191–206.

Metzger, B. E., Vileisis, R. A., Ramikar, V. and Freinkel, N. (1982) 'Accelerated starvation' and the skipped breakfast in late normal pregnancy. *Lancet*, **1**(8272), 588–92.

Michael, S., Reilly, C. S. and Caunt, M. (1991) Policies for oral intake during labour: a survey of maternity units in England and Wales. *Anesthesia*, **46**, 1071–73.

Morton, K. E., Jackson, M. C. and Gillmer, M. D. G. (1985) A comparison of the effects of four intravenous solutions for the treatment of ketonuria during labour. *British Journal of Obstetrics and Gynecology*, **92**, 473–9.

Newton, C. and Champion, P. (1997) Oral intake in labour: Nottingham's policy formulated and audited. *British Journal of Midwifery*, **5**, 418–23.

Nimmo, W. S., Wilson, J. and Prescott, L. F. (1975) Narcotic analgesics and delayed gastric emptying during labour. *Lancet*, **1**, 890–3.

Nimmo, W. S., Wilson, J. and Prescott, L. F. (1977) Further studies of gastric emptying during labour. *Anaesthesia*, **32**, 890–3.

O'Driscoll, K., Jackson, J. A. and Gallagher, J. T. (1969) Prevention of prolonged labour. *British Medical Journal*, **2**, 447–80.

O'Sullivan, G. M., Sutton, A. J., Thompson, S. A., Carrie, L. E. and Bullingham, R. E. (1987) Non-invasive measurement of gastric emptying in obstetric patients. *Anesthesia and Analgesia*, **66**(6), 505–9.

O'Sullivan, G., Kubli, M. and Scrutton, M. (2000) Eating or drinking during labour: is it time to change the rules? *Seminars in Anesthesia, Perioperative Medicine and Pain*, **19**(3), 157–63.

Paterson, P., Sheath, J., Taft, P. and Wood, C. (1967) Maternal and fetal ketone concentrations in plasma and urine. *Lancet*, **i**, 862–5.

Porter, J. S., Bonello, E. and Reynolds, F. (1997) The influence of epidural administration of fentanyl infusion on gastric emptying in labour. *Anaesthesia*, **52**, 1151–6.

Roberts, R. B. and Shirley, M. A. (1976) The obstetrician's role in reducing the risk of aspiration pneumonitis with particular reference to the use of oral antacids. *American Journal of Obstetrics and Gynecology*, **124**, 611–17.

Robinson, A. M. and Williamson, D. M. (1980) Physiological roles of ketone bodies as substrates in mammalian tissues. *Physiological Reviews*, **60**, 143–87.

Romney, S. L. and Gabel, P. V. (1966) Maternal glucose loading in the management of fetal distress. *American Journal of Obstetrics and Gynecology*, **96**, 698–708.

Sandar, B. K., Elliott, R. H., Windram, I. and Rowbotham, D. J. (1992) Peripartum changes in gastric emptying. *Anaesthesia*, **47**, 196–8.

Scheepers, H. C., Thans, M. C. J., de Jong, P. A., Essed, G. G., Le Cessie, S. and Kanhai, H. H. (2001) Eating and drinking in labor. The influence of practitioner's advice on womens' behavior. *Birth*, **28**(2), 119–23.

Scheepers, H. C., Thans, M. C. J., de Jong, P. A., Essed, G. G., Le Cessie, S. and Kanhai, H. H. (2002) A double-blind randomised, placebo controlled study on the influence of carbohydrate solution intake during labour. *British Journal of Obstetrics and Gynecology*, **109**(2), 178–81.

Scrutton, M. J. L., Metcalfe, G. A., Lowy, C., Seed, P. T. and O'Sullivan, G. (1999) Eating in labour. A randomised controlled trial assessing the risks and benefits. *Anaesthesia*, **54**(4), 329–34.

Shambaugh, G. E., Koehler, R. A. and Freinkel, N. (1977) Fetal fuels II. *American Journal of Physiology*, **223**(6), 457–61.

Sleutel, M. and Golden, S. (1999) Fasting in labor: relic or requirement. *Journal of Obstetrics, Gynaecology and Neonatal Nursing*, **28**, 507–12.

Swartz, H. (2001) pregnancy toxemia (ketosis) in does and ewes. University of Missouri. http://www.case-agworld.com/cAw.LU.ket.html.

Swift, L. (1991) Labour and fasting. *Nursing Times*, **87**(48), 64–5.

Tarnow-Mordi, W. O., Shaw, J. C. L., Lin, D., Gardner, D. A. and Flynn, F. V. (1981) Iatrogenic hyponatraemia of the newborn due to maternal fluid overload: a prospective study. *British Medical Journal*, **283**(6292), 639–42.

Teabeaut, J. (1952) Aspiration of stomach contents: an experimental study. *American Journal of Pathology*, **28**, 51–67.

Thomas, J. and Paranjothy, S. (2001) Royal College of Obstetricians and Gynaecologists Clinical Effectiveness Support Unit. *National Sentinel Caesarean Section Audit Report*. RCOG Press, London.

Tortora, G. J. and Grabowski, S. R. (1993) *Principles of Anatomy and Physiology*, 7th edn. Harper Collins, New York, p. 839.

Van Nieuwenhoven, M. A., Brouns, F. and Brummer, R. J. (1999) the effect of physical exercise on parameters of gastrointestinal function. *Neurogastroenterology and Motility*, **11**, 431–9.

Van Thiel, D. H., Gavaler, J. S. and Stremple, J. (1976) Lower esophageal sphincter pressure in women using sequential oral contraceptives. *Gastroenterology*, **71**, 232–4.

Van Thiel, D. H., Gavaler, J. S., Joshi, S. N., Sara, R. K. and Stremple, J. (1977) Heartburn of pregnancy. *Gastroenterology*, **72**(4 Pt 1), 666–8.

Wong, C. A., Loffredi, M., Ganchiff, J. N., Zhao, J., Wang, Z. and Avram, M. J. (2002) Gastric emptying of water in term pregnancy. *Anesthesiology*, **96**(6), 1395–400.

Wright, P. M. C., Allen, R. W., Moore, J. and Donnelly, J. P. (1992) Gastric emptying during lumbar epidural extradural analgesia in labour; effect of fentanyl supplementation. *British Journal of Anaesthesia*, **68**, 248–51.

Yiannouzis, C. and Parnell, C. (1992) A randomised controlled trial measuring the effects on labour of offering a light, low fat diet. *Abstract.* Miriad, Books for Midwives, London. *Unpublished.*

Zimmerman, D. L., Breen, T. W. and Fick, G. (1996) Adding fentanyl 0.0002% to epidural bupivacaine 0.125% does not delay gastric emptying in laboring parturients. *Anesthesia and Analgesia,* **82**, 612–16.

CHAPTER 4

Feeding the newborn baby

Breast milk and breast milk substitutes

Sally Inch

Introduction

Mammary glands (after which the particular class of vertebrates to which humans belong are named) began their evolution some 120 million years ago, as specialised epidermal secretions started to develop nutritional and bacteriostatic functions. For the last 240,000 years, milk production has proved a crucial factor in mammalian survival in a wide range of habitats.

Human breast milk (as with all other mammalian milks) is species-specific, adapted and optimised by the process of natural selection over 8,000 generations, which has included competitive interaction with viruses, bacteria and protozoans. Thus, human milk has functions other than optimal nutrition for the human infant; it is a complex mixture of cells, membranes and molecules (Mitchie, 2001) (see Tables 4.1 and 4.2).

Historically, human breast milk has been the only truly safe way of feeding human young and it is still the case in many parts of the world that a baby who is not fed at the breast is at increased risk of dying. Less than 200 years ago most attempts to feed a human baby on anything other than breast milk and keep him or her alive were spectacularly unsuccessful, even in the relatively affluent West. For example, in 1829 the mortality rate at the Dublin foundling hospital was reportedly as high as 99.6% (Palmer, 1993, p. 143).

Historically, the need for a human child to receive human milk was not questioned and, in the great majority of cases, it was the child's mother that provided the milk. However, in parts of some societies, another (lactating) woman would be paid to provide breast milk for a child who was not her own – a wet nurse.

Table 4.1 Constituents of human milk: white blood cells.

Constituent	Function – if known
B cells	Aided by cytokines, B cells give rise to antibodies (IgA and IgM) targeted against specific microbes
Macrophages	Kill bacteria and fungi outright in the baby's gut, produce lysosyme, prostaglandins, complement components and activate other components of the immune system
Neutrophils	May act as phagocytes ingesting bacteria in the baby's digestive system
T cells	Kill infected cells directly or send out chemical messages to mobilise other defences. They proliferate in the presence of organisms that cause serious illness in infants. They can also cross the gut mucosa intact and manufacture compounds that can strengthen the child's own immune system.

The status of the wet nurse varied according to the society, from that of someone with the ability to confer kinship to that of just another form of domestic servant.

For centuries only wealthy women could afford to pay another woman to feed their child and therefore it was regarded as a status symbol – though a double-edged one, as noblewomen were freed from lactation (and its contraceptive effect) only to find themselves repeatedly pregnant. This pattern is now being repeated in developing countries, where breast milk substitutes have undermined breastfeeding while artificial means of contraception have not kept pace.

With the advent of commercially available breast milk substitutes in the late 19th century, those who were less well off could afford the status symbol of not feeding their child themselves. Infant mortality was high at the time, so its association with the substance on which a child was fed from birth was not quickly made. Over time, breast milk substitutes and delivery systems improved and the degree to which they were inferior to breast milk continued to be masked by the more obvious environmental factors that were associated with illness. It is only as research methods have improved that the effects of the differences between breast milk and commercial substitutes have become more apparent, and those making comparisons are able to document the disadvantages of formula milk feeding.

Some of these disadvantages, such as poorer cognitive development and visual acuity, increased weight gain, increased incidence of atopic disease, diabetes and necrotising enterocolitis, are probably due to compositional/nutritional differences between breast milk and breast milk substitutes (Heinig and

Table 4.2 Constituents of human milk: molecules.

Component		Function – if known
Anti-infective factors	Antibodies of secretory IgA class	Bind to microbes (and their toxins) in the baby's gut and thereby prevent them from adhering to (and passing through) the walls of the gut into the body's tissues
	B12 binding protein (Haptocorrin)	Reduces the amount of 'available' B12 and folate, which bacteria need in order to grow
	Folate binding protein	
	Bifidus factor	Promotes the growth of Lactobacillus bifidus, a harmless bacterium, in the baby's gut. Growth of such non-pathogenic bacteria helps to crowd out dangerous varieties
	Fatty acids	Disrupt membranes surrounding certain viruses and destroy them
	Lactoferrin	Binds to iron, a mineral many bacteria need to survive. Can also bind to a bacterial surface and cause cell death. Survives in and can pass through infant gut. Antiviral effect against CMV, HIV, Herpes simplex; antifungal against Candida albicans
	Lysosyme	Kills bacteria by disrupting their cell walls. Resists digestion to protect the gut. Concentrations in milk rise as lactation progresses – up to 2 yrs
	Complement	All 9 complement components are found in colostrum and mature milk. They collectively protect against respiratory and enteric infections.
	Lactoperoxidase	Transforms thiocyanate (part of saliva) into hypothiocyanate, which can kill gram positive and negative bacteria
	Fibronectin	Increases the microbial activity of macrophages; helps to repair tissues that have been damaged by immune reactions in the baby's gut
Glycoproteins	Mucins/lactadherin butyrophilin	Adhere to bacteria and viruses (e.g. Rotavirus and E. coli) thus preventing them from attaching to mucosal surfaces
	Oligosaccharides	Bind to certain enteric and respiratory bacterial pathogens and their toxins thus preventing them from attaching to mucosal surfaces
	Glycosaminoglycans	Inhibit the binding of HIV gp120 to its host cell CD4 receptor, the first step in infection by the virus
Growth factors	Epidermal growth factor (EGF)	Stimulate the baby's digestive tract to mature more quickly. Once the initially 'leaky' membranes lining the gut mature, infants become less vulnerable to micro- organisms
	Nerve growth factor (NGF)	

Component		Function – if known
	Insulin-like growth factor (IGF)	Immunomodulatory function
	Transforming growth factor (TGF)	
Hormones	Thyroxine (T3, T4)	
	Thyroid stimulating hormone (TSH)	Promotes maturation of the newborn's intestine and development of intestinal host–defence mechanism
	Thyrotropin releasing hormone (TRH)	
	Corticosteroids	Response to stress in adult
	Adrenacorticotrophic hormone (ACTH)	
	Luteinizing hormone releasing factor (LHRF)	
	Gonadotropin releasing hormone (GnRH)	
	Somatostatin	
	Insulin	Neonatal glycaemia
	Oxytocin	
	Prolactin	Enhanced development of B and T lymphocytes/ immunomodulatory and neuro-endocrine effects in later life
	B-casomorphin (opioid peptide)	Lowers response to pain, elevates mood
	Erythropoietin	Stimulates red blood cell synthesis
	Calcitonin	
Anti-inflammatory agents and cytokines	Alpha I-antitrypsin	May prevent the absorption of endogenous and bacterial proteases, thus contributing to the passive protection or extra intestinal organs such as the liver
	Alpha J-antichymotrypsin	
	Interleukins	Homeostasis of the intestinal barrier and regulation of aberrant immune responses to pathogens. Some protect the breast itself
	Interferon (IFN-y)	Enhances anti microbial activities of immune cells (lymphocytes)
	Tumour necrosis factor (TNF)	Anti-inflammatory function
	Prostaglandin E and F (PGE & F),	Cyto-protective

Component		Function – if known
Digestive enzymes	Amylase (survives exposure to acid and pepsin in the stomach of young infants)	Its presence in milk significantly enhances carbohydrate digestion, as pancreatic amylase may be absent for the first 2–6 months of life
	Lipoprotein lipase	Aid gastric lipolysis – releasing free fatty acids and monoglycerides (from triglycerides), which have anti protozoan/bacterial/viral activity
	Bile salt stimulated lipase	

Data for Tables 4.1 and 4.2 derived from:

Garofalo, R. P. and Goldman, A. S. (1998) Cytokines, chemokines and colony stimulating factors in human milk: the 1997 update. *Biology of the Neonate: Fetal and Neonatal Research*, **74**(2), 134–43.

Hamosh, M. (1999) *Breastfeeding: Unravelling the Mysteries of Mothers' Milk.* http://www.medscape.com/viewarticle/408813.

Heitlinger, L. A., Lee, P. C., Dillon, W. P. and Lebenthal, E. (1983) Mammary amylase: a possible alternate pathway of carbohydrate digestion in infancy. *Pediatric Research*, **17**(1), 15–18.

Lönnerdal, B. (2003) Nutritional and physiologic significance of human milk proteins. *American Journal of Clinical Nutrition*, **77**(6), 1537S–43S.

Newman, J. (1995) How breastmilk protects newborns. *Scientific American*, **273**(6), 76.

Peterson, J. A., Patton, S. and Hamosh, M. (1998) Glycoproteins of the human milk fat globule in the protection of the breastfed infant against infections. *Biology of the Neonate: Fetal and Neonatal Research*, **74**(2), 143–63.

Udall, J. N., Dixon, M., Newman, A. P., Wright, J. A., James, B. and Bloch, K. J. (1985) Liver disease in alpha-1-antitrypsin deficiency: a retrospective analysis of the influence of early breast vs. bottle-feeding. *Journal of the American Medical Association*, **253**, 2679.

Weaver, L. T. (1997) Digestive system development and failure. In: *Seminars in Neonatology – Necrotising Enterocolitis* (eds. A. R. Wilkinson and P. K. H. Tam). WB Saunders Co.

Xanthou, M. (1998) Immune protection of human milk. *Biology of the Neonate: Fetal and Neonatal Research*, **74**(2), 121–34.

Dewey, 1996); others, such as an increased incidence of gastro-intestinal illness, otitis media and respiratory and urinary tract infections, are likely to be due to the presence of immunological components in breast milk (Heinig and Dewey, 1996) that will always be absent from inert breast milk substitutes.

Furthermore, in biological terms the body of a pregnant woman is prepared, hormonally, for eventual lactation (with increased fat stores, calcium mobilisation, etc.) and the body of a woman who has just given birth 'expects' to feed a baby. In evolutionary terms the breasts, ovaries and uterus were not intended to be exposed to the hormones of the menstrual cycle, particularly oestrogen, continually from menarche to menopause. The suspension of the menstrual cycle that occurs during lactation prevents more pregnancies worldwide than all other methods of contraception put together (Thapa *et al.*, 1988). It also reduces the exposure of the primary and secondary sexual organs and skeletal system to the effect of ovarian hormones (Collaborative Group on Hormonal Factors in Breast Cancer, 2002). Thus, for the parturient woman, *not* breastfeeding is associated with a higher incidence of breast and ovarian cancer, hip fracture and fertility (Heinig and Dewey, 1997).

It will, however, take more than an increased awareness of the real differences between breast milk and breast milk substitutes to reverse the cultural trend in the UK and other parts of the world where breastfeeding has been undermined. It also needs to be acknowledged that breastfeeding is a learned skill and that a woman's ability to learn has been reduced by the loss of those skills from what are now bottle-feeding cultures. Health professionals will thus need to acquire the ability to teach the women in their care how to breastfeed effectively, before optimal nutrition can be assured for future generations.

Composition and function of human milk

Popular nutritionists often focus on the need for protein in the human diet. This has led to the widely held view that the higher the protein content of the nation's food, the healthier the nation will be. Yet the human species, which has risen above all others largely by virtue of its brain size and capacity, has one of the lowest levels of protein in the milk produced to suckle the young. What is overlooked is that, whereas protein is qualitatively the most important feature in the structure of muscle, lipid (fat) is the most important in the brain and peripheral nervous system (Sinclair, 1992).

Human young are born immature by comparison with many other mammals and the brain grows rapidly after birth. The significant postnatal increase in brain weight is mainly due to the development of myelin, which consists of 70% structural lipid on a dry weight basis. Consequently, lipid factors will be important to postnatal development and evidence is growing that an incorrect lipid balance in milk (particularly in relation to long chain polyunsaturated fatty acids) may influence brain development (Farquarson *et al.*, 1992; Sinclair, 1992; Makrides *et al.*, 1994). This section will therefore pay particular attention to the controversies and challenges that surround this particular aspect of infant nutrition. The other aspect of human milk that will be considered in this section is its non-nutritional function. Human milk has evolved to do far more than simply nourish the infant and even substances that might be thought of as purely nutritional often have other functions as well.

Water is the major constituent of human milk, closely followed by the disaccharide lactose. The lactose concentration of milk rises steeply as milk production begins and pulls water into the milk-producing cells; thus lactose concentration is positively correlated with milk yield. In mature milk, lactose is present at an average concentration of 68 g/L and is one of the most stable constituents of human milk. Other sugars, present at much lower concentrations, include glucose, nucleotide sugars, glycolipids, glycoproteins and oligosaccharides. As well as providing energy, some of these also have anti-infective functions (see Table 4.2).

The proteins in human milk (15.8 g/L in early secretions, slowly decreasing to 8–9 g/L as lactation becomes established, and largely unaffected by maternal diet) provide an important source of amino acids to rapidly growing breastfed infants. Many human milk proteins also play a role in facilitating the digestion and uptake of other nutrients in breast milk. Examples of such proteins are bile salt-stimulated lipase and amylase, which may aid lipid and starch digestion, and beta-casein, lactoferrin, and haptocorrin, which may assist in the absorption of calcium, iron, and vitamin B_{12}, respectively. Human milk proteins also exert numerous physiological activities benefiting breastfed infants in a variety of ways. These activities include enhancement of immune function, defence against pathogenic bacteria, viruses and yeasts, and development of the gut and its functions (Lönnerdal, 2003).

The fats in human milk provide about 50% of the total energy value (Sinclair, 1992; Picciano, 1998). The total lipid content rises more than three-fold from the colostrum up to the 3rd month and then more slowly up to the 12th month (Chen *et al.*, 1997; Agostoni *et al.*, 2001), providing a mean of 35–36 g/L for the first year of lactation (Mitoulas *et al.*, 2003). For an individual mother, the *amounts* of most fatty acids delivered to the infant over a 24 hour period and the fatty acid composition of milk and serum seems to change little during lactation and has been found to be similar in two consecutive lactations in the same woman (Spear *et al.*, 1992; Mitoulas *et al.*, 2003). However the *proportions* (g/100 g total fatty acids) of fatty acids have been found to differ significantly between mothers and over the first year of lactation (Mitoulas *et al.*, 2003).

Ninety-eight per cent or more of the fat in human milk is in the form of triglycerides (0.5–1% occurs as phospholipid and 0.2–0.5% as sterols, of which cholesterol is the major one, ranging from 10–20 mg/100 ml milk). As well as being a source of energy, the breakdown products of fats (chiefly fatty acids) are essential to normal brain development, the structure and function of cell membranes, and prostaglandin synthesis (Sinclair, 1992). The 'released' fatty acids also have varying degrees of anti-infective function in both human and non-human milk and act by breaking down the cell walls of viruses, bacteria and protozoans. The presence of bile salt-stimulated lipase in human milk speeds up the breakdown (digestion) of triglycerides (compared with fat in breast milk substitutes) and increases its anti-infective properties (Hamosh, 1998) (See Table 4.2).

Over 100 different kinds of fatty acids have been identified in human milk, some saturated (46%) and some unsaturated (54%), of which some are monounsaturated (containing a single double bond in the molecule) and some polyunsaturated (containing two or more double bonds in the molecule). The molecules can be of different lengths, depending on the number of carbon atoms present in the chain. Two of these fatty acids (alpha-linolenic and linoleic acid) cannot be made in the human body and have to be obtained from the diet; they are thus referred to as *essential* fatty acids. However, in order to exert their full and specific biological effect, the molecules have to be desaturated and elongated to DHA (docosahexanoic acid) and AA (arachidonic acid). These forms are also plentiful in breast milk and compensate for the rather slow conversion rates in the neonate at a time when the longer chain forms are needed quickly for the rapidly growing brain and retinal membranes.

The lack of AA and DHA in the diet of infants who were not breastfed has been shown to result in marked differences in the fatty acid profile of neonatal brains (Farquarson *et al.*, 1992; Makrides *et al.*, 1994). There is also a demonstrable impact of not breastfeeding on visual acuity, cognitive function and even intelligence (Lucas and Cole, 1990; Anderson *et al.*, 1999), which are thought to be related to the availability of these LC-PUFAs (long chain polyunsaturated fatty acids). These observations, along with growing concerns about LC-PUFA deficiency in the diet of both adults and children, have meant that this has been a major focus of research over the past two decades.

In the late 1980s, the lack of commercially purified sources of AA (an omega 6 series LC-PUFA) led researchers to experiment with the nucleotide supplementation of breast milk substitutes in an attempt to speed the conversion of the parent fatty acids (Gil *et al.*, 1988; Pita *et al.*, 1988). Others worked on the ratio of the parent fatty acids to try to achieve the optimal conversion rates (Clark *et al.*, 1992). As purified sources became available, AA was added to breast milk substitutes by first one and then all of the major manufacturers over the course of the 1990s; even though it was still questionable as to whether their mere addition would make any measurable difference to visual and cognitive function, even if changes could be demonstrated in plasma and red blood cell levels (Hamosh, 1998). Subsequently, some studies have shown a positive effect on visual acuity and cognitive function (Willatts *et al.*, 1998), while others have demonstrated a lack of effect on visual acuity and cognitive function in both term and preterm babies (Lucas *et al.*, 1999; Fewtrell *et al.*, 2002). Recent Cochrane reviews suggest that any apparent functional benefits of the addition of LC-PUFAs to breast milk substitutes are only temporary (Simmer, 2004; Simmer and Patole, 2004).

Maternal diet and its relationship to fats in breast milk

Numerous studies have demonstrated that changes in the composition of external sources of fatty acids to the lactating mother (Jensen *et al.*, 2001), and/or cultural differences in dietary intake, are reflected in the fatty acid composition of breast milk samples, particularly monounsaturated, n-6, n-3 and trans fatty acids (Craig-Schmidt *et al.*, 1984; Chappell *et al.*, 1985; Ogunleye *et al.*, 1991; Innis, 1992; Chen *et al.*, 1997; Hayat *et al.*, 1999; Smit *et al.*, 2002). The impact of these changes in composition, and what influences them, are considered below.

Medium chain fatty acids

Medium chain fatty acids (C6:0–C14:0) can be synthesised *de novo* in the mammary gland, as evidenced by the fact that medium chain fatty acids are higher in milk (8.36–21.37%) than in serum (1.59–9.6%) throughout lactation (Spear *et al.*, 1992). This ability of the breast to synthesise fats may, in part, explain the fact that total milk fat is less variable than composition in an individual woman.

Long chain (polyunsaturated) fatty acids

In a longitudinal study of 10 Italian mothers, Agostoni *et al.* (2001) found that the concentrations (mg/dL) of C20:4 and C22:6 fatty acids remained stable from colostrum up to the 12th month of nursing, while their percentage levels were highest in colostrum and decreased afterwards in association with the increase in total fats. The C18:2n6 and C18:3n3 fatty acids amounts progressively increased, following the trend of total fats. These data indicate that (providing the maternal diet does not change radically) the secretion of arachidonic acid and docosahexaenoic acid during lactation remains constant, in spite of changes in total fat and in the linoleic acid and alpha-linolenic acid contents of milk. Thus, when a baby is breastfed, his or her rapidly growing brain will have a constant and adequate supply of these LC-PUFAs. As noted above, babies who are supplied only with the precursors of AA and DHA will be unable to convert them fast enough and this will be reflected in the different proportions of the different fatty acids that make up their brain tissue.

Hayat *et al.* (1999) analysed the milk of 19 fully breastfeeding Kuwaiti mothers and found that the content of LC-PUFAs in human milk lipids did not correlate with their parent fatty acids, like linoleic and alpha-linolenic acids. However, the human milk LC-PUFAs *were related to* the content of LC-PUFAs in the maternal diet. Mothers reporting a high fish consumption showed significant amounts of C22:6 (DHA) omega 3 and C20:5 (EPA), omega 3 fatty acids (Hayat *et al.*, 1999). Earlier, Spear *et al.* (1992) had demonstrated that long-chain polyunsaturated fatty acids (C20:1–C22:6) of the n-3 and n-6 series were higher in serum (6.76–12.53%) than in milk (1.57–4.42%).

Dietary supplements to increase LC-PUFAs

In the UK, the low levels of the omega 3 in the diet of the general population are currently a cause for concern (Crawford, 2004) because of their relationship to neurological function and behaviour. Recent studies have shown that LC-PUFA deficiencies or imbalances are associated with childhood developmental and psychiatric disorders, including attention deficit hyperactivity disorder (ADHD), dyslexia, dyspraxia and autistic spectrum disorders (Richardson, 2004; Richardson and Montgomery, 2005). Several researchers have investigated the effect of dietary supplements to increase the percentage of omega 3 derivatives obtained by the newborn and breastfeeding infant. Giving a DHA supplement (fish oil) to pregnant women was shown, in one small study, to have no effect on umbilical cord blood values of DHA. This suggests that, for dietary supplements to have no direct benefit, term infants must have accrued sufficient amounts of DHA while *in utero*, in spite of and/or at the expense of their mothers (Malcolm *et al.*, 2003).

In another small study, giving the precursor (alpha-linolenic acid) to lactating women by supplementing their diet with flaxseed oil did not increase the amounts of docosahexaenoic acid in their milk (Francois *et al.*, 2003). Giving DHA supplements to breastfeeding mothers had previously been shown to increase the amount of DHA in their milk (Makrides *et al.*, 1996) and to have some effect on the rate of decrease as lactation progresses, but no effect was (later) found on either infant visual function or cognitive or behavioural development (Gibson *et al.*, 1997). This was possibly because of the 'saturable curvilinear nature of the relationship of breast milk DHA to infant plasma and erythrocyte phospholipid DHA' (Heird, 2001, p. 185) – 'enough' perhaps being 'as good as a feast'.

Trans fatty acids

Trans fatty acids are unsaturated fatty acids with at least a double trans configuration, resulting in a more rigid molecule, akin to a saturated fatty acid. These do appear naturally in dairy fat, but the relatively high levels found in Western diets, as opposed to Chinese or Mediterranean diets (Chen *et al.*, 1997), are probably due to high intakes of processed foods which often use hydrogenated oils. In a study of 103 Canadian mothers with exclusively breastfed two-month old infants (Innis and King, 1999), the major dietary sources of trans fats were bakery products and breads (32%), snacks (14%), fast foods (11%) and margarines and shortenings (11%). This study found a wide range of trans fatty acid concentrations in the breast milk of these mothers, from 2.2%–18.7% of total fatty acids, with a mean (±SEM) percentage of 7.1 ± 0.3%, which is almost twice the level (4%) currently set as the maximum permitted in the manufacture of breast milk substitutes (Infant Formula and Follow-on Formula (Amendment) Regulations, 1997).

In September 2003, a subgroup of the UK Scientific Advisory Committee on Nutrition (Maternal and Child Nutrition) recommended that the maximum permitted level of trans fats in formula be lowered further still to no more than 3% of total fatty acids (SACN, 2003). Furthermore, the fact that the breast milk levels were similar to those calculated for the diet suggested that the estimated value of 6.9 g trans fatty acids/day was a reasonable estimation of the trans fatty acid intake of the women in this study (Innis and King, 1999). Previous estimates of average daily intakes by adults in the United States, Canada, Europe, and Australia based on food usage, food-frequency questionnaires, or duplicate portion analysis range from 1 ≈ 3 to 17 g/person (Hunter and Applewhite, 1991; Emken, 1995).

The (rising) levels of trans fatty acids in westernised diets is of concern because animal and *in vitro* studies are consistent with the hypothesis that trans fatty acids may interfere with the desaturation of 18:2n-6 by inhibiting the desaturase enzymes and thus slowing the conversion of C18:2n6 and C18:3n3 to C20:4n6 and C22:6n3 respectively (Koletzko, 1995). The study by Innis and King (1999) found a significant inverse relationship between milk concentrations of trans fats and 18:2n-6 and 18:3n-3, confirming the work of Chen *et al.* (1995).

Trans fatty acid consumption has implications in adult health for the development of hypertension, cardiac disease (Emkin, 1995) and some cancers (Chin *et al.*, 1992) and in infants for its potential impact on brain and retinal membrane development. Innis and King (1999) also showed a relation between the concentration of a specific trans fatty acid, conjugated linoleic acid (CLA), in milk and in the plasma lipids of breast-fed infants. CLAs are positional and geometric isomers of 18:2n-6 (linoleic acid) that occur naturally, as linoleic acid is acted upon by bacteria in the stomachs of herbivores (plant eaters), such as cows. CLAs are therefore found in several foods (particularly dairy products and beef). They appear to have some biological activity (Watkins *et al.*, 1997; Li and Watkins, 1998). In animal studies they have been shown to alter bone formation rates, possibly as a result of its effect on prostaglandin E2 biosynthesis. In contrast with other *trans* fatty acids, CLAs were found to be preferentially accumulated, by 1–2-fold, in the infants' plasma phospholipids rather than in triacylglycerols. (The animal studies (above) suggested possible tissue specificity for CLA (Watkins *et al.*, 1997).)

More recently, a small randomised controlled trial (RCT) of CLA supplements given to lactating women found that the fat content of their breast milk was significantly lower during CLA treatment, as compared to placebo treatment ($p < 0.05$). Data indicated no effect of treatment on milk output (Masters *et al.*, 2002). Whether CLAs have any direct physiologic effects on breast-fed infants is not yet known.

Socio-economic status and fat consumption

The consumption of high levels of saturated fat and trans fatty acids and low levels of polyunsaturated fats is strongly linked to socio-economic status (although not in the same direction in all cultures/societies). International comparisons indicate a continuing, if narrowing, north–south gradient across Europe. In Ireland (Kelleher *et al.*, 2002), the Netherlands (Hulshof *et al.*, 2003), Australia (Turrell *et al.*, 2003), Finland (Laaksonen *et al.*, 2003) and Norway (Holmboe-Ottesen, 2004), there is clear evidence of inverse social-class gradients in intake of fruit and vegetables and dairy products and in reported patterns of healthy eating. Median carbohydrate and vitamin C intake levels are higher among socio-economic occupational groups 1 and 2 and mean saturated fat intake is lower. Conversely, in Greece and China (Trichopoulou *et al.*, 2002; Kim *et al.*, 2004 respectively) it is still the case that households of lower socio-economic occupational groups follow a healthier diet, in terms of greater availability of vegetable oils, fresh vegetables, legumes, fish and seafood.

In Italy, the relationship of socio-economic occupational group to healthier diet is in the process of changing, with most of the eating habits considered to be potentially harmful (high consumption of meat or fats and alcohol and low consumption of olive oil and fish) becoming more frequent in northern than in southern Italy. These habits were inversely correlated with educational level, especially in the south (Vannoni *et al.*, 2003). In China, as socio-economic status improves, lifestyle becomes less healthy (Kim *et al.*, 2004). Thus, concerns about dietary fat, health or lifestyle issues that alter food choices may impact not only on a mother's own health, but may also influence the quality of fatty acid nutrition of her breastfed infant.

It is timely that in the UK the Welfare Food Scheme, first established in 1940 and which provided tokens to families on low incomes which could be exchanged for liquid milk or breast milk substitutes, has been reformed in the shape of the Healthy Start Initiative (Department of Health, 2002). Healthy Start, which is due to be implemented in 2006, will broaden the nutritional base of the scheme to allow fruit and vegetables (as well as liquid milk or breast milk substitutes) to be obtained through the exchange of fixed value vouchers at a range of outlets, including local food co-ops and supermarkets. It will also mean that, in this respect at least, child health clinics will cease to give a mixed message about their commitment to breastfeeding as they will no longer be the exchange point for vouchers for breast milk substitutes.

Substitutes for mother's own milk

This section will consider what was done in the past if a mother could not or chose not to feed her own baby. It will also chart the rise of commercial alternatives to breast milk.

Although, historically, the vast majority of women fed their own babies, wet nursing has been recorded since well before the birth of Christ. In many of the societies in which this happens now, including our own, it is an act of friendship and/or compassion and quite different from that of hiring another woman to feed the baby. In the past, although a wet nurse may have been hired to feed a baby whose mother had died, in many cases she was hired to demonstrate the mother's social standing in her community; a status symbol. Thus for some it became something to aspire to, even though it was evidently detrimental for the babies as they were more likely to succumb to diseases (Palmer, 1993, p. 133).

Wet nursing also removed the contraceptive protection of breastfeeding – a combination of lactational amenorrhoea and (depending on the culture) sexual abstinence whilst breastfeeding. However, until the mass production of formula milks, wet nursing was, as it still is in many countries, the only viable alternative to the mother feeding her baby. During the 19th century, as the position of women in society changed and the workplace and home separated, a great many babies succumbed in the process of looking for artificial methods (dry nursing), which included direct suckling of animals, particularly goats, by the baby (Palmer, 1993).

The industrialised society provided both the necessity and the means for the mass production of artificial food for babies. In the main these were based on cows' milk to which other ingredients were added (e.g. pea flour, wheat flour and bicarbonate of potash) and were offered for sale in liquid, condensed or powdered form. Such was the ignorance of the composition of human milk that these items were advertised as 'the perfect food' for infants (Palmer, 1993, p. 163). With a few notable exceptions (such as the child reared on beer who lived to be 70 years old; Still, 1931), the alarming mortality rates (usually from diarrhoea) amongst babies who were fed on these often bacteriologically contaminated substances seems to have given little pause for thought by the communities where this was common practice, such as areas of southern Germany, and Finland in the 19th century, because the practice continued (Palmer, 1993, p. 144).

As knowledge about the constituents of human milk and cows' milk increased in the late 19th and early 20th century, doctors devised recipes for imitating human milk, which they presented in the form of complex mathematical and chemical formulae; striving to make infant feeding 'scientific and exact' for each baby (Pritchard, 1904 (cited by Fisher, 1982); Palmer, 1993, p. 175). Meanwhile commercially prepared infant milks, available over the counter, reduced the necessity for a mother to visit (and thus pay) a doctor. The potential conflict between manufacturers and the medical profession was averted when the two formed an alliance in which mothers could buy formula milk in packages that bore no instructions for use other than to 'consult her doctor' before using the product. At the same time, new commercially prepared 'formulae' (such as Simulated Milk Adaptation) could be 'tested on unsuspecting babies in wards and hospitals' (Palmer, 1993, pp. 176–7). The relationship between health professionals and the manufacturers of breast milk substitutes has a long, lucrative and ignoble history; one which ultimately can only be addressed at policy level.

Formula milks

The more that is known about the composition of breast milk, the harder it is to imitate. Similarly, the more that is known of the difference in health outcomes between breastfed and formula fed babies, the more important it becomes to regulate the composition and marketing of breast milk substitutes. This section will look at what legislation exists to safeguard infants who are fed breast milk substitutes and what still need to be done.

The composition of breast milk substitutes in the UK is currently controlled by the Infant Formula and Follow-on Formula Regulations 1995 (UK) and its subsequent amendments. These regulations set out the permitted/prohibited sources of proteins, fats and carbohydrates; and the permitted range for levels of specified amino acids, nucleotides, fatty acids, vitamins, major minerals and trace elements, as well as the total energy density of the formula, per 100 ml, when reconstituted.

In 1995 only cows' milk protein and soya protein isolates were listed for use (in the regulations above) in the manufacture of infant formulae. Nevertheless, a goats' milk formula, manufactured in New Zealand, has been sold in the UK since 1992. In 2002, at the request of the European Commission, the UK-based company submitted a dossier to the newly formed European Food Standards Agency, which in turn was asked to evaluate the data in order to give an opinion on the suitability of goats' milk protein as a source of protein in infant formulae and in follow-on formulae (Request No. EFSA-Q-2003-019). (This was with a view to amending the Commission Directive 91/321/EEC to include goats' milk protein as a suitable protein source). Their finding, published in February 2004, was that 'the data submitted are insufficient to establish the suitability of goats' milk protein as a protein source for infant formula' (EFSA, 2004, executive summary). Meanwhile, in September 2003, the UK's Scientific Advisory Committee on Nutrition (SACN) questioned the benefit of using any milk protein other than from cows, or any plant protein, including soya (SACN, 2003).

In January 2004 the Chief Medical Officer (CMO) advised all doctors, via his on-line Update No. 37 (http://www.dh.gov.uk/assetRoot/04/07/01/76/04070176.pdf), that soya-based infant formulas should not be used as the first choice for the management of infants with proven cow's milk sensitivity, lactose intolerance, galactokinase deficiency and galactosaemia. The main concern was that soya-based formulas' high phytoestrogen content could pose a risk to the long-term reproductive health of infants – according to a 2003 report from the Committee on Toxicity (COT), an independent scientific committee that advises the UK Department of Health and other government agencies.

The CMO also quoted the advice from SACN, namely that there is no particular health benefit associated with the consumption of soya-based infant formula by infants who are healthy (no clinically diagnosed conditions) and no unique clinical condition that particularly requires the use of soya-based infant formulas. The CMO recommended that soya-based formulas should only be used in exceptional circumstances to ensure adequate nutrition. For example, they may be given to infants of vegan parents who are not breastfeeding or infants who find alternatives (such as amino acid formulae) unacceptable.

Adverse reactions to 'foreign' proteins

The response to the well-documented inability of some babies (2–7.5% of the population; Bahna, 1987; Adler and Warner, 1991; Host *et al.*, 1999), to tolerate cows' milk-based formula, has given rise to the development of hydrolysed protein formulae, as well as those based on amino acid mixtures. Even extensively hydrolysed products can sometimes cause a child with cows' milk allergy to respond adversely, evidence that only amino acid based products can truly be regarded as non-allergic. It follows that the 'HA' (hypoallergenic) formula milks introduced in the UK in August 2002, that are only partially hydrolysed, should not be fed to infants with a known milk allergy, despite their claim to be 'hypoallergenic'. These milks were the subject of legal action in the USA in 1988 when several allergic babies suffered from anaphylactic shock as a result of their use. As a result the company was obliged to drop the 'HA' claim (Baby Milk Action, 2002a).

In July 2002, the response of the UK Minister of Health to concerns about the use of such claims for this product in the UK was that it would not be placed on shelves and would only be available from pharmacies through special order. The packaging would also carry a warning that the product was *not* for use for babies with cow's milk allergy. Appropriately, modified soya and goats' milk formula are also both currently marketed in the UK and elsewhere as suitable for children suffering from or at risk of cows' milk allergy. They are advocated for this purpose in writings and internet resources directed at a lay audience. Unfortunately, not only has clinically significant cross-allergenicity between cow's and goat's milk been noted (Bellioni-Businco *et al.*, 1999), but at least one life-threatening cross-reaction has also been reported (Pessler and Nejat, 2004).

Although the incidence of documented allergic responses to soya is lower than that to cow's milk (0.5–1.1%) (American Academy of Pediatrics, 1998), it is not without hazard. Two large double-blind, placebo-controlled studies of infants with atopic dermatitis documented that soy positivity was demonstrated in 4–5% of children (Sampson, 1988; Businco *et al.*, 1992). In addition, up to 60% of infants with cow milk protein-induced enterocolitis will be equally sensitive to soy protein (Eastham, 1989; Burks *et al.*, 1994; Whitington and Gibson, 1977). Much of this information is reflected in the advice available to the general public on the Food Standards Agency website (http://www.food.gov.uk/), and yet at the time of writing (May 2005) all the formulae discussed above were still available for the general public to purchase without prescription.

Other problems with formula milks

Although they may have come a long way since the mid-19th century and Liebig's 'perfect infant food' – made from wheat flour, cows' milk, malt flour, pea flour and bicarbonate of potash (Palmer, 1993, p. 163) – the fact remains that breast milk substitutes can only ever imitate the substances in breast milk if:

- they are *identifiable*,
- the *technology exists* to synthesise them, and
- it is *economic* to synthesise them.

Although minimum and maximum permitted levels of named ingredients for formula milks for infants are laid down by statute, the recommendations for the upper and lower limits of nutrients are often based on limited data, data from adults or data from other species (Walker, 1993). Researchers are increasingly questioning precisely what goes into breast milk substitutes and compositional recommendations are frequently revised (e.g. SACN, 2003).

The manufacturers themselves make over a hundred changes to the 'formula' every year (Messenger, 1994). It follows, therefore, that all infants who consumed the breast milk substitutes prior to the change or addition, must have received food deficient in the substances newly defined as being necessary for optimal growth and development. Furthermore, the mere addition of a substance to the mixture does not necessarily mean that it will be available to the infant that consumes it. The ability of the baby to make use of the substance may depend on the form in which it is presented. For example, iron is only present in breast milk substitutes as an inorganic salt, of which only 10% can be absorbed; whereas in breast milk it is bound to a carrier protein, lactoferrin, making 70% of the iron 'available' for use (Akre, 1989; Williams, 1993). Indeed, the addition of one substance may cause another to fail to be utilised and the baby may end up with a deficiency. For example, if too much linoleic acid is added, alpha-linolenic metabolism may be inhibited (Farquharson *et al.*, 1992).

Clinical trials with bovine lactoferrin added to infant formula have not shown any enhancing effect on iron absorption or iron status (Fairweather-Tait *et al.*, 1987; Chierici *et al.*, 1992), which may be because bovine lactoferrin does not bind to the human lactoferrin receptor (Davidson and Lönnerdal, 1988). It is also possible that a positive effect of lactoferrin is found only when it is present in breast milk; when added to infant formula other constituents of the formula may interfere with iron utilisation from lactoferrin. It is also likely that the form in which lactoferrin is added to formula (dry blended or dissolved), and the subsequent processing of the formula (by heat treating), affects the ultimate activity of lactoferrin when fed to infants (Lönnerdal, 2003).

It goes without saying that something that began as cows' milk or soya beans can contain nothing that is species-specific to humans. It can also contain none of the living cells, enzymes, growth factors, hormones, or anti-infective factors listed in Tables 4.1 and 4.2; not even those of bovine origin. The manufacturing process reduces the starting material to an inert, dry, powder.

Processing errors

As with all processed foods, there is the potential for inadvertent excesses or deficiencies during the manufacturing process. For example, in 2004 the Chinese news agency Xinhua reported that an inquiry had revealed that 45 sub-standard milk powders, produced by 141 factories, were on sale in one Chinese city. Police in Anhui province subsequently detained five wholesalers of fake formula milk. Around 200 babies in Anhui alone were fed formula of little nutritional value and the whole episode caused the worst cases of malnutrition Chinese doctors had seen in 20 years, according to the media reports (RCM, 2004). In the same year a German manufacturer was reported to be paying at least £8.7 million in compensation to Israeli families whose infants died or suffered developmental damage after they were fed a milk substitute lacking the B vitamin, thiamin. Three babies died in 2003 after being fed the soy-based formula and 13 other infants were harmed by drinking the product.

There is also the danger of accidental contamination. Documented cases include contamination with inadvertent additions of aluminum, iodine and halogenated hydrocarbons, as well as contamination due to interaction between the can and its contents, particularly with regard to lead and plasticisers (Walker, 1980; Minchin, 2001; Walker, 1993.)

Bacterial contamination also appears to be a widespread problem. A 1988 analysis of 141 powdered human milk substitutes obtained from 35 different countries found bacterial organisms in 52.5% of the products evaluated. The species most frequently isolated included *Enterobacter agglomerans, Enterobacter cloacae, Enterobacter sakazakii* and *Klebsiella pneumoniae* (Muytjens *et al.*, 1988). Although in none of these products was the level of contamination higher than the maximum limit recommended by the Food and Agricultural Organization of the United Nations, the study highlights the fact that powdered infant formula is not sterile; and one major formula manufacturer has recently stated that current manufacturing processes are not sufficient to remove all contamination (IBFAN, 2002). Although in none of these products was the level of contamination higher than the maximum limit recommended by the Food and Agricultural Organization of the United Nations, the study highlights the fact that powdered infant formula is not sterile.

As if to underline this point, the death (from meningitis) in 2002 of a 5-day-old Belgian baby who received contaminated formula whilst in hospital received widespread media coverage. The baby was born healthy, but was fed with dried infant formula from a batch which was contaminated with *Enterobacter Sakazakii*, which was the cause of the meningitis (Baby Milk Action, 2002b).

Errors during preparation

The potential for error does not end with the manufacture of the breast milk substitutes. Those who buy it may use it inappropriately. This is most apparent where the purchaser cannot read the instructions on the tin or packet, either because they are illiterate or the instructions are in the wrong language. The cost of the breast milk substitutes may sometimes result in it being over-diluted to make it go further (RCM, 2003). In the more affluent West, feeds are often made up with too much powder for a given amount of

water. Sometimes this is deliberate, when an extra scoop is added suppos-
edly to 'satisfy' the baby, but more commonly it is a result of inaccuracies
in either the measuring scoop or the fact that the instructions to either level
it off or pack it down differ from brand to brand (RCM, 2003). All powdered
formula available in the UK is now reconstituted using 1 scoop (provided
with the powder) to 30 ml of water. Clear instructions about the volumes of
powder and water are also printed on the container. Nevertheless, over- and
under-concentration of formula may still occur.

The problem of accidentally over-concentrated feeds, which can result in
obesity, intestinal obstruction, hypernatremia and other metabolic stresses,
might be overcome if manufacturers supplied only packets containing a standard amount of dry powder, or bottles/cartons of ready to feed mixture (Jeffs,
1989; Lucas et al., 1992). However, although these are now readily available,
the price is likely to deter mothers from using them exclusively in favour of the
dried powder.

In 1988, 274 mothers (recruited from 19 clinics in two areas of Australia,
one predominantly middle class, one working class) who were bottle feeding
their infants aged from 1 to 9 months, were interviewed by researchers (Lilburne et al., 1988). Particular attention was paid to mixing technique and storage of reconstituted formula. Following the interview, a sample of milk from
a previously prepared bottle was taken to measure osmolarity and to count the
number of bacterial colonies. Errors in reconstituting the formulae, compared
with the manufacturer's instructions, were made by 100 (30%) mothers. In 52
cases these were potentially serious errors, usually erring on the side of preparing an over-concentrated formula. This finding from the interviews was confirmed by osmolarity analysis of 34 milk samples. Twenty-two per cent of samples collected grew potential pathogens.

This study was one of five included in the systematic review of formula feed
preparation conducted by Renfrew et al. in 2003. All found errors in reconstitu-
tion, with a tendency to over-concentrate feeds, although under-concentration
also occurred. The review concluded that there was a paucity of evidence available to inform the proper use of breast milk substitutes and a large array of
different preparations for sale in the UK. Given the impact that incorrect recon-
stitution of formula feeds can have on the health of large numbers of babies, the
reviewers felt that there was an important and urgent need to examine ways of
minimising the risks of feed preparation.

One way of doing this might be to ensure that all women who intend to
bottle feed, and who begin doing so in hospital (in the UK, currently 30% of
all those who give birth (Hamlyn et al., 2002), have the opportunity to make
up feeds using what they will use when they go home. In reality this means
that they would need to bring their own equipment into hospital with them. It
would also mean that the 'ready to feed' formula, currently in use in many UK
hospitals, would need to be withdrawn from general use. This runs counter to

the current infection control ethos of removing risk from the hospital setting by means of pre-packed and single use 'equipment'. But perhaps this risk needs to be balanced against the evidence that there is a social class gradient in both the prevalence of bottle feeding and the risk of gastro-enteritis associated with bottle feeding; which compared with breastfed babies is 3.5 times higher in social class 1, and 10 times higher in social class 5 (Howie *et al.*, 1990; Forsyth, 2004). This suggests that it is not only what is in the bottle that increases the risk, but the bottle itself in terms of its cleanliness. Denying women who are bottle feeding in hospital the opportunity to make up feeds and clean equipment under 'supervision' may run the risk of increasing the incidence of gastroenteritis in their babies after they leave hospital. The 2000 Infant Feeding Report revealed that only 9% of first-time mothers who were bottle feeding were taught how to make up a bottle (Hamlyn *et al.*, 2002). Enabling women who elect to bottle feed from birth to make up feeds with their own baby milk powder and their own equipment while they are in hospital will of course have no impact on the much greater number (82% in Lilburne's Australian study in 1988) who begin breastfeeding in hospital and then partially or wholly bottle feed days or weeks later.

A leaflet entitled 'Preparing a bottle feed using baby milk powder' is available to anyone as a single A4 sheet of instructions (in English and other languages). It can be downloaded, free of charge, from the UNICEF UK Baby Friendly Initiative website. A similar companion leaflet, 'Sterilisation of baby feeding equipment', is also available. These leaflets are independently produced and health facilities can 'customise' them with their own logo if they wish. The Department of Health in the UK has recently produced a free illustrated booklet with similar guidance.

It is generally assumed in the UK that boiled tap water will be free from bacterial contamination and any harmful chemicals, but from time to time this is shown not to be the case. In some areas of the UK, mothers who feed their babies on formula milk have to be provided with a separate supply of water (or are advised to boil the water for 10 minutes) because water from the tap has become contaminated (House of Commons Hansard Debates for 28 February 1989).

If bottled water is used, a still, non-mineralised variety suitable for babies must be chosen and it should be boiled as usual. Softened water is usually unsuitable.

Milk delivery

A breastfed baby who (temporarily) needs to be given his mother's milk by some other means than directly from the breast can be given the milk from a cup, spoon, dropper, syringe, bottle or teat, or via a naso-gastric tube. For a baby who is to be formula fed from birth, however, a bottle and teat is the predominant means of delivering the formula milk, certainly in the UK. Feeding bottles should meet the UK standard – made of food-grade plastic with relatively smooth interiors. Crevices and grooves in a bottle may make cleaning difficult. Patterned or decorated bottles may make it less easy to see if the bottle is clean. Concern has been expressed in the past about the nitrosamine content of rubber teats, and in some countries mothers have been urged to boil the teat several times with fresh water before using (Minchin, 2001). Silicone teats are now widely available but these have been known to split and need to be checked regularly for signs of damage. It is often easier for the baby to use a simple soft long teat than industry-labelled orthodontic teats. Despite manufacturers' advertising claims, no bottle teat is like a breast. A bottle teat occupies only the oral cavity, whereas the teat formed from the breast and nipple is sucked up into the baby's palate, encouraging the eustachian tube to open properly (Hall, 1994; Thompson, 1994). The observed increase in the incidence of otitis media amongst bottle-fed babies may thus have a mechanical component as well as an immunological one.

Although a teat and bottle is the system most widely used by mothers to feed formula milk to their babies (as it 'mimics' the sucking and swallowing that the baby does at the breast) many health professionals appear to believe that feeding from a bottle and a teat is so different and so damaging to a baby's ability to breastfeed that they go to great lengths (in the place where they have influence/control – the hospital) to avoid exposing the breastfed baby to either. A very recent study, conducted in an un-named UK hospital, found that staff used cups, syringes, droppers, tubes and fingers to give supplements to babies, without any evidence that these methods conferred any benefit (nor did any harm) (Cloherty *et al.*, 2005). Furthermore they appeared to pay more attention to the route of, rather than the need for, supplemental feeds for breastfed babies. This is particularly unfortunate in view of strong evidence that such supplements are themselves the biggest single predictor of early cessation of breastfeeding.

The manufacture and use of breast milk substitutes

The environmental impact of the manufacture and use of breast milk substitutes, on the current scale, is hugely negative. The cows graze on land that could be used for agriculture and are fed other foods that could have been fed to humans (soya, molasses), which is itself grown on land that may have been cleared forest, using fertilisers that pollute rivers and ground water. Cows produce 20% of the global emissions of methane, the second most important 'greenhouse'

gas, and ammonia from their excrement further pollutes soil and water and contributes to acid rain (Radford, 1991).

The cows' milk has to be transported (using fuel), heat-treated (using fuel),
spray-dried at high temperatures (more fuel) and added to an assortment of fac-
tory-produced ingredients (yet more fuel). It is then packed into containers for
transport to the consumer (even more fuel). Packaging and labelling requires
tin, aluminium, plastic, foil and paper or card. Large amounts of water, fuel
and synthetic materials are involved in feeding the product to infants. Post-con-
sumer, most of these items then make their way into landfill (leachate and water
pollution) or incinerators (air pollution, including dioxins and PCBs) (Radford,
1991).

The use of breast milk substitutes contributes to government debt in
developing countries, increased ill health in all countries and malnutrition
and death (mostly from diarrhoea) in many. It drains health care budgets
where these exist and family budgets everywhere. It contributes to the ill
health of mothers worldwide through increased risk of cancer, osteoporosis
and the loss of the (child spacing) contraceptive effect of lactation (Radford,
1991).

On its current scale, it exists primarily to make money for the 25 or so
companies worldwide involved in the production either of the substitutes or the
means of delivery (bottles and teats). Millions of pounds are spent each year on
advertising these products by any legal means.

The International Code for the Marketing of Breast Milk Substitutes

In 1974, the consequences of the marketing practices of the leading breast milk
substitute manufacturer on the health of mothers and babies in developing countries was published by War on Want (Muller, 1974. The furore that followed
(including a failed libel suit by the company) resulted in an international boycott in 1977, triggering a US senate Committee of Inquiry (CIIR, 1993). This
led, four years later, to the adoption of the International Code for the Marketing
of Breastmilk Substitutes by the World Health Assembly (WHO, 1981). This
Code was, and still is, designed to protect breastfeeding, rather than to prohibit
bottle feeding. Its main points follow.

For products within its scope, the International Code bans:

- Advertising
- Free samples (unless for the purpose of professional evaluation or
  research)

- Contact between company representatives and pregnant women or mothers of infants and young children
- Promotion through health care facilities (e.g. no posters, no brand names on pens or writing pads, no leaflets for mothers)
- Gifts to health workers or mothers
- Labels which have pictures of babies or pictures or text which idealise the use of infant formula

And the Code requires that:

- Labels are in the appropriate language for the country and contain stipulated warnings and messages
- Stipulated warnings and messages appear in educational materials relating to infant feeding, whether written, audio or visual
- Information given to health professionals is limited to matters that are factual and scientific

Free supplies

Free supplies of products covered by the Code are banned 'in any part of the health care system' (International Baby Food Action Network, 2005) by resolution WHA 47.5, which was passed in 1986 when it became clear that companies were using some of their advertising budget to provide these. The international boycott was lifted in 1984 when the companies publicly agreed to abide by the Code and reinstated in 1988 when it became apparent that they were not. Currently Code compliance of all manufacturers is monitored internationally by IBFAN.

Every three years, IBFAN publishes a report on compliance with the International Code of Marketing of Breastmilk Substitutes and relevant World Health Assembly Resolutions. Their May 2004 report, *'Breaking the Rules – Stretching the Rules'* (IBFAN, 2004), discussed each of the 16 (formula manufacturing) companies under different Code themes. It also highlighted the predominant marketing trends over the period 2000–2004:

- *Health facilities still come out to be the preferred avenue for companies to reach mothers.* This is especially so in countries which have not implemented the Code or where measures are inadequate. Countries with strong measures, which are properly enforced, are better at keeping company promotion out of health facilities.
- *Closely intertwined with promotion in health facilities is the pursuit of health professionals by companies.* In Thailand, where the voluntary Code has

expired, companies are vying with each other to entice doctors and nurses with innovative gifts in varieties and numbers not seen elsewhere. Mothers too are deluged with gifts during their stay in hospital and when they return for check-ups.

■ *The problem of promotion in health facilities is compounded by the fact that the Code is weak in certain areas.* Companies exploit these weaknesses by pushing at the boundaries of what is allowed. One striking example is informational materials for health professionals. Since information to mothers is restricted, companies adeptly mark materials as 'information for health professionals' and list the required statements and warnings in small print, while the text is addressed as if to mothers. Such attractive company materials are often supplied in bulk to health facilities, testimony to the fact that mothers are intended as the captive audience; one company even states this on its materials.

■ *Claims which ride on 'closeness to breast milk' abound in advertisements, leaflets and the so-called scientific and factual information for health professionals.* The one dominant theme over the last three years has been the emphasis on fatty acids such as DHA/AA, naturally found in breast milk, but imitated (derived from fungi, algae or fish oil) and added to formula to purportedly give babies a higher IQ. Eleven out of the 16 international companies included in their report jumped on the bandwagon of selling 'intelligence in a bottle'. IBFAN quote the main supplier of oils and other additives to most formula makers as saying in 2004 that:

> Infant formula is currently a commodity market, with all products being almost identical and marketers competing intensely to differentiate their products. Even if our product (a blend of fatty acids, DHA/ RA) has no benefit, we think it would be widely incorporated into formula, as a marketing tool and to allow companies to promote their formula as 'closest to human milk').

According to Baby Milk Action, the organisation based in Cambridge UK which campaigns against the unethical marketing of baby milks, awareness of the impact of inappropriate commercial sponsorship is growing. In September 2004 they reported that, in May 2004, the Breakthrough Breast Cancer Charity refused £1 million from Nestlé (Baby Milk Action, 2004). The 8th Nordic Conference on Nutrition organised by the Norwegian Nutrition Society, held in Tonsberg, Norway in June 2004, decided not to apply to Nestlé for financial support (Baby Milk Action, 2004). In the UK, the organisers of the 12th International Conference of the International Society for Research in Human Milk and Lactation (ISRHML) held in Queens' College, Cambridge in September 2004, decided not to accept funding from the baby food industry – as it had done in previous years (Baby Milk Action, 2004).

Together with UNICEF, Baby Milk Action and IBFAN (its partner in the global network) have been urging the refusal of such money because it creates conflicts of interest and opportunities for undue influence. However, in the UK, where the International Code is only partially incorporated into the Infant Formula and Follow-on Formula Regulations (Department of Health, 1995) (first passed in 1995, with subsequent amendments), companies are allowed to advertise infant formulae in publications specialising in baby care and distributed through the health care system, in scientific publications and for the purposes of trade prior to the retail stage.

This means that professional bodies, such as the Royal College of Midwives, despite (1) their avowed commitment in their 2004 Position Statement (No. 5) to both breastfeeding and the International Code (RCM 2004); (2) their acknowledgement that part of the rapid decline in breastfeeding duration from birth to six months is due to the 'aggressive marketing of breast milk substitutes'; and (3) their recommendation that training (in health care facilities) 'should be provided by employers without the involvement, sponsorship or provision of promotional materials by manufacturers of formula milk'; can, and do, accept money from formula manufacturers to fund (among other things) their professional journal, which is sent to every member and associate member of the RCM.

It also means that hospitals can accept funding for new facilities, such as the new hearing testing room set up in one London hospital in 1995 which carried a large sign over the door bearing the company's name. In the year following the opening of this room, sales in the local clinic of this company's milk increased by 560% (Baby Milk Action, 1997).

While formula manufacturers are permitted to sponsor health workers' education by advertising in their professional journals and providing health care facilities with 'educational' material advertising their products, health professionals are likely to continue to believe the manufacturers' slogan that 'you can't get any closer to mothers' milk' (Becker, 1992, p. 137–42). They will therefore have little incentive to acquire the knowledge and skills necessary to help women breastfeed successfully.

Currently, the only 'defence' against the commercial exploitation of the weaknesses of the UK law is the requirement, by the UNICEF UK Baby Friendly Hospital Initiative (part of the Global WHO/UNICEF Initiative), that as well as fully implementing the Ten Steps To Successful Breastfeeding (as set out in the joint WHO/UNICEF booklet 'Promoting, Protecting and Supporting Breastfeeding', 1989) hospitals who wish to obtain the Baby Friendly Award must fully comply with all elements of the International Code. Until the UK law is brought into full alignment with the International Code, breastfeeding will continue to be undermined by those whose commercial interest is served by seeing breastfeeding fail.

Human milk banks: another substitute for mothers' own milk

The current (international) system of collecting and freezing human milk from screened donors is an extension of the much older service of wet nursing. Instead of feeding the baby directly at another mother's breast, the mother with milk to spare collects it and sends it to her local milk bank where it can be used for any baby, including those too small or too sick to suckle directly. Milk donors are screened for blood-borne diseases such as hepatitis and HIV, and in some parts of the world the milk is then given fresh to the babies that need it. In the UK, the milk is pasteurised before it is re-frozen and stored prior to use. In the late 1970s and early 1980s there were over 60 human milk banks in the UK. Most of them closed in the late 1980s, driven both by the fear of HIV transmission and the rising popularity of preterm formulas. By the early 1990s there were only six milk banks left in the UK.

Slowly this number has risen, encouraged by research which demonstrated the effectiveness of pasteurisation as a means of destroying HIV (Eglin and Wilkinson, 1987) and the importance of human milk in the prevention of necrotising enterocolitis (Lucas and Cole, 1990). The total number of milk banks in the UK in 2005 stands at 17. The most pressing need in the UK is not for donors, but for more milk banks and/or a system for transporting milk to geographical areas where it is needed.

In the Breastfeeding Awareness Week of 1998 (arranged by the UK Department of Health, since its inception in 1993), the UK Human Milk Banking Association (UKAMB) was launched and spearheaded by the oldest milk bank, that at Queen Charlotte's and Chelsea Hospital. Its purpose is to make human milk more readily available to preterm infants by setting up a milk bank network and to encourage and support the setting up of new milk banks. One of its first tasks was to update the British Paediatric Association Guidelines for Human Milk Banks, first published in 1994 (2nd edn 1999, 3rd edn 2003), which provides a template for those wishing to set up new milk banks.

Choosing not to breastfeed

Although knowledge of the benefits of breastfeeding is important, it would be naive to think that all women need is enough information and every baby would be breastfed. There may be evidence that a proportion of women who feed their babies with formula milk are unaware of the differences in health outcomes, but there is also evidence to suggest that many women choose to bottle feed knowing that breast milk is best for their baby (Hally *et al.*, 1984; Jones *et al.*, 1986; Graffy, 1992; Hoddinott, 1998), for 'while it is "known" that breastfeeding is better, our society is not structured to facilitate that choice' (Retsinas, 1987, p. 129).

Nor is it truly a choice for many women. It has been suggested that 38% of the UK population persistently formula feed (or use mixed feeding) from birth because of social adherence to culturally acquired patterns of feeding behaviour (Woolridge, 2004).

The characteristics of women who choose not to breastfeed are well known from past research, particularly successive quinquennial Infant Feeding Reports; they are predominantly young, poorly educated and in the lower socio-economic occupational groups (e.g. <18 years of age, left school at 16, never worked). However, there are important variations within different ethnic groups and many women with these characteristics may well start by breastfeeding (as opposed to never breastfeed), or mix feed from birth (Thomas and Avery, 1997; Woolridge *et al.*, 2004). Data from RCTs may be lacking, but given the biology of breast milk it would seem likely, and there is evidence from cohort studies (Howie *et al.*, 1990; Kelly, 2004), that some breast milk is better for the infant than no breast milk.

The best predictor of whether a woman will commence breastfeeding is if she has breastfed before – it is therefore hugely important to encourage and help mothers to feed their first baby, as this is likely to affect the way that they feed subsequent babies. The Infant Feeding Report for 2000 did demonstrate an increase in breastfeeding initiation in social class 5 compared with 1995, but unfortunately by six weeks the numbers still breastfeeding were the same as 1995 (Hamlyn *et al.*, 2002). If the support infrastructure is missing, no amount of breastfeeding promotion is going to improve the health inequalities between the higher and lower social classes.

Women are more likely to do what they have done (or seen) before, as predicted by the theory of planned behaviour (Ajzen, 1991) and most women have either seen or fed another woman's baby by bottle. However, actually seeing a baby being breastfed can strongly influence the decision to breastfeed, both positively and negatively, depending on the context (Hoddinott and Pill, 1999). This finding may be of particular relevance in the context of women from lower socio-economic groups for whom theoretical knowledge may have less power than embodied knowledge. It has therefore been suggested that women intending to breastfeed might benefit from an antenatal 'apprenticeship' with a known breastfeeding mother. Peer group support can influence both the initiation and the continuation of breastfeeding (Fairbank *et al.*, 2000) and introducing pregnant women to other mothers with young babies, as is often done as part of parent education classes (as well as through drop-in breastfeeding centres and baby cafés), may be helpful.

Changes are also needed in the social environment, such as greater provision for breastfeeding outside the home (e.g. in shopping centres and restaurants) and the implementation of housing programmes which eliminate overcrowding and thus the necessity for young mothers to share accommodation with other relatives (MacIntyre, 1982; McIntosh, 1985; Woolridge, 2004). Feeding in public may be a huge issue for women in lower socio-economic occupational groups. 'Public' has to be defined in terms of the woman's individual life – if she is living with her parents she is always 'in public', and breastfeeding in public may be seen as inviting unwelcome sexual voyeurism (Renfrew, 2004; Woolridge, 2004).

Focus groups of such women discuss breastfeeding in terms of its disadvantages – formula feeding is seen to have few disadvantages (Renfrew, 2004; Woolridge, 2004). Changing the socially accepted norm for a particular peer group, as with smoking and drink/driving, will happen only slowly and then only when women's perceived lack of social support and/or the requirement to be separated from their children have been addressed with better help with breastfeeding, milk expression, working arrangements and maternity leave.

If the decision to formula feed (or not) is heavily constrained by social circumstances, it is not surprising that the part played by health professionals in assisting a mother to choose is probably not very great (Hoddinott, 1998), but in so far as the professional has an influence, it should be positive and unequivocal (Crawford, 1992; Freed *et al.*, 1995). Given the powerful effect of breastfeeding to ameliorate some of the health outcomes associated with poverty (breastfed babies in social class 5 have health outcomes equivalent to or better than formula fed babies in social class 1; Forsyth, 2004), mothers and babies deserve no less.

References

Adler, B. R. and Warner, J. O. (1991) *Food Intolerance in Children*. Royal College of General Practitioners Members Reference Book, pp. 497–502.

Agostoni, C., Marangoni, F., Lammardo, A. M., Galli, C., Giovannini, M. and Riva, E. (2001) Long-chain polyunsaturated fatty acid concentrations in human hindmilk are constant throughout twelve months of lactation. *Advances in Experimental Medicine and Biology*, **501**, 157–61.

Ajzen, I. (1991) The theory of planned behavior. *Organizational Behavior and Human Decision Processes*, **50**, 179–211.

Akre, J. (ed.) (1989) *Infant Feeding – The Physiological Basis*. Chapter 2: Lactation, p. 23. WHO Bulletin Supplement Vol. 67.

American Academy Of Pediatrics: Committee on Nutrition (1998). Soy protein-based formulas: recommendations for use in infant feeding. *Pediatrics*, **101**, 148–53.

Anderson, J. W., Johnstone, B. M. and Remley, D. T. (1999) Breastfeeding and cognitive development: a meta-analysis. *American Journal of Clinical Nutrition*, **70**, 525–35.

Baby Milk Action (1997) Sponsorship is advertising. `http://www.babymilkaction.org/pages/uklaw.html#7`.

Baby Milk Action (2002a) Update Issue 31 July 2002 Nestlé formula in UK – is it legal? `http://www.babymilkaction.org/update/update31.html`.

Baby Milk Action (2002b) Belgian baby death. `http://babymilkaction.org/press/press2aug02.html`.

Baby Milk Action (2004) Press release 10 September 2004: International conference says no to baby food industry sponsorship. `http://www.babymilkaction.org/press/press10sept04.html` [Accessed 30/09/05].

Bahna, S. L. (1987) Milk allergy in infancy. *Annals of Allergy*, **59**, 131–6.

Becker, G. (1992). Breastfeeding knowledge of hospital staff in rural maternity units in Ireland. *Journal of Human Lactation*, **8**, 137–42.

Bellioni-Businco, B., Paganelli, R., Lucenti, P., Giampietro, P. G., Perborn, H. and Businco, L. (1999) Allergenicity of goat's milk in children with cow's milk allergy. *Journal of Allergy and Clinical Immunology*, **103**, 1191–4.

Burks, A. W., Casteel, H. B., Fiedorek, S. C., Williams, L. W. and Pumphrey, C. L. (1994) Prospective oral food challenge study of two soybean protein isolates in patients with possible milk or soy protein enterocolitis. *Pediatric Allergy and Immunology*, **5**, 40–5.

Businco, L., Bruno, G., Giampietro, P. G. and Cantani, A. (1992) Allergenicity and nutritional adequacy of soy protein formulas. *Journal of Pediatrics*, **121**, S21–S28.

Chappell, J. E., Clandinin, M. T. and Kearney-Volpe, C. (1985) *Trans* fatty acids in human milk lipids: influence of maternal diet and weight loss. *American Journal of Clinical Nutrition*, **42**, 49–56.

Chen, Z.-Y., Pelletier, G., Hollywood, R., Ratnayke, W. M. N. (1995) Trans fatty acid isomers in Canadian human milk. *Lipids*, **30**, 15–21.

Chen, Z. Y., Kwan, K. Y., Tong, K. K., Ratnayake, W. M., Li, H. Q. and Leung, S. S. (1997) Breast milk fatty acid composition: a comparative study between Hong Kong and Chongqing Chinese. *Lipids*, **32**, 1061–7.

Chierici, R., Sawatzki, G., Tamisari, L., Volpato, S. and Vigi, V. (1992) Supplementation of an adapted formula with bovine lactoferrin. 2. Effects on serum iron, ferritin and zinc levels. *Acta Paediatrica*, **81**, 475–79.

Chin, S. F., Liu, W., Storkson, J. M., Ha, Y. L. and Pariza, M. W. (1992) Dietary sources of conjugated α-lienoic isomers of linoleic acid, a newly recognized class of anticarcinogens. Journal of Food Composition Analysis, 5, 185-97.

CIIR (1993) *Baby Milk: Destruction of a World Resource*. Catholic Institute for International Relations, London.

Clark, K. J., Makrides, M., Neumann, M. A. and Gibson, R. A. (1992) Determination of the optimal linoleic acid to alpha-linolenic acid ratio in infant formula. *Journal of Pediatrics*, **120**, S151–8.

Cloherty, M., Alexander, J., Holloway, I., Galvin, K. and Inch, S. (2005) The cup-versus-bottle debate: a theme from an ethnographic study of the supplementation of breastfed infants in hospital in the United Kingdom. *Journal of Human Lactation*, **21**, 151–62.

Collaborative Group on Hormonal Factors in Breast Cancer (2002) Breast cancer and breastfeeding: collaborative reanalysis of individual data from 47 epidemiological studies in 30 countries, including 50 302 women with breast cancer and 96 973 women without the disease. *Lancet*, **360**, 187–95.

Craig-Schmidt, M. C., Weete, J. D., Faircloth, S. A., Wickwire, M. A. and Livant, E. J. (1984) The effect of hydrogenated fat in the diet of nursing mothers on lipid composition and prostaglandin content of human milk. *American Journal of Clinical Nutrition*, **39**, 778–86.

Crawford, J. (1992) Understanding our own breastfeeding experiences. *JBI Newsletter*, No. 4, 1 June, 1–2.

Davidson, L. A. and Lönnerdal B (1988) Specific binding of lactoferrin to brush border membrane: ontogeny and effect of glycan chain. *American Journal of Physiology*, **254**, G580–5.

Department of Health (1995) *The Infant Formula and Follow-on Formula Regulations 1995*. Statutory Instrument 1995 No. 77. HMSO, London.

Department of Health (2002) *Healthy Start: Proposals for reform of the welfare system*. Department of Health, London. http://www.dh.gov.uk/asset-Root/04/10/25/09/04102509.pdf.

Eastham, E. J. (1989) Soy protein allergy. In: *Food Intolerance in Infancy: Allergology, Immunology, and Gastroenterology* (ed. R. N. Hamburger). Carnation Nutrition Education Series. Vol 1. Raven Press, New York, pp. 223–36.

Emken, E. A. (1995) *Trans* fatty acids and coronary heart disease risk: physiochemical properties, intake, and metabolism. *American Journal of Clinical Nutrition*, **62**(suppl.), 659S–69S.

Fairbank, L., Woolridge, M. J., Renfrew, M. J., O'Meara, S., Sowden, A., Lister-Sharp, D. and Mather, L. (2000) Effective health care: promoting the initiation of breastfeeding. *NHS Centre for Reviews and Dissemination/University of York*. July 2000. Vol. 6 No. 2.

Fairweather-Tait, S. J., Balmer, S. E., Scott, P. H. and Ninski, M. J. (1987) Lactoferrin and iron absorption in newborn infants. *Pediatric Research*, **22**, 651–4.

Farquharson, J., Cockburn, F., Patrick, W. A., Jamieson, E. C. and Logan, R. W. (1992) Infant cerebral cortex phospholipid fatty-acid composition and diet. *Lancet*, **340**(8823), 810–13.

Fewtrell, M. S., Morley, R., Abbott, R. A., Singhal, A., Isaacs, E. B., Stephenson, T., MacFadyen, U. and Lucas, A. (2002) Double-blind, randomized trial of long-chain polyunsaturated fatty acid supplementation in formula fed to preterm infants. *Pediatrics*, **110**, 73–82.

Fisher, C. (1982) Mythology in midwifery – or 'making breastfeeding scientific and exact'. *Oxford Medical School Gazette*, **33**(2), 30–3.

Forsyth, S. (2004) Influence of infant feeding practice on health inequalities during childhood. Paper presented at the annual UNICEF-UK Baby Friendly Conference: Reducing inequalities in breastfeeding: evidence and support for success. Clyde Auditorium, Scottish Exhibition and Conference Centre, Glasgow, 10–11 November.

Francois, C. A., Connor, S. L., Bolewicz, L. C. and Connor, W. E. (2003) Supplementing lactating women with flaxseed oil does not increase docosahexaenoic acid in their milk. *American Journal of Clinical Nutrition*, **77**(1), 226–33.

Freed, G. L., Clark, S. J., Sorenson, J., Lohr, J. A., Cefalo, R., Curtis, P. (1995) National assessment of physicians' breastfeeding knowledge and experience. *Journal of the American Medical Association*, **273**, 472–6.

Garofalo, R. P. and Goldman, A. S. (1998) Cytokines, chemokines and colony stimulating factors in human milk: the 1997 update. *Biology of the Neonate: Fetal and Neonatal Research*, **74**(2), 134–43.

Gibson, R. A., Neumann, M. A. and Makrides, M. (1997) Effect of increasing breastmilk docosahexanoic acid on plasma and erthyrocyte phospholipid fatty acids and neural indicies of exclusively breastfed infants. *European Journal of Clinical Nutrition*, **51**, 578–84.

Gil, A., Lozano, E., De-Lucchi, C., Maldonado, J., Molina, J. A. and Pita, M. (1988) Changes in the fatty acid profiles of plasma lipid fractions induced by dietary nucleotides in infants born at term. *European Journal of Clinical Nutrition*, **42**, 473–81.

Graffy, J. (1992) Mothers' attitudes to and experience of breast feeding: a primary care study. *British Journal of General Practice*, **42**(355), 61–4.

Hall, C. (ed.) (1994) Health page (25). *The Independent*, 1 November.

Hally, M. R., Bond, J., Crawley, J., Gregson, B., Philips, P. and Russell, I. (1984) Factors influencing the feeding of first-born infants. *Acta Paediatrica Scandinavia*, **73**(1), 33–9.

Hamlyn, B., Brooker, S., Oleinikova, K. and Wands, S. (2002) *Infant Feeding Report 2000*. The Stationery Office, London.

Hamosh, M. (1998) Protective functions of proteins and lipids in human milk. *Biology of the Neonate: Fetal and Neonatal Research*, **74**(2), 163–77.

Hayat, L., al-Sughayer, M. A. and Afzal, M. (1999) Fatty acid composition of human milk in Kuwaiti mothers. *Comparative Biochemistry and Physiology Part B: Biochemistry and Molecular Biology*, **124**(3), 261–7.

Heinig, M. J. and Dewey, K. G. (1996) Health advantages of breast feeding for infants: a critical review. *Nutrition Research Review*, **9**, 89–110.

Heinig, M. J. and Dewey, K. G. (1997) Health effects of breast feeding for mothers: a critical review. *Nutrition Research Review*, **10**, 35–56.

Hoddinott, P. (1998) Why don't some women want to breastfeed and how might we change their attitudes? *Unpublished MPhil thesis*, University of Wales College of Medicine, Cardiff, pp. 62–5.

Hoddinott, P. and Pill, R. (1999) Qualitative study of decisions about infant feeding among women in east end of London. *British Medical Journal*, **318**(7175), 30–4.

Holmboe-Ottesen, G., Wandel, M. and Mosdol, A. (2004) Social inequality and diet. *Tidsskrift for Den Norske Laegeforening*, **124**(11), 1526–8.

Host, A., Koletzko, B., Dreborg, S., Muraro, A., Wahn, U., Aggett, P., Bresson, J. L., Hernell, O., Lafeber, H., Michaelsen, K. F., Micheli, J. L., Rigo, J., Weaver, L., Heymans, H., Strobel, S. and Vandenplas, Y. (1999) Dietary products used in infants for treatment and prevention of food allergy. Joint statement of the European Society for Paediatric Allergology and Clinical Immunology (ESPACI) Committee on Hypoallergenic Formulas and the European Society for Paediatric Gastroenterology, Hepatology and Nutrition (ESPGHAN) Committee on Nutrition. *Archives of Disease in Childhood*, **81**(1), 80–4.

House of Commons Hansard Debates for 28 February 1989. http://www.parliament.the-stationery-office.co.uk/.

Howie, P. W., Forsyth, J. S. and Ogston, S. A. (1990) Protective effect of breast feeding against infection. *British Medical Journal*, **300**, 11–16.

Hulshof, K. F., Brussaard, J. H., Kruizinga, A. G., Telman, J. and Lowik, M. R. (2003) Socio-economic status, dietary intake and 10 y trends: the Dutch National Food Consumption Survey. *European Journal of Clinical Nutrition*, **57**(1), 128–37.

Hunter, J. E. and Applewhite, T. H. (1991) Reassessment of trans fatty acid availability in the US diet. *American Journal of Clinical Nutrition*, **54**, 363–9.

IBFAN (2002) *How Safe Are Infant Formulas? The Death of a One-week Old Formula-fed Baby in Belgium*. http://www.ibfan.org/english/news/press/press10may02.html [Accessed 30/09/05].

IBFAN (2004). *Breaking the Rules – Stretching the Rules.* http://www.ibfan. org/english/pdfs/btr04.pdf [Accessed 30/09/05].

IBFAN (2005) *The International Code of Marketing of Breastmilk Substitutes.* http://www.ibfan.org/english/resource/who/fullcode.html [Accessed 30/09/05].

Innis, S. M. (1992) Human milk and formula fatty acids. *Journal of Pediatrics,* **120**(suppl.), S56–61.

Innis, S. M. and King, D. J. (1999) *trans* Fatty acids in human milk are inversely associated with concentrations of essential *all-cis* n-6 and n-3 fatty acids and determine *trans*, but not n-6 and n-3, fatty acids in plasma lipids of breast-fed infants. *American Journal of Clinical Nutrition,* **70**(3), 383–90.

Jeffs, S. G. (1989) Hazards of scoop measurements in infant feeding. *Journal of the Royal College of General Practitioners,* **39**, 113.

Jensen, R. G., Lammi-Keefe, C. J., MacBurney, M. and Wijendran, V. (2001) Parenteral infusion of a lactating woman with intralipid: changes in milk and plasma fatty acids. *Advances in Experimental Medicine and Biology,* **501**, 163–8.

Jones, D. A., West, R. R. and Newcombe, R. G. (1986) Maternal characteristics associated with the duration of breastfeeding. *Midwifery,* **2**, 141–6.

Kelleher, C., Friel, S., Nolan, G. and Forbes, B. (2002) Effect of social variation on the Irish diet. *Proceedings of the Nutrition Society,* **61**(4), 527–36.

Kelly, M. (2004) *How the Baby Friendly Initiative makes a difference – Case studies (Northgate Medical Centre).* Paper presented at the annual UNICEF-UK Baby Friendly Conference: Reducing inequalities in breastfeeding: evidence and support for success. Clyde Auditorium, Scottish Exhibition and Conference Centre, Glasgow, 10–11 November.

Kim, S., Symons, M. and Popkin, B. M. (2004) Contrasting socioeconomic profiles related to healthier lifestyles in China and the United States. *American Journal of Epidemiology,* **159**(2), 184–91.

Koletzko, B. (1995) Potential adverse effects of trans fatty acids in infants and children. *European Journal of Medical Research,* **1**, 123–5.

Laaksonen, M., Prattala, R., Helasoja, V., Uutela, A. and Lahelma, E. (2003) Income and health behaviours. Evidence from monitoring surveys among Finnish adults. *Journal of Epidemiology and Community Health,* **57**(9), 711–17.

Li, Y. and Watkins, B. A. (1998) Conjugated linoleic acids alter bone fatty acid composition and reduce ex vivo prostaglandin E2 biosynthesis in rats fed n-6 or n-3 fatty acids. *Lipids,* **33**(4), 417–25.

Lilburne, A. M., Oates, R. K., Thompson, S. and Tong, L. (1988) Infant feeding in Sydney: a survey of mothers who bottle feed. *Australian Paediatrics Journal,* **24**(1), 49–54.

Lönnerdal, B. (2003) Nutritional and physiologic significance of human milk proteins. *American Journal of Clinical Nutrition*, **77**(6), 1537S–43S.

Lucas, A. and Cole, T. J. (1990) Breast milk and neonatal necrotising entero-colitis. *Lancet*, **336**, 1519–23.

Lucas, A., Morley, R., Cole, T. J., Lister, G. and Leeson-Payne, C. (1992) Breast milk and subsequent intelligence quotients in children born pre-term. *Lancet*, **339**, 261–4.

Lucas, A., Stafford, M. and Morley, R. (1999) Efficacy and safety of LU-PUFA supplementation of infant formula milk: a randomised trial. *Lancet*, **354**, 1948–54.

MacIntyre, S. (1982) *Rhetoric and Reality: Mothers' Breastfeeding Intentions and Experiences*. Mimeo, Institute of Medical Sociology, Aberdeen.

Makrides, M., Neumann, M. A. and Byard, R. W. (1994) Fatty acid composition of brain, retina and erythrocytes in breastfed and formula fed infants. *American Journal of Clinical Nutrition*, **60**, 189–94.

Makrides, M., Neumann, M. A. and Gibson, R. A. (1996) Effect of maternal docosahexaenoic acid (DHA) supplementation on breast milk composition. *European Journal of Clinical Nutrition*, **50**(6), 352–7.

Malcolm, C. A., McCulloch, D. L., Montgomery, C., Shepherd, A. and Weaver, L. T. (2003) Maternal docosahexaenoic acid supplementation during pregnancy and visual evoked potential development in term infants: a double blind, prospective, randomised trial. *Archives of Disease in Childhood*, **88**(5), F383–90.

Masters, N., McGuire, M. A., Beerman, K. A., Dasgupta, N. and McGuire, M. K. (2002) Maternal supplementation with CLA decreases milk fat in humans. *Lipids*, **37**(2), 133–8.

McIntosh, J. (1985) Barriers to breastfeeding: choice of feeding method in a sample of working class primiparae. *Midwifery*, **1**, 213–24.

Messenger, H. (1994) Don't shoot the messenger. *Health Visitor*, **67**(5), 171.

Minchin, M. (2001) *Towards Safer Artificial Feeding*. Alma Publications, Australia.

Mitoulas, L. R., Gurrin, L. C., Doherty, D. A., Sherriff, J. L. and Hartmann, P. E. (2003) Infant intake of fatty acids from human milk over the first year of lactation. *British Journal of Nutrition*, **90**(5), 979–86.

Muller, M. (1974) *The Baby Killer*. War on Want, London.

Muytjens, H. L., Roelofs-Willemse, H. and Jaspar, G. H. J. (1988) Quality of powdered substitutes for breast milk with regard to members of the family Enterobacteriaceae. *Journal of Clinical Microbiology*, **26**(4), 743–6.

Ogunleye, A., Fakoya, A. T., Niizeki, S., Tojo, H., Sasajima, I., Kobayashi, M., Tateishi, S. and Yamaguchi, K. (1991) Fatty acid composition of breast milk from Nigerian and Japanese women. *Journal of Nutritional Science and Vitaminology*, **37**(4), 435–42.

Palmer, G. (1993) *The Politics of Breastfeeding*. Rivers Oram Press/Pandora List.

Pessler, F. and Nejat, M. (2004) Anaphylactic reaction to goats' milk in a cows' milk-allergic infant. *Pediatric Allergy and Immunology*, **15**(2), 183–5.

Picciano, M. F. (1998) Human milk: nutritional aspects of a dynamic food. *Biology of the Neonate: Fetal and Neonatal Research*, **74**(2), 84–94.

Pita, M., Fernandez, M. R., De-Lucchi, C., Medina, A., Martinez-Valverde, A., Uauy, R. and Gil, A. (1988) Changes in the fatty acids pattern of red blood cell phospholipids in duced by type of milk, dietary nucleotide supplementation, and postnatal age in preterm infants. *Journal of Pediatrics, Gastroenterology and Nutrition*, **7**, 740–7.

Radford, A. (1991) *The Ecological Impact of Bottle Feeding*. Baby Milk Action, London. (Document first launched at XIII IOCU World Congress, Hong Kong, July 1991)

RCM (2003) *Successful Breastfeeding. A Handbook for Midwives*. Churchill Livingstone, London.

RCM (2004) *Position Statement No. 5*. http://www.rcm.org.uk/ [Accessed 30/09/05].

RCM Journal (2004) News and appointments. May Issue, p. 3.

Renfrew, M. J. (2004) Breastfeeding: state of the art. Report of a meeting at the Forum on Maternity and the Newborn of the Royal Society of Medicine. *Midwives*, **7**(7), 306–9.

Renfrew, M. J., Ansell, P. and Macleod, K. L. (2003) Formula feed preparation: helping reduce the risks; a systematic review. *Archives of Disease in Childhood*, **88**(10), 855–8.

Retsinas, J. (1987) Nature versus technology: the breastfeeding decision. *Sociological Spectrum*, **7**, 121–9.

Richardson, A. J. (2004) Long-chain polyunsaturated fatty acids in childhood developmental and psychiatric disorders. *Lipids*, **39**(12), 1215–22.

Richardson, A. J. and Montgomery, P. (2005) The Oxford–Durham study: a randomized, controlled trial of dietary supplementation with fatty acids in children with developmental coordination disorder. *Pediatrics*, **115**(5), 1360–6.

SACN (2003) (Scientific Advisory Committee on Nutrition). Minutes of the meetings are available on: http://www.sacn.gov.uk/meetings/subgroups/maternal/2003_09_29.html.

Sampson, H. A. (1988) The role of food allergy and mediator release in atopic dermatitis. *Journal of Allergy and Clinical Immunology*, **81**, 635–45.

Simmer, K. (2004) Longchain polyunsaturated fatty acid supplementation in infants born at term (Cochrane Review). In: *The Cochrane Library, Issue 2.* John Wiley & Sons, Chichester.

Simmer, K. and Patole, S. (2004) Longchain polyunsaturated fatty acid supplementation in preterm infants (Cochrane Review). In: *The Cochrane Library, Issue 2.* John Wiley & Sons, Chichester.

Sinclair, C. M. (1992) *Fats in Human Milk. Topics in Breastfeeding, set IV.* Lactation Resource Centre.

Smit, E. N., Martini, I. A., Mulder, H., Boersma, E. R. and Muskiet, F. A. (2002) Estimated biological variation of the mature human milk fatty acid composition. *Prostaglandins, Leukotrienes and Essential Fatty Acids,* **66**(5–6), 549–55.

Spear, M. L., Hamosh, M., Bitman, J., Spear, M. L. and Wood, D. L. (1992) Milk and blood fatty acid composition during two lactations in the same woman. *American Journal of Clinical Nutrition,* **56**(1), 65–70.

Still, G. F. (1931) *The History of Paediatrics.* Oxford University Press, London, p. 305.

Thapa, S., Short, R. V. and Potts, M. (1988) Breastfeeding, birth spacing and their effects on child survival. *Nature,* **335**, 679–82.

Thomas, M. and Avery, V. (1997) *Infant Feeding in Asian Families.* The Stationery Office, London.

Thompson, A. (1994) *Doctor,* 27 October, p. 23.

Trichopoulou, A., Naska, A., Costacou, T. and DAFNE III Group (2002) Disparities in food habits across Europe. *Proceedings of the Nutrition Society,* **61**(4), 553–8.

Turrell, G., Hewitt, B., Patterson, C. and Oldenburg, B. (2003) Measuring socio-economic position in dietary research: is choice of socio-economic indicator important? *Public Health Nutrition,* **6**(2), 191–200.

Vannoni, F., Spadea, T., Frasca, G., Tumino, R., Demaria, M., Sacerdote, C., Panico, S., Celentano, E., Palli, D., Saieva, C., Pala, V., Sieri, S. and Costa, G. (2003) Association between social class and food consumption in the Italian EPIC population. *Tumori,* **89**(6), 669–78.

Walker, M. (1993) A fresh look at the risks of artificial infant feeding. *Journal of Human Lactation,* **9**(2), 97–107.

Watkins, B. A., Shen, C. L., McMurtry, J. P., Xu, H., Bain, S. D., Allen, K. G. and Seifert, M. F. (1997) Dietary lipids after histomorphometry and concentrations of fatty acids and insulin-like growth factor in chick tibiotarsal bone. *Journal of Nutrition,* **127**(6), 1084–91.

Whitington, P. F. and Gibson, R. (1977) Soy protein intolerance: four patients with concomitant cow's milk intolerance. *Pediatrics,* **59**, 730–2.

WHO (1981) *International Code of Marketing of Breastmilk Substitutes*. World Health Organization, Geneva.

WHO/UNICEF (1989) *Protecting, Promoting and Supporting Breast-feeding: the Special Role of Maternity Services*. A joint WHO/UNICEF Statement. WHO, Geneva.

Willatts, P., Forsyth, J. S., Di Modugno, M. K., Varma, S. and Colvin, M. (1998) The effect of longchain polyunsaturated fatty acids in infant formula on problem solving at 10 months of age. *Lancet*, **352**, 688–91.

Williams, A. (1993) In: *Forfar and Arneil's Textbook of Paediatrics*, 4th edn (eds. A. G. M. Campbell and N. McIntosh). Churchill Livingstone, London, p. 372.

Woolridge, M. (2004) The LIFT Project: effective interventions to promote breastfeeding. Paper presented at the annual UNICEF-UK Baby Friendly Conference: Reducing inequalities in breastfeeding: evidence and support for success. Clyde Auditorium, Scottish Exhibition and Conference Centre, Glasgow, 10–11 November.

CHAPTER 5

Reflections on HIV and feeding babies in the United Kingdom

Magda Sachs

Introduction

The discovery that human immunodeficiency virus (HIV) can be transmitted from a mother to her baby during breastfeeding has challenged international infant feeding policy and triggered fierce debate about how to respond. In this chapter the issue is reviewed, with particular reference to recent research; including data illustrating the impact of different patterns of infant feeding on transmission. International agency responses as well as policies in the United Kingdom are outlined, and the current situation in the UK discussed. The case of HIV, important in itself, throws light on assumptions about and practices of infant feeding in the UK, and these are considered.

Twenty-five years ago, AIDS (acquired immune deficiency syndrome) had not been named or identified as a single disease and its cause was unknown. Today it is held to be one of the greatest challenges facing the international community. In the relatively brief space of a quarter of a century, people living with HIV/AIDS, communities, governments, researchers and international agencies have had to develop an understanding of the disease and create and implement responses: both in treating individuals and in stemming its spread. It is twenty years since the recognition that HIV could be transmitted through breastfeeding and our understanding is still imperfect.

HIV/AIDS is transmitted through body fluids: primarily blood, semen, vaginal fluids, and breast milk. For each route of transmission different sets of responses have developed. Perhaps because early cases of HIV/AIDS were identified in intravenous drug users and male homosexuals, huge stigma has been attached to those who are HIV+, and early education on prevention often focused on simply avoiding behaviour which might result in transmission. However, strategies have changed. Intravenous drug users have been urged to practice safer needle use if they continue to inject drugs. A whole new concept of 'safe sex' has been developed in response to sexual transmission, with an emphasis on using condoms, monogamy and avoiding certain sexual practices; these have been taught and promoted (with varying estimates of success).

Blood transfusion services have developed screening and testing procedures. There have been attempted formulations of synthetic blood, and it is possible that had a suitable substitute existed it might have become the preferred method of dealing with problems of transmission through transfusion. In the area of infant feeding, a substitute already existed, and the initial response to the possibility of transmission through breast milk was simply to advocate replacement of breastfeeding with infant formula in a bottle. This has been challenged in high-prevalence, resource-poor regions, but remains the recommendation in the UK. While this may be partially explained by differences in technologies and medical infrastructure, it also suggests that the value our society gives to breast-feeding is actually rather low.

My personal interest in HIV and infant feeding has been expressed through writing, speaking at a variety of conferences, lecturing to midwives and trainee midwives at several universities, and participating in many conversations (some online). These opportunities to deliver my ideas in public, to hear responses, share others' views and answer questions have aided me in refining my thinking. It has also meant that I have been contacted for information for specific individuals. These experiences inform the four case scenarios included in this chapter (although all are composites and do not relate to any single woman's circumstances). Each constructed case highlights practical issues and dilemmas for health care staff and women and they are presented as aids to reflection.

Understanding of HIV/AIDS and infant feeding is likely to change with additional research and experience in practice, and practitioners working with mothers need to be kept updated. However, a truly overwhelming number of original research reports (often several from the same study), commentaries, overviews, opinion pieces and letters have been published on this issue. The majority of these focus on developing countries; it is often difficult to know how to relate these to practice in the UK. Literature reviews can help place individual research into context. When using these, however, it is necessary to keep in mind that authors may have strong views, which may colour – or at least tinge – conclusions (as is, indeed, also the case with this present chapter). In 1999, for example, two International Board Certified Lactation Consultants (IBCLCs) published reviews, largely focusing on HIV and breastfeeding in developing countries. (By this stage the orthodoxy was for HIV+ women in western, developed countries to avoid breastfeeding). White (1999) reported being 'horrified' at the 'very significant' risk of transmission through breastfeeding and strongly critiqued what she saw as UNICEF's lack of timely response, due to a reluctance to advocate formula use (p. 1). Morrison (1999a,b) emphasised the competing risks of HIV infection and formula feeding, with attendant risks of infant morbidity and mortality, and urged caution in advocating the use of formula.

The World Health Organization published literature reviews in 1998 and in 2004 (WHO/UNICEF/UNAIDS, 1998; WHO/UNICEF/UNFPA/UNAIDS, 2004); the latter provides an excellent summary of the research that has been conducted, areas in which questions still remain, and an indication of studies currently under way which are expected to yield important results. Despite implicitly relating to the global situation, these have little specific to say to those working with women in developed countries. Foster and Lyall (2005) provide guidelines for caring for babies of HIV+ women in the UK, but do not explore infant feeding in depth. The current review attempts to draw links between such international and UK literature and to highlight areas for debate. Throughout, the discussion relates to HIV-1, as HIV-2 is rare.

Breastfeeding – how much mother-to-child-transmission does it account for?

Transmission of HIV to babies (often referred to as MTCT, or 'mother-to-child-transmission') can occur during pregnancy (*in utero*), at the time of birth, and postnatally, during breastfeeding. HIV testing of newborns is complicated by the presence of residual maternal antibodies, so it is not possible to know whether babies are HIV-positive immediately after they are born (Piwoz *et al.*, 2004b). Knowing – or having best estimates of – the proportion of transmission through each of these routes is theoretically important to enable health care providers to target and evaluate interventions.

The first case reports of transmission of HIV to babies via breastfeeding were published in the mid-1980s (Read and Committee on Pediatric Aids, 2003). It is useful to remember that, at this time, modes of transmission were not well understood, and case reports may not have given what we might now regard as all the relevant information. For example, in the celebrated case of Elizabeth Glaser, who was infected via a blood transfusion (White, 1999), the possibility that her baby, Ariel, had also received a transfusion was not thoroughly investigated: attention focused on breastfeeding (Marian Thomson, personal communication). At this time, too, HIV/AIDS was still strongly associated with stigmatised groups such as gay men and drug users, and early cases in 'innocent' people, such as newborn babies, prompted strong emotional reactions, as they muddied early perceptions of HIV as 'the gay plague' (Uddin, 2003).

HIV was detected in breast milk samples during the 1990s: however the implications of the presence of cell-free and cell-associated virus in milk is not well understood. Nor is the association between levels in maternal plasma and breast milk clear (WHO/UNICEF/UNFPA/UNAIDS, 2004). Dunn *et al.* (1992) conducted a meta-analysis of data then available and calculated rates of transmission via breastfeeding. They estimated that 14% of HIV+ women who breastfeed would transmit HIV to their baby via breastfeeding (this is the rate of transmission over and above any transmission *in utero* and during birth). Six sets of birth cohort study data, each with breastfed and non-breastfed babies, were included, from the USA, Europe, Australia and Africa. The rate of a positive HIV test in babies whose mothers had been diagnosed HIV+ was compared between babies who had never been breastfed and those who had ever been breastfed: the authors commented on the difficulty of finding studies which included both breast and formula feeding women, as women in western, developed countries were already discouraged from breastfeeding and very few African women completely avoided breastfeeding (comparison of the rate of positive HIV tests of babies of HIV+ African women who breastfed with HIV+ European women who never breastfed would be subject to many confounding factors).

Forty-two cases of women who acquired HIV after their babies were born (and were therefore in the period of seroconversion and high infectivity (Piwoz *et al.*, 2004b)) were analysed separately, and a rate of 29% transmission via breastfeeding estimated in these circumstances. Subsequent studies have indicated that women with a low CD4+ cell count at the time of delivery and with severe clinical disease also have an increased chance of transmitting to their babies (WHO/UNICEF/UNFPA/UNAIDS, 2004). Subsequent modelling of the risk of transmission via breastfeeding, using information from data collected since the Dunn analysis, estimated risks ranging between 5% and 20% transmission (de Cock *et al.*, 2000; WHO/UNICEF/UNFPA/UNAID, 2004). Most recently, the Breastfeeding and HIV International Transmission Survey Group (BHITS, 2004) analysed data collected in nine trials on 4085 breastfed children, which were testing the impact of vitamin therapy or antiretrovirals on transmission. This calculated that the risk of transmission remained roughly constant during the period of breastfeeding and was around 4% for every six months of breastfeeding (BHITS, 2004; Coutsoudis, 2005). Many published analyses continue to use the Dunn figures.

In concern about breastmilk transmission, it is easy to overlook one vital point: *the majority of HIV+ women who breastfeed do not transmit HIV to their babies through breastfeeding.* Breastfeeding is not an automatic route of transmission (even where women are very ill). Thus while avoiding breastfeeding avoids the major cause of postnatal transmission (but not transmission during pregnancy or at birth), there is a dilemma in balancing the benefits of reducing transmission with the negative consequences of formula feeding.

The wide range of rates of transmission in the different data sets analysed by Dunn *et al.* (1992) offered a clue that factors other than just some breastfeeding influenced this. Most of the women included in the analysis breastfed for a short time (e.g. a median of four weeks in Europe; seven weeks in France); it seems unlikely that their babies would have received much of a period of exclusive breastfeeding. Personal experience – having two children and working as a volunteer breastfeeding counsellor – during these years suggests that early use of water, glucose solution and formula feeds was common. This issue of mixed feeding has turned out to be crucial. It should be emphasised that even the most recently calculated risks of breastfeeding are mainly derived from studies in which babies were mixed-fed.

Exclusive breastfeeding

For decades, research on many aspects of infant feeding compared health outcomes between groups of babies who were breastfed and groups who were replacement fed (never breastfed). Any one study might group together, in the 'breastfed group', babies who were breastfed and given water, formula/animal milk, or semi-solids (mixed-fed) with those who were given nothing other than breast milk. This had the result of 'dampening' comparisons of infant morbidity (health) and mortality (death) outcomes on the basis of mode of feeding (Armstrong, 1991; Sachs, 2002). In order to address this, definitions of breastfeeding practices were developed by the World Health Organization (WHO, 1991), with exclusive breastfeeding defined as (p. 2):

> The infant has received only breast milk from his/her mother or a wet nurse, or expressed breast milk, and no other liquids or solids, with the exception of drops or syrups consisting of vitamins, mineral supplements or medicines.

Labbock (2000, p. 19) notes that prior to this definition, the term exclusive breastfeeding could mean that 'breastfeeding was the infant's only source of milk, but other foods might be given'. Unfortunately, and confusingly, this use may still be found. WHO (1991) used the term 'predominant breastfeeding' to describe situations where the baby receives breast milk, as well as other foods or drinks, while 'mixed feeding' is generally used in HIV literature.

WHO recently commissioned a review of evidence of the optimal duration of exclusive breastfeeding (Kramer and Kakuma, 2001) and recommended six months' exclusive breastfeeding as global policy (WHO, 2003). The UK Department of Health has also adopted this (Department of Health, 2002). Goldman (2001) and Walker (2001) reviewed available evidence on infant gastrointestinal and immunological systems, concluding that they are developmentally ready for the introduction of foods or drinks other than breast milk at six months. Humans are born relatively developmentally immature and the period of exclusive breastfeeding may be likened to a continuation of the support received via the placenta in pregnancy. During this time, the immune system and the gut mucosal lining mature; a number of factors present in breast milk appear to be designed to foster this (Labbok *et al.*, 2004). Six months' exclusive breastfeeding thus represents not only a period of protection from too many challenges by a range of foods and pathogens, but also time necessary for the full development of the infant immune response and gut integrity. (Six months is intended to represent the best estimate of the period that an infant requires to reach a stage of readiness for the challenge of complementary feeding. Individuals may require a shorter or longer time – unfortunately little helpful evidence exists which might help identify such individuals.)

Mechanisms of HIV transmission via breastfeeding are not well understood, but the infant's gut mucosal surfaces are a likely site of entry of virus present in the milk. Gut permeability may be increased if anything other than breast milk 'challenges' the immature gut, allowing HIV virus to pass through the mucosal barrier (Rollins *et al.*, 2001; WHO/UNICEF/UNFPA/UNAIDS, 2004). A study in Belarus, unrelated to HIV transmission, found a higher incidence of diarrhoea among babies who were not exclusively breastfed (Kramer *et al.*, 2001), demonstrating real differences in health outcomes between mixed and exclusive breastfeeding. The increasing understanding that exclusive breastfeeding differs from mixed feeding has led researchers to examine this in the context of HIV.

Exclusive breastfeeding and HIV – first research results

A randomised trial investigating vitamin A supplementation of 549 pregnant HIV+ women in Durban, South Africa, included a prospective, observational component of transmission on the basis of the feeding patterns (Coutsoudis *et al.*, 1999, 2001a, 2003). Pregnant women entering the study were counselled and made an informed choice on whether to breastfeed or formula-feed; those breastfeeding were given information on exclusive breastfeeding. Women were then followed up until their babies were 15 months old. The early results from this study challenged the accepted role of breastfeeding in HIV transmission, as babies who were exclusively breastfed to three months and those never breastfed had similar rates of transmission, while the mixed fed group showed higher rates (Coutsoudis, 1999). Results to 15 months showed that transmission rates for babies exclusively breastfed to four months were similar to never-breastfed babies at four months, and continued to remain similar to transmission rates for never-breastfed babies until after six months (Coutsoudis, 2001a). The rate of transmission then continued to increase above that of the never-breastfed babies. It is important to note that almost no babies in this study were exclusively breastfed to six months, so it is not possible to do more than conjecture about the effect of mixed feeding after six months' exclusive breastfeeding.

This study has had important effects in shaping policies and future directions in research. Weaknesses of the study design include that its purpose was to study the effects of vitamin A (no effect of supplementation was found on transmission); that it was not a randomised controlled trial of feeding; and that the adherence to feeding options was not closely monitored (Coutsoudis, 2005). The data also strengthened the previously theoretical idea of 'early cessation'; that is, exclusive breastfeeding to six months and then either fairly rapid, or abrupt, weaning of the baby from the breast to appropriate replacement milks and solids (WHO/UNICEF/UNAIDS, 1998; Piwoz *et al.*, 2001).

Publication of this study reinvigorated debate about breastfeeding policy for HIV+ women, not only in developing countries, but in the UK too. (Note that the first results appeared in the same year as both the Department of Health policy (1999a) and the Camden Case – see below). Confirmation in further studies has been called for as a minimum requirement for basing policy on these findings; however, it takes time to devise, obtain ethical approval, recruit, collect and analyse data (especially where outcomes over some months or years are collected), and report. The results of a study collecting information on the effects of exclusive and mixed breastfeeding in Zimbabwe (ZVITAMBO study) have recently become available (Piwoz *et al.*, 2004a; Iliff *et al.*, 2005) and show that mixed breastfeeding more than doubles the rate of transmission through breastfeeding in the first six months. Analysis also indicates a dose response, with predominantly breastfed babies (given breast milk and non-milk liquids) experiencing lower rates than mixed fed babies (given breast milk and non-human milk and/or solid food), but higher rates than exclusively breastfed babies. A further important finding is that two-thirds of postnatal transmission occurred after six months, supporting the idea of 'early cessation' as an intervention (Piwoz *et al.*, 2004a; Iliff *et al.*, 2005).

The advent of HIV and increasing understanding of the importance of exclusive breastfeeding has sharply highlighted the fact that the cultural norm in Africa and other parts of the developing world may be for most women to breastfeed, but for almost no women to breastfeed without the use of additional drinks or semi-solid porridges (Kyenkya-Isabirye and Armstrong, 1992; Haider *et al.*, 2000). For the period 1995–2000, UNICEF (2001) cites a global rate of 45% exclusive breastfeeding in the first four months; 37% in less developed countries; and 33% in sub-Saharan Africa. In the UK, women who begin breastfeeding also have high rates of early cessation and introduction of other fluids, milks or semi-solids (Hamlyn *et al.*, 2002).

Outside the context of HIV, Haider *et al.* (2000) showed that provision of regular support by peers could increase exclusivity; similarly in Honduras, regular knowledgeable support helped women meet the everyday challenges of continuing exclusive breastfeeding (Cohen *et al.*, 1999). Women around the world struggle to find a period of time in which their usual duties – caring for other children, preparing food, waged work, work for the household and social obligations – can be shared with others, or expectations of them decreased, so that they have time and flexibility to respond to the needs of their babies for frequent access to the breast. In western countries such as the UK, even women from higher socio-economic groups may find that the expectations of returning to work, social obligations and meeting cultural norms such as an unbroken night's sleep are significant barriers to sustaining exclusive breastfeeding (Sachs, 2002).

Field trials supporting exclusive breastfeeding for HIV+ women in Africa have met with various challenges. The traditional use of teas and semi-solids and sharing baby care mean practical obstacles. Because the promotion of exclusivity began in the context of HIV, practising it may mean family members or neighbours concluding that women are HIV+ from their method of feeding, thus stigmatising the practice. Such obstacles need to be understood, thought through and locally relevant solutions found in order to support women (Coutsoudis *et al.*, 2003; Burke, 2004; Kooniz-Booher *et al.*; 2004, Rollins *et al.*, 2004; Thairu *et al.*, 2005). It should be noted that using formula from day one in a community where the norm is to breastfeed may also be tantamount to announcing one is HIV+ (Uddin, 2003).

In confronting heterosexual transmission of HIV, policy makers and health workers have become acutely aware of the impact of gender inequalities on the world's women. Financial dependence and traditions of subordination to husbands have meant that women may feel helpless to ask to use condoms within marriage or when working as prostitutes. Women in the developing world who are diagnosed HIV+ during pregnancy may be the first people in the family to take home the diagnosis and may be blamed as the source, with subsequent poor treatment or abandonment by their families, so discouraging women from taking HIV tests (Seidel *et al.*, 2000). Indeed, focusing on women in prevention of HIV transmission to babies tends not to target the initial transmission to women in the first place; usually via heterosexual contact. This is the wider context of the issue of how to feed the baby (Uddin, 2003).

Randomised trial of formula versus breastfeeding for HIV+ women

Soon after publication of the Coutsoudis *et al.* (1999) early results, came the first randomised clinical trial of breast and formula feeding (Nduati *et al.*,

2000). This study recruited 425 HIV+ women in Nairobi, Kenya, into the trial when they were 32 weeks pregnant. Women who had access to the municipal water supply (expected to reduce preparation risks of using infant formula, but not representative of the circumstances of many women in Africa) were eligible. Babies were followed up to 24 months. The results showed a difference in HIV transmission between the breastfeeding and formula feeding arms: breast-fed babies had 16.2% higher chance of transmission. Mortality of babies at 2 years was similar between the two groups, with 24.4% of breastfed babies and 20% of those fed formula dying. The authors concluded that using breast milk substitutes significantly improved chances for 'HIV-1-free survival' of infants, although, by the age of two, the women in each group had a similar chance that their child had died (Nduati *et al.*, 2000). No data was collected on women's reactions: given that the chances of their baby dying were similar, was it important to mothers whether their baby had died as a result of AIDS or not? Did they have any thoughts about the method of feeding in retrospect? We do not know.

Randomised trials are considered to be the 'gold standard' in terms of giving clear indications of causality (in this case that breastfeeding caused HIV transmission). To achieve robust results, the sample selected for study needs to be representative of a wider population – which in this case would be the new mothers of Nairobi (although it would be hoped to suggest more general, relevant conclusions). Nduati *et al.* (2000, p. 1170) indicated that 2315 HIV+ women were eligible for inclusion, and 425 (18%) consented to participate. This raises questions as to the applicability of outcomes based on the minority of women who were prepared to have their choice between breast and bottle feeding allocated on the basis of a randomised draw to others: are they representative of others (Humphrey and Iliff, 2001)?

Bulterys (2000) also raised the possibility that randomising the women at 32 weeks may have caused subsequent antenatal and birthing care to vary, which might have affected rates of transmission *in utero* or at birth. If this were the case, the babies in the two arms of the trial may have had different rates of HIV+ status at birth, making the impact of feeding method difficult to assess.

This study is a landmark in infant feeding research. It had previously been held that recruiting women to a study in which infant feeding methods were allocated randomly would be neither feasible nor ethical. The extreme situation of HIV may have altered ethical considerations, but it is interesting to note that even these women who had consented to participate had difficulty adhering to protocols. Ninety-six per cent of the women in the breastfeeding arm were reported to have complied with breastfeeding; there was insufficient detailed information to determine whether any had breastfed exclusively – mixed feeding is the usual pattern in Kenya (Coutsoudis *et al.*, 2000). Thirty per cent in the formula feeding arm admitted that they had not avoided breastfeeding completely. This is probably a marker of the strength of cultural pressure to breastfeed, and to be seen to breastfeed, in this African city. Programmes offering free formula milk to HIV+ women in Africa have found social and cultural – as well as practical – barriers to exclusive formula feeding (de Wagt and Clark, 2004; Rollins *et al.*, 2004). Policy in western countries such as the UK assumes that any barriers to formula feeding are negligible (Foster and Lyall, 2005).

Health outcomes for HIV+ women and their children

Rates of infant HIV and mortality are not the only outcomes of interest in infant feeding comparisons. Issues of maternal and infant health are also important. Data was collected in the Nairobi study on mortality risks for HIV+ women during breastfeeding (Nduati *et al.*, 2001). Breastfeeding women had a cumulative probability of death at 24 months of 10.5%, compared to 3.8% for formula feeding women. This difference, though striking, appears to result from pre-existing differences in the sample, rather than the effect of breastfeeding on women's health. Coutsoudis *et al.* (2001b) found no differences in morbidity and mortality between the groups of HIV+ women choosing different feeding methods in Durban. A study in Tanzania showed similar results (Sedgh *et al.*, 2004) and it appears that 'mortality among infected women in the period following delivery is associated with HIV infection and not with infant feeding modality' (WHO/UNICEF/UNFPA/UNAIDS, 2004 p.7).

Examination of infant morbidity data shows that breast and bottle-fed babies in the Nairobi trial experienced similar incidences of diarrhoea (155 in formula fed vs. 149 in breastfed babies per 100 person years) and identical rates of pneumonia (Mbori-Ngacha *et al.*, 2001). Coutsoudis *et al.* (2003), in data from the Durban study, found that 60% of never-breastfed babies had three or more episodes of illness, compared to 32% of breastfed babies. A meta-analysis of interventions (not feeding method) to prevent MTCT could make no comment on the effect of breastfeeding on the mortality of the babies of HIV+ women, due to the characteristics of the study samples (Newell *et al.*, 2004). This is an area which requires fuller exploration.

Some babies are HIV+ at birth, and it is important not to forget their needs when making feeding recommendations, although this has been little studied. In the UK it is estimated that, despite interventions, 2% of children born to HIV+ women will be diagnosed HIV+ (European Collaborative Study, 2001). Kent (in press) observes that what is important for individual women who are deciding how to feed their babies are the risks of each possible choice; and formula feeding is not risk-free. Indeed he notes that he was unable to 'find published studies indicating that formula-fed infants are likely to have better health outcomes than exclusively breastfed infants under *any* circumstances' (Kent, 2001a, p. 8). Research has focused primarily on HIV transmission, not on health outcomes.

A small study in Italy showed that breastfed babies had a slower progression to AIDS and longer survival than formula fed babies (Tozzi *et al.*, 1990). Unpublished data from Los Angeles confirms this (Frederick *et al.*, 1997): in neither study is breastfeeding likely to have been exclusive. Outside the context of HIV, health outcomes for babies (on a population basis) are poorer if they are mixed rather than exclusively breastfed, and poorer still if they are never breastfed. The challenge is to balance these health risks with risks of HIV transmission through breastfeeding.

Factors affecting transmission rates

As noted, not all women who practice mixed feeding transmit HIV to their babies. A number of studies have collected observational information indicating that mastitis and infant oral thrush appear to increase the chances of HIV transmission (Rollins *et al.*, 2004; WHO/UNICEF/UNFPA/UNAIDS, 2004). Mastitis, which may itself be more prevalent where mothers are mixed-feeding and breast drainage may be more erratic, is theorised to increase the 'leakiness' of the cell junctions in maternal duct tissue and increase the amount of virus in the milk (WHO/UNICEF/UNAIDS, 1998; Semba and Neville, 1999; Willumsen *et al.*, 2003). Mastitis may also be a marker for ineffective breastfeeding, occurring when the breast is not well drained. It therefore may soon lead to mixed feeding, meaning that the association between mastitis and higher transmission could be the result of reverse causality (WHO, 2000a). Piwoz *et al.* (2004b) applied epidemiological methods to risk estimates from previous studies and speculated that mastitis may account for up to 50% of the transmission through breastfeeding. Thrush, and any other condition in which the infant's oral mucosa are breached, may similarly allow a portal for infection. Studies currently under way include some which explicitly aim to decrease incidence of breast pathologies in HIV+ breastfeeding women (Rollins *et al.*, 2004).

HIV is heat sensitive and can be inactivated by pasteurisation (Orloff *et al.*, 1993). Investigation into ways of decreasing the risk of HIV transmission via breast milk has examined methods of heat-treating. Using equipment as basic as a large saucepan and a peanut butter jar, milk expressed by hand can be treated to inactivate HIV virus by women at home (Chantry *et al.*, 2000; Jeffery and Mercer, 2000). Heat-treating milk reduces levels of many components (Lawrence and Lawrence, 1999), meaning lower levels of immune system protection (however, it should be remembered that these elements are absent from formulae). Expression and heat treatment method may be difficult for many women to commit to carry out from birth, but Rollins *et al.* (2004) suggest its value for breastfeeding women during any episodes of mastitis. It may also have a role during the transition from exclusive breastfeeding to complete replacement feeding if rapid cessation is chosen.

Breast milk is a living fluid with a variety of immunological components, such as immunoglobulins, lactoferrin and mucins, which help develop the infant immune system (Kourtis *et al.*, 2003; Labbok *et al.*, 2004). The presence of these may help account for the fact that breastfeeding, even mixed breast-feeding, does not result in 100% transmission from HIV+ women (Piwoz *et al.*, 2004b). Further study might indicate whether there may be differences in the level of such components in the milk of HIV+ and HIV- women (WHO/UNICEF/UNFPA/UNAIDS, 2004).

Lactoferrin has been found, in a laboratory study, to inhibit HIV replica-tion, suggesting it may suppress HIV infection (Moriuchi and Moriuchi, 2001). McClain (2002) searched out numerous patents on components of human milk, including lactoferrin, held by pharmaceutical companies and others. This raises the bizarre possibility that human milk components could be isolated, bioengi-neered and marketed as components for formula milks or as therapeutic inter-ventions for the prevention of HIV transmission, while the infants in question have their own mother's milk withheld.

The activities of companies manufacturing breast milk substitutes, some of which are subsidiaries of pharmaceutical companies, have been scrutinised, as breastfeeding advocates feared they might attempt to use the threat of HIV to promote their products (IBFAN/ICDC, 2001). UNICEF, during the period in which it supported governments with supplies of formula, chose not to accept donations from companies (de Wagt and Clark, 2004), fearing that this could allow them to present themselves as 'saviours not culprits' (Martyn, 2001, p. 10). In response to such concerns, the World Health Assembly stressed that HIV+ women's infant feeding decisions should be independent of commercial influences (WHA, 2001).

Since the publication of the Cousoudis *et al.* (1999) and Nduati *et al.* (2000) studies, there has been increasing recognition that a myriad of factors need to be considered in order to ensure that either exclusive formula feeding or exclusive breastfeeding can be practised by women. Policy has varied during the last two decades, as it followed the current state of understanding of MTCT via breast-feeding.

Policy recommendations

International policy has evolved in response to increasing knowledge and research. WHO made a statement in 1987 and, in the then current state of uncer-tainty as to the magnitude of the proportion of transmission via breastfeeding, emphasised the importance of protecting, promoting and supporting breastfeeding, speaking only of individual situations in which a mother might safely use replacement feeding (WHO, 1987). In 1992 the recommendations continued to stress the importance of breastfeeding in resource-poor settings, but stated that: 'In settings where infectious diseases are not the primary causes of death during infancy, pregnant women known to be infected with HIV should be advised not to breast-feed' (WHO, 1992 p.2). Thus, the 'advice depends on the circumstances' (Cutting, 1992, p. 788).

Results of trials of antenatal antiretroviral drugs appeared to promise prevention: this research was conducted with women who were not breastfeeding and it was feared that the benefits of the drugs would be negated by subsequent breastfeeding (WHO/UNICEF/UNAIDS, 1998; de Wagt and Clark, 2004; Foster and Lyall, 2005). A 1997 policy statement stated that HIV+ women should be offered a choice of feeding method. This document asserts that when babies can 'be ensured uninterrupted access to nutritionally adequate breast-milk substitutes that are safely prepared and fed to them, they are at less risk of illness and death if they are not breast-fed' (WHO/UNICEF/UNAIDS, 1998, p. 20). It should be noted that this assertion is very poorly supported by evidence; research has mainly focused on transmission of HIV and not on comparison of health outcomes. The 1998 recommendation seems to represent the high tide of enthusiasm for replacement feeding, with implementation in a variety of field programmes in Africa in which free or subsidised formula was provided for HIV+ women. A rapid assessment, carried out in 2000, concluded that promotion of formula feeding in order to prevent MTCT was having a profound effect on general promotion, protection and support for breastfeeding and could be 'disastrous for breastfeeding in Sub-Saharan Africa' (Latham and Kisanga, 2001, p. 5).

As noted above, White (1999) castigated UNICEF for not responding even sooner; however, the 1997 recommendations galvanised concern from many within the wider breastfeeding community (Latham and Greiner, 1998), with the World Alliance on Breastfeeding Action (WABA) taking the lead in providing information via email to those interested around the world. At this time UNICEF, traditionally a strong proponent of breastfeeding, began supporting governments in programmes to prevent MTCT, including providing formula free of charge to HIV+ mothers in countries where governments requested this. A generic label was developed so that supplies could be provided within the scope of the WHO Code. De Wagt and Clark (2004) provide an overview of this experience and note the problems encountered, including the appearance of implicit endorsement of formula feeding by health workers. This could contribute to 'spillover', or the effects of the provision of information and support for formula feeding, or free or subsidised formula to HIV+ women; which may lead women who are HIV– or untested to decide to formula feed (Coutsoudis *et al.*, 2002).

In 2000 a technical consultation made recommendations setting forth the 'AFASS' conditions in which formula feeding could be recommended to women: 'When formula feeding is acceptable, feasible, affordable, sustainable and safe, avoidance of all breastfeeding by HIV-infected mothers is recommended' (WHO, 2000b, p. 8). These five conditions have been further defined by WHO (2004). It could be said that, internationally, the emphasis shifted back towards the advice depending on the circumstances. In 2002, HIV and MTCT experts and representatives from the breastfeeding community met to examine the issues together. Labbok (in WABA and UNICEF, 2003, p. 3) opened the meeting noting that 'After nearly a decade of seeing the conflict build between those who were trying to prevent every case of HIV/AIDS, and those who were trying to have the best overall public health outcomes for infants and young children [...] the Colloquium led to [...] moving forward together'.

The WHO research evidence summary was updated in 2004, as were guidelines for decision-makers, a guide for health-care managers and supervisors, and a 'Framework for Priority Action' was produced. A comparison of the 1998 and 2004 research summaries is instructive: aside from obvious differences in the actual content of research conducted, the 2004 document strongly sets the discussion in the context of ensuring optimal feeding for all babies through the Global Strategy (WHO and UNICEF, 2003), which itself draws together previous instruments in this area such as the Innocenti Declaration, The WHO/UNICEF Code of Marketing of Breastmilk Substitutes, and the Baby Friendly Hospital Initiative. Governments are expected to make a high-level political commitment to improving infant feeding practices, specifically setting the feeding of the babies of HIV+ women inside a strong framework of protection, promotion and support of breastfeeding and appropriate complementary feeding. Current recommendations are that HIV+ women should either formula feed exclusively or breastfeed exclusively and, 'whatever choice a mother makes, she should be supported' (WHO, 2004, p. 4–3). Mixed feeding should be avoided, particularly in the early months.

Counselling HIV+ women

In order to ensure that the feeding method chosen meets the AFASS criteria, HIV+ women should be offered guidance that is 'personal to the individual woman' (WHO/UNICEF/UNFPA/UNAIDS, 2004, p. 4). A manual for training health workers in maternal and child health and in primary care settings was produced, covering training in counselling skills, information about MTCT and also information on best breastfeeding management practice (WHO/UNICEF/UNAIDS, 2000); updated materials combine training on all aspects of prevention of MTCT so that all health workers can give consistent information (WHO, 2004). Quality counselling relies on training, ongoing retraining and support for counsellors. Barriers to effective counselling in practice include strong opinions of the counsellors as to which feeding method is best, and inadequate knowledge of practical aspects of different feeding options (de Paoli *et al.*, 2002; WHO/UNICEF/UNFPA/UNAIDS, 2003a,b). The manual notes that 'counselling means ***more than advising***' and should not involve making a decision for a woman (WHO/UNICEF/UNAIDS, 2000, p. 29 emphasis in original). Coutsoudis (2005) remarks that counsellors 'need to have the ability to translate complex scientific concepts on risk in a way that is understood by women who do not have a grasp of these dilemmas' (p. 90). The concepts of counselling and making 'informed choices' are western ones which may be difficult for both counsellor and woman, in some cultures, to enact: women may expect respected health workers to tell them what to do (Morrison *et al.*, 2001). De Paoli *et al.* (2002) found that counsellors in Tanzania perceived 'good' counsellors as those who got women to accept testing and interventions; a review of unpublished literature from MTCT prevention programmes concluded that counsellors in many areas were biased towards a particular feeding method (Koniz-Booher *et al.*, 2004). It is open to conjecture how different this in the UK context; discussions of infant feeding choices are not often framed in terms of relative risk. The WHO manual, or any other standard text, does not appear to be used in the UK.

International recommendations have developed with explicit focus on countries with a high prevalence of HIV and a limited resource base. Policy in western countries, including the UK, has taken a different path.

Policy on HIV and mother-to-child-transmission in the United Kingdom

Policy in the UK has stressed antenatal screening to identify HIV+ women and to offer them interventions. Anonymous HIV testing of pregnancy blood samples was undertaken in several areas in order to establish population prevalence of HIV from 1988 (Nicoll *et al.*, 1998) and the option of an HIV test in pregnancy offered to women considered to be at high risk (Department of Health, 1994). In 1999, this policy changed to a universal offer of HIV tests to all pregnant women, with targets for uptake: 50% by the end of 2000 and 80% by 2002 (Nicoll and Peckham, 1999). The expected beneficial effects of universal testing rested on every woman identified as HIV+ (and who continued with her pregnancy) accepting three interventions: antiretroviral drugs for herself in pregnancy and for her baby; a caesarean section; and avoidance of breastfeeding (Nicoll *et al.*, 1999; Bott, 2000a; Ottewill, 2000; Foster and Lyall, 2005). Concern was expressed about the harmful effects of these interventions on the babies of HIV+ women born HIV–, many of whom would have been negative even without intervention (Harrison and Corbett, 1999; Davies, 2000). The setting of testing targets, with little additional time given for pre-test counselling, raises ethical issues; Davies (2000) contrasted the level of counselling by midwives with that offered at a GUM clinic. Comments on the policy in practice continue to indicate a variety of views with some midwives unhappy at undertaking this task (Kaufmann, 2001).

Soon after the first reports that HIV might be passed to babies via breastfeeding, the Department of Health and Social Security issued advice that HIV+ women and women in 'high-risk' groups should be discouraged from breastfeeding (Department of Health and Social Security, 1988). This advice was criticised because of the scanty nature of the evidence of such transmission, and because the result of advising this to all women considered at high risk would be that 'all African women or partners of African men [would] be discouraged from breastfeeding' (Lancet, 1988, p. 144). A modification of the guidance was issued the following year, stressing that only those who were known to be HIV+ should be advised not to breastfeed (Department of Health and Social Security, 1989). It is interesting to note that this first UK public health recommendation was made so rapidly and on the basis of little consensus about transmission of HIV through breastfeeding. One is prompted to wonder what level of evidence would be required now to overturn this policy: surely more than a few case reports of women who exclusively breastfed without transmitting HIV to their babies?

The advice also stated that 'Since bottle feeding, if incorrectly performed, carries its own risks for the infant, arrangements should be made for those who decide against breastfeeding to receive additional assistance in the safe and successful use of infant formula feeding' (Department of Health and Social Security, 1989, p. 2). It is instructive to note that bottle feeding is considered risky in the UK only if unsafely performed. This was prior to the publication of a study in Dundee showing a difference in the incidence of gastrointestinal disease between babies breastfed for 13 weeks and those never breastfed (Howie *et al.*, 1900). These authors explicitly offered their conclusions as evidence of a protective effect of breastfeeding in developed countries. Since then, numerous research studies have contributed to our understanding of the health differences between breastfed and never breastfed babies (UNICEF UK Baby Friendly Initiative, 2004). A cultural understanding of formula feeding as a generally benign activity, which has implicitly become the norm; with breastfeeding conceived of as offering advantages above this norm, rather than setting the normative standard itself, is powerfully revealed.

The 1988 advice also made recommendations about milk banks, including the stipulation that all donors be tested for HIV; 'this directive had the effect of closing the majority of milk banks in the UK' (Spiro, 1992, p. 35; Balmer and Wharton, 1992). This has impacted on the availability of banked human milk for ill and premature babies in the UK over the past 15 years, with incalculable health consequences (Lucas, 1987; Lucas and Cole, 1990). Thus, babies (and families) not directly affected by HIV have been affected in a form of 'spillover'. The discovery that heat treatment kills the HIV virus and new protocols for donors and pasteurisation have led to a slow revival of milk banks (United Kingdom Association for Milk Banking, 2004).

At the time of introducing universal HIV testing, the Department of Health (1999a) issued a policy that did not unequivocally state that HIV+ women should not breastfeed, but asserted that most HIV+ women 'opt to avoid breastfeeding' (p. 2), and if a woman 'insists on breastfeeding' (p. 7) she should be advised about early cessation and good positioning of the baby at the breast. Although this admits the possibility that a woman might breastfeed, this use of the word 'insist' appears loaded. In general, one of the roles of midwives is to discuss infant feeding choices with women during pregnancy. Despite evidence that babies who are not breastfed have an increased risk of adverse health outcomes, the usual policy is to preserve women's right to choose the method of feeding, and to support her choice: I have never heard health care staff referring to women who 'insist' on formula feeding even though this has health consequences for their babies. UK policy was revised (Department of Health, 2001) and further updated (Department of Health, 2004b); and this wording changed to the more neutral 'chooses not to feed artificially' (p. 10; p. 12). A leaflet was produced for mothers (Department of Health, 1999b) intended to persuade women to accept HIV testing: its language assumes that anyone who tests positive will accept the three interventions listed above, while no mention is made of potential risks of any of these. Davies (2000) suggests that this leaflet patronises women and presents the interventions with no mention of possible attendant risks.

One spur for the policy revision (Department of Health, 2001) was uncertainty over legal issues, after the publicity surrounding a case where parents of a five-month-old were taken to court by Camden social services in 1999. The mother had been diagnosed with HIV nine years previously, but was well and healthy without taking anti-retrovirals. The couple had engaged an independent midwife and the baby was born at home. The family's new GP discovered the HIV diagnosis when notes were transferred to the surgery. The GP, and subsequently paediatrician and social worker, asked the parents to have the baby tested for HIV; they refused, and were taken to court. The case focused on the issue of testing, but the judge made it clear that, should the baby test positive, there would be pressure on the parents to give her drug therapy, and if she tested negative, there would be pressure for the mother to stop breastfeeding. The court stated that the parents must bring their baby for testing: instead they left the country, going underground (Brahams, 1999; Dyer, 1999; BBC News,1999a,b, 2000a).

This mother had reportedly decided that the benefits of breastfeeding out-weighed the risks to her child (BBC News, 1999a). The case did not directly test what a UK court would rule if an HIV+ mother chose to breastfeed, but it created a charged atmosphere of worry and concern. The Department of Health (2001) noted the absence of legal direction, leaving the position for an individual health worker caring for a breastfeeding HIV+ woman unclear. A text for solici-tors working with HIV+ clients draws the conclusion: 'Women contemplating an HIV test before or during pregnancy need to know that once they have given birth, their choices may be overridden if the doctors treating their child do not agree with their decisions' (Burt and Thackray, 2000, p. 118).

In 2000, The Royal College of Midwives held a seminar to discuss the HIV issue: the report from the day lists recommendations; these and a 1998 RCM position paper are the most up-to-date guidance for midwives on HIV and infant feeding (Janet Fyle, personal communication, August 2004; Royal College of Midwives, 1998; Royal College of Midwives, 2000). The 1998 document 'advises that breastfeeding should not be encouraged for known HIV positive women in the UK' (p. 1), but at the same time **'women who choose to breast-feed should have their decision respected and be given sympathetic support'** (p. 3; emphasis in original). The presentations and discussions at the seminar reflected the tensions felt by midwives at attempting to adhere to both parts of this policy (Royal College of Midwives, 2000). Recommendations are listed in the seminar report (and more briefly in the policy (Department of Health, 2001; Department of Health, 2004b)) and include a responsibility for every maternity unit, midwifery manager and midwife to ensure there are local protocols, dis-cussions and updated knowledge on the issues. Strategies – which are audited – should be in place to facilitate informed choice on infant feeding in general, with specific strategies for the support of formula feeding for HIV+ women, and support for HIV+ women who wish to breastfeed. Midwives are urged to share their experiences to promote best practice; however, no published audit or assessment of this type has been found.

The Department of Health policy (2004b, p. 16) states that 'the paediatri-cian should promote infant formula feeding'; a model perinatal care plan for the babies of HIV+ women merely includes antenatal discussion of 'avoidance of breastfeeding' (Dhar, 2001, p. 2), suggesting that no other option need be presented. The Royal College of Midwives (2000) recommends that multidisci-plinary protocols be developed and that women's choices should be respected. Anecdotal evidence suggests that the issue of possible social service involve-ment affects different midwives differently (Royal College of Midwives, 2000). If an HIV+ mother sees several professionals, she may meet with contrasting attitudes, due both to individual outlook and to differing professional proto-cols. It is notable that there have been several literature reviews by midwives, suggesting possible ways of supporting HIV+ women in the UK who choose to breastfeed, indicating that some are prepared to support this (Drozdowska,

2001; Finigan, 2002; Wright, 2004). In lecturing to midwives and midwifery students I have met with contrasting reactions, ranging from an enthusiasm for supporting women with exclusive breastfeeding to incomprehension that any HIV+ woman could contemplate breastfeeding. A study of UK midwifery education found that, even in the classroom situation, lecturers and students were uncomfortable talking about HIV: it invoked 'prejudice, stigma and fear which cannot always be disassociated from professional practice' (Grellier, 2000, p. 65). This appears to leave women in a difficult situation where the type of advice and support they will receive for making and sustaining their choice of infant feeding is unpredictable.

Very little work has been done to establish what women in the UK think about universal testing and the interventions on offer. One small study found that most women approved of testing, but a minority were more doubtful (Baxter and Bennett, 2000); no discussion of the interventions was included. A few HIV+ women have shared their personal feelings about MTCT interventions. Beatrice (2000) concealed her caesarean from friends and hid even from her mother and two older children that she did not breastfeed, because these actions would signal her HIV status in her community. Hickman did not accept drug therapy or have a caesarean, but also did not breastfeed, and revealed her anguish at this (in Royal College of Midwives, 2000). Both women talk about the physical pain of feeling their breasts full of milk they could not give to their babies.

Advice on primary prevention – measures to avoid becoming infected while a woman is pregnant or breastfeeding such as condom use and safer sex – is an important part of international and European policy to prevent MTCT (WHO/UNICEF/UNFPA/UNAIDS, 2004; UNFPA/UNAIDS/UNICEF/WHO Europe, 2004), and is mentioned in the Department of Health policy (2001, 2004b). However, no information is given in the UK leaflet for pregnant women intended for use before the antenatal HIV test (Department of Health, 1999b). Bott (2000b) asserts that suggesting use of condoms is unrealistic, since women will have trouble getting their male partners to agree. For many African women, avoiding breastfeeding may be just as problematic. The logic of universal testing during pregnancy would suggest that all women in the UK should receive information about protecting themselves against sexual transmission during pregnancy and breastfeeding at the time the issue is raised into their awareness. The policy instead suggests giving information about primary prevention to women who might be at high risk (Department of Health, 2001, 2004b); this represents something of a return to the policy of 1988, in which women received information based on the health worker's estimation of her risk category.

Drug therapies offered to HIV+ individuals are not cures, but manage symptoms and are expected to delay disease progression; doses offered to babies immediately after birth are intended to be prophylactic. Data, especially long-term data, on any adverse effects of maternal antiretroviral therapy during pregnancy on the unborn child, are scant (Coll *et al.*, 2002). In the UK, there is long-term follow-up of HIV– children born to HIV+ women, in addition to pae-diatric involvement with all children born HIV+ to help to monitor future health outcomes (Sharland *et al.*, 2002). Galliard *et al.* (2004) describe ongoing stud-ies in resource-poor settings examining the effects of maternal drug regimens on infants during breastfeeding. While it is expected that antiretroviral therapy during breastfeeding should reduce transmission via breast milk, there are also concerns that babies may develop possible drug resistance (John-Stewart *et al.*, 2004). As the combinations of drugs used in resource-poor settings may not be the same as those available in the UK, it is unclear how useful such research might be for UK mothers considering medication and breastfeeding (Foster and Lyall, 2005).

A caesarean involves major abdominal surgery, with implications for recov-ery and possible postnatal infection risk. Although operative delivery may reduce risks of transmission (European Collaborative Study, 2001), an element of choice seems to be acknowledged: an HIV specialist health visitor work-ing in London states that, depending on her state of health, 'if a woman feels strongly that she would like a normal delivery this can be considered' (White, 2002, p. 169), while Foster and Lyall (2005) note that avoiding a caesarean may be important for women expecting to return to a country where she may not be able to access an operative delivery for a subsequent birth.

In summary, UK policy remains to discourage HIV+ women from breast-feeding, but allows women the final choice of feeding method, subject to the possible intervention of social services. All women are offered the HIV test in pregnancy. Department of Health policy acknowledges that HIV+ women in the UK are not typical of the pregnant population. The Royal College of Obstetri-cians and Gynecologists (2004) began monitoring HIV in pregnancy in 1989 and, by the end of June 2004, 3820 HIV+ women, with 4630 pregnancies, had been identified in the UK. (For comparison, there were 563,000 deliveries in England alone in 2002–03 (Department of Health, 2004a, p. 3).) Some HIV+ mothers are injecting drug users, but the proportion of these has decreased over time (Nicoll *et al.*, 1998). More than two-thirds of the UK's HIV+ pregnant women are in London (Royal College of Obstetricians and Gynaecologists, 2004) and more than 80% were born in sub-Saharan Africa, a trend which seems set to increase (Cortina-Borja, 2004). Thus the UK policy of avoidance of breastfeeding is often being suggested to women from a distinctly different cultural background. It is clear that many of these women are grateful for the care they can access in the UK and are eager to do anything they can to reduce the risks of transmission to their babies. However, it is unclear, even if they find formula feeding person-ally acceptable, whether this choice will be accepted in their community, or if they will face stigma and discrimination. Further hurdles may make it difficult to ensure formula feeding is feasible, affordable, sustainable and safe.

No estimate is available as to how many HIV+ women in the UK are asylum seekers (arriving in the UK with a claim for protection from persecution under the terms of the 1951 Geneva Convention), although one HIV specialist midwife reported that the majority of her caseload was from this group (O'Driscoll, 2002). A report from the All-Parliamentary Group on AIDS notes that 'two of the most stigmatised groups in today's media and society are immigrants and people living with HIV/AIDS' (All-Party Parliamentary Group on AIDS, 2003, p. 16). Current government asylum policy includes 'dispersal': asylum claimants are sent to different areas, where local councils have contracted with the national asylum service to house them. Individuals are placed and can be moved at very short notice and have no control over this aspect of their lives. Medication regimes may be interrupted and risks of *in utero* transmission of HIV increased (All-Party Parliamentary Group on AIDS, 2003). Continued receipt of benefit is dependent on complying with housing allocation. Housing conditions may be unsuitable for the safe preparation and storage of formula feeds (McLeish, 2002). Dispersal may account for the rise in HIV cases reported in 2001 and 2002 outside London (Cortina-Boria *et al.*, 2004). Health professionals in dispersal areas may have little previous experience in caring for Africans, and local HIV services may be unable to cope with increases in numbers (All-Party Parliamentary Group on AIDS, 2003). Individuals whose asylum claim fails may be made destitute (put on the street without income) or sent back to their country of origin (Shentall, 2004). A formula-feeding mother, finding herself in such situations, could have difficulties in sustaining safe feeding practices.

Concerns about the effect of asylum policy on MTCT and HIV treatment of individuals have been voiced. In 2002 an HIV+ woman took court action for the provision of vouchers for formula milk, which would have otherwise cost 10% of her weekly income (Dyer, 2002). An HIV charity noted 'it is illogical for the government to encourage women to be tested for HIV, give them drugs... and advise caesareans... then give no support for them to avoid breastfeeding' (BBC News, 2000b). If women do not always have formula available, they may put their babies to the breast – insecurity of supply fosters mixed feeding: the mode with highest risks of transmission (McLeish, 2002). A recent survey revealed that doctors find that dispersal of HIV+ asylum seekers may compromise care and lead to increased transmission, including MTCT (Creighton *et al.*, 2004). Local attempts to ameliorate such problems have included asking for donations from infant formula companies (Kumalo, 2002) – a response which may appear pragmatic, but which could provide a publicity opportunity for companies: something which is regulated under the WHO Code. Exclusive breastfeeding, without consistent support, could also be difficult for women in these circumstances. Current policies may encourage mixed feeding, subverting public health aims of reducing HIV transmission.

Another group of women from sub-Saharan African in the UK are health care staff. Concern has been raised that a number of such staff are HIV+, and that this might affect patients in their care (BBC News, 2001; BBC News, 2002).

No study appears to have investigated childbearing in this group of women and their choices about infant feeding. At the RCM seminar in 2000, it was noticeable that a number of specialist HIV midwives from London hospitals were African women (personal observation). Some could themselves be HIV+: personal experience and beliefs may therefore influence the information or guidance they give women in their care. This could be fruitful to explore, but no research in this area has been found.

Perceptions that breast milk is risky

Several incidents have been reported in western countries (although not in the UK), where a baby has been breastfed by a woman other than the mother without the mother's permission (usually in nursery care). Mothers have cited their horror that their baby might have been exposed to HIV (*Dallas Morning News*, 2003; *News-Medical*, 2004). This may be how women express their feeling of outrage at having the physical intimacy with their baby broken into; however, it indicates that breastfeeding and HIV transmission are linked in public consciousness. At least one US hospital has developed a protocol for this situation, which includes HIV testing for the mother who fed the baby (Warner and Sapsford, 2004).

Such fear of harm to babies coming from the milk of a polluted other strongly echoes concerns in previous centuries about the quality of milk from wet nurses. For centuries parents were urged to scrutinise the moral character and sexual habits of those they hired (Fildes, 1986). Indeed, this long-held unease about the reliability of women poor enough to hire out their breasts could be identified as one marketing opportunity that early breast milk substitutes were developed to exploit (Golden, 1996). There is no record of research examining whether such perceptions affect the infant feeding choices of women who are HIV– in the UK; however in view of the concern expressed internationally with the possibility of spillover effects, this is an area of interest.

Refusal of interventions – ethics and rights

Wolf *et al.* (2001) consider whether clinicians should have recourse to the courts if parents refuse interventions. They do not include caesareans in their discussion, but treat refusal of antiretroviral therapy on the grounds of concern about the side effects as rational, and therefore not needing court intervention. Cultural factors might make breastfeeding allowable, and they cite the hypothetical case of Muslim women under a religious injunction to breastfeed, who might therefore make a case for doing so. In response to this, Murray (2002, p. 87) challenged the idea that any HIV+ woman should breastfeed as 'no risk exposure to an infant is allowable' and asserting that formula is 'safe and risk-free'. In contrast, a response from Greiner *et al.* (2002) specifically challenged the assumption that bottle feeding is risk-free. These divergent responses indicate how contentious such issues are for clinicians.

It also is interesting to note that Wolf *et al.* appear to suggest that some cultural factors might override medical advice. This raises questions as to whether women should be treated primarily as individuals or as members of a particular culture, and who decides which cultural view of breastfeeding is considered to override other considerations. One might also ask if this is an implicit statement that western culture does not value breastfeeding?

Kent (2001b) proposes that, in considering human rights and breastfeeding, that instead of opposing women's and babies' interests, breastfeeding be considered a form of 'group rights' which belongs to the mother–infant pair, so that no one may interfere with women's rights to choose how to feed their babies. In the context of HIV, Kent (in press) questions the use of coercion to ensure that women formula feed, emphasising instead that women should be given the best information on which to make a choice. In contrast, Cook and Dickens (2002) cite FIGO ethics committee (1996, p. 39) that 'it may be unethical for an HIV-infected mother to breastfeed her child' when she has practical access to formula feeding.

Kent (in press) points out that, although in the absence of HIV there is overwhelming evidence for the inferiority of breastmilk substitutes, we generally do not propose to require women to breastfeed. If it were established that exclusive breastfeeding provided the lowest risk of transmission, would we expect judges to order women to do so and take those who used formula milk to court? Surely not, yet looking at this logical 'flip side' of current practice reveals our cultural biases and assumptions.

Counselling and women's choices in the UK

International recommendations include providing each HIV+ woman with individual counselling and the opportunity to examine her options given her own circumstances (WHO/UNICEF/UNFPA/UNAIDS, 2004). If formula feeding is acceptable, feasible, affordable, sustainable and safe (AFASS), this may be advised. The UK has not explicitly adopted this approach, although, in view of the realities of some women's lives highlighted above, it might have much to recommend it. European policy states that a local assessment should always be made of the risks and benefits of various feeding options and notes that, while most women in Europe may find formula acceptable, feasible, affordable, sustainable and safe, others may not (UNPFA/UNAIDS/ UNICEF/WHO Europe, 2004). The updated policy (Department of Health, 2004b) does acknowledge that if a woman is moving outside the UK, this should be a factor to consider in feeding decisions. If assessment of the AFASS criteria for each woman were explicitly adopted, the first criterion is that the mother must find formula feeding acceptable. If she does not, as was the case for the mother in the Camden Case (BBC News, 1999b), these conditions are not met. Even if every woman diagnosed HIV+ in the UK decides not to breastfeed, surely each one deserves a discussion of her individual circumstances and the chance to make a real decision. Is it acceptable that women's choices are compromised because of a blanket assumption that AFASS conditions are universally met in the UK?

Despite the difference revealed in transmission rates via breastfeeding between mixed and exclusive breastfeeding, discussion in the UK appears to continue to assume that women will inevitably practise the former. As acknowledged, there are real barriers for women in achieving exclusive breastfeeding. It is not a cultural norm for African women or for women in the UK generally; however, individuals may feel they have the resources for this to be feasible and sustainable, especially if they receive health worker support. Currently the general recognition by health workers and women that exclusive breastfeeding differs from mixed feeding is low in the UK (Sachs, 2002). Improved professional knowledge of how to support the initiation and continuation of exclusive breastfeeding would benefit not only any HIV+ women who choose this, but also all other breastfeeding women. Early recognition and treatment of mastitis and thrush, as well as teaching women preventative strategies, may be of particular value.

Another option is expressing and heat-treating milk – a small home pasteurizer is now available on the UK market for a modest cost, comparable to some weeks of purchasing formula. This method allows the possibility of transitioning to breastfeeding in the event that the baby was discovered to have been born HIV+. It might also be used during episodes of mastitis during exclusive breastfeeding, or at the time of rapid cessation (Rollins *et al.*, 2004).

Substantial investment in the infrastructure of milk banks throughout the UK could allow banked, donated, pasteurised human milk to be offered to every child born to an HIV+ woman. This might appear a utopian suggestion, but, in a wealthy society such as the UK, the main constraint is simply lack of will, based on our lack of value for breast milk and breastfeeding. In South Africa, a small charity collects donated milk for AIDS orphans, allowing women unaffected by HIV to contribute generously to the survival of these most vulnerable children (iThembaLethu, 2002).

WHO policies on HIV and infant feeding are intended for implementation globally, with European countries explicitly directed to use them (European Commission, 2004, p. 22); however, UK policy differs in its emphasis. The government has also not embraced other aspects of international recommendations on wider policies on infant feeding. The Global Strategy (WHO, 2003) recommends renewed government commitment, a national policy, implementation of the WHO Code, support for BFI and, above all, a high level of will. It is notable that, although the UK has had two HIV and Infant Feeding policies (and an update of the second), there is no national infant feeding policy; and, although the recommendation of exclusive breastfeeding has been endorsed, training materials for health professionals and leaflets for mother have yet to appear. An evaluation of the situation in Europe shows that there is no room for complacency in the current ability to protect, promote or support breastfeeding in the UK (European Commission, 2003). Much remains to be planned and implemented before women who wish to breastfeed exclusively would be likely to find appropriate support from the health services, employers, or communities. The Global Strategy notes that formula fed infants are at particular risk, and a review by Renfrew *et al.* (2003) indicates that, even in the UK where formula feeding has long been practised, there are unmet needs for support to ensure it is done safely.

Conclusions

HIV has uniquely challenged breastfeeding. It has illuminated our attitudes, throwing into stark relief the generally low cultural value of breastfeeding in the west. It has also exposed the realities of women's feeding choices, which have resulted in widespread global patterns of mixed feeding. Initial reaction to the threat of breast milk transmission was to abandon breastfeeding. Recommendations for women in resource-poor regions of the world appear to have shifted from the uncompromising pursuit of achieving full formula feeding for all HIV+ women to balancing risks and endorsing either exclusive formula feeding or exclusive breastfeeding while ensuring that wide social and health service support is available for exclusive breastfeeding in general. As the highest tide of enthusiasm for replacing breastfeeding recedes slightly, it is noticeable that we are left with the orthodoxy that HIV+ women in developed countries must avoid it. The exact legal position of health workers who might be asked to support breastfeeding for an HIV+ woman remains unclear.

At the same time, investigation of the mechanisms of HIV transmission has helped to deepen our understanding of breastfeeding and the biological differences between exclusive and mixed breastfeeding. The results of the Durban study (Cousoudis *et al.*, 1999, 2001) showed that exclusively breastfed babies had MTCT rates similar to never-breastfed babies in the early months, with mixed fed babies having the greatest risk of HIV. The Nduati *et al.* (2000) study showed that formula feeding could reduce HIV transmission, but did not improve mortality during the first two years, even in a relatively 'safe' African setting. Results of pilot programmes which subsidised or gave formula to women in resource-poor settings sharpened awareness of the infrastructure necessary for reducing the riskiness of replacing breastmilk with even the best available substitutes. The latest recommendations emphasise a choice between two exclusive feeding methods, with individual calculation of which is best, and recognise the support need to sustain either. The acute case of HIV has demonstrated the breadth of social and personal support required to help women achieve adequately safe infant feeding.

In the UK, the relative lack of what might be termed 'breastfeeding social capital' – the capacity for families, communities, government, employers and health professionals to value and foster breastfeeding – has been made evident. A rush to advise women not to breastfeed has left its mark. Although recent research demonstrates how the choice of feeding methods cannot be clear-cut, the presumption remains that formula feeding is the only choice for women in the UK. Our speedy sacrifice of human milk banks flagged up our deeply ambivalent attitude to the life-giving fluid which comes from women's bodies.

Globally, research continues and looks set to focus on safer breastfeeding practice to reduce risks of HIV transmission. Questions of importance for everyone interested in infant feeding issues in the UK remain. What evidence would we accept as good enough to change our current advice to HIV+ women, of avoiding breastfeeding, to a more even-handed policy, which would emphasise an informed assessment of each woman's individual circumstances? How can we start a discussion of these issues involving many sections of society? Can we build our capacity so that, if we want to, we have the knowledge, expertise and social support available to enable women (whatever their HIV status) to breastfeed exclusively for six months if they so choose? Finally, what will we do if, or when, we discover a new disease that may be transmitted via women's milk? Have we learned any useful lessons? Or would we be doomed to repeat our immediate abandonment of breastfeeding in the face of uncertainty?

Case 1

At an antenatal session where you are discussing screening tests, a pregnant woman is deciding whether she will have the HIV test. She asks you what the implications are for her feeding choices. 'I want to breastfeed my baby, but I heard about this HIV+ woman who was taken to court because she was breastfeeding. What could happen to me if I test positive?'

In this situation:

- What information do you need?
- Where will you get this information? Is it available to hand in the place where you conduct pre-screening counselling? Is it covered in the information you give to every woman before she decides whether to have an HIV test?
- What issues of professional ethics and policy of your employing Trust do you need to consider? Will other health care professionals who meet this woman feel able to support the decision she comes to?
- What support would you need for yourself in this situation? Where would you get this?
- Are there particular cultural issues you need to consider if the mother is British-born or if she is African?

Case 2

A pregnant woman, diagnosed HIV+ a few years ago, comes to the booking-in visit. She has been quite well since her diagnosis, and this is a planned pregnancy. She asks you what options she has for feeding her baby and what issues she should consider when she is making her feeding choice. She would also like a leaflet or contact numbers.

- What information do you need?
- Where will you get this information?
- What issues of professional ethics and policy of your employing Trust do you need to consider? Will other health care professionals who meet this woman feel able to support the decision she comes to?
- What support would you need for yourself in this situation? Where would you get this?
- Are there particular cultural issues you need to consider if the mother is British-born or if she is African?

Magda Sachs

Case 3

You visit a new mother and her baby in her home. You know from her notes that she is HIV+. When you see her, everything is going well; she has chosen to breastfeed and she and her baby are off to a good start. She asks you if there are any particular things she needs to know about breastfeeding, in view of her HIV status.

- What information do you need?
- Does professional practice in your local area already adequately support exclusive breastfeeding up to 6 months and good breastfeeding management for all women? Is there a referral structure for women experiencing difficulties?
- What issues of professional ethics and policy of your employing Trust do you need to consider?
- What support would you need for yourself in this situation? Where would you get this?
- Are there particular cultural issues you need to consider if the mother is British-born or if she is African? Are there further issues to cover if she is an asylum seeker?

Case 4

A woman with a three-month old baby has been breastfeeding and things are going well. She has just been told that she has been in a situation in which she has been exposed to HIV infection, and she needs to know what to do about feeding her baby.

In this situation:

- What will be the immediate information you need? What will you suggest for her to do for the baby's next feed?
- What further information do you need? Where will you get this?
- What support would you need for yourself in this situation? Where would you get this?
- What issues of professional ethics and policy of your employing Trust do you need to consider? What other professionals are available and should be involved?
- What further sources of support would you suggest for this woman?
- Are there particular cultural issues you need to consider if the mother is British-born or if she is African?

192

References

All-Party Parliamentary Group on AIDS (2003) *Migration and HIV: Improving Lives in Britain*. All-Party Parliamentary Group on AIDS, London.

Armstrong, H. C. (1991) International recommendations for consistent breast-feeding definitions *Journal of Human Lactation*, **7**, 51–4.

Baby Milk Action (2001) Nestlé uses HIV to push infant formula in Africa in battle with Wyeth. *Baby Milk Action Newsletter*, **30**, 3.

Balmer, S. E. and Wharton, B. A. (1992) Human milk banking at Sorrento Maternity Hospital, Birmingham. *Archives of Disease in Childhood*, **67**, 556–9.

Baxter, J. and Bennett, R. (2000) What do pregnant women think about antenatal HIV testing? *RCM Midwives Journal*, **3**, 308–11.

BBC News (1999a) Baby must have HIV test. http://news.bbc.co.uk/1/hi/health/437358.stm [Accessed September 1999].

BBC News (1999b) Parents flee over baby's HIV test. http://news.bbc.co.uk/1/hi/health/450855.stm [Accessed September 1999].

BBC News (2000a) HIV baby case to go to Europe. http://news.bbc.co.uk/1/hi/health/574883.stm [Accessed February 2000].

BBC News (2000b) Asylum policy 'risks spreading HIV'. http://news.bbc.co.uk/1/hi/health/702982.stm [Accessed April 2000].

BBC News (2001) HIV nurses 'pose no risk'. http://news.bbc.co.uk/1/hi/health/1113408.stm [Accessed November 2004].

BBC News (2002) Testing plan over HIV nurse fears. http://news.bbc.co.uk/1/hi/health/2143624.stm [Accessed November 2004].

Beatrice (2000) Choices. *Positively Women Newsletter*, May/June, 3 and 8.

Bott, J. (2000a) HIV screening issues for midwives. *British Journal of Midwifery*, **8**, 72–8.

Bott, J. (2000b) HIV screening during pregnancy: gender issues. *British Journal of Midwifery*, **8**, 174–7.

Brahams, D. (1999) Court order for HIV-1 test for baby. *Lancet*, **354**, 884.

The Breastfeeding and HIV International Transmission Study (BHITS) (2004) Late postnatal transmission of HIV-1 in breast-fed children: an individual patient data meta-analysis. *The Journal of Infectious Diseases*, **189**, 2154–66.

Bulterys, M. (2000) Breastfeeding in women with HIV (letter). *Journal of the American Medical Association*, **284**, 956.

Burke, J. (2004) Infant HIV infection: acceptability of preventative strategies in central Tanzania. *AIDS Education and Prevention*, **16**, 415–25.

Burt, A. and Thackray, J. (2000) Families and children. In *Advising Clients with HIV and AIDS* (eds. I. Manley and A. Sherr), pp. 80–118. Butterworths, London.

Chantry, C. J., Morrison, P., Panchula, J., Rivera, C., Hillyer, G., Zorill, C. and Diaz, C. (2000) Effects of lipolysis or heat treatment on HIV-1 provirus in breast milk. *Journal of Acquired Immune Deficiency Syndromes*, **24**, 325–9.

Cohen, R. J., Brown, K. H., Rivera, L. L. and Dewey, K. G. (1999) Promoting exclusive breastfeeding for 4–6 months in Honduras: attitudes of mothers and barriers to compliance. *Journal of Human Lactation*, **15**, 9–18.

Coll, O., Fiore, S., Floridia, M., Grosch-Worner, I., Giaquinto, C., Guiliano, M., Lindgren, S., Lyall, H., Mandelbrot, L., Newell, M. L., Peckham, C., Rudin, C., Semprini, A. E., Taylor, G., Thorne, C. and Tovo, P. A. (2002) Pregnancy and HIV infection: a European consensus on management. *AIDS*, **16**(suppl. 2), S1–S18.

Cook, R. J. and Dickens, B. M. (2002) Human rights and HIV-positive women. *International Journal of Obstetrics and Gynecology*, **77**, 55–63.

Cortina-Borja, M., Cliffe, S., Tookey, P., Williams, D., Cubitt, W. D. and Peckham, C. S. (2004) HIV prevalence in pregnant women in an ethnically diverse population in the UK: 1998–2002. *AIDS*, **18**, 535–40.

Coutsoudis, A., Pillay, K., Spooner, E., Kuhn, L. and Coovadia, H. M. (1999) Influence of infant-feeding patterns on early mother-to-child transmission of HIV-1 in Durban, South Africa: a prospective cohort study. South African Vitamin A Study Group. *Lancet*, **354**, 471–6.

Coutsoudis, A., Coovadia, H. M., Pillay, K. and Kuhn, L. (2000) Breastfeeding in women with HIV (letter). *Journal of the American Medical Association*, **284**, 956–7.

Coutsoudis, A., Pillay, K., Kuhn, L., Spooner, E., Tsai, W. Y. and Coovadia, H. M. (2001a) Method of feeding and transmission of HIV-1 from mothers to children by 15 months of age: prospective cohort study from Durban, South Africa. *AIDS*, **15**, 379–87.

Coutsoudis, A., Coovadia, H., Pillay, K. and Kuhn, L. (2001b) Are HIV-infected women who breastfeed at increased risk of mortality? *AIDS*, **15**, 653–5.

Coutsoudis, A., Goga, A. E., Rollins, N., Coovadia, H. M. and Child Health Group (2002) Free formula milk for infants of HIV-infected women: blessing or curse? *Health Policy And Planning*, **17**, 154–60.

Coutsoudis, A., Pillay, K., Spooner, E., Coovadia, H. M., Pembrey, L. and Newell, M. L. (2003) Morbidity in children born to women infected with human immunodeficiency virus in South Africa: does mode of feeding matter? *Acta Paediatrica*, **92**, 890–5.

Coutsoudis, A. (2005) Breastfeeding and the HIV positive mother: the debate continues. *Early Human Development*, **81**, 87–93.

Creighton, S., Seithi, G., Edwards, S. G. and Miller, R. (2004) Dispersal of HIV positive asylum seekers: national survey of UK healthcare providers. *British Medical Journal*, **329**, 322–3.

Cutting, W. A. M. (1992) Breastfeeding and HIV infection: advice depends on the circumstances. *British Medical Journal*, **305**, 788.

Dallas Morning News (2003) Daycare owner charged with breast-feeding someone else's baby. 3 June.

Davies, S. (2000) HIV universal voluntary testing in pregnancy – should midwives routinely recommend the test? *MIDIRS Midwifery Digest*, **10**, 280–4.

de Cock, K. M., Fowler, M. G., Mercier, E., de Vincenzi, I., Saba, J., Hoff, E., Alnwick, D. J., Rogers, M. and Shaffer, N. (2000) Prevention of Mother-to-Child HIV Transmission in resource-poor countries. *Journal of the American Medical Association*, **283**, 1175–82.

de Paoli, M. M., Manongi, R. and Klepp, K. I. (2002) Counsellors' perspectives on antenatal HIV testing and infant feeding dilemma facing women with HIV in Northern Tanzania. *Reproductive Health Matters*, **10**, 144–56.

de Wagt, A. and Clark, D. (2004) *A review of UNICEF experience with the distribution of free infant formula for infants of HIV-infected mothers in Africa*. Academy for Educational Development, Washington, DC. Available at: http://womenchildrenhiv.org/wchiv?page=wx-resource&rid=830–41985&topic=if&ty.

Department of Health (1994) *Guidelines for Offering Voluntary Named HIV Anti-body Testing to Women Receiving Ante-natal Care*. Department of Health, London.

Department of Health (1999a) *HIV and Infant Feeding*. Department of Health, London.

Department of Health (1999b) *Better for Your Baby?* Department of Health, London.

Department of Health (2001) *HIV and Infant Feeding*. Department of Health, London.

Department of Health (2002) *New Recommendation Offers Mothers Support to Mark National Breastfeeding Awareness Week*. http://www.dh.gov.uk/PublicationsAndStatistics/PressReleases/PressReleasesNotices/fs/en?CONTENT_ID=4046831&chk=QSo7AP.

Department of Health (2004a) *NHS Maternity statistics, England: 2002–03*. http://www.publications.doh.gov.uk/public/sb0410.pdf.

Department of Health (2004b) *HIV and Infant Feeding* (updated). Department of Health, London.

Department of Health and Social Security (1988) *HIV Infection, Breastfeeding and Human Milk Banking*. PL/CMO(88)13 PL/CNO(88)7. Department of Health and Social Security, London.

Department of Health and Social Security (1989) *HIV Infection, Breastfeeding and Human Milk Banking in the United Kingdom.* PL/CMO(89) 4 PL/CNO(89)3. Department of Health and Social Security, London.

Dhar, J. (2001) *Perinatal Care Plan.* BHIVA. http://www.bhiva.org/chiva/protocols/plan.html.

Drozdowska, T. M. (2001) Informed choice: infant feeding and HIV. *British Journal of Midwifery,* **9**, 368–71.

Dunn, D. T., Newell, M. L., Ades, A. E. and Peckham, C. S. (1992) Risk of human immunodeficiency virus type 1 transmission through breastfeeding. *Lancet,* **340**, 585–8.

Dyer, C. (1999) Baby to be tested for HIV against parents' wishes. *British Medical Journal,* **319**, 658.

Dyer, C. (2002) Asylum seeking mother to fight for milk tokens. *The Guardian,* 9 May.

European Collaborative Study (2001) HIV-infected pregnant women and vertical transmission in Europe since 1986. *AIDS,* **15**, 761–70.

European Commission, Directorate Public Health and Risk Assessment (2004) *EU Project on Promotion of Breastfeeding in Europe. Protection, Promotion and Support of Breastfeeding in Europe: a Blueprint for Action.* European Commission, Luxembourg.

European Commission, Directorate Public Health and Risk (2003) *EU Project on Promotion of Breastfeeding in Europe. Protection, Promotion and Support of Breastfeeding Europe: Current Situation.* European Commission, Directorate for Public Health, Luxembourg.

FIGO (2003) *Recommendations on Ethical Issues in Obstetrics and Gynecology by the FIGO Committee for the Ethical Aspect of Human Reproduction and Women's Health.* FIGO, London.

Fildes, V. (1986) *Breast Bottles and Babies: a History of Infant Feeding.* Edinburgh University Press, Edinburgh.

Finigan, V. (2002) Infant feeding choices for mothers who are HIV positive. *Professional Nurse,* **18**, 19–21.

Frederick, T., Mascola, L., Tucker, D., Jackson, J. and George, J. (1997) Breastfeeding and disease progression among perinatally HIV-infected children in Los Angeles County (LAC). *AIDSLINE MED/97926745 4th Conference on Retroviruses and Opportunistic Infections,* Chicago, January, abstract no. 720.

Foster, C. and Lyall, H. (2005) Current guidelines for the management for UK infants born to HIV-1 infected mothers. *Early Human Development,* **81**, 103–10.

Gaillard, P., Fowler, M. G., Dabis, F., Coovadia, H., Van Der Horst, C., Van Rompay, K., Ruff, A., Taha, T., Thomas, T., De Vincenzi, I., Newell, M. L.

and Ghent IAS Working Group on HIV in Women and Children (2004) Use of antiretroviral drugs to prevent HIV-1 transmission through breast-feeding: from animal studies to randomized clinical trials. *Journal of Acquired Immune Deficiency Syndromes*, **35**(2), 178–87.

Golden, J. (1996) *A Social History of Wet Nursing in America: from Breast to Bottle*. Cambridge University Press, Cambridge.

Goldman, A. S. (2001) Immune system development in relation to the duration of exclusive breastfeeding. In: *Developmental Readiness of Normal Full Term Infants to Progress from Exclusive Breastfeeding to the Introduction of Complementary Foods* (eds. A. J. Naylor and A. L. Morrow). The Linkages Project & Wellstart International, Washington.

Greiner, T., Sachs, M. and Morrison, P. (2002) The choice by HIV-positive women to exclusively breastfeed should be supported (letter). *Archives of Pediatric and Adolescent Medicine*, **156**, 87–8.

Grellier, R. (2000) 'Everyone is scared of it inside so they start being a bit irrational': HIV/AIDS education within midwifery. *Midwifery*, **16**, 56–67.

Haider, R., Ashworth, A. and Kabir, I. (2000) Effect of community-based peer counsellors on exclusive breastfeeding practices in Dhaka, Bangaldesh: a randomised controlled trial. *Lancet*, **356**, 1643–7.

Hamlyn, B., Brooker, S., Olienikova, K. and Woods, S. (2002) *Infant Feeding 2000*. The Stationery Office, London.

Harrison, R. and Corbett, K. (1999) Screening of pregnant women for HIV: the case against. *Practicing Midwife*, **2**, 24–9.

Howie, P. W., Forsyth, J. S., Ogston, S. A., Clark, A. du V. and Flory, C. (1990) Protective effect of breast feeding against infection. *British Medical Journal* **300**, 11–16.

Humphrey, J. and Iliff, P. (2001) Is breast not best? Feeding babies born to HIV-positive mothers: bringing balance to a complex issue. *Nutrition Reviews* **59**, 119–27.

IBFAN/ICDC (2001) *The International Code, HIV and Breastfeeding*. IBFAN/ICDC, Penang http://www.ibfan.org/english/codewatch/lwtd01/lwtdhiv01.html.

Iliff, P. J., Piwoz, E. G., Tavengwa, N. V., Zunguza, C. D., Marinda, E. T., Nathoo, K. J., Moulton, L. H., Ward, B. J., Humphrey, J. H. and ZVITAMBO study group (2005) Early exclusive breastfeeding reduces the risk of postnatal HIV-1 transmission and increases HIV-free survival. *AIDS*, **19**(7), 699–708.

iThembaLethu (2002) *Breast Milk Bank*. http://www.ithembalethu.org.za/bmbank.htm [Accessed 10 September 2004].

Jeffery, B. S. and Mercer, K. G. (2000) Pretoria pasteurisation: a potential method for the reduction of postnatal mother to child transmission of the human immunodeficiency virus. *Journal of Tropical Pediatrics*, **46**, 219–23.

John-Stewart, G., Mbori-Ngacha, D., Epkini, R., Janoff, E. N., Nkengasong, J., Read, J. S., Van de Perre, P., Newell, M. L. and Ghent IAS Working Group on HIV in Women and Children (2004) Breast-feeding and transmission of HIV-1. *Journal of Acquired Immune Deficiency Syndromes*, **35**, 196–202.

Kaufmann, T. (2001) Feedback on HIV antenatal testing. *RCM Midwives Journal*, **4**, 216–17.

Kent, G. (2001a) Should HIV-positive mothers use infant formula? *The Health Exchange*, April, 8–9.

Kent, G. (2001b) Breastfeeding: a human rights issue? *Development*, **44**, 93–8.

Kent, G. (in press) HIV/AIDS, infant feeding and human rights. In: *Adequate Food as a Human Right: its Meaning and Application in Development*, (eds. U. Kracht and W. Barthe Eide). Intersentia, Belgium.

Kooniz-Booher, P., Burkhalter, B., de Wagt, A., Illif, P. and Willumsen, J. (eds.) (2004) *HIV and Infant feeding: a compliation of programmatic evidence*. Published for UNICEF and the US Agency for International Development by the Quality Assurance Project (QAP). University Research Co, Bethesda.

Kourtis, A. P., Butera, S., Ibegbu, C., Belec, L. and Duerr, A. (2003) Breast milk and HIV-1: vector of transmission or vehicle of protection? *Lancet*, **3**, 787–93.

Kramer, M. S. and Kakuma, R. (2001) Optimal duration of exclusive breast-feeding (Cochrane Review). In: *Cochrane Library, Issue 1*, 2002. Update Software, Oxford.

Kramer, M., Chalmers, B., Hodnett, E., Sevkovskaya, A., Dzikovich, I., Shapiro, S., Collet, J. P., Vanilovich, I., Mezen, I., Ducruet, T., Shishko, G., Zubovich, V., Mknuik, D., Gluchanina, E., Dombrovskiy, V., Ustinovitch, A., Kot, T., Bogdanovich, N., Ovchinikova, L., Helsing, E. and PROBIT Study Group (Promotion of Breastfeeding Intervention Trial) (2001) Promotion of breastfeeding intervention trial (PROBIT): a randomised trial in the Republic of Belarus. *Journal of the American Medical Association*, **285**, 413–20.

Kumalo, P. V. (2002) Bottle feeding intervention in asylum seekers in the *UK International Conference on AIDS*, Abstract No. F11979.

Kyenkya-Isabirye, M. and Armstrong, H. (1992) Is there a problem with breast-feeding in Africa? *Breastfeeding Review*, **2**, 254–8.

Labbok, M., Clark, D. and Goldman, A. S. (2004) Breastfeeding: maintaining an irreplaceable immunological resource. *Nature*, **4**, 565–72.

Labbok, M. (2000) What is the definition of breastfeeding? *La Leche League Breastfeeding Abstracts*, **19**, 19–20.

Lancet Editorial (1988) HIV infection, breastfeeding and human milk banking. *Lancet*, **2**, 143–4.

Latham, M. C. and Greiner, T. (1998) Breastfeeding versus formula feeding in HIV infection (letter). *Lancet*, **352**, 737.

Latham, M. C. and Kisanga, P. (2001) *Current Status of Protection, Support and Promotion of Breastfeeding in Four African Countries*. Unpublished monograph prepared for UNICEF.

Lawrence, R. A. and Lawrence, R. M. (1999) *Breastfeeding: a Guide for the Medical Profession*. Mosby, St Louis.

Lucas, A. (1987) AIDS and human milk bank closures. *Lancet*, **1**, 1092–3.

Lucas, A. and Cole, T. J. (1990) Breast milk and neonatal necrotising entercolitis. *Lancet*, **336**, 1519–23.

Martyn, T. (2001) Saviours or culprits? HIV, infant feeding and commercial interests. *The Health Exchange*, April, 10–12.

Mbori-Ngacha, D., Nduati, R., John, G., Reilly, M., Richardson, B., Mwatha, A., Ndinya-Achola, J., Bwayo, J. and Kreiss, J. (2001) Morbidity and mortality in breastfed and formula-fed infants of HIV-1-infected women: a randomised clinical trial. *Journal of the American Medical Association*, **286**, 2413–20.

McClain, V. (2002) Breastmilk as big business. http://www.anotherlook.org/ [Accessed 1 September 2004].

McLeish, J. (2002) *Mothers in Exile: Maternity Experiences of Asylum Seekers in England*. Maternity Alliance, London.

Moriuchi, M. and Moriuchi, H. (2001) A milk protein lactoferrin enhances human T cell leukemia virus type 1 and suppressed HIV-1 infection. *Journal of Immunology*, **166**, 4231–6.

Morrison, P. (1999a) HIV and infant feeding: to breastfeed or not to breastfeed: the dilemma of competing risks Part 1. *Breastfeeding Review*, **7**, 5–13.

Morrison, P. (1999b) HIV and infant feeding: to breastfeed or not to breastfeed: the dilemma of competing risks Part 2. *Breastfeeding Review*, **7**, 11–18.

Morrison, P., Latham, M. C. and Greiner, T. (2001) UNAIDS policy ought to promote exclusive breastfeeding but instead may lead to its decline in Africa (eletter). http://bmj.bmjjournals.com/cgi/eletters/322/7285/512/e#12999.

Murray, P. E. (2002) Exposure to possible risk is unethical (letter). *Archives of Pediatic and Adolescent Medicine*, **156**, 87.

Nduati, R., John, G., Mbori-Ngacha, D., Richardson, B., Overbaugh, J., Mwatha, A., Ndinya-Achola, J., Bwayo, J., Onyango, F. E., Hughes, J. and Kreiss, J. (2000) Effect of breastfeeding and formula feeding on transmission of HIV-

1: a randomised clinical trial. *Journal of the American Medical Association*, **283**, 1167–74.

Nduati, R., Richardson, B. A., John, G., Mbori-Ngacha, D., Mwatha, A., Ndinya-Achola, J., Bwayo, J., Onyango, F. E. and Kreiss, J. (2001) Effect of breastfeeding on mortality among HIV-1 infected women: a randomised trial. *The Lancet*, **357**, 1651–5.

Newell, M. L., Coovadia, H., Cortina-Borja, M., Rollins, N., Gailliard, P. and Dabis, F. (2004) Mortality of infected and uninfected infants born to HIV-infected mothers in Africa: a pooled analysis. *Lancet*, **364**, 1236–43.

News-Medical (2004) HIV test after wrong woman's breast milk given to baby. http://www.news-medical.net/print_article.asp?print=yes&id=1098 [Accessed 4 May 2004].

Nicoll, A., McGarrigle, C., Brady, A. R., Ades, A. E., Tookey, P., Duong, T., Mortimer, J., Cliffe, S., Goldberg, D., Tappin, D., Hudson, C. and Peckham, C. (1998) Epidemiology and detection of HIV-1 among pregnant women in the United Kingdom: results from national surveillance 1988–96. *British Medical Journal*, **316**, 253–8.

Nicoll, A., Steele, R. and Mortimer, P. (1999) Pregnant women and testing for HIV. *Practicing Midwife*, **2**, 34–7.

Nicoll, A. and Peckham, C. S. (1999) Reducing vertical transmission of HIV in the UK. *British Medical Journal*, **319**, 1211–12.

O'Driscoll, S. (2002) HIV positive women seeking asylum (letter). *RCM Midwives Journal*, **5**, 268.

Orloff, S. L., Wallingford, J. C. and McDougal, J. S. (1993) Inactivation of human immunodeficiency virus type 1 in human milk; effects of intrinsic factors in human milk and of pasteurisation. *Journal of Human Lactation*, **9**, 13–19.

Ottewill, M. (2000) Antenatal screening for HIV: time to embrace change. *British Journal of Nursing*, **9**, 908–14.

Piwoz, E., Huffman, S. L., Lusk, D., Zehner, E. R. and O'Gara, C. (2001) *Early Breastfeeding Cessation as an Option for Reducing Postnatal Transmission of HIV in Africa*. Academy for Educational Development, Washington.

Piwoz, E., Illiff, P., Zunguza, C., Marinda, E., Nathoo, K., Moulton, L. and Ward, B. (2004a) Early introduction of non-human milk and solid foods increases the risk of postnatal HIV-1 transmission in Zimbabwe (conference abstract). *XV International AIDS Conference*, Bangkok, Thailand. Abstract number eJIAS mOpPb2008. http://www.medscape.com/ejiashome.

Piwoz, E. G., Ross, J. and Humphrey, J. (2004b) HIV transmission during breastfeeding: knowledge, gaps and challenges for the future. *Advances in Experimental Medicine and Biology*, **544**, 195–211.

Read, J. S. and Committee on Pediatric AIDS (2003) Human milk, breastfeeding, and transmission of Human Immunodeficiency Virus Type 1 in the United States. *Pediatrics*, **112**, 1196–205.

Renfrew, M. J., Ansell, P. and Macleod, K. L. (2003) Formula feed preparation: helping reduce the risks; a systematic review. *Archives of Disease in Childhood*, **88**, 855–8.

Rollins, N., Meda, N., Becquet, R., Coutsoudis, A., Humphrey, J., Jeffrey, B., Kanshana, S., Kuhn, L., Leroy, V., Mbori-Ngacha, D., McIntyre, J., Newell, M. L. and Ghent IAS Working Group on HIV in Women and Children (2004) Preventing postnatal transmission of HIV-1 through breast-feeding: modifying infant feeding practices. *Journal of Acquired Immune Deficiency Syndromes*, **35**, 188–95.

Rollins, N. C., Filteau, S. M., Coutsoudis, A. and Tomkins, A. M. (2001) Feeding mode, intestinal permeability, and neopterin excretion: A longitudinal study in infants of HIV-infected South African women. *Journal of Acquired Immune Deficiency Syndromes*, **28**, 132–9.

Royal College of Midwives (1998) *HIV & AIDS; Position Paper 16a*. Royal College of Midwives, London.

Royal College of Midwives (2000) *HIV & Infant Feeding: Report of a Seminar*. Royal College of Midwives, London.

Royal College of Obstetricians and Gynecologists (2004) National study of HIV in pregnancy. *RCOG Newsletter*, **59**, 1.

Sachs, M. (2002) Exclusive breastfeeding. *MIDIRS Midwifery Digest*, **12**, 245–8.

Sedgh, G., Spiegelman, D., Larsen, U., Msamanga, G. and Fawzi, W. W. (2004) Breastfeeding and maternal HIV-1 disease progression and mortality. *AIDS*, **18**, 1043–9.

Seidel, G., Sewpaul, V. and Dano, B. (2000) Experiences of breastfeeding and vulnerability among a group of HIV-positive women in Durban, South Africa. *Health Policy and Planning*, **15**, 24–33.

Semba, R. D. and Neville, M. C. (1999) Breast-feeding, mastitis and HIV transmission: nutritional implications. *Nutrition Reviews*, **57**, 146–53.

Sharland, M., Gibb, D. M. and Tudor-Williams, G. (2002) Advances in the prevention and treatment of paediatric HIV infection in the United Kingdom. *Archives of Disease in Childhood*, **87**, 178–80.

Shentall, L. (2004) HIV and immigration. *Insight* (George House Trust newsletter), June/July, 3.

Spiro, A. (1992) HIV and breastfeeding. *New Generation*, March, 35.

Thairu, L. N., Pelto, G. H., Rollins, N. C., Bland, R. M. and Ntshangasa, N. (2005) Sociocultural influences on infant feeding decisions among HIV-infected women in rural Kwa-Zulu Natal, South Africa. *Maternal and Child Nutrition*, **1**, 2–10.

Tozzi, A. E., Pezzotti, P. and Greco, D. (1990) Does breast-feeding delay progression to AIDS in HIV-infected children? (letter). *AIDS*, **4**, 1293–4.

Uddin, S. (2003) *The No-Nonsense guide to HIV/AIDS*. New Internationalist Publications/Verso, Oxford.

UNFPA/UNAIDS/UNICEF/WHO Europe (2004) *Strategic Framework for the Prevention of HIV Infection in Infants in Europe*. World Health Organization, Copenhagen.

UNICEF UK Baby Friendly Initiative (2004) *Health Benefits of Breastfeeding* (updated list). http://www.babyfriendly.org.uk/benefits.asp.

UNICEF (2001) UNICEF *Statistics: Breastfeeding and Complementary Feeding*. http://www.childinfo.org/eddb/brfeed/current1.htm [Accessed 2 January 2005].

United Kingdom Association for Milk Banking (2004) http://www.ukamb.org/ [Accessed 2 September 2004].

WABA and UNICEF (2003) *HIV and Infant Feeding: a Report of a WABA-UNICEF colloquium*. WABA, Penang.

Walker, A. W. (2001) Gastrointestinal development in relation to the duration of exclusive breastfeeding. In *Developmental Readiness of Normal Full Term Infants to Progress from Exclusive Breastfeeding to the Introduction of Complementary Foods* (eds. A. J Naylor and A. L. Morrow). The Linkages Project & Wellstart International, Washington.

Warner, B. B. and Sapsford, A. (2004) Misappropriated human milk: fantasy, fear and fact regarding infectious risk. *Newborn and Infant Nursing Reviews*, **4**, 56–61.

White, E. (1999) *Breastfeeding and HIV/AIDS: the Research, the Politics and the Women's Responses*. McFarland & Co, Jefferson.

White, J. (2002) Caring for HIV 'indeterminate' infants and their parents. *Community Practitioner*, **75**, 168–70.

WHO (1987) *Breast-feeding/Breast Milk and Human Immunodeficiency Virus (HIV)*. World Health Organization, Geneva.

WHO (1991) *Indicators for Assessing Breastfeeding Practices. Report of an Informal Meeting*. World Health Organization, Geneva.

WHO (1992) *Consensus Statement from the WHO/UNICEF Consultation on HIV Transmission and Breast-feeding*. World Health Organization, Geneva.

WHO (2000a) *Mastitis: Causes and Management*. World Health Organization, Geneva.

WHO (2000b) *New Data on the Prevention of Mother-to-child Transmission of HIV and Their Policy Implications: Conclusions and Recommendations.* World Health Organization, Geneva.

WHO (2002c) *Report of the Expert Consultation on the Optimal Duration of Exclusive Breastfeeding.* World Health Organization, Geneva.

WHO (2004) *Prevention of Mother-to-Child Transmission of HIV; generic training package; Participant Manual.* World Health Organization, Geneva.

WHO and UNICEF (2003) *Global Strategy for Infant and Young Child Feeding.* World Health Organization, Geneva.

WHO/UNICEF/UNAIDS (1998) *HIV and Infant Feeding: a Review of HIV Transmission Through Breastfeeding.* World Health Organization, Geneva.

WHO/UNICEF/UNAIDS (2000) *HIV and Infant Feeding Counselling: a Training Course; Trainer's Guide.* World Health Organization, Geneva.

WHO/UNICEF/UNFPA/UNAIDS (2003a) *HIV and Infant Feeding: Guidelines for Decision-makers* (revised). World Health Organization, Geneva.

WHO/UNICEF/UNFPA/UNAIDS (2003b) *HIV and Infant Feeding: a Guide for Health-care Managers and Supervisors* (revised). World Health Organization, Geneva.

WHO/UNICEF/UNFPA/UNAIDS (2004) *HIV Transmission Through Breastfeeding: a Review of the Available Evidence.* World Health Organization, Geneva.

Willumsen, J. F., Filteau, S. M., Coutsoudis, A., Newell, M. L., Rollins, N. C., Coovadia, H. M. and Tomkins, A. M. (2003) Breastmilk RNA viral load in HIV-infected South African women: effects of subclinical mastitis and infant feeding. *AIDS,* **17**, 407–14.

Wolf, L. E., Lo, B., Becherman, K. P., Dorenbaum, A., Kilpatrick, S. and Weintrub, P. S. (2001) When parents reject interventions to reduce postnatal human immunodeficiency virus transmission. *Archives of Pediatric and Adolescent Medicine,* **155**, 927–33.

World Health Assembly (2001) *WHA 54.2 Infant and Young Child Feeding.* http://www.who.int/gb/ebwha/pdf_files/WHA54/ea54r2.pdf. World Health Assembly, Geneva.

World Health Assembly (2004) *Resolution 54.2.* http://www.ibfan.org/english/resource/who/whares542.html. World Health Assembly, Geneva.

Wright, H. (2004) Breastfeeding and the transmission of HIV. *British Journal of Midwifery,* **12**, 88–92.

CHAPTER 6

Exploring attitudes towards infant feeding

Sue Battersby

Introduction

Infant feeding is a highly charged and emotional subject for both mothers and health professionals. There has been a concerted effort by health professionals and the government in the UK over the last 15 years to increase both the breastfeeding initiation and continuation rates. Despite this effort, the increase in these rates has been slow, particularly in the lower socio-economic occupational groups (Hamlyn *et al.*, 2002). The mother often takes the decision about the method of infant feeding in early pregnancy, or even before becoming pregnant (Earle, 2000). The decision is not usually taken lightly and, whether the mother decides to breast or bottle feed her baby, depends on a variety of conscious and unconscious psychological, physical and social factors. Her attitude to infant feeding will be one of the factors involved in this process. The midwives' and health professionals' attitudes towards infant feeding may also be influential on the mother's decision and may influence the nature of the support and guidance given to mothers. The literature on infant feeding has largely focused upon challenging the unhelpful practices that hinder breastfeeding promotion and support by proposing practical and technical solutions. Little research has been conducted which addresses the complex issue of attitudes (Smale, 1998). Jamieson (1997) suggests that breastfeeding practices are interlinked with cultural attitudes and that professionals need to be aware of their own social and cultural learning which will influence their views.

The focus of this chapter is to examine the attitudes related to infant feeding. The chapter will begin by defining what is meant by attitudes and will discuss the formation of women's attitudes towards infant feeding. This will include an exploration of the issues that may influence the formation of these attitudes and how these issues may impinge on the woman's choice of infant feeding. Consideration will be given to how women's attitudes to infant feeding may be changed. Midwives and health professionals' attitudes to infant feeding will then be examined and any additional influences that may affect their attitudes will be identified. This is important as midwives often possess the same social background as many of the women for whom they care, but their personal and professional values may either enhance or impinge upon that care. The potential effect of the midwives' attitudes on the mothers' decision to breastfeed and how the midwives' attitudes can affect the support and guidance given to breastfeeding mothers will then be examined. The midwives' attitudes towards women who bottle feed with infant formula will be considered. Finally, a model will be presented to enable midwives and health professionals to examine their attitudes and to think about how they can improve care and support for both breast and bottle feeding mothers.

Defining attitudes

Eiser (1986) stated that the term 'attitude' is probably used more frequently than any other in social psychology, but what do we mean by attitude? If we have a certain attitude towards something or someone it implies that we have feelings or thoughts of like or dislike, approval or disapproval, attraction or repulsion about that thing or person. This is a rather simplistic view, however. The study of attitudes is somewhat more complex and, although there are studies looking at the attitudes of health professionals towards breastfeeding in particular, few authors define the concept. Ajzen (1988, p. 4) asserts what most contemporary social psychologists seem to agree with is that 'the characteristic attribute of attitude is its evaluative (pro-con, pleasant-unpleasant) nature'. The definition to be used within this chapter is that provided by Ajzen (1988) and defines an attitude as:

> ... a disposition to respond favourably or unfavourably to an object, person, institution, or event.

Early theorists advocated that attitudes were composed of three elements; a cognitive (knowledge), affective (emotional) and a behavioural (conative) element (Katz and Stotland, 1959). Although the different elements of attitudes have been questioned, what remains important is that to have an attitude towards an object or thing one must have some knowledge of the domain in question.

Deaux *et al.* (1988) argue that it is not necessary to have a great deal of knowledge to form an attitude, but there must be sufficient knowledge to be able to represent the object to memory and, as a consequence, be able to think about it.

Attitude formation is a similarly complex notion. As Deaux *et al.* (1988) explain, there are many routes to attitude formation. The most obvious way of acquiring an attitude is through direct experience that leads on to an evaluation of the object. Direct experience enables learning to occur through a heuristic approach, i.e. an approach the enables an individual to develop attitudes through their own individual perspective. At the same time, social learning also forms a major factor in the development of attitudes. As Byron and Bryne (1987, p. 17) state:

> ...learning attitudes is a large part of socialisation, the process by which a wild helpless creature (a newborn baby) is transformed into a responsible and capable member of human society.

This means that attitudes are influenced by the society in which we live and as such are a large part of socialisation. Furthermore, attitudes are developed through a lifelong process and so are reinforced by cultural norms, experiences and beliefs.

Mothers' attitudes towards infant feeding

Mothers' attitudes towards infant feeding are not developed in isolation. They are, as already stated, developed in response to cultural norms, experiences and beliefs. Attitudes to infant feeding are formed within the family, which exists within a culture. Many women make the decision on how to feed their baby prior to conception or early in pregnancy, regardless of whether they intend to breast or bottle feed (Losch *et al.*, 1995). In her study of influences upon choices of method of infant feeding, Earle (2000) found that the majority of women, including those who intended to bottle feed, were aware of the benefits of breastfeeding for both infants and mothers. This demonstrates that, although women were knowledgeable about breastfeeding, for many of them other significant factors were involved in the decision of how they should feed their babies. Factors influencing a woman's decision could include direct experience with a previous child of her own or indirectly through the experiences of a relative or close friend. Alternatively, it could be an individual expression, which had resulted from her fear of her inability to successfully breastfeed (Hallawell and Brittle, 1995).

Women's experiences of infant feeding

The direct experiences of mothers are likely to have a profound effect upon their attitudes towards infant feeding. Previous experiences of infant feeding have been shown to have a direct impact on the mothers' choice of infant feeding method in a subsequent pregnancy. A mother who has previously had a positive experience of infant feeding will often adopt the same method of feeding for any subsequent children (Foster *et al.*, 1997). Role modelling family members, peers and friends has a strong influence on the formation of attitudes to infant feeding. In traditional societies, childbearing and nursing mothers are surrounded by a support system of female family members that not only offer support, but also pass down the art and knowledge of breastfeeding. There is well documented evidence that demonstrates the association between the mother's own mother's method of infant feeding and the method that a woman adopts herself (Foster *et al.*, 1997). Therefore if a woman was breastfed herself she is more likely to breastfeed her own children. Furthermore, it has been found that the mother's own mother has been found to be very influential in a woman's choice of infant feeding (Losch *et al.*, 1995). However, in some societies, particularly in areas of social and economic deprivation, there may be a long history of formula feeding with an associated loss of traditional knowledge of breastfeeding. Formula feeding has become the social norm and, as a consequence, many women in those areas will not have seen a relative or friend breastfeeding and will therefore have no or very limited direct experience of breastfeeding. With limited knowledge and no direct experience, it can be very difficult to form a positive attitude towards breastfeeding.

Many women opt to bottle feed their infants, with 31% commencing artificial feeding, as their initial method of feeding, in the UK (Hamlyn *et al.*, 2002). There are a number of possible reasons for this. One reason may be that there is a widespread lack of confidence in breastfeeding, which Renfrew *et al.* (2000) argue is endemic throughout the British culture. This lack of confidence could be a result of the increasing medicalisation of childbirth and infant feeding which has led to a growing doubt that the female body is able to reproduce or provide sustenance for the infant without the need for medical or technical intervention. A second reason may be that there is a strong belief in the western world that technology is scientific and therefore best. Some may see formula, quite erroneously, as equivalent to or even an advancement on breast milk because it is seen as being scientifically formulated to meet the needs of babies and infants.

Paternal attitudes towards infant feeding

The father's role and attitudes towards infant feeding may also have an influence on the mother's decision. Wylie and Verber (1994) and Losch *et al.* (1995) reported that the male partner has a strong influence upon the choice of infant feeding method. The partners will have been exposed to the same process of socialisation and will therefore have also developed attitudes towards infant feeding. Fraley *et al.* (1992) found that there were attitudinal differences between those fathers who intended their infant to be breastfed and those who intended their infant to be bottle fed. The fathers who wished their infant to be breastfed did so because they believed it was better for the baby, whilst those who wished their infant to be bottle fed believed breastfeeding spoils the breasts and it interferes with sex. Men may also feel that breastfeeding prevents their involvement and bonding with the newborn child (Earle 2000). Midwives have strived to make men more participative in childbearing and childrearing and have included fathers in antenatal classes, encouraging them to change nappies, bath their baby and care for the infant. Some mothers feel that their partners should also participate in feeding the infant. Earle (2000) interviewed 12 women about their decision to bottle feed. The women felt that bottle feeding would ensure more paternal involvement and provide them with periods away from childcare, thereby easing their role into motherhood.

Cultural perceptions of the female breast

Conflicting cultural believes about women's breasts can undermine a woman's desire to breast feed (Dykes and Griffiths, 1998) and also create problems for those who do breastfeed. Within western society, there has been an increasing sexualisation of women's breasts to the extent that within many countries, including England, breasts are viewed primarily as sexual objects and both men and women see breastfeeding as primitive and crude, especially if undertaken for more than the first few months. It appears that it is more acceptable in society to expose breasts within the tabloid press for erotic purposes than for breasts to be exposed for the purpose of feeding an infant. This leads to a conflict for women who have been taught through socialisation that the sexual aspects of women and the maternal aspects should be independent of each other (Stearns, 1999). Constantly viewing breasts as sexual can lead to feelings of disgust and embarrassment at the thought of breastfeeding for many women (Dykes and Griffiths, 1998).

Baumslag and Michels (1995) highlighted that women who are self-conscious about baring their breasts will seek alternative ways of infant feeding.

Palmer (1993) also believes that the sexualisation of the female breast has led to the breasts being appropriated by men, which has resulted in some men discouraging their partners to breastfeed. For those who choose to breastfeed the conflict may cause embarrassment when breastfeeding within the public domain (Pugliese, 2000).

Body image

Body image, which is also linked with sexuality, has achieved a very high profile within western culture, and Minchin (1998, p. 66) has singled out 'the cult of fitness and body consciousness' as having an impact upon mothers' decisions to breastfeed or not. Within societies, certain body shapes are deemed as fashionable and the shape and size of the breast are seen as critical within this context. A common misapprehension made by both women and men is that breastfeeding causes 'sagging' of the breasts. This cosmetic appearance is viewed as unacceptable by both men and women and may discourage some women from breastfeeding or cause their partners to be unsupportive towards it. This view is supported by the findings of Barnes *et al.* (1997) who reported an association between extreme attitudes to body shape and the reluctance to breastfeed. A notable finding from the study was that women who were preoccupied with their body shape were less likely to express intentions to breast feed. Conversely, a study by Stapleton (2002) found that some women with eating disorders purposely breastfed in the belief that it would help them to lose weight after the birth of their baby.

Good mothering

Current discourses on good mothering can also influence a woman's attitude towards infant feeding. Breastfeeding has become synonymous with good mothering (Murphy, 1999), and the current discourses on mothering emphasise that good mothers are supposed to breastfeed. Breastfeeding mothers are presented as choosing the most natural, unselfish and best possible feeding method for their infant. Health professionals are constantly expounding the mantra that 'breast is best' and UNICEF (1998, p. 13) states that all mothers should be informed of the benefits of breastfeeding in the antenatal period. Feminist texts highlight the tendency to portray breastfeeding as the natural responsibility of real women as mothers and consequently, those mothers who opt not to breastfeed their infant, especially when they know of the benefits both to themselves and their infants, open themselves to the charge of not being a good mother (Carter, 1995; Murphy, 1999).

Pain *et al.* (2001) studied the experiences of breastfeeding women in the North East of England. They reported that, although the women had formed their own strong opinions about how best to care for their babies, all felt under pressure to live up to the ideals of good mothering. The belief that 'breast is best' has the power to overcome the mother's own wishes, especially when breastfeeding is perceived in the same context as being a good mother. Murphy (1999, p. 187) postulates that, 'the "good mother" is deemed to be one who prioritizes her child's needs, even (or especially) where this entails personal inconvenience or distress'.

Even if a woman has had a negative experience of breastfeeding and, although she may wish to bottle feed any subsequent children, the desire to conform and be a good mother may override her negative experience and she may decide to breastfeed again. The participants in a qualitative study undertaken by Pain *et al.* (2001) highlighted how they felt that breastfeeding was perceived as part of a performance of good mothering in front of hospital staff, community midwives, family and friends, especially in the early postnatal period.

Recently there has been a return to the discourse which states that 'breast is best' by both mothers, health professionals and the media and there has been an increasing amount of criticism about mothers being 'bullied' if they do not wish to breastfeed (Burchill, 1999; Hope, 2000; Battersby, 2003a). Women who discontinue breastfeeding, whatever the reason, have to negotiate feelings of failure because they feel that others place value judgements on the basis that 'good' mothers breastfeed and 'successful' mothers continue to do so (Pain *et al.*, 2001).

The influence of the media

The influence of the media on attitudes towards infant feeding has recently been researched in both England and Australia (Henderson, 1999, Henderson *et al.*, 2000). The media portrays the norms of society and can form part of the socialisation process, which influences attitude formation. Henderson *et al.* (2000) studied British television programmes and newspaper articles for a month and recorded all references, both visual and verbal, made to infant feeding. The contents of 1396 television programmes, which included health and parenting programmes, medical drama, soap opera, news, documentary, daytime non-fiction and intermission advertisements, were analysed. They found 235 references to infant feeding within their television sample and 38 references within the 13 national newspapers sampled. The analysis of the television coverage demonstrated that bottle feeding occurred more frequently than breastfeeding, with only one scene being identified showing a baby that was being put to the breast. Bottle feeding was also presented as being less problematic than breastfeeding. The themes that arose related to breastfeeding were of the body being out of control, such as when the breasts were leaking milk, embarrassment and sexuality of breasts. Breastfeeding was represented as the domain of the higher social classes, whereas bottle feeding was associated with the 'ordinary' family. The representations of infant feeding within the press were mostly related to breastfeeding and were simply cursory comments, the majority of which were related to the problematic nature of breastfeeding. There were no visual images of breastfeeding, but there was one article on sperm donation that was illustrated with a baby feeding from a bottle. In Australia, similar findings were found in the press and popular magazines (Henderson, 1999). Whilst breastfeeding was seen as 'natural', it was also seen as problematic. Representations were strongly suggestive of the 'do's and 'don't's of practice, removing it from a natural process to one that needed strict guidance and control. The health professionals were portrayed as adopting a paternalistic role in order to persuade mothers to breastfeed.

There also appears to be a puritanical aspect within British society that leads to the censorship of adverts that refer to breastfeeding. It was reported in an Australian newspaper how, in a recent advert to encourage voting in the European elections, the Eurocrats chose the image of a baby deciding which nipple to feed from as the basis for their film campaign to encourage people to use their vote. The picture of an exposed nipple, however, proved too much for the British film censors, who decided that it had to be cut from the production before it could outrage cinema-goers in Britain (Barkham, 2004). An 'Iron Bru' advert several years earlier had a similar demise, when a poster promoting the drink by showing a baby breastfeeding with a thought bubble announcing its mother had been drinking 'Iron Bru', was banned because of complaints from the public. Not all European countries, however, have this puritanical view. In many Scandinavian countries, such as Sweden and Norway, breastfeeding is widely used to promote a wide range of products, including 'Norwegian Sild', a canned fish product.

Consumerism and infant feeding

Consumerism is a topic that is not often discussed within the midwifery discourse surrounding breastfeeding, but is certainly worthy of consideration. Woollett (1987) believes the purchasing of formula and the array of goods that go with it, can be seen as part of the general interest in convenience and processed food and the ownership of consumer durables. Mulford (1995) believes that, in the modern culture, the feeding bottle has become the icon for 'baby'. It is used in many settings as the symbol for baby-changing facilities, whilst gift-wrapping paper and birth congratulation cards frequently contain images of the feeding bottle. At the same time, many dolls are sold with feeding bottles as accessories. Whilst these images focus on bottle feeding as acceptable and, in many instances, the norm, there has also been a concomitant increasing focus on breastfeeding as pathological and lactation as a precarious body function requiring the guidance of health professionals (Wolf, 2000). Some women may decide not to breastfeed because of the current discourse, which portrays breastfeeding as difficult. However, some women will decide to breastfeed knowing that, if difficulties arise, infant formula is easily accessible.

Manufacturers are realising that if more women choose to breastfeed there are increasing opportunities for them to exploit women. Infant feeding is a multimillion dollar industry and with the increasing promotion of breastfeeding, manufacturers are identifying commercial products that they perceive as important and essential for the breastfeeding mothers. There has been a steady increase in the number of adverts for breast pumps, feeding bras, nipple ointments and breast pads. The need to have all these products to breastfeed a baby helps to reinforce the discourse that, although breastfeeding is 'natural', it can also be problematic. At the same time, the edict that states that breastfeeding is the cheaper option is being eroded through consumerism, which dictates that in order to breastfeed successfully a mother requires a wide range of expensive products.

Changing attitudes

Women can change their attitudes to infant feeding through the acquisition of new information. New knowledge, in the form of informal, small group, interactive and discursive breastfeeding education sessions, have been shown to change the attitude of antenatal women who have previously decided on bottle feeding (Fairbank *et al.*, 2000). Trying to increase a woman's knowledge of breastfeeding by the use of leaflets alone, on the other hand, has not been shown to be influential, unless it was included with other interventions (Fairbank *et al.*, 2000). Breastfeeding peer support workers have also been shown to be influential in helping women to select breastfeeding as their choice of infant feeding, especially in areas of social and economic deprivation where normally women would choose to bottle feed (Battersby, 2002a). In my evaluation of breastfeeding peer support programmes, peer support workers were shown to be able to impart knowledge of breastfeeding to women, without appearing coercive or bullying, through meeting the women antenatally either in their home, antenatal clinic or infant feeding workshops. Women who initially intended to bottle feed became very positive towards breastfeeding after personal experience of breastfeeding, and some even went on to train as breastfeeding peer supporters (Battersby, 2002a).

Simply changing a woman's attitude towards breastfeeding is not sufficient to bring about change. Breastfeeding is a social behaviour and for mothers to be successful there needs to be a conducive and supportive environment for breastfeeding. The task of converting public opinion back to the notion of breastfeeding as normal and 'first choice' is enormous and daunting. It is hoped that the slow but steady increase in breastfeeding rates, as revealed in the latest Infant Feeding Survey (Hamlyn *et al.*, 2002), will help to change attitudes towards breastfeeding, but a variety of other interventions also need to be adopted. These could include sessions on infant feeding within schools, including nursery schools, developing public awareness of the benefits of breastfeeding through promotional activities (e.g. those undertaken in National Breastfeeding Awareness Week) and better representation of breastfeeding within the media and television. Interventions should also include ways of developing better knowledge and understanding of the importance of breastfeeding by health professionals.

Midwives' attitudes to infant feeding

It is only recently that the issue of midwives' attitudes towards infant feeding have been addressed within the midwifery press; and this has been mostly through commentary rather than research. Many of these comments are related to breastfeeding. Renfrew *et al.* (2000, p. 11) state that:

> ... it would not seem appropriate for the first point of contact between an expectant mother, or one that is newly delivered, to be with someone who has entrenched views or adverse attitudes towards breastfeeding.

Midwives, as members of a particular society, will have similar direct experiences of, and socialisation to, infant feeding as the mothers for whom they care. Their personal attitudes, values and beliefs associated with infant feeding will be a consequence of their own socialisation process (Dykes, 1995). Therefore the issues addressed previously will also be relevant to midwives. The attitudes of midwives towards breastfeeding are usually perceived as being positive, but this may not be wholly accurate. Welford

(1995) explains that midwives' social attitudes to breastfeeding are varied, just as those of the rest of the population are, and consequently there will be some midwives who may not be comfortable with promoting breastfeeding or supporting breastfeeding mothers.

Through working with and observing midwives, and through current unpublished research that I am undertaking, there appears to be emerging a number of stances that midwives may take in regard to infant feeding (see Table 6.1). There has been an increasing amount of press coverage of the midwife (Type 1) who is perceived, both by other midwives and by women, as being over-zealous towards breastfeeding and who women feel have an anti-bottle feeding attitude. This leads women to feel like they are being coerced into breastfeeding against their will (Hope, 2000; Burchill, 1999). There is the middle of the road midwife (Type 2) who is pro-breastfeeding but also tries to be supportive of mothers who are bottle feeding, believing that all mothers have a right to informed choice; the majority of midwives will fall into this category. The third type of midwife (Type 3) is in the minority, but she is anti-breastfeeding and strongly believes that bottle feeding mothers are unsupported and neglected. Midwives need to consider which category they fall into and consider whether their attitudes support and protect women in their care, or whether their attitudes undermine women's confidence and ability to care for their infants.

Brosseau (1994) believes that many things shape midwives' attitudes towards breastfeeding, and these may originate consciously or subconsciously. As already stated, midwives will develop their attitudes towards infant feeding by the same processes as other women in their society. However, Brosseau (1994) highlights three factors that she believes particularly shape the health profession's attitudes towards breastfeeding. These factors are: personal experience; media and consumerism; and education. The issues are relevant to the formation of attitudes towards both breastfeeding and bottle feeding.

Table 6.1 The formation of midwives' attitudes to infant feeding.

Midwife			Feelings
Type 1	Pro breastfeeding	Anti bottle feeding	All babies should be breastfed regardless of the mother's wishes
Type 2	Accepts breastfeeding	Accepts bottle feeding	All women have a choice
Type 3	Anti-breastfeeding	Pro-bottle feeding	Believes many midwives over-zealous towards breastfeeding and bottle feeders neglected

Midwives' personal experiences of infant feeding

Many midwives feel that, as a professional, they are able to push aside their own personal feelings related to infant feeding and give the mother the holistic care they require. Renfrew *et al.* (2000) advocate that, should a health care professional have any ambivalent or adverse personal views based on their own experiences, these should not be allowed to enter into or colour their practice. However, in reality this is sometimes difficult to achieve.

The fact that a midwife's personal experiences can colour her impression of birth and affect the care that she gives to women in labour has been suggested by Thomas (2000) and, if that is the case, it is therefore also highly likely that a midwife's own personal experiences of breastfeeding can also affect the care she gives to a mother. There is limited research that has considered midwives' personal experiences of breastfeeding, and none that has considered midwives who have bottle fed their infants. This lack of research is not surprising when there is a paucity of research investigating women's experiences of breastfeeding. The studies that have explored this issue have demonstrated the complexity of breastfeeding, whilst also highlighting the individualistic nature of the meaning of breastfeeding for individual mothers (Bottorff, 1990; Dignam, 1995; Britton, 1997; Dykes and Williams, 1999). However, a study by McMulkin and Malone (1994) highlighted that midwives' professional experience and educational experiences of breastfeeding had very little influence on their personal experiences, although this study did not explore what effect the midwives' personal experience may have on her practice.

The influence of personal experiences on the support given to women

Personal experiences can be reflected in the way that midwives support the women in their care. Many midwives who have had personal experience of breastfeeding believe that it gives them a greater ability to understand women's concerns, feelings and actions, whilst others feel it enables them to empathise with and relate to mothers (Battersby, 2002b). It is difficult, however, to determine how a midwife will use her personal experiences in practice. A midwife who has successfully breastfed would be in a position to support and encourage a mother through her experience of breastfeeding. Alternatively, she may have breastfed her child or children successfully for a long period with relatively few problems and this could make it difficult for her to empathise with women who are having difficulty breastfeeding.

The midwife who has had a bad experience when breastfeeding may be more empathetic towards the women she cares for, or alternatively she could feel it is easier to encourage the mother to offer a formula feed. Finigan (2004, p. 229) believes that some midwives who bottle fed their babies may have difficulty giving information to breastfeeding women because they may have had difficulties themselves with breastfeeding, which has coloured 'their objectivity'. This is supported by Jamieson (1997), who suggests that a professional who has either had experience of bottle feeding or a bad personal experience of breastfeeding, either professionally or personally, may find that this has enforced a negative attitude and this may indicate a lack of belief in women's ability to breastfeed. It was very poignant when reading the comments made by midwives in my study of midwives' experiences of breastfeeding to find a midwife who believed, because she had failed to breastfeed successfully, she was a failure, not only as a mother but also as a midwife (Battersby, 2002b). Jamieson (1997) further argues that a negative attitude developed through a bad personal experience is especially powerful.

Media, consumerism and the midwife

The media and consumerism will affect midwives the same as the mothers they care for, therefore the issues related to media and consumerism discussed earlier are also relevant to midwives. An issue that is more pertinent to midwives and health professionals is the covert ways in which formula companies seek to endorse their products within the health care setting. The subject of formula milk advertisements will be addressed in the ways midwives learn about formula milk products, but there are also many other strategies that formula milk companies utilise. Many maternity hospitals and health care establishments have made a concerted effort to remove from their premises products and merchandise with milk company logos; this includes free samples of formula, information leaflets, notepads, wall calendars, diary covers, pens etc. It has been recognised that these products give subliminal messages to midwives and women that breastfeeding may be best, but there is always formula there if it is needed. Many milk companies also offer to sponsor conferences and similar activities. This is a tempting proposition for many establishments and groups, especially in the era where lack of finances is a limiting factor, but accepting sponsorship from these companies can endorse the company's product in the mind of the participants. Recently, milk companies have developed a new strategy of sponsoring bursaries for student midwives. This gives out the message that, if students will support milk companies, milk companies will support them. There are very few ways that breast milk can compete with the multimillion dollar formula milk companies, but the UK Department of Health is trying in a modest way to improve people's perception of breastfeeding by issuing free promotional products, such as pens and key rings, for National Breastfeeding Week each year. The more health professionals utilise and distribute these products the more the breastfeeding message will get across to their colleagues and the public.

Midwifery education

Midwives' knowledge of breastfeeding

Midwives play an important role in the promotion and support of breastfeeding. In order to give support to breastfeeding mothers, there has been a shift away from giving advice. Giving information enables a woman to make her own decisions rather than having them imposed upon her by health professionals. Despite this shift, there is evidence that conflicting advice is prevalent among health professionals and concerns have been raised about the deficits in health practitioners' knowledge of breastfeeding (Simmons, 2002). In England, the inclusion of infant feeding topics within basic midwifery curricula has been inconsistent. UNICEF UK Baby Friendly Initiative (2001, p. 3) recently questioned the standard of breastfeeding education for student midwives and health visitors because they found:

> ...without exception those facilities which have achieved or are working towards a baby friendly award have found it necessary to upgrade their staff training to reach the required standard. Many organisations and individuals have questioned why this catch-up training should be needed.

This deficit could have come about because midwives have been educated in a range of educational institutions and their education has occurred over a wide period of time. I found when interviewing midwives about their midwifery education related to infant feeding, that midwives who had been trained for six years or longer could recall very little infant feeding training, except for being taught the anatomy of the breast and the physiology of lactation (Battersby, 1999). Their practical education was even more variable than the classroom education, with some midwives believing that breastfeeding was very low profile and that they acquired few practical skills to enable them to assist breastfeeding mothers. The midwives complained that within their midwifery education, the focus was on 'getting those forty deliveries', and other areas, such as infant feeding, were perceived as inferior. A very important issue that arose from this study was that none of the midwives, regardless of when they qualified, felt that their infant feeding training had prepared them for practice. In Australia, Cantrill *et al.* (2003) found similar results in their study of how midwives learn about breastfeeding.

Knowledge and breastfeeding support

Similar to their attitudes and personal experiences of infant feeding, midwives knowledge of breastfeeding will likewise be variable and this will depend upon their basic midwifery education, their exposure to breastfeeding mothers and their post-basic education. As already identified, midwifery education in relation to infant feeding has been recognised as being inconsistent and inadequate in some instances (UNICEF UK Baby Friendly Initiative, 2001; Simmons, 2002). In units and communities where the Baby Friendly Award has been achieved, the level of knowledge for the midwives will have been increased as part of the requirements of the award. Conversely, in other maternity units, the midwives do not appear to have the depth of knowledge about breastfeeding required to give good support to breastfeeding mothers, and because the knowledge base is often inadequate, this can result in misinterpretation and bias (Simmons, 2002). To try to prevent this occurring, UNICEF UK Baby Friendly Initiative (2001) has introduced 'Best Practice Standards for Midwifery and Health Visiting Education'. These would ensure that all students, by the end of their programme of education, have the level of knowledge and practical skills to promote breastfeeding and to give evidence-based assistance and support to mothers wishing to breastfeed their infant. Qualified midwives and health professionals also need a high level of knowledge and understanding to enable them to support breastfeeding mothers appropriately. Many maternity units are now working towards Baby Friendly status and many are developing innovative approaches to improve midwives knowledge of breastfeeding. Many have in-service training, which can take various formats, including statutory breastfeeding updates, breastfeeding workshops, breastfeeding competencies, and staff attending breastfeeding courses, and many units now employ infant feeding specialists. However, it takes time and commitment from midwives, and again this may vary depending upon the midwife's understanding of the importance of breastfeeding, her attitude to breastfeeding and her personal experiences.

Ways of knowing

Another important aspect of knowledge is the difference in the 'ways of knowing'. Feminists argue that knowledge has been predominantly determined and defined by men, and Belenky *et al.* (1986) state that men have drawn upon their own viewpoints and visions to construct theories, write history and set values that have become the guiding ideology for both men and women. This is because, until the mid to late 20th century, many women were excluded from universities and therefore, it has been judged, by men, that women's values, ways of knowing and modes of learning are identical to those of men. Rose (1992, p. 32) argues that masculine knowledge emphasises cognitive and objective rationality, and is based on reductive explanations and on the dichotomous partitioning of the social and natural worlds. It is only more recently that there has been any acknowledgement that women may utilise different 'ways of knowing'. Belenky *et al.* (1986) found that women went through various stages of learning, which include silence, received knowledge, subjective knowledge, procedural knowledge and constructed knowledge. There were women in their study who found their voices silenced because they felt powerless to challenge the voice of authority, whilst also having no confidence that they could learn through their own experiences. They felt that their views would not be listened to and were consequently silenced. Belenky *et al.* (1986, p. 4) recognised that for any woman, 'the "real" and valued lessons learned did not necessarily grow out of their academic work but in relationships with friends and teachers, life crises, and community involvement'.

This highlights the fact that midwives' learnt experiences may be more meaningful than the classroom teaching they received during their midwifery education. Many midwives have gained their infant feeding knowledge after qualifying, and this will have included both their direct personal and professional experiences. Personally they will have learnt through exposure to infant feeding outside of midwifery, from having a child themselves or being involved with friends and peers who have had children. Professionally they will have increased their knowledge base by caring for women, from post basic education, study days and through the implementation of infant feeding policies. Unfortunately, many midwives may find conflicts between the different types of knowledge gained. They may find that the objective knowledge of the classroom conflicts with the subjective knowledge they have gained through their experiences.

In their evidence for the ten steps to successful breastfeeding, WHO (1998, p. 48) state that 'no other food or drink other than breast milk should be given, unless medically indicated', but many midwives feel that giving just one formula feed can help a tired mother to continue breastfeeding. Cloherty *et al.* (2004) found in their study that some midwives were still offering mothers supplementation as a short-term and pragmatic solution for a mother's tiredness and distress. This belief may have arisen through either the midwife's own personal experience or the observation of the women in her care. Recently, a midwife's article which debated the issue of whether women should be allowed to give supplementary feeds, especially if they are tired, sparked off a torrent of responses in the *Midwives Journal* (Anon, 2003). Some midwives strongly agreed with the article, whilst others condemned the midwife and her practices. Within the context of clinical experience, many would argue that the theoretical knowledge based upon research evidence is the 'real' knowledge of breastfeeding. Within this context, personal experience with the inherent embodied knowledge could be seen as subjective and of little importance. Consequently, midwives may feel that the knowledge they have gained through their own personal experiences counts for nothing, and this could undermine their ability to assimilate evidence-based knowledge. To assist them, midwives need to reflect on their personal experiences and relate them to the theoretical perspectives. This should enable them to consider strategies, other than the giving of formula feeds, to help tired mothers.

Midwives' knowledge of formula

Midwives are bombarded by adverts for formula milk, more than the majority of other health professionals, through their professional journals. Virtually every edition of the Royal College of Midwives (RCM) journal carries an advert for formula; this is paradoxical, particularly when the RCM was one of the organisations that supported a total ban on advertising baby milks at the consultation stages of the Infant Formula and Follow-on Formula Regulations, 1995 (RCM, 2002). In 2003, the RCM Head of Communications and Marketing stated that many of the journal advertisements were for specialist formula that midwives might not otherwise encounter (Morrison, 2003). Yet in the very same edition of the *Midwives Journal*, there were four adverts for standard formulas, but none for specialist formulas. The Head of Communications and Marketing went on to say that these adverts are carefully vetted to ensure they meet the RCM's high standard. The College's commitment to women having the right to informed choice is emphasised and implies that these adverts are a good method of providing the midwives with information to pass onto mothers. The Head of Communications and Marketing does not appear to acknowledge that, as a source of information, these adverts are biased to the brands they advertise. Midwives do need to know about the different types of formula available, the constituents added to formula and the reasons behind their inclusion. Kaufmann (1999) identified a lack of independently funded consumer information on formula milk, which often leads women to turn to commercial advertising. This is also the case for midwives, as suggested by Morrison (2003); but adverts are not the correct format for midwives' learning. Midwives should receive this information in an unbiased manner, both in their pre- and post-basic midwifery education and in infant feeding update sessions, and preferably from nutritionists rather than company representatives.

Midwives' support for bottle feeding

There is increased concern among mothers and some midwives that women feel they are being denied the information that would enable them to bottle feed their infant safely. This view was endorsed by Walton (2004), who accuses midwives of failing to give mothers who have decided to bottle feed information or support for bottle feeding because they want to be with the 'in crowd'. This is a very important issue, as studies have suggested that more than half of UK mothers make up feeds incorrectly (Lucas *et al.*, 1992). The recommendation by UNICEF UK Baby Friendly Initiative (1998), which states that no group instruction that demonstrates the making up of formula feeds should be given antenatally, has been taken by some midwives to mean that no instruction at all should be given to bottle feeding mothers. UNICEF UK Baby Friendly Initiative states very clearly that mothers should be given this information, but on either a one-to-one or one-to-two basis in the postnatal period when the skill is more relevant. This is not meant to deter midwives from giving mothers important information on the safe making-up of formula feeds if they wish to bottle feed, but to encourage good practice. It is questionable whether group instruction is a suitable environment in which to learn a skill; plus the group environment may inhibit mothers from asking important questions.

Acquisition of new knowledge

Jamieson (1997) argues that attitudes that undermines breastfeeding also reduce the ability of health professionals to learn skills that promote breastfeeding. Fairbank *et al.* (2000) indicated in their review of the evidence, that the breast-feeding knowledge of health professionals can be increased by intensive lactation training courses and in-service training courses, but that these may not necessarily alter their attitudes. What has been shown to be more effective in changing attitudes and to have a positive effect on hospital breastfeeding promotion practice is the use of a package of intervention, which has also included a training component (Fairbank *et al.*, 2000). Van Esterik (1995) proposes that, within the study of breastfeeding, there is a convergence of different ways of knowing – convergence of scientific knowledge, experimental knowledge and experiential knowledge. Therefore midwifery education and in-service training related to breastfeeding need to give consideration to all three of these sources of knowledge. Scientific knowledge of breastfeeding is continually increasing and this new knowledge must be incorporated into any training component. Educationalists and trainers usually have no difficulties in this area because of the wealth of knowledge available. Teaching skills for breastfeeding has increasingly been included in many texts and journals and incorporated into education and training, at both pre- and post-basic levels. However, the area that has received minimal attention is how to encourage health professionals to consider their own personal experiences of infant feeding and to use these experiences constructively when supporting breastfeeding women.

Reviewing personal attitudes to infant feeding

In order to support and promote breastfeeding, it is important that midwives have a positive attitude towards breastfeeding, but at the same time they must be able to help and support women who have decided to bottle feed their infants without making them feel guilty or inferior. When training to be a breastfeeding counsellor for the voluntary breastfeeding organisations, e.g. the National Childbirth Trust, La Leche League, the Breastfeeding Network or the Association of Breastfeeding Mothers, all candidates are asked first to address their own infant feeding history. They are asked to consider their emotions and feelings associated with that history and how these could impinge on the care that they give to women. This should be an integral part of all pre-registration programmes for midwives and health professionals. For qualified midwives and health professionals, it should be introduced either as a part of in-service training, breastfeeding courses or on an individual basis. This will help them to identify any areas of negativity or overzealousness, and assist them to initiate behavioural changes which would benefit the women for whom they care.

The following programme has been developed to assist midwives and health professionals to review their own infant feeding history (Battersby, 2003b) and can be used either in a group format or by individuals. The exercise can be undertaken in stages over a period of time, or in one process.

Exercise 1

This entails answering a list of questions which has been compiled to help assist health professionals to analyse their own attitudes towards infant feeding. The questions that have been posed will enable the health professional to consider her or his own perceptions of infant feeding. It is important that sufficient thought is given to each question and that the questions are answered honestly, not as the reader thinks they should be answered.

- How were you fed as an infant? Has your mother talked to you about it?
- How have your family and friends fed their babies? Is it predominantly breastfeeding or infant formula feeds?
- Have you any children of your own? How did you feed them? Why did you choose this method?
- If you do not have children of your own, which method of infant feeding would you adopt if or when you have your own children? Why?
- Do you perceive breastfeeding as being easy or hard? What makes you think this?
- Do you perceive that there are any health benefits for breastfeeding in a developed nation? List these.
- Is infant formula as good as breast milk? Why?
- Do you feel that the UK is predominately a breast or bottle feeding nation? What makes you think this?
- Which women are more likely to breastfeed their babies?
- Do you think women should breastfeed their babies in public places?

Exercise 2

On completion of the first exercise, the next stage is to consider where the views and attitudes that have been expressed in the answering of the previous questions originated. The midwife or health professional could do this by completing a table similar to the one below. Then the health professional should write down any infant feeding experience she or he may have encountered in the second column; starting with the earliest memory, knowledge or experience and finishing with the most recent. This should include influences from family, friends, peers and the media. When this exercise has been completed, the health professional should consider whether these experiences have had any influence on their personal attitude towards infant feeding and, if so, they should complete the third column, stating whether these were perceived as positive or negative.

Date/age	Experience	Influence (positive/negative)

An alternative exercise to the one above is the completion of a time line. Here a straight line is drawn and any positive experiences are placed with a mark above the line and any negative influences are placed with a mark below the line. Following this there is a need to reflect on why some experiences were positive and others negative. Consideration is also given to whether the positives outweigh the negatives or vice versa.

Exercise 3

These first two exercises focus on a micro-view of attitude formation that looks at the issues affecting the individual, which may include the family, school, peers, midwifery training and personal experiences. A process that will further help to identify personal attitudes and feelings towards infant feeding is by considering cultural issues within society. This can be undertaken by the observation of a variety of photographs or pictures that portray images of the breasts, breastfeeding and bottle feeding. Photographs such as those seen in magazines and the tabloid press are ideal, as are adverts promoting infant feeding products and equipment. A further selection of pictures should include women breastfeeding and bottle feeding babies and older infants in a variety of settings. The midwife or health professional needs to consider their thoughts and feelings regarding each of the pictures. Which pictures do they find acceptable? Which ones do they dislike? Are there any that generate strong feeling? What are these feelings? What do they believe to be the roots of these feelings? It is important not just to state the feeling but to analyse the feelings. A chart similar to the one below may help in this process.

Photograph	Comment
1	What do I think of the picture? Why?
2	What do I think of the picture? Why?
3	What do I think of the picture? Why?
4	What do I think of the picture? Why?
5	What do I think of the picture? Why?

Exercise 4

The final stage in the review process is the drawing together of the issues that have arisen in the review, considering them in relation to how they may affect the care given to women. The midwife or health professional concludes the review by asking themselves the following questions, adapted from Hallawell and Brittle (1995, p. 53):

- Am I aware of my own attitudes to infant feeding?
- Do I know how these have developed?
- How strongly held are those attitudes?
- Can I perceive how my attitudes influence others?
- Can I modify my attitudes if necessary?
- Can I communicate necessary information to women without it becoming distorted by my own attitudes?

The whole process of review should be taken seriously and not rushed. There must be adequate time for consideration of the issues and it should be an empowering exercise. These exercises have been used as part of breastfeeding educational programmes, and normally three hours are allocated to complete the exercises and allow meaningful discussions to develop. If time is limited, the participants can be asked to complete the work prior to the session and the answers then used to stimulate discussion. The process assists midwives, other health professionals and students to identify their attitudes towards infant feeding, enabling them to recognise opposing views that surround infant feeding and highlighting many of the associated tensions that exist. Through the completion of the process, it is hoped that the participants would improve the care given to women regardless of whether they are breastfeeding or bottle feeding their infants.

Conclusion

The understanding and formation of attitudes is complex, but is generally accepted as being either a positive or a negative disposition towards an object or thing. Within this chapter, the attitudes towards infant feeding were considered. For women, attitudes are formed in response to the cultural norms of the society in which they live. They are also influenced by their own personal experiences of infant feeding and through contact with family and friends. Partners' attitudes have also been found to be influential in the woman's decision of infant feeding method. Other factors that may affect a woman's attitude towards infant feeding include cultural perceptions of the female breast, body image, media and consumerism and the current discourses on breastfeeding.

Recognition of the importance of breastfeeding, both for the mother and the baby, has increased over the last decade, as the benefits of breastfeeding have been intensively researched. There has also been an increasing recognition that women in socially and economically disadvantaged areas are least likely to breastfeed and are therefore placing themselves and their infants at increased health risks (Hamlyn *et al.*, 2002). Women may decide to bottle feed, although they know the benefits of breastfeeding. This is important, as many health professionals use the discourse of 'breast is best' to promote breastfeeding and do not take into consideration social and psychological factors that influence the woman's decision. It has been increasingly recognised that in order to increase the initiation rate of breastfeeding there needs to be a change in the attitudes of both individuals and society. Losch *et al.* (1995) have highlighted the importance of introducing health promotion programmes that target both the woman and the woman's social network. This will require a diversity of strategies to be initiated by both health professionals and the government.

Midwives have a major role in supporting breastfeeding and bottle feeding mothers and should consider their own attitudes to infant feeding to assist them to give evidenced-based but sensitive support to all women, regardless of their infant feeding method. Midwives' attitudes will have developed as part of their socialisation, but will have the added influence of their professional education and experience. The midwife needs to remember that direct personal experience has a strong influence on attitude formation and therefore care needs to be taken to ensure that personal experience is used constructively, not destructively. A negative attitude developed through a bad experience is especially powerful. The midwife's attitude to breastfeeding may either help or hinder a woman's success at breastfeeding. A negative attitude and a lack of support for bottle feeding may result in a mother incorrectly making up formula feeds or incorrectly sterilising equipment, both of which may put her infant at increased risk of illness.

It has been shown that increasing knowledge alone does not necessarily change attitudes. Therefore educationalists and trainers must consider including in their programmes the opportunity for midwives to review their own perceptions of infant feeding. The model presented within this chapter could assist midwives to identify issues within their educational and personal experiences that may impinge on the care that they give to any woman, regardless of her infant feeding method.

References

Anon (2003) Breastfeeding – where has the common sense gone? *RCM Midwives Journal*, **6**(12), 529.

Ajzen, I. (1988) *Attitudes, Personality and Behaviour*. Open University Press, Milton Keynes.

Barkham, P. (2004) Nipple causes ripple in land that invented Page 3 girls. *Sidney Morning Herald*, 24 May. `http://www.smh.com.au/2004/05/23/1085 250871369.html?oneclick=true` [Accessed 16 January 2005].

Barnes, J., Stein, A., Smith, T. and Pollock, J. I. (1997) Extreme attitudes to body shape, social and psychological factors and a reluctance to breastfeed. *Journal of the Royal Society of Medicine*, **90**, 551–9.

Battersby, S. (1999) Midwives' experiences of breastfeeding: Can the attitudes developed affect how midwives support and promote breastfeeding? *Proceedings of the 25th Triennial Congress of the International Confederation of Midwives*, Manila, pp. 53–7.

Battersby, S. (2002a) *Breastfeeding is Best Supporters (BIBS): an evaluation of the merged Breastfeeding Peer Support Programmes*. `http://www.sheffield.ac.uk/surestart` [Accessed 16 January 2005].

Battersby, S. (2002b) Midwives' embodied experiences of breastfeeding. *MIDIRS Midwifery Digest*, **12**(4), 523–6.

Battersby, S. (2003a) Breastfeeding and bullying: who's putting the pressure on? In: *Midwifery Best Practice* (ed. S. Wickham), pp. 170–2. Books for Midwives, Edinburgh.

Battersby, S. (2003b) *Infant Feeding Workbook*. Sheffield University, Sheffield.

Baumslag, N. and Michels, D. L. (1995) *Milk, Money and Madness: The Culture and Politics of Breastfeeding*. Bergin & Garvey, Westport, Connecticut.

Belenky, M. F., Clinchy, B. M., Goldberger, N. R. and Tarule, J. M. (1986) *Women's Ways of Knowing; The Development of Self, Voice and Mind*. Basic Books Inc., USA.

Bottorff, J. L. (1990) Persistence in breastfeeding: a phenomenological investigation. *Journal of Advanced Nursing*, **15**, 201–9.

Britton, C. (1997) 'Letting it go, letting it flow': women's experiential accounts of the letdown reflex. *Social Sciences in Health*, **3**(3), 176–87.

Brosseau, J. (1994) How the attitudes of health professionals towards breastfeeding are shaped and their impact on breastfeeding. *AARN News Letter*, **50**(9), 10–11.

Burchill, J. (1999) Breast-feeding? It sucks! *The Guardian*, 12 May, pp. 8–9.

Byron, R. A. and Byrne, D. (1987) *Social Psychology: Understanding Human Interaction*, 5th edn. Allyn and Bacon, Boston.

Cantrill, R. M., Creedy, D. K. and Cooke, M. (2003) How midwives learn about breastfeeding. *Australian Midwifery Journal*, **16**(2), 11–16.

Carter, P. (1995) *Feminism, Breasts and Breastfeeding*. Macmillan Press Limited, London.

Cloherty, M., Alexander, J. and Holloway, I. (2004). Supplementing breast-fed babies in the UK to protect their mothers from tiredness or distress. *Midwifery*, **20**, 194–204.

Deaux, K., Dane, F. C., Wrightman, L. S. and Sigelman, C. K. (1988) *Social Psychology in the 1990s*, 6th edn. Brooks/Cole Publishing Company, Pacific Grove, California.

Dignam, D. M. (1995) Understanding intimacy as experienced by breastfeeding women. *Health Care International*, **16**, 477–85.

Dykes, F. (1995) Valuing breastfeeding in midwifery education. *British Journal of Midwifery*, **3**(10), 544–7.

Dykes, F. and Griffiths, H. (1998) Societal influences upon initiation and continuation of breastfeeding. *British Journal of Midwifery*, **6**(2), 76–80.

Dykes, F. and Williams, C. (1999) Falling by the wayside: a phenomenological exploration of perceived breast-milk inadequacy in lactating women. *Midwifery*, **15**(4), 232–46.

Earle, S. (2000) Why some women do not breast feed: bottle feeding and the father's role. *Midwifery*, **16**, 323–30.

Eiser, J. (1986) *Social Psychology: Attitudes, Cognition and Social Behaviour*. Cambridge University Press, Cambridge.

Fairbank, L., O'Meara, S., Renfrew, M. J. Woolridge, M., Sowden, A. J. and Lister-Sharp, D. (2000) A systematic review to evaluate the effectiveness of interventions to promote the initiation of breastfeeding. *Health Technology Assessment*, **4**(25).

Finigan, V. (2004) Breastfeeding – the great divide: the controversy as seen through a midwifery lens. *MIDIRS Midwifery Digest*, **14**(2), 227–31.

Foster, K., Lader, D. and Cheesborough, S. (1997) *Infant Feeding 1995. A Survey of Infant Feeding Practices in the UK*. HMSO, London.

Fraley, K., Freed, G. L. and Schanler, R. J. (1992) Attitudes of expectant fathers regarding breast-feeding. *Pediatrics*, **90**, 224–7.

Hallawell, B. and Brittle, R. (1995) *The Individual in Society*. Scutari Press, London.

Hamlyn, B., Brooker, S., Olienikova, K. and Wands, S. (2002) *Infant Feeding 2000*. The Stationery Office, London.

Henderson, A. M. (1999) Mixed messages about the meaning of breast-feeding representations in the Australian press and popular magazines. *Midwifery*, **15**, 24–31.

Henderson, L., Kitzinger, J. and Green, J. (2000) Representing infant feeding: content analysis of British media portrayals of bottle feeding and breast feeding. *British Medical Journal*, **321**, 1196–8.

Hope, J. (2000) To breastfeed or not? *The Daily Mail*, 26 April, 24–5.

Jamieson, L. (1997) Knowledge and Skills Involved in Infant Feeding. In: *Essential Midwifery* (eds. C. Henderson and K. Jones), pp. 265–84. Mosby, London.

Katz, D. and Stotland, E. (1959) A preliminary statement to a theory of attitude structure and Change, In: *Psychology: a Study of a Science*, Vol. 3 (ed. S. Koch). McGraw-Hill, New York.

Kaufmann, T. (1999) Infant feeding: politics vs pragmatism *RCM Midwives Journal*, **2**(8), 244–5.

Losch, M., Dungy, C. I., Russell, D. and Dusdicker, L. B. (1995) Impact of attitudes on maternal decisions regarding infant feeding. *Journal of Pediatrics*, **126**(4), 507–14.

Lucas, A., Lockton, S. and Davies, P. (1992) Randomised trial of ready-to-feed compared with powered formula. *Archives of in Disease in Childhood*, **67**, 935–9.

McMulkin, S. and Malone, R. (1994) Breastfeeding – midwives' personal experiences. *Modern Midwife*, **4**(5), 10–12.

Minchin, M. (1998) *Breastfeeding Matters*, 4th edn. Alma Publications, Sydney, Australia.

Morrison, S. (2003) Reply from Simon Morrison, RCM head of communications and Marketing. *Midwives* (RCM Journal), **6**(8), 357.

Mulford, C. (1995) Swimming upstream: breastfeeding care in a non-breastfeeding culture. *Journal of Obstetric, Gynecologic, and Neonatal Nursing*, **24**(5), 464–74.

Murphy, E. (1999) 'Breast is best': infant feeding decisions and maternal deviance. *Sociology of Health and Illness*, **21**(2), 187–208.

Pain, R., Bailey, C. and Mowl, G. (2001) Infant feeding in North East England: contested spaces of reproduction. *Area*, **33**(3), 261–72.

Palmer, G. (1993) *The Politics of Breastfeeding*. Pandora Press, London.

Pugliese, A. R. (2000) Breastfeeding in public. *New Beginnings*, November/December, 196–200.

Renfrew, M. J., Woolridge, M. W. and McGill, H. R. (2000) *Enabling Women to Breastfeed: a Review of Practices Which Promote or Inhibit Breastfeed-*

ing – with Evidence-based Guidance for Practice. The Stationery Office, London.

Rose, H. (1994) *Love, Power and Knowledge: Towards a Feminist Transformation of the sciences*. Polity Press, Cambridge.

Royal College of Midwives (2002) *Successful Breastfeeding*. RCM, London.

Smale, M. (1998) Working with breastfeeding mothers: the psychosocial context. In: *Psychological Perspectives on Pregnancy and Childbirth* (ed. S. Clement), pp. 183–204. Churchill Livingstone, Edinburgh.

Simmons, V. (2002) Exploring inconsistent advice: 2. *British Journal of Midwifery*, **10**(10), 616–19.

Stapleton, H. (2002) Women with eating disorders: a study of their perceptions of childbearing and maternity services. In: *International Confederation of Midwives. Midwives and women working together for the family of the world*, ICM proceedings CD-ROM Vienna 2002. ICM, The Hague.

Stearns, C. A. (1999) Breastfeeding and the good maternal body. *Gender and Society*, **13**(2), 308–25.

Thomson, A. (1989) Why don't women breast feed? In: *Midwives, Research & Childbirth*, Vol. 1 (eds. Robinson, S. and Thomson, A.), pp. 215–240. Chapman & Hall, London.

Thomas, G. (2000) Be nice and don't drop the baby. In: *The New Midwifery; Science and Sensitivity in Practice* (ed. L. A. Page), pp. 173–18. Churchill Livingstone, Edinburgh.

UNICEF UK Baby Friendly Initiative (1998) *Implementing the Ten Steps to Successful Breastfeeding*. UNICEF, London.

UNICEF UK Baby Friendly Initiative (2001) *UNICEF UK Baby Friendly Initiative: Baby Friendly Best Practice Standards for Midwifery and Health visiting Education*. http://www.babyfriendly.org.uk/education.asp [Accessed 3 February 2005].

Van Esterik, P. (1995) The politics of breastfeeding: an advocacy perspective. In: *Breastfeeding: Biocultural Perspectives* (eds. P. Stuart-Macadam and K. Dettwyler), pp. 145–65. Aldine De Gruyter, New York.

Walton, G. (2004) Time to grow up. *The Practising Midwife*, **7**(11), 49.

Welford, H. (1995) Breastfeeding: promoting good practice. *Modern Midwife*, **5**(11), 29–30.

WHO (1998) *Evidence for the Ten Steps to Successful Breastfeeding* (Revised). Family and Reproductive Health, Division of Child Health and Development. World Health Organization, Geneva.

Wolf, J. H. (2000) The social and medical construction of lactation pathology. *Women and Health*, **30**(3), 93–109.

Woollett, A. (1987) Who breastfeeds? The family and cultural context. *Journal of Reproductive and Infant Psychology*, **5**, 127–31.

Wylie, J. and Verber, I. (1994) Why women fail to breastfeed: a prospective study from booking to 28 days post partum. *Journal of Human Nutrition and Dietetics*, **17**, 115–20.

CHAPTER 7

Gujarati women and infant feeding decisions

Alison Spiro

Introduction

The decision to breastfeed in industrialised countries is complex, enmeshed within social, historical, political, economic and religious contexts. In many parts of the world breastfeeding may be the only option, but where there are improvements in economic conditions together with the marketing of formula milks, infant feeding becomes situated within human relations in kin groups, as Scheper-Hughes (1992) has described in her ethnography of an area of Brazil. This chapter will argue that there is no simple choice about the method of infant feeding, but that kinship, power, dependency, religion, ideas of the body and the person are influential. Here the focus will be on Hindu and Jain Gujarati women living in the North London suburb of Harrow and will draw on qualitative research conducted for my doctoral thesis. My thesis was a study of Gujarati women and children living in Harrow. It addressed the issues concerning women in the household that include their relations with other kin and wider social networks, caring for children, feeding, protecting them from evil influences and their key involvement in ritual practice. Households were studied using the methods of participant observation and in-depth taped, unstructured interviews. Different caste groups, religious and social classes were included in the study group, but the majority were Hindu, with some Jain. Data was also included from a three-month period of research in Ahmedabad in India, and this informed the Harrow data (Spiro, unpublished PhD). In the following text, pseudonyms are used for all quotations to protect the anonymity of my informants.

Many Gujaratis migrated to Britain in the 1970s from Kenya and Uganda, when the political situation there became difficult. Large numbers settled in

North London and Leicester, followed by relatives and marriage partners from India. Now 20–30% of school children in Harrow and Brent are of Gujarati origin. They retain their strong kinship, religious and moral values, and sense of identity, but also see themselves as British and participate fully in economic and political life.

Health professionals working with South Asian women may find the relationships between women in the household difficult to understand and may see older women as interfering in the caring of the infant. This chapter will seek to place the new mother and her child within the cultural context, where a child experiences multiple carers and learns to be a member of a wide social group, often relating more closely to a grandmother or aunt than to his or her own mother. The challenge here is for professionals to embrace this difference and work sensitively with it.

Attitudes to breastfeeding and decision making

Infant feeding decisions are made by Gujarati women within the context of family life and through consultation with immediate kin and close friends. In the past, Gujarati men have viewed these as situated within the realm of domestic life, which does not concern them; but this may be changing in the Western context, with men sharing a greater role than their fathers did in childbirth and childcare. In rural and poor urban areas of India, breastfeeding is the only method of feeding that ensures child survival.

In wealthier urban India, East Africa or Britain, decisions about breastfeeding are made taking into account the views of older women, religious and moral imperatives, supernatural beliefs and ritual practice. The new mother's body is not only capable of issuing a pure, life-giving, white fluid in the form of breast milk, but also potentially polluting and a danger to others through its blood loss. She becomes the focus of attention by older women, and rituals and special foods are made to ensure her safe transition to motherhood.

I will begin by examining these aspects of kinship that impact on the new mother and her infant from birth through to the post-birth period. I will explore the way in which the child is integrated within the family and the involvement of other women in his or her care, so becoming dependent on many carers. Breastfeeding is an integral part of this process, one in which the child learns about the world and the relationships around him or her. I will then examine the way the woman's body is fed, acted on in ritual, controlled in space and time and, in the Western context, subjected to biomedical management and time schedules.

The impending birth of a child is a time for celebration and caution, drawing together close kin and friends. Most Hindu and Jain households in Britain and

India observe certain rituals of childhood that must be conducted in the correct sequence. Although variations in practices are found, there are always common threads. These rituals begin in the seventh month of pregnancy, when some families perform the *kholo bharvo* ritual, although others may incorporate it into the first ritual after the birth. During this ceremony, the pregnant woman's mother and mother-in-law exchange rice in the folds of their saris, ending with the woman's own mother, with whom she will stay after the birth. This implies that she will move from the joint family home, where she lives with her husband's family, for the first 40 days after the birth. Joint family life is still popular in all socio-economic groups and is seen as a Hindu and Jain ideal, where domestic chores are shared and care of the young and elderly are an integral aspect of the household members' *dharma* or moral duty. Twenty years ago the demise of the joint family was predicted (Warrier, 1988) and that Western nuclear living practices would take over, but my data suggest that this is not the case, with many young couples still living with the husband's family. If they do move into a home of their own, it will be in close proximity, meals will be shared frequently and the grandparents will care for children in the joint home. The seventh month ritual not only symbolises this move to the maternal home, but also indicates the close involvement and responsibility that both grandmothers will have in the care of the child.

Feeding the child implies sustaining the growth of the physical body and also the transmission of cultural knowledge about kin relations, power in the family, and moral and religious continuity. Many Gujaratis believe that while the child is in the womb, he or she is experiencing the mother's emotions and receiving knowledge about kin and moral values through body fluids. Likewise, when breastfeeding, a child is learning about the world around him or her through the milk; so the future character of the child is affected by the way the mother feels. Meera, a mother who was breastfeeding her four-month-old son explained to me:

> Most people say that if you breastfeed and you are thinking good thoughts, then he will grow up nicely, not as a hooligan who won't listen to his parents. If the mother is stubborn, then the kid tends to be stubborn too. I have seen it so many times like that in India.

After the birth of the child (not directly after the pregnancy ceremony, as was the case previously in India), the newly delivered mother and child are cared for by the mother's parents in their home. Here she will be instructed in breastfeeding and in the care of the child, with her mother taking much of the responsibility for the physical care. If the infant is premature or small, he or she may be required to stay in a neonatal unit and it will be the maternal grandmother's, or *nani's*, responsibility to instruct her daughter in the care of her child there. Observations I have carried out in a local unit have demonstrated this, with the common scenario of the mother and *nani* sitting next to the incubator, often with the *nani* taking the main role in caring for the infant. When asked why this happens, I have been told that, because it is the mother's first child, she needs to be shown what to do; but when placed within the context of shared mothering, it can be seen to be the beginning of a relationship with the *nani* that will continue throughout childhood and beyond.

Most Hindus and Jains value colostrum, the first milk the baby receives from the breast, although some Muslim women believe it contains negative products of labour and refuse to give it. Older women may doubt its quantity and whether it is sufficient for the infant's needs. In India, pre-lacteal feeds are often given in the form of water mixed with herbs or spices and honey. This is not practised so much in the UK, although Reena told me that honey was given to her baby on the tips of her female relative's fingers, welcoming him to the family group. More value is placed on the white, mature milk that is seen as a pure gift from God and the way a child gets to know his mother, as Kanta, a grandmother, explained:

> You must feed your own milk; it is made especially for your child. If you breastfeed, the child knows his mother. If you bottle feed, he doesn't know his mother. If the bottle breaks, the child cries because the bottle is broken, but if the mother dies, the child does not care.

Sala, another Gujarati grandmother, saw breastfeeding as situated within nature as well as being integrated with religion and traditions:

> All animals have milk and it is natural to feed their young, so we should do it. It is nature's way of looking after the baby. You only have breast milk after having a baby, and you must feed your own milk, it is made especially for your child.

Hansa, a mother breastfeeding her two-month-old baby, explained that it was also part of a person's spiritual path through life:

> Breastfeeding a child is thought to be one of the best things you can do. It is part of your *karma*, or life force. If you breastfeed someone, you do them a very big favour.

The infant is seen as pure after birth, but in a state of transition from life in the womb to living outside, and because of this uncertain status it needs protection from any supernatural forces, notably *najar* or the evil eye. Initially, there is strong support for breastfeeding from older female kin, who believe that the mother has an obligation to give her milk because it is a gift from God. Breast milk is a pure substance, which comes directly from the body and so avoids any malevolent gaze or pollution that might have occurred outside the body. Expressing breast milk or receiving donated milk may be problematic for some Gujarati women, because once the milk is outside the body it could attract the eye of jealous people and become contaminated, making the child unwell. Donated milk contains body fluids from other women and could transmit negative elements of her milk and alien cultural values. Mita, a midwife and mother, told me how concerned she was about negative energies in donated breast milk:

> Breast milk used to be so much in fashion, when people were collecting it and putting it in milk banks. Then women started to think, do I really want to give my child milk from another woman, who might have a different kind of personality, different thoughts, do I want to use it? I feel the same way. I have no way of proving it, but I believe it so strongly I would like research to show that this is the case. The same with food. It doesn't matter what ingredients you have in cooking, if you don't have a portion of love in it, the food is never good.

The new mother stays in her parent's home and is given special foods to help her recover from the birth, strengthen her back, improve her breast milk, and replenish her body, which will have become depleted in minerals and energy. Most families are vegetarian and the diet will be rich in green vegetables and aubergines. Root vegetables should be avoided because they are thought to upset the mother and baby's stomach. A special food called *katlu* is made with maize flour, butter, gum, honey, nuts and spices, and is cut into squares; at least two pieces should be eaten each day, but some women are reluctant to do this because it is high in calories and fat. New mothers are expected to drink *sua*, which is boiled water mixed with spices, to rid their bodies of the toxic effects of the birth process, but many find it bitter to taste and hard to drink. *Nani* will usually massage the baby and her daughter daily after their morning bath, but in India wealthier families will call in a local woman to do this, who is often very vigorous in the way she uses her hands on the baby's limbs. Afterwards, both mother and baby sleep for several hours. In stricter families, the mother will be confined to her room for the first few days and not allowed into the kitchen for the first two weeks and must not touch the household shrine for the whole of the 40 days. A special ritual is done when the child is six days old, called the *chhati*. Here the *mataji* or goddess Randalma is called upon to protect the mother and her child from malign supernatural forces; this is also a symbolic coming together of maternal and paternal kin in their joint responsibilities to the child. It can be a small, informal affair involving immediate family, or a larger gathering where a priest is invited and wider kin and friends are invited. During the ritual, the father's sister, or *foi*, plays the main role by rolling the baby in front of a small shrine and shielding his or her eyes from the light of the candle. The god of fate, Vidhata, is thought to write the child's future on a piece of white paper with a red pen which is left under the child's mattress during the night after the ritual. The *foi* is also expected to choose the child's name, so paving the way for her close involvement in decision making in the future. The child's mother is not allowed to play a role in this ritual because of her state of impurity due to her blood loss. Usually after two weeks she will be allowed to move freely around the house, but she and the baby will be unlikely to leave the house until after the *sava mahino*, a month and a quarter after the birth. Then she and the baby will have a ceremonial bath, dress in new clothes and visit the temple, after which she will return to her husband's family home. This period of rest, good nutrition and freedom from household chores enables the mother to establish breastfeeding and to regain physical and spiritual strength after the birth, and is enjoyed by most women. Those women who have been educated in Britain, however, may find the close involvement of maternal and paternal kin in decision making about the baby difficult and may find it even harder once they return to the husband's joint family home, where the mother-in-law, or *sasu*, will play a large part in the care of the child.

When the Gujarati woman gets married, she moves into the household as an outsider and is expected to do the menial tasks of cleaning and cooking. When she has a child, however, her status rises through the sharing of some bodily substances of the family through her child. She becomes involved in more decision making in the household and shares the chores with other women. Her *sasu* remains the most powerful figure in the family when decisions about child rearing arise and will direct the rituals that need to be done to protect the child from supernatural forces. She will tie black threads around the child's wrists, ankles, waist or neck and may put black marks on the feet or hands, behind the ears and around the eyes, so the child is less attractive to the jealous eye. Both grandmothers are actively involved with the child, the *nani* initially and then the father's mother, or *dadi*, after the first 40 days. The grandmother often performs the physical care of the child in the form of washing, changing nappies, comforting and carrying and is frequently seen rocking the baby, sitting cross-legged on the floor. The child soon develops a close bond with these other women. Although the mother is actively involved in breastfeeding, the close 'love-laden' bond (Seymour 1999, p. 85) between mother and child that is expected in the West is actively discouraged in South Asian families, and dependency on many carers is encouraged. Initially the baby will sleep with the mother and breastfeed on demand at night. In India, children always share beds with their parents. When breastfeeding stops or another baby is born, the older child co-sleeps with the *dadi*, so the bond between them deepens further.

I asked Mrs Purohit, a grandmother who has two grandsons living a mile away with her son and his wife, whether sleeping together was an important aspect of child rearing and she replied:

It is for many grandmothers, it is how we get close. Shiv is now three years old and he sleeps with me, in my bed, every Thursday night. It makes us very close. My husband goes to the box room. I can teach him so much, and read the Gayatri slok [worship to the goddess Gayatri] in the morning. My other grandson, who is now six, comes to our house every night after school and sleeps with me on Saturday nights. He says to me – when I put my head on your lap, my worries disappear.

Many adults have described to me the closer relationship they have had with their grandmothers than with their own mothers. Sanjay, a father of a two-year-old boy, told me of the relationship he had with his grandmother:

I was so close to my grandmother that I shared a bed with her until I was 16. When she died, I went into a deep depression and took a long time to recover.

Co-sleeping is an important aspect of parenting. Even if the couple move with their children to a flat or house of their own, the older children will probably co-sleep with their *dadi* at least once a week. This may continue until puberty and in rare cases even beyond. Through co-sleeping and breastfeeding, a child learns about his or her kin and religious ideals, and builds up close bonds with many carers. This web of interdependency continues throughout life and within it the moral obligations to kin arise, which override all other considerations.

Grandparents will devote their lives to caring for grandchildren while the child's parents are at work and older members will be also be cared for in the house. There is no expectation of financial gain or other reward for this care, but it becomes an integral part of the *karma* of the person and their journey through life. A Gujarati grandmother walked into my baby clinic one day, proudly carrying her new grandson with her husband walking behind her and the baby's mother behind him, and announced to me and all others present:

Our baby is lucky, he has three mothers: me, my husband and his mother.

Western-trained health professionals may find this close involvement of other women difficult to understand and may feel they are undermining the mother in what they believe to be a universal right of parents to have sole control over decisions about their children. The psychoanalytic model of childcare has underpinned much of the parenting models used in the West. Several theorists have tried to apply the psychoanalytic model to aid the understanding of the South Asian psyche. Kakar (1981) uses a Freudian stance and tries to describe the development of the ego through multiple attachments with many caregivers, but he appears to contradict his own Indian childcare practices. Kurtz (1992), on the other hand, tries to develop a theory of Hindu child rearing by re-shaping Western psychoanalytic theory through emphasising the link between mother-hood with the great goddesses and their interchangeable status, which he argues can be applied to human mothers. His aims are to establish a new psychoana-lytic approach in line with the structure of Hindu divinity. Seymour (1999) does not attempt to apply a Western model and her observations suggest that children were socialised to identify with the family as a whole and to value the collec-tive unit above their own individual interests. She sees problems in the Western theories of child development that focus on individuation when they are applied in societies where group attachment is stronger than it is to a single caretaker. Her descriptions of other women in the household caring and making decisions about children are similar to those I have observed in Harrow and Ahmedabad.

> While nursing, a mother responds physically to her child but withholds empathic attention thus encouraging the child to seek emotional satisfac-tion in relationships with others, not in an exclusive relationship with her (Seymour 1999, p. 82).

Seymour (1999, p. 270) predicts that changes may occur as Western-style educational achievement and professional goals encourage a move away from a culturally ideal interdependent self toward a more independent and autono-mous self. This may happen in the next generation, but my data suggest that the Gujarati grandmothers of today are ensuring the continuity of the system of interdependence by beginning in early childhood. An understanding of this is essential for all professionals working with South Asian families in any aspect of parenting and presents a challenge to all who have been brought up and edu-cated in a society where the nuclear family is the norm and individual choice respected.

South Asian women in Britain today are more likely to breastfeed and con-tinue doing so for longer than their Western counterparts (Hamlyn *et al.*, 2002). Katbamna (2000) recognised the strong preference that Gujarati women in the UK have for breastfeeding, which contrasted with that of Bangladeshi women, who were more likely to introduce bottle feeds. There is evidence from a local breastfeeding audit that I carried out in 2002 in Harrow that South Asian women (mostly Gujarati) are more likely to breastfeed initially, but by the time the child is six weeks old many have introduced formula feeds (unpublished Harrow PCT audit, 2002). The reasons for this may be the involvement of other women in decisions about infant feeding and their beliefs that formula feeding may make babies fatter. This may also be an opportunity for grandmothers or aunts to demand a share in the feeding process at an earlier stage in the child's life than was ever possible in India. Grandmothers who migrated to Britain in the 1960s and 1970s were probably exposed to advertisements for formula milk show-ing chubby babies, and may think that Indian babies are thinner and smaller because they were breastfed. Mita, a midwife, described to me how this attitude might have developed:

> The women who came from India, especially from the villages, are often little, quite small compared with women in this country, and their husbands are also of small frame. The mother-in-law believes that this is because of breast milk, having seen babies in this country, which are much bigger, and may think it is because of the bottle. With their experience of breastfeeding, they think it is the better option to bottle-feed. *They* couldn't bottle feed because they were not rich enough to do it.

Nikhita was a mother who had two small children. The younger one was six months old and she was breastfeeding him. She told me how the discrepancy in size between Asian babies and white babies influences how breastfeeding is viewed in the Asian community:

> Asian mothers believe that formula milk makes babies heavier. They compare Asian babies with white babies of the same age and the white children are always bigger. Breastfeeding is more common in the Indian culture than it is in the Western culture. There is an assumption that they are formula fed and that is why they are bigger. If you have ten babies, then the white ones will always be bigger. The other thing in our community is that if anyone makes a comment about me not producing enough milk, it really rattles me. I feel like saying that I am feeding him, he is not going hungry. First of all you fight it and then you say, I've had enough, and pack it in. It depends how strong you are, you might pack it in, or just keep going.

Sometimes the pressure to give the babies formula feeds is so strong that women feel they cannot continue to fight it, as Ameeta found when her relationship with her mother and father-in-law became very difficult. She came directly from India following an arranged marriage in 2000 and had little support in this country.

> I was living in my mother-in-law's house. She wanted me to stop breastfeeding, so that she could feed my son. She took him away and bottle-fed him. I was left with milk pouring out of my breasts and I didn't know what to do, because I couldn't disagree with her. I was like a guest in her house.

The decisions about whether breastfeeding should continue are often made by the older women in the household in consultation with the mother, but in this case Ameeta felt that she could not argue with her mother-in-law, who was the most powerful voice in the household, and even her husband could not disagree with her.

In areas where there are mothers of South Asian origin, there is a strong case for breastfeeding promotion campaigns to be targeted at influential women in the household, not just at pregnant women and their partners. The health hazards associated with giving formula are poorly understood by this population. On the other hand, formula milk is viewed as scientific and often seen promoted alongside biomedicine in pharmacies, clinics and some hospitals.

The woman's body, time and biomedical management

In the second part of this chapter, I will focus on the Gujarati woman's lived body experiences in Britain, in the context of industrial time and biomedical management. This shift involves movement from her being seen as a passive object being acted on by kinship, religion and rituals, to one where she is actively negotiating and navigating herself through what could sometimes be seen as a stormy sea full of waves, adverse tides and currents. Gujarati women describe the process of breastfeeding in natural metaphors involving water flows, rather than the industrial metaphors used by Western women. Problems were associated with 'lack of flow' instead of 'lack of supply', suggesting a connection with nature rather than production, which is linked with a mechanistic view of the body. Ameeta told me how her milk did not flow and she resorted to giving her baby bottle feeds:

> No matter how hard I tried to breastfeed, the milk just did not flow. I tried for a week and got the feeling that the child was hungry because he used to take a lot of water from the bottle. I think it was my mother who said that you are not going to flow; the best thing is to put him on powdered milk. She said that he is losing weight, which he was.

Meera also identified that the breastfeeding problems other women had were associated with the lack of flow:

> Breast milk is precious. They say that, during pregnancy, the milk is being prepared for the baby. If the milk doesn't flow then there is something wrong with you. A lady down the road had a lot of milk, but no way was it coming out. They used a pump and what not, but no way it came. So she had to give bottle milk.

Western women use production and industrial metaphors, which suggest how breastfeeding has been removed from the natural flows of the mother's body and situated in the context of work, based around the clock as a way of exercising controls over nature (Khan, 1989). The deep entrenchment of these concepts in Western thought is demonstrated in the popularity of childcare manuals that advocate strict time regimes of childrearing, rather than responding to a child's communication of need. Women in the West may have lost touch with their natural body rhythms and flows following industrialisation. Ideas of the body as a machine that can be turned on and off as required, where 'supply' must meet 'demand' and milk 'let down' when required, are taken for granted. The verb 'to breastfeed' itself is mechanistic, indicating the transfer of milk to the baby in isolation from the woman's body as a whole, separated from emotions, nurturing, and the natural and social world around them. Concepts of linear time arose with industrialisation, with time schedules for feeding, moving the woman away from being in control of her body's natural processes and her 'organic cycle of life' (Khan, 1989, p. 21). Biomedicine took charge of these body fluids in the form of strict feeding regimes, determining how and when breastfeeding should happen, leaving women feeling powerless. Khan attempts to situate time back within the body and describes the times of pregnancy, birth and lactation as 'maialogical' from the Greek word 'maia' meaning mother or nurse (p. 27). Using a maialogical perspective, she argues that childbirth becomes the founding moment of the relation of self to other, grounded in the body, where both the one being born and the one giving birth are taken into account (Khan, 1989). She describes the experience she had when breastfeeding her own son:

> After being at work with deadlines, schedules and meetings, everything marked off by the clock, I would float with him into a different time. It was more cyclical, like the seasons, the tides, like the milk which kept its own appointment with him, without my planning it out. I lived those years in two kinds of times – agricultural and industrial (Khan, 1989, p. 21).

Older Gujarati women have told me that the younger generation in Britain and urban India may not have time for breastfeeding, but in rural India it was different. Here time in pregnancy and breastfeeding is seen as 'time out' from their normal work, a good time for women, and a time for rest. They saw breastfeeding as a vital time for recuperation after the birth and anticipated health problems later in life, especially associated with their back, if this did not happen. Several younger mothers who came to Britain after arranged marriages, spoke to me about their previous experiences in India. Joyti came from rural Gujarat and she told me:

> In India, women have plenty of time for breastfeeding. They sit together and talk. Some will go to the farm early and return to breastfeed.

Bina agreed with Joyti and said:

> The ladies of our caste do not work after they have children. They are at
> home and do housework, so it is easier to breastfeed than here.

Joyti continued and said:

> I liked working on the farm. They used to grow peanuts, potatoes and
> onions. We used water from the well. I miss it.... They have a much
> better life than here... they have freedom. If they have extra work, then
> they call other ladies to help. When we are breastfeeding we are free
> from work. At night when babies wake up and are crying, bottle-feeding
> is hard. It is easy to breastfeed in bed.

Breastfeeding was seen here as a positive time for women to relax and
socialise. Rather than being hard work or demanding, it was a time of release
from the hard physical labour of the farms. In the West, childbirth and lactation
have become times needing to be controlled by the clock, rather than natural
times which respond to the bodies of the mothers and their infants, or 'maialogical' times. Biomedicine has sought to manage both these natural processes
within predetermined time restraints, resulting in women losing contact with
their natural body flows and 'maialogical' time. Strict schedules, feed charts,
scales and growth charts have reinforced the biomedical stance and served to
distance the mother from her body and that of her baby. An awareness of body
rhythms, flows and breastfeeding as body praxis has been lost and undermined,
and women's bodies treated as unreliable and needing surveillance.

The medical management of breastfeeding dates back to the 15th century;
at that time there was agreement between religious and medical writers that
the mother was the best nurse for her child (Fildes, 1986). The emphasis from
the importance of the mother–child relationship in the 16th and 17th centuries
changed to the good health of the mother and child in the 18th century. The term
'breastfeeding' suggests this emphasis on the contents of the breast or the milk
itself and the process of its transfer to the baby. Foucault (1978) argues that
biomedicine in the West now occupies the social space left by the erosion of
religion, and Turner (1992, p. 22) develops this further by suggesting:

> The development of society in terms of the differentiation of religion,
> medicine, law and government, eventually brought about a separation
> of the functions of doctor and the priest, and then a transfer of moral
> regulation from the church to the clinic.

The implications of the medicalisation of breastfeeding in Western countries
are profound, not only because of the increasing control and surveillance it

places on women's bodies, but because of the wider social, cultural and economic effects. Both van Esterik (1989) and Maher (1992) have recognised some of these issues:

> Medicalisation individualises human problems and removes them from their social and economic context (van Esterik, 1989, p. 115).

Maher argues that biomedicine treats breastfeeding as if it were situated in a social vacuum and cultural factors such as gender relations that determine women's work, conjugal or kinship roles, or reproduction as a political strategy are rarely discussed (Maher, 1992, p. 175):

> The medical model as regards breastfeeding appears to belong to an out-dated positivist tradition, which is anthropologically interesting but highly dangerous, if it is to inform policies towards women. It may be too costly for women to regard it merely as an object of analysis and not as an attitude to oppose and overcome.

Haraway (1991) also argues that the domination of women is deeply embedded in the natural sciences. She sees that science has become a 'reified fetish' in the way that it has been created by humans and then they forgot that they had done so. It has become the new 'truth', replacing religion, and advocates a new feminism that replaces science as culture and sees nature not as an enemy that needs to be destroyed. Women's bodies should not be alienated and turned into commodities but viewed as active agents (Haraway, 1991).

Indian women's bodies have been seen as 'problems' in biomedical literature and have been the focus of research looking into high infant mortality rates, low birth weight babies, rickets, TB and anaemia. Katbamna (1993) argues that however well meaning the research may have been, there has been inadequate consultation with the Asian community and the inferiority of the Asian culture and its dietary habits have been emphasised, so resulting in victim blaming:

> It is assumed that given time, the attitude of the next generation of Asian women will be brought into line with those of the indigenous women, with the help of the health professionals (Katbamna, 1993, p. 10).

Women from South Asia in Britain are more likely to breastfeed initially and continue for longer than those from the indigenous community (Hamlyn *et al.*, 2002), so here, in this country, is an opportunity to learn about a positive aspect of women's bodies within a social world of kin that still believe that breastfeeding is an important way to nurture a child and teach him or her about the world. It is apparent that breastfeeding is an integral part of every aspect of my ethnography on Gujarati kinship, within the context of Hindu and Jain religion, and can never be isolated in discreet areas. Biomedicine is respected and the support given by midwives and health visitors appreciated, but where family ties are strong, the advice given by powerful older women is more likely to be followed. Women have to navigate through this choppy sea of conflicting ideas and information and make sense of it for their own bodies. The way in which decisions are made about breastfeeding will be different for each woman depending on the support she receives from her own kin and her own sense of power and control.

The woman's body in religion, supernatural beliefs and gender

The woman's body is portrayed in Hindu and Jain temples as something to be revered and worshipped, often in the form of goddesses, or *mata* (meaning either mother or goddess). Breasts are often exposed in temple art in representations of the *mata*, and are not seen as sex objects but as images of fertility, producers of a pure, white, sacred fluid. Women have a close affinity with the *mata* and act as mediators between humans and the divine through ritual. Adherence to purity observances during menstruation and childbirth strengthens the bond they have with the *mata* and heightens the protection that will in turn be afforded to the new mother and her child. Failure to observe expected rites may anger the goddess and result in misfortune or ill health in the household. Girls and young women who are virgins and have not yet menstruated are considered pure and may represent the *mata* in ritual, and their inclusion increases the validity and efficacy of the occasion. Usually seven virgins are invited for each image of the *mata* included in the ritual, and their presence is seen as a good omen for the household, emphasising the closeness between women and the goddesses. Raheja and Gold (1994) also see this strength in their analysis of Rajastani women's songs which challenge the image of the Hindu woman as split between her 'sexual potency' and 'procreative and nurturing capacities'. They argue that the split image approach to Hindu women comes from a male perspective and that women see themselves as 'participants in a society strongly oriented toward fertility' (Raheja and Gold, 1994, p. 37). Breastfeeding is an essential part of this nurturing; breast milk has come from the gods and must not be wasted, but fed to the baby for whom it has been specially made. Most Gujarati households worship Krishna as the main God and the divine embodiment of Vishnu. In Hindu epic he is portrayed as the divine lover, effeminate and seductive, who danced with the *gopi* (milk maids or girl cow herds). The links he had with cows and milk strengthens the association between milk and the divine. The annual autumn festival of *navatri*, which is nine nights of dancing, celebrates women's fertility through a special dance with sticks, performed in epic, by Krishna with the *gopi*.

Every important religious ritual uses cow's milk as one of the five immortal substances, its level of purity surpassing all the others. The cow itself is called *gai-mata* (mother cow), who is venerated as one of the goddesses, the mother of all, and the milk she produces is essential not only for health, but also in linking humans with the divine. Milk is particularly suitable for children who are intrinsically pure, so the food given to them is similar to that given to the gods and is considered safe. Cooked foods, by contrast, are vulnerable to evil influences or negative forces and may be responsible for introducing an unclean element into the child's body. So weaning may be delayed, depriving children of the needed nutrients, especially minerals that are present in a mixed diet.

Health visitors working with South Asian families will be aware of this dependence on cow's milk in children's diets. It may also be a sign of wealth in India, where poor families are unable to buy it, but in the UK milk is cheap and in abundant supply. Children are often given excessive volumes of cow's milk or formula after weaning from the breast, which suppresses their appetites for food and may lead to anaemia. The challenge here is to understand the link that milk has with purity and to work with families to establish which home-cooked foods, such as lentils and green vegetables, could also be used. Commercially prepared foods may be viewed with suspicion because of the uncertainty surrounding their preparation and cooking, and the possibility of negative energies having entered the foods. Feeding bottles are often covered with cotton or woollen cloths to prevent the milk being seen by others. Someone outside the kin network may look at the milk with a jealous eye and spoil the milk by introducing negative energies into it, which could make the child unwell.

When a mother breastfeeds, she also needs to take care that other women who might be jealous do not see her and evoke supernatural powers that may spoil her milk. Nikhita, a mother of two children, both of whom she breastfed, explained some of the precautions a mother should take to protect her children from the evil eye:

> Because we have this thing about the evil eye, Asian women will not feed in front of other Asian women. They feel that the woman might cast an evil eye on their child, and then you will stop producing milk. They are very cautious who they feed in front of, and will probably restrict it to just direct family. If there is someone else there, they will not come out and feed their child. It is not the shame of showing a boob, it is out of fear of casting the evil eye. She may be jealous and think, oh, she's got a beautiful baby, or she's having milk, and I couldn't do it. Or it could be that she has a boy, and I've got a girl. It could be a hundred and one things, and she could be from one of the most modern families.

My mother-in-law told me not to feed in front of anyone, because we don't want anyone casting an evil eye on him. I would have breastfed him if there were no other Asian mothers present. We don't think white people have the same jealousy.

Nikhita's mother-in-law gave her advice on the avoidance of the evil eye and where to feed her son, but other women in the kinship network may also have been consulted. Children and newly delivered mothers are in a state of transition and are particularly vulnerable to attack from supernatural forces in the forms of the evil eye and ghosts. A mother is discouraged from showing too much pride or loving behaviour towards her child in front of others, or she herself may transmit the 'sweet evil eye' to her child. Beliefs in the evil eye pervade social life and may restrict mixing with others. I described the rituals after childbirth earlier in the chapter, which were guided by older women in the family; likewise certain practices are followed to protect children from misfortune. Here Nikhita's mother-in-law was controlling the space where breastfeeding could happen in order to protect her grandson and her daughter-in-law.

Most South Asian women will also refrain from breastfeeding in front of men in the household. Exposure of certain parts of the body is considered disrespectful of men and elders. In India, the shoulders and legs should be covered with the Punjabi suit or sari, although the midriff is visible with the sari. Women can breastfeed very discreetly with the baby tucked under a fold of a sari, or under a loose top, but will usually only do so in front of other female kin.

Men are beginning to take a more active role in being involved in decisions on infant feeding and participate in discussions in antenatal classes. After the birth of their infants, if they live in joint households, they tend to leave any feeding support that their wives need to their mothers or aunts. In a nuclear setting, especially if there are few relatives in Britain, they may be more involved. Women negotiate where and when to feed their infants usually with their female kin, but increasingly men, especially in the professional social groups, are becoming involved in these decisions.

Conclusion

This chapter has sought to demonstrate the different aspects of social life that contribute to attitudes and inform bodily praxis about breastfeeding. It is rarely an individual act but one made, whether consciously or not, in tune with close kin, in line with religious values and supernatural beliefs, ideas of the body and self; within the constraints of industrial society and biomedicine. Gujarati women in Britain have continued to breastfeed more than their Western counterparts and do so for longer. Health professionals trained to have a psychoanalytic approach to parenting, which highlights the supremacy of the mother–child bond, may find the close involvement of female kin difficult to understand. Multiple mothering encourages a long-term relationship with many kin and is the beginning of the network of interdependency that makes up Gujarati kinship. The challenge to health professionals is to understand some of these cultural processes that influence decisions on infant feeding, and adjust their advice to support and encompass them. The influence of older women needs consideration when planning antenatal education classes, postnatal support groups and parenting sessions. Campaigns to promote breastfeeding need to be targeted at older female relatives as well as parents if they are to be effective with South Asian communities.

References

Fildes, V. (1986) *A History of Infant Feeding*. Edinburgh University Press, Edinburgh.

Foucault, M. (1978) *The History of Sexuality*. Tavistock Publications, London.

Hamlyn, B., Brooker, S., Olienikova, K. and Wands, S. (2002) *Infant Feeding 2000*. The Stationery Office, London.

Haraway, D. (1991) *Simians, Cyborgs and Women*. Routledge, London.

Harrow Primary Care Trust (2002) *Breastfeeding Audit*. Unpublished.

Kakar, S. (1981) *The Inner World: A Psycho-Analytic Study of Childhood and Society in India*. Open University Press, Delhi.

Katbamna, S. (1993) *The Experiences of Bangladeshi, and Gujarati Women in Childbirth*. Unpublished PhD Thesis, Cranfield University.

Katbamna, S. (2000) *Race and Childbirth*. Open University Press, Buckingham.

Khan, R. P. (1989) Women and time in childbirth and during lactation. In: *Taking our Time, Feminist Perspectives on Temporality* (eds. F. Forman and C. Sowton). Pergamon Press, Oxford.

Kurtz, S. (1992) *All the Mothers are One: Hindu India and the Cultural Reshaping of Psychoanalysis*. Columbia University Press, New York.

Maher, V. (1992) *The Anthropology of Breastfeeding: Natural Law or Social Construct*. Berg, London.

Raheja, G. and Gold, A. (1984) *Listen to the Heron's Words. Reimagining Gender and Kinship in North India*. University of California Press, London.

Scheper-Hughes, N. (1992) *Death Without Weeping*. University of California Press.

Seymour, S. (1999) *Women, Family and Childcare in India. A World in Transition.* Cambridge University Press, Cambridge.

Spiro, A. (2003) *Moral Continuity: Gujarati Kinship, Women, Children and Rituals.* Unpublished PhD Thesis, Brunel University.

Turner, B. (1992) *Regulating Bodies.* Routledge, London.

van Esterik, P. (1989) *Motherpower and Infant Feeding.* Zed Books, Michigan.

Warrier, S. (1988) Marriage, maternity and female economic activity: Gujarati mothers in Britain. In *Enterprising Women: Ethnicity, Economy and Gender Relations* (eds. S. Westwood and P. Bhachu). Routledge, London.

Glossary

The following words are used in the text in the Gujarati vernacular:

Chatti	The ceremony done six days after birth, when Vidhata, the god of fate is invited to write the child's future.
Dadi	Father's mother.
Dharma	Religious duty or the way of truth.
Foi	Father's sister.
Gai-mata	The cow goddess. Cows are venerated and cared for by local people in India. To kill a cow is worse than killing a Brahman.
Gopi	The milk maids believed to have danced with Krishna.
Karma	Action which accumulates and attaches itself to the soul, so determining a person's fate after death and whether he or she is fit for reincarnation.
Katlu	A sweet food made of nuts, glue, honey and ghee, given to mothers after birth.
Mata	Mother or goddess. *Mataji*-with the respectful suffix.
Nani	Mother's mother.
Najar	The evil eye, or the eye of jealousy.
Sasu	Mother-in-law.
Sava mahino	One month and a quarter.
Sua	Boiled water, containing spices, given to mothers to drink after childbirth, to rid their bodies of impurities.

CHAPTER 8

'Breastfriends' Doncaster: the story of our peer support project

Mavis Kirkham, Angela Sherridan, Daniella Thornton
and Mary Smale

Background

Doncaster is a working class northern town with breastfeeding rates well below the national average. In many of the deprived areas of Doncaster, bottle feeding has been the norm for three generations. Mothers who wish to breastfeed are therefore likely to have few people within their circle of friends and family with whom they can discuss the experiences of breast-feeding. Support networks are very important for new mothers, especially when they are embarking upon life's most important project for the first time. In the absence of breastfeeding experience within their support net-work, new mothers are likely to receive well meaning advice to 'give him a bottle' derived from the experience of all those they love and respect. Thus there are real problems in promoting breastfeeding in a situation where the social default position is usually that of bottle feeding.

Enthusiastic midwives, health visitors and an NCT breastfeeding counsellor had worked hard to improve breastfeeding initiation and several projects had endeavoured to provide support for breastfeeding mothers in Doncaster in the late 1990s. Work with a breastfeeding drop-in session, staffed by midwives and health visitors, had shown the need for breastfeeding knowledge and experience within the community.

At this stage, we reached the conclusion that the aim must be to attempt to change the culture of Doncaster towards breastfeeding. This change in culture was needed to create a situation where everyone knew someone who was breast-feeding or who had successfully breastfed and breastfeeding was something that people talked about. It was clear that a breastfeeding resource was needed which was within the community and part of the experience of the social networks of new mothers.

Research has shown that knowing and seeing peers breastfeed can influence young women to choose breastfeeding (Gregg, 1989). Breastfeeding peer support has been shown to work well in other areas (Gribble, 1996; Brown, 1998), and we were keen to set up a peer support project in Doncaster.

Breastfriends Doncaster 2000

Late in 1999, a Department of Health Breastfeeding Initiative small grant provided the opportunity to set up a peer support project for young breastfeeding mothers in Doncaster. The project was originally planned by three midwives (Debbie Ellis, Angela Sherridan and Mavis Kirkham) and two NCT breastfeeding counsellors (Mary Smale and our local counsellor Rachel Hymans). The project team, which included a health visitor and a midwife teacher, met with health visitors and community midwives to gain their support in recruiting volunteers. Some health visitors observed that women in their area simply did not breastfeed so they could not recruit any volunteers, but overall the project was received with enthusiasm. Recruitment leaflets, designed by the project team, were given to community midwives and health visitors and their clients. These leaflets were soon scrapped and replaced by leaflets and posters felt to be more appropriate by the first set of volunteers. The design was very different and very much their own!

The training sessions were held in Doncaster Women's Centre, a town centre site, in the hope that it would be more accessible and attractive to young mothers than NHS premises. It was felt to be important to base the project amongst many other women's activities. The breastfeeding drop-in sessions were also transferred from the hospital to the Women's Centre and used as a base for volunteers to gain ongoing support and informal training.

The initial recruitment day was attended by five young mothers. Fares and childcare costs were provided if required. We had hoped for 10 mothers, but our meetings with health visitors suggested that this may have been unrealistic. The initial mutual introductions often included the phrase 'but I thought I was the only one breastfeeding'. The way out of isolation and the potential for friendship and mutual support was apparent from the start.

The training undertaken by the volunteers

The training programme used was based, in part, on approaches developed by the National Childbirth Trust breastfeeding counselling training programme. The approach we adopted was rooted in their 'counselling skills' model which emphasised research-based information and the provision of support for women's own decision making. This model of training has been developed over subsequent courses and published (Smale, 2004).

Two training courses were delivered, one to each of the two intakes of volunteers (10 women in total). Each training course comprised of 20 hours of classroom-based learning activities conducted over the space of a few weeks. Within the short time frame available volunteers were able to achieve a basic level of competency in the all-round skills needed to support childbearing women. The training courses were subject to ongoing evaluation and the forms completed by the volunteers were integral to the continuous cycle of curriculum development.

Overall, attendance at the training sessions was excellent. Occasionally sessions were missed due to unavoidable circumstances such as bereavement, illness and attendance at hospital appointments. All 10 volunteers who were recruited to the training programme completed the course.

The aims of training

The training was intended to empower the volunteers to become advocates for breastfeeding, and to provide practical support to women within their local communities. It was designed to help volunteers to:

- build on their listening and information giving skills
- understand the limits and scope of their role and enable them to recognise and refer concerns they felt that they could not, or should not, deal with
- be aware of the need to avoid competition with health professionals
- avoid reliance on directive methods
- develop self-awareness
- understand the basics of the physiology of breastfeeding in order to help women to breastfeed effectively
- understand some of the social constraints on women and to help them identify strategies to improve their chances of breastfeeding

All aspects of the volunteers' role were explored in integrated sessions which took account of the participants as individual women and as actors within their own sub-cultures.

The training model and methods used

The key philosophies underlying the approach included modelling of respect for the individual within the group (Rogers, 1993) and working from the known to the unknown (Bruner, 1996). The approach was designed to make it possible for the Breastfriends volunteers to inform each other about breastfeeding issues and add some wider understanding, whilst simultaneously seeking to avoid 'professionalising' their knowledge on this subject.

Figure 8.1, which models the key issues that influence a mother's breastfeeding experiences, was developed in collaboration with a National Childbirth Trust (NCT) colleague. It provided a framework for the volunteers' training.

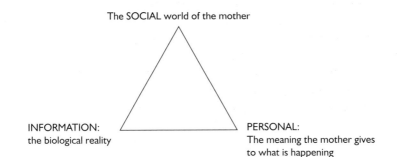

The SOCIAL world of the mother

INFORMATION:
the biological reality

PERSONAL:
The meaning the mother gives
to what is happening

Figure 8.1 The key issues that influence a mother's breastfeeding experiences.

Aspects of breastfeeding

This pedagogic approach enabled the volunteers to reflect upon their own experiences of their childbearing journeys, particularly the experience of infant feeding. It emphasised the interrelatedness of all aspects of this journey and continuously underpinned the knowledge base, which was taught simultaneously. The physiology of breastfeeding was thus taught in conjunction with reflections on personal experience. Volunteers learned to reframe their experiences if necessary, and finally to integrate these experiences with their classroom learning experience. This approach tended to de-emphasise breastfeeding as a biomedical event and to relocate it within a personal, cultural and political context.

The way in which the personal, breastfeeding experiences of the volunteers were actively sought and incorporated into the educational process provided an explicit opportunity for them to come to terms with their individual histories. It also encouraged them to value their own experiential and embodied knowledge, and to consider such knowledge as one of a number of legitimate resources, especially when working within medicalised environments which stress particular forms of 'evidence'.

Volunteers practised listening to one another's accounts of their childbearing journeys. Over time, this 'listening practice' taught them to be more sensitive, empathetic listeners. They became more able to hear personal meanings and less likely to assume diagnostic ways of thinking. The need to work in an active listening skills model was made explicit and reinforced throughout the course. For example, there were handouts and activities about why 'advice' may not empower women to make choices in the way that information-giving does. This is not just a matter of avoiding insurance difficulties and avoiding treading on health professionals' toes. Listening skills use is not about the *taking* of a history from a woman by an expert but about listening to *her* story. It is easy for peer supporters to be subverted into advice-giving if this is the model they hear most. We do not know how important this fundamental difference in communication style is seen to be in other courses since the ethics underlying the communication style chosen are often not mentioned in course descriptions. These tend to focus instead on biomedical content, referring in passing to 'advice' given.

Volunteers were also given the opportunity to consider personal material, which might not be appropriate to share in their volunteering role. The likelihood of inappropriate self-disclosure during encounters with breastfeeding mothers was thus thought to be reduced because a 'safe place' had been created wherein volunteers could discharge difficult experiences and be helped to make sense of them. The possibility of continuing such a dialogue with each other and with their 'supervising' health professional later has been realised in other areas where sensitive and deeply committed people have been involved in offering support to the volunteers. These health professionals are characterised by a respect for peer supporters' embodied, psychological and social experience of breastfeeding. They skilfully 'cherish' the peer supporters.

The training model did not follow a prescribed curriculum, nor were examinations a feature of the volunteers' learning experience. Adult learners, particularly perhaps those who have not previously engaged with educational initiatives, will not necessarily proceed in a linear and logical manner through course material. Adults are 'life-centred in their orientation to learning' (Newman and Peile, 2002). Flexibility in the delivery of the curriculum was thus essential, but this was balanced with a need to work through the skills and knowledge required in an appropriate and sensitive way.

External contributions to the training programme were provided by a small number of local midwives and health visitors. They played an important role in linking the volunteers with the wider community of health professionals.

A child protection worker also contributed her knowledge and skills. As mentioned earlier, the volunteers were recruited in two phases. This enabled the first group of volunteers to contribute their knowledge and experience to the training cycle, for example, by answering questions raised by the second group of volunteers and by talking with them on an individual basis, as the need arose. All of the volunteers felt that the training programme had prepared them very well for their roles, although one was of the opinion that the course was not quite long enough; she felt that she was only just beginning to 'open up'.

The course was interactive and experiential, with the volunteers participating in short bursts of different activities. The training was demanding in terms of the attention required and the volunteers encountered many distractions during the learning process, such as attending to the demands of their breastfeeding toddlers. As most were unfamiliar with recent formal learning it was important to deliver information that was stimulating and that maintained concentration. In order to familiarise the volunteers with different ways of working, activities were arranged which required them to work in pairs, on their own and in groups of different sizes.

Volunteers were taught, and were reminded constantly, about the need to refer medical problems. They were also encouraged to admit to 'not knowing' the answer when they were asked difficult questions. Indeed, learning activities included volunteers having to practise saying 'I don't know', and then asking for the help they needed. This activity was developed into a formal exercise. A variety of scenarios were given and the volunteers were asked to place each one on a continuum line, with 'I am fairly sure I could help this mother' at one end and 'I definitely need help with this one!' at the other end.

Teaching materials included an array of visual images of women breastfeeding, together with written information such as leaflets and magazine articles and extracts from videos. The teaching aids were designed to stimulate discussion amongst the volunteers about the positive and negative responses which breastfeeding provokes. Throughout the training period, the volunteers were encouraged to reflect upon and critically evaluate such material, and to constantly appraise and re-frame their own attitudes towards breastfeeding practices. The classroom exercises were not just about the subject of breastfeeding, but were designed to provide multiple opportunities for the volunteers to develop their self-awareness and confidence in speaking knowledgeably and with authority.

Many of the sessions employed a 'hands-on' approach using everyday objects as demonstration tools. In one such session a sponge soaked in dyed water and oil was squeezed out over a succession of containers. The process of handling, and squeezing out the sponge, conveyed a very realistic impression of the difference between the watery fore-milk (mainly the dyed water) and the increasingly creamy hind-milk (with more oil).

Learning aids

Volunteers were given handouts covering a range of subjects related to breast-feeding. The handouts were colour-coded in accordance with the diagram displayed earlier in this section. The colour green signified 'factual' information and usually had a physiological or biomedical basis, for example, illustrating the 'let-down' reflex. A blue section contained information about the way in which volunteers might consider working with families and their own peer groups. A third, red, section dealt with listening skills.

The volunteers were also given a comprehensive reference folder containing a range of literature on topics related to breastfeeding, a booklist, phone numbers for national and local agencies which might be of interest to new mothers, and a list of relevant community-based facilities. The volunteers also circulated their own home and mobile phone numbers and were given the phone numbers of the two liaison midwives, key members of the team and other referral agencies. This extensive network ensured that the volunteers could always access support when they needed to do so. In later courses such support has proved invaluable in maintaining groups. Health professionals have offered information and emotional support for this work and acted as advocates with less involved colleagues.

Ongoing training

This was achieved informally through the provision of mutual support, either face to face or over the phone, and by weekly attendance with health professionals at a community-based drop-in breastfeeding session. Ongoing training was also delivered via attendance at monthly sessions with the trainer for the Breastfriends Initiative. The content of these formal sessions was responsive, determined by the volunteers and the relevant health professionals prior to the scheduled event.

Outcomes

The progress made by the group towards skilled listening was inspiring. This was no easy task as it required that the volunteers 'unlearn' the powerful and seductive model of 'advice-giving' to which they had been exposed during their own child-bearing careers. The volunteers produced a slogan that illustrated their unique way of supporting women in their desire to breastfeed: *'We do not pester, pressurise or preach.*' By the end of the training course, the volunteers demonstrated great skill in their use of open questions when discussing feeding issues, and in their use of empathy during interactions with one another. Volunteers were also able to demonstrate that they understood the information conveyed to them by explaining what had been said to a third person. The training process seemed to have inspired confidence in the volunteers and heightened their awareness of their ability to contribute, both within their peer group and within their local communities.

Evaluation

The original Breastfriends 2000 project is the only one to have had a formal evaluation (Curtis *et al.*, 2001). This was carried out at the end of the first year of Breastfriends. It was therefore based upon the initial work of 10 volunteers.

The evaluation was carried out by Penny Curtis and Helen Stapleton, researchers from the Women's Informed Childbearing and Health Research group at the University of Sheffield. Three focus groups were held to gain insight into the experiences of volunteers, health professional and breastfeeding mothers who had come into contact with the project. With only three focus groups, recruited through project networks, the authors point out that there was a risk that those who came to the focus groups did so because of their commitment to the project, thus biasing the data. Nevertheless the researchers felt able to draw some conclusions from their clear and interesting findings.

Participants in all the focus groups spoke of the local bottle feeding culture and the problems it posed. Since breastfeeding was a minority choice, many women anticipated breastfeeding in isolation. They lacked positive role models, expected to encounter difficulties with breastfeeding and they commonly anticipated failure.

The language used by all participants to describe aspects of breastfeeding was seen as being of 'enormous symbolic significance'.

Breastfeeding is described in terms of 'success' and 'failure'. There is no equivalent value judgement applied to bottle-feeding. At no stage did any participant refer to an 'unsuccessful bottle-feeder'. The assumption that this brings with it is that a woman who chooses to breastfeed runs the risk of failing as a mother. Moreover, success and failure seemed to be defined in relation to duration of breastfeeding and the distinction was always implicit. Without explicit criteria, against which women could compare their own breastfeeding experiences, they frequently found themselves to be wanting. Women who had not persevered and breastfed for extended periods were likely to feel disappointed with themselves, and to label themselves as failures. The experience of women who had breastfed for relatively short periods of time tended to be ignored or rejected by health professionals. In this respect, the approach taken by the Breastfriends volunteers was notably different. They were wholly committed to breastfeeding and saw all of women's attempts as positive. Although they were aware of the implicit assumptions about an appropriate and sufficient duration of breastfeeding (and indeed applied notions of failure to their own past experiences), they were actively striving to challenge the boundaries between success and failure (Curtis *et al.*, 2001, p. 47)

In all the focus groups, examples were given of how the Breastfriends were achieving cultural change by normalising breastfeeding.

There was general agreement in all groups that the Breastfriends volunteers, although small in number, were beginning to have discernible effects within their communities [...]. Health professionals were convinced that these young women were beginning the long process of 'normalising' breastfeeding within communities with a long-term commitment to bottle feeding. The volunteers have become a source of practical and experiential knowledge around breastfeeding that has previously been inaccessible to many women. They are acknowledged to constitute important role models, and mothers and health professionals saw this very positively. For both these groups, though especially the breastfeeding mothers, the fact that all of the Breastfriends volunteers had fed their babies for a 'long' duration, was particularly significant (Curtis *et al.*, 2001, p. 49).

The positive differences between Breastfriends and health professionals were raised in terms of their knowledge, the time they had for women and their availability as mothers within their local communities.

The different participants within the focus groups attested to the existence of different forms of breastfeeding knowledge. Professionals' discussions were characterised by reference to formal knowledge. The 'Breast is Best' message that they are required to emphasise is anchored in research-based knowledge of the physiology of lactation. In their day-to-day practice, professionals are coming under increasing pressure to justify what they do on the basis of 'evidence', which is defined in relation to established, formal scientific criteria. Professionals referred to a 'political correctness' with respect to breastfeeding and felt that this restricted their freedom to act. The mothers, however, whether volunteers or clients, referred to a much broader notion of breastfeeding knowledge (Curtis *et al.*, 2001, p. 48).

The Breastfriends valued their training which was rooted in a model that legitimated their own experiential and embodied knowledge of breastfeeding.

Both the professionals and the mothers were highly positive about this knowledge. While professionals articulated an undefined assumption that they should dispense the 'right' information to women, mothers seemed willing to access a variety of different knowledges and to try different approaches in order to find what worked best for them. There was a general consensus about the important role that the volunteers played as a source of 'practical' information about breastfeeding. This was defined as the practicalities of integrating breastfeeding into a woman's everyday life and her other mothering commitments. This type of knowledge seems to have been almost completely lost within a longstanding bottle feeding culture (Curtis *et al.*, 2001, p. 48).

Differences between health professionals' responses to the project were reported, particularly in the focus groups of professionals and mothers.

There were clear indications of tensions between professionals; those who had helped to recruit volunteers and had facilitated their work felt an 'ownership' over the project that others did not. There was a perception that 'other' midwives and health visitors had failed to make an effective commitment to Breastfriends and this aroused some hostility within the discussion group (Curtis *et al.*, 2001, p. 50).

It was also clear from the professionals' focus group that this effort to deprofessionalise breastfeeding expertise was seen, by these professionals, as helping them in their professional project rather than being a radically different approach.

While it is clear that the health professionals represented in the focus group acknowledged that the Initiative was a 'good thing', this affirmation was conditional. Discussion clearly articulated a 'them and us' distinction, in which the volunteers (them) were perceived of as a useful group, which could be 'used' by the professionals (us). Midwives and health visitors had to work to control what the volunteers did, but if they accomplished this management work, the Breastfriends could take some pressure off them by providing 'appropriate' support to women in their caseloads.

There was very little evidence from professionals of a two-way learning process. Although a number of professionals noted that working alongside the volunteers had challenged some of their own attitudes towards breastfeeding, only one suggested that she had been stimulated to change her practice as a result. Furthermore, although midwives and health visitors noted with surprise that some of the volunteers had opted not to attend their antenatal classes they had, nonetheless, been highly successful as lay supporters.

This was not, however, seen as a potential learning issue, and the appropriateness of antenatal classes was not discussed.

As the Breastfriends' Initiative matures, and the volunteers explore new ways of working that circumvent the health professionals' gatekeeping role, new tensions between midwives, health visitors and lay supporters may become evident. If the volunteers are to continue to develop as a community resource, issues concerning power and control will need to be acknowledged and confronted. The tensions between health professionals and lay supporters pose a potential threat to the continuing success of this scheme, a danger waiting in the wings (Curtis *et al.*, 2001, p. 51–2).

This evaluation showed considerable foresight.

Breastfriends at work

Two training cycles were completed in 2000 and were followed by monthly study sessions that centred around needs identified by the volunteers. Feedback from the first set of volunteers led to the second initial training being spread over two weeks with shorter days. The first set of volunteers played a considerable part in training and orientating the second set. Volunteers from both sets continued to meet for the Friday afternoon drop-in to ensure ongoing support.

Different volunteers have worked in different ways. Most have had their main contact with mothers through clinics, classes, drop-in sessions or hospital ward visits organised by health professionals. Volunteers are dependent upon local health professionals for access to such sites and health professionals have varied greatly in the extent to which they invited Breastfriends onto their territory. Within these settings, there have been occasions when health professionals committed to the project have stepped in to help volunteers work more effectively. For instance, the support of the Head of Midwifery ensured that Breastfriends could take their own breastfed babies onto postnatal wards, although this had initially been seen as against the rules for ward visitors.

Some volunteers put notices in local shops and one organised a website. All have also had wide informal links with their personal network of family and friends. They have tended to work in pairs for mutual support, though not always in the same pairings.

All but one of those trained as Breastfriends in 2000 continued to work as peer supporters for far longer than was originally anticipated. The exception became an assistant in Mothercare, where she gave support to breastfeeding mothers as part of her job.

The original ten Breastfriends were based in five areas across Doncaster; this was logistically very difficult to co-ordinate. The peer supporters were assigned to midwives and health visitors who would buddy them in their local community. The health professionals' commitment to the project and their support for the peer supporters varied due to their own enthusiasm and the time they could realistically allocate to this work.

For professionals to work well with Breastfriends, it was important that the volunteers' role was understood and they were listened to and enabled to work. This very much depended upon the health professional and became quite frustrating at times when the peer supporters would attend the weekly drop-in sessions at the Women's Centre and share differing stories of how their local midwives or health visitors had or had not enabled them to work with local women. The youngest of the Breastfriends 2000, who had several children, was disapproved of by her health visitor and not allowed to access her clients or work within her clinic sessions. This Breastfriend, therefore, worked through her own network, i.e. through a local Sure Start area and in Doncaster Women's Hospital. The health visitor concerned went on to change areas and has since become considerably more positive towards Breastfriends.

Another Breastfriend was very outspoken to her assigned health professional, calling her a 'silly cow'. Professional training had not included how to handle interpersonal disharmony and this proved a challenge for both parties. Yet over time and through the support and feedback from the project team, mutual respect developed between the Breastfriend and the health professional.

There was sometimes disharmony within the group, as there were considerable social differences. In one area, some peer supporters were seen by others as 'snobby cows' whereas other were labelled 'rough'. This division was addressed by the group and the follow-up sessions were quite innovative. We thought of ways to merge the group together with varying teaching methods, group bonding trips to local attractions and meals out as a thank you for the voluntary work they were doing.

One peer supporter was well respected in a very working class area. She found the that name 'Breastfriend' did not work in that setting. Local women wanted her knowledge and support, but without the Breastfriends, label which they described as 'cheesy' and as signifying becoming 'one of them' with health professionals. After discussion with Angela and Daniella, she stopped using the name and continued to work in her area.

The flexibility and commitment of both the Breastfriends and those supporting the project has been impressive throughout.

Breastfriends spreads

The Sure Start midwife in Denaby and Conisborough was an enthusiastic supporter of Breastfriends. She recruited mothers to the original Breastfriends Doncaster project. The next Breastfriends project was set up by her. Denaby and Conisborough Sure Start started training Breastfriends for their area during 2001. This was then a new Sure Start project covering two former pit villages and operating from small and somewhat dilapidated premises. Mary ran the training in the open entrance area to the building, constantly interrupted as every visitor to the building joined in the conversation and stopped to pat the guide dog of a blind volunteer. The Sure Start midwife found it very difficult to engage other health professionals in the project. She described some colleagues as 'amicable to the project, but they didn't do anything on the ground'. No health professionals referred women to the volunteers, except for the Sure Start midwife herself. Some health visitors felt that the volunteers were too young, others felt that volunteers from Denaby were 'not suitable' to work in Conisborough. Conisborough women, however, were described by volunteers as 'very open' to Breastfriends from out of their area. The Denaby and Conisborough Breastfriends networked amongst friends and relations. Mary kept in touch with several of them for a while and they all said that no one had been referred to them. The Sure Start midwife had 12 women recruited for a second round of Breastfriends training in Denaby when the funding was withdrawn. Since then there have been staff changes in that area and it is possible that Breastfriends may start there again in the future.

After several unsuccessful bids for funding to make a video of the project, Sheffield University Department of Midwifery and Children's Nursing agreed to provide the funding. The 'Help Yourself to Breastfeeding' video went on sale in 2001. We were proud to produce the first video of working class, northern women's experience of breastfeeding. The video has sold well and not just in the north of England.

Breastfriends in Education

In 2002 we gained a second Department of Health Breastfeeding grant for a project developed from Breastfriends called Breastfriends in Education.

The initial proposal for this project stated its aims:

To extend a successful young women's breastfeeding peer support project by training volunteers in group work in educational settings. The project will be integrated into school curricula in a particularly deprived area where bottle feeding has been the norm for three generations. It will then be extended. Boys and girls will have an opportunity to explore breastfeeding issues, which are not part of their culture, with skilled and confident local breastfeeding volunteers. These volunteers can offer new knowledge, new role models and new possibilities whilst remaining grounded in local realities.

Children in one large comprehensive school and all its feeder schools will be involved initially. The project will then extend. The influence on attitudes will be much wider than the classes involved.

These aims were achieved in the main, though there were many problems in the course of the project, resulting in considerable changes in plans.

The training was highly experiential, similar to existing Breastfriends training but with an emphasis on working with groups rather than one to one. It included the volunteers developing their own teaching materials. Training was half-time for two weeks with follow-up study half-days and debriefings over the six months. We planned two six-month cycles of training. The first cycle was conducted by Mary and included the training of two existing Breastfriends and two local midwives as future trainers. The second cycle was to be taught by these local trainers supervised by Mary, but unfortunately it was not conducted as we had no funding for Breastfriends training at that point.

The project centred on work in a large comprehensive school in a deprived area of Doncaster. The Head of Personal and Social Education, an enthusiastic supporter of the project, timetabled sessions with all the Year 9 mixed classes of boys and girls (aged 14). Two groups of volunteers, each consisting of a midwife and two Breastfriends with their babies, worked in that school. Group 1 did two sets of three classes, Group 2 did one set of three classes. Thus three groups of pupils had three classes.

We achieved access to only one other secondary school. The only way we could access this school was by agreeing to integrate our sessions with the childcare lessons, which were only attended by girls, despite being a mixed school. Two sessions were held with 14–15-year-old girls. There were approximately 25 girls in each group. It was not possible to timetable any follow-up sessions in this school.

Nine junior schools act as feeders for the secondary school in which we mainly worked. We made approaches to all of these, but were only able to establish links with four. We applied to the school governors for permission to carry out sessions in these four schools, but were granted permission to access just one. Unfortunately, most of our approaches and our applications to school governors to conduct sessions in junior schools were rejected or ignored. In the school that granted us access, we held two sessions for three groups of children in their senior year (there were approximately 30 children per group). Our sessions were linked with recent classes on citizenship. For that reason the midwife was asked to attend in uniform and describe her job as one to which children could aspire. We accepted this as a condition of access. The teacher was not present at these sessions, but her cousin, a breastfeeding mother known to the class, was present, thus freeing the teacher for other activities.

As well as the sessions in schools, two sessions were held with student nursery nurses. One session was held with teenagers in an after-school drop-in centre. Another one-off session was held within a project for teenage mothers.

Overall the sessions went well and all were enjoyed and evaluated well by those who took part. The volunteers were very flexible in their approach. This was essential in terms of responding to pupils. It was also essential as the sessions were used by teachers to serve very different agendas. The sessions were fitted in to the National Curriculum as citizenship, childcare and personal and social education. The volunteers responded appropriately in each case.

The teachers and school nurses at our main secondary school were very supportive. Yet we were aware that their position was difficult with regard to breastfeeding. Initially volunteers were requested to be 'very discreet' if they breastfed during sessions. It was in this most supportive school that the name of the project was changed to remove the word 'breast'. Informal feedback from teachers suggests that breasts have powerful sexual connotations, even in the context of infant feeding. Lessons with 'breasts' in their title are therefore seen as potentially threatening to the emotional order of the school. The screening of our proposal by school governors is a procedure designed for sex education sessions. The renaming of the project at our most supportive school, so as to remove any reference to breasts, also demonstrates this problem.

Negotiating access to schools was very time-consuming and involved more gatekeepers than we had anticipated. Where we gained access, it was because individuals who shared our aims managed to fit us into parts of the curriculum where they had some control of class content. As volunteers and midwives, we were outsiders who had to adjust to the requirements of each school. It was interesting that the midwife was required to wear her uniform to demonstrate her status in the junior school. This was in contrast to our earlier decision to avoid wearing uniforms in an attempt to aid communication and demonstrate equality between midwives and Breastfriends. We had to fit the different agendas of the schools, as breastfeeding has no place, in its own right, in the National Curriculum.

Almost all the pupils who took part in the sessions were enthusiastic. There were three instances of challenging behaviour: one was dealt with by a teacher; one challenging boy was challenged back by a midwife; and some noisy junior school boys were described by one Breastfriend as 'OK once you show a bit of authority'. The challenging pupils all went on to participate appropriately.

A 'titter session' dealt with embarrassment and rude words at the outset. Our collection of words for breasts was large and runs from 'babylons' to 'twin towers'. Labels saying how pupils were fed when they were infants gave a very personal aspect to the facts and discussion that followed. This also initiated discussion at home, where some children asked their parents how they had been fed as babies.

The volunteers have grown in confidence and skill. They initially described themselves as 'dreading it', being 'scared stiff' or 'very nervous' and, in one case, 'nearly passing out with fear'. Yet the teachers and midwives who were part of the sessions described them as 'confident', 'flexible' and 'responding well'. They dealt with every eventuality and are keen to help train future volunteers.

This project is considered to be a success and is much discussed by professionals and young people in Doncaster. The Healthy Schools Co-ordinator for Doncaster is enthusiastic about the project and has asked us to 'roll it out across Doncaster'. However, she has no funding to help us do this, nor can she facilitate our access to individual schools.

Breastfriends goes on

After mid-2001 there was a lull. The initial volunteers continued to work, though we gradually ran out of funds to pay their travel and childcare expenses. Although the project received lots of favourable publicity locally and nationally, there was no money left to train further volunteers. Breastfriends spoke at a number of conferences and we received many letters from people wanting to visit the project. As the project had no base and was then running with minimal funds, we organised two study days at the University of Sheffield. One day addressed Breastfeeding Peer Support and the other was concerned with Breastfeeding Education in Schools. Both study days were well attended and highly successful.

We applied unsuccessfully to a number of sources of funding. None would fund a project that was already under way. We spoke to a number of service providers in health and community development across Doncaster; they all praised the project but went on to explain that it didn't quite come under their remit and they had no money to spare. The ongoing commitment of the volunteers was unfailing; together with the project team, they attended a vast number of meetings, complete with babies and toddlers, only to be disappointed when we did not gain the funding that we sought. Daniella and Marie, both from an area that had excellent links with supportive health professionals, became the only peer supporters left as the others gradually found other forms of employment and devoted their time to their children.

At the end of 2002, Sure Start Moorends and the Willows agreed to fund Thorne Breastfriends and training started there in January 2003. At this stage, true to the enabling approach, Mary stepped back from being the trainer and concentrated on equipping and supporting others to be trainers. Angela and Debbie (the midwives who started the project) and Daniella and Marie (the peer supporters from the second set of Breastfriends trained in 2000) were trainee trainers, who became equipped to take on the training role in future. Debbie, who was on maternity leave at the time, brought in her third son and breastfed him whilst doing the training. The volunteers identified with her and would ring and confide in her as she was 'real' and at the same point in life as they were. Having two peer supporters carrying out part of the training showed what volunteers could achieve, and the new peer support trainees had people they could talk to about the practicalities and potential of being a Breastfriend. The project was evaluated extremely well by the seven mothers who took part.

Sure Start Adwick and Bentley agreed to fund a Breastfriends project from March 2003 to April 2004. Daniella became the co-ordinator there in her own local area, supported by Debbie and Angela. Mary, our original trainer, acted as a supervisor to the training. We were all delighted that one of the original Breastfriends was now running the Breastfriends training.

Daniella has since trained a second set of volunteers in Bentley and Adwick. This second group of volunteers met at Daniella's house, because the only alternative venue available was a church hall and one of the volunteers was a Jehovah's Witness who did not feel comfortable there. This also alleviated the need for crèche support as the children were in the same room as their mothers and played with Daniella's children's toys. The informal setting of a home worked really well and was appreciated by the trainees – they felt comfortable and relaxed. It was the first time Daniella had run the training alone and she was very nervous, but found that it 'just came naturally' as she had done the training so many times before. All the trainees were very supportive and congratulated her afterwards for doing a good job and said that they had learned a lot more than they thought. She still has close links with three of the four trainees.

In January 2004, Intake and Belle Vue Sure Start set up a breastfeeding peer support project, co-ordinated by Angela and Daniella, who were by then very experienced in working together as midwife and volunteer trainers. They chose the name Bosom Buddies Breastfeeding Encouragement and Support Team. Each group has its own identity as well as its own name. Other groups have been trained using the approach developed originally for Doncaster in the East Yorkshire, York and North Lincolnshire areas and are in touch with each other, with occasional meetings and informal support. For example, on some occasions a peer supporter meets a mother with a special situation and may find it helpful to talk to a peer supporter in another area who has had this experience herself.

In the autumn of 2004 a post was created to co-ordinate breastfeeding peer support projects across Doncaster and to support new projects. The post is part-time and for a year and a half, but it is the first move to foster projects across the area. There was a lot of competition for the post. The person who was appointed to the post was one of the first set of Breastfriends trained in Bentley by Daniella.

Breastfriends, the New Generation

At the end of 2003 a teenage breastfeeding co-ordinator post was created to roll out training for 'Breastfriends, the New Generation'. The training will be Open College Network (OCN) accredited through partnership with Doncaster

Women's Centre. Daniella was appointed to this post. We see this as fitting recognition of the skills she has developed and the work she has undertaken as a Breastfriend.

Extending breastfeeding peer support to teenagers is not an easy task. There are few people breastfeeding in Doncaster as it is, never mind teenagers! Much of Daniella's time has been spent visiting centres and groups, where pregnant or teenage mothers go, to talk to them and try to identify young mothers who have breastfed and would be interested in doing the training. The first training sessions have now started; there are only two volunteers but both are enthusiastic. It was felt that it was important to go ahead despite the small number of volunteers, as this may interest others in future training sessions. The basis of the training is the same as Breastfriends training, but it has had to be adapted and added to, to make it fit the OCN criteria and to make it more hands on and interesting for teenagers.

Reflections on the project

Did it work?

When we applied for the first Breastfriends funding in 1999, our overall aim was:

- To increase the number of women, especially young women, from deprived areas of Doncaster who initiate and continue breastfeeding, using an empowerment approach.

We also listed our objectives:

- To present breastfeeding as a viable option for women in Doncaster.
- To equip young mothers to support others in breastfeeding within their community.
- To equip these helpers to take up a wider local educational role with regard to breastfeeding, especially within schools.
- To use these helpers in the recruitment and training of future helpers.
- To create a multidisciplinary team of health professionals and representatives of voluntary support groups who will support and evaluate the project and liaise and inform local midwives and health visitors.

Breastfeeding rates have risen in Doncaster since 1999 but it would be impossible to prove, and arrogant to claim, that this is due to the efforts of Breastfriends alone.

There are Breastfriends projects in some parts of Doncaster but not in others. The fragmented service of Breastfriends in some parts of Doncaster parallels the fragmentation of Sure Start areas, which cover several parts of Doncaster but not all and differ in their organisation, some including Breastfriends and some not. There is no Breastfriends network across Doncaster, which would be a real lever towards the cultural change that we seek. We trust that the creation of the new co-ordinator's post will mark the start of such a network. Breastfriends in Education only addressed a small part of Doncaster's education system for less than one year. Again, our best efforts have not produced the funding to extend that service. Yet progress has been made and the posts now held by Daniella and her colleague were beyond our hopes in 1999.

We sought to focus this project on young mothers, yet most of the Breastfriends were in their early 20s when recruited. We have not done much work with teenage mothers. In all the focus groups involved in the project evaluation, consisting of mothers, midwives, health visitors and volunteers, there was a tendency to demonise younger mothers (Curtis *et al.* 2001). We hope that 'Breastfriends, the New Generation' will make the skills and achievements of Breastfriends available to younger mothers, as part of a project which they feel is theirs.

Cultural change is slow, but we feel that it is happening. The project has had lots of local publicity and breastfeeding is discussed locally. In 2001, Mavis had the happy experience of overhearing two women, whom she did not know, discussing the project in positive terms in Doncaster fishmarket. Yet our successes contain their own dilemmas, from which we seek to learn.

Empowerment?

This project is a deliberate attempt to deprofessionalise breastfeeding and enable mothers to act as resources of breastfeeding skills and knowledge within their community. Given the extent to which breastfeeding, and much of life, has been placed in the hands of professional experts, this may have been a naive aim. Whilst we are still convinced that this is the path towards cultural change in favour of breastfeeding, it is not without its ups and downs.

'Empowerment' is a word that has become a part of the language of professionals to refer to aspects of their work (Ramcharan and Borlans, 1997). Yet the behaviour of a few midwives and health visitors towards Breastfriends suggests that they see power as a finite commodity, resisting any decrease in their own power which they perceive may follow from increasing the power of others. We saw this with the gatekeeping of some midwives and health visitors who did not invite Breastfriends into their territory. Breastfriends were seen as too young, too working class, from a less desirable part of town or otherwise inappropriate to be invited into their clinics or classes. In Daniella's experience, getting referrals was the hardest thing; a lot of the health professionals tended to gatekeep and were not confident in the volunteers' abilities as they were not familiar with the Breastfriends training. In her view, it took her four years to be truly accepted and respected as a complementary service by health professionals. This is interesting, as in Angela's view, as a midwife involved in the project but not working in Daniella's local area, the professional support in that area was fantastic compared to other areas.

Ironically, it may be that efforts to improve midwives' and health visitors' training with regard to breastfeeding have increased their feeling of ownership of breastfeeding knowledge. The following two quotations come from an evaluation of the Doncaster Women's Hospital Breastfeeding Helpline.

> Our knowledge is also a lot better, so we handle a lot of things ourselves anyway ... more recently I've been more inclined to just do it myself. [Health visitor] (Trewick *et al.*, 2001, p. 50)

> Some years ago, yes, I was very actively involved with the NCT and I have used them in the past. But since I've also done the Invest In Breast course, that obviously empowers you with a lot more information .... So, no, I very rarely use other groups now. [community midwife] (Trewick *et al.*, 2001, p. 37)

These quotations raise important issues as to how breastfeeding knowledge is seen. It may be that some health professionals simply felt threatened by someone else being involved in 'their' area of expertise on 'their' territory. Midwives certainly feel that they must give the 'right' information to their clients (Curtis *et al.*, 2001, p. 28; Kirkham and Stapleton, 2001) and this may lead them to feel anxious that they cannot control what others say. Yet, this creates a dilemma as there may be a considerable difference between the 'right' information, which professionals give, and the knowledge which women seek and feel that they need. In the focus group of midwives and health visitors held to evaluate the project, it was observed that:

> Despite the health professionals' exclusive focus on formal knowledge, it was the volunteers' experiential, embodied knowledge of breastfeeding that appeared to increase their credibility and status with participants in this focus group. Yet participants were rarely heard to acknowledge women's embodied knowledge of infant feeding as a valid source of information for other women (Curtis *et al.*, 2001, p. 28).

Professionals can experience difficulties with the splitting off and effective silencing of their own embodied experience in favour of biomedical, formal, evidence-based information. Midwives often qualify an opinion with 'as a mother ...' before reverting to the professional line 'as a midwife'. Breastfriends have the considerable advantage that their training enables them to work through their own experience and integrate it into their knowledge base. The training of midwives and health visitors has traditionally addressed only one of the three key issues in the Breastfriends model of training (see above). This emphasis upon information without consideration of its social and personal context means that the words of midwives and health visitors may not be grounded in the reality of women's lives. Efforts are now being made to enable student midwives to 'debrief' their relevant experiences as part of their education (Battersby, 2004), but this is within a curriculum packed with facts, not within a model which gives equal emphasis to the personal and the social alongside biological information. Breastfriends have done some interesting education sessions with student midwives in the University of Sheffield.

Ours is not the only model of training for breastfeeding peer supporters. No research has been done as to who should best deliver such training and what educational model is most useful. Our model takes time and thought, and is probably more work for all concerned than the delivery of information alone. We chose our model because we are sure that information is of limited use without a social and personal context. If breastfeeding peer support training expands it will be a real challenge to maintain such a model within the health service, where professional education is very different. Indeed, if peer support were to be made available to all, massive issues of bureaucratisation and professionalisation would have to be faced. We hope it may be possible to achieve the cultural change we seek before that occurs.

Another striking contrast between Breastfriends and health professionals concerns time. Mothers praised Breastfriends because they had time for them. Midwives work under great pressures of time, which is often experienced as not giving women time to speak (Stapleton *et al.*, 2002). This makes it difficult for them to work on the equal footing and in the relaxed manner in which friends speak and which Breastfriends used as their model.

> Health professionals have greater status and power than the women who seek care. In order for them to feel comfortable and on an equal footing, professionals must make a deliberate effort to understand women's needs and provide for them (Gready *et al.*, 1995).

It is very difficult to understand women's needs without listening to them as individuals. Breastfriends have considerable training in listening, which is not the experience of health professionals, who also tend to control conversation with clients as a way of managing time (Kirkham and Stapleton, 2001). Women usually do not experience, and may not expect to experience, an 'equal footing' in consultations with midwives. Pressures of time and the professional emphasis upon evidence-based information put women at a real disadvantage in their conversations with health professionals. As a respondent in another study observed (Kirkham and Stapleton, 2001):

They don't 'discuss' things with you. They 'tell' you things. Like you're still at school .... With breastfeeding, they told me all the advantages and disadvantages but I knew them already. I wanted to know what it would feel like ... about feeling embarrassed and if it would hurt for long. My mum couldn't help me on that. She'd bottle-fed all of us.

As the 16-year-old quoted above so clearly illustrates, dialogue is as important as information in the decision-making around breastfeeding. More time and education could improve professional communication skills. Nevertheless, as the professionals in our evaluation observed (Curtis *et al.*, 2001, p. 28), their role does separate them, to some extent, from the women with whom they work.

In a climate of litigation and increasingly rule-governed practice, midwives and health visitors feel they are under considerable pressure to do the 'right' thing as well as to give the 'right' information (Kirkham and Stapleton, 2001). This can be a lonely position to be in. A number of studies show how midwives feel a great need for support, which they find to be lacking in their professional lives (e.g. Kirkham and Stapleton, 2000). This stands in sharp contrast to the training and ongoing support for Breastfriends. Just as mothers appreciated the support of Breastfriends, the volunteers appreciated the support of the project team. In this respect, our project was part of a long tradition of projects concerned with mentoring (Taylor, 2002, p. 193):

... perhaps the most common outcome of studies on mentoring is the enhanced satisfaction the protégés experience in their chosen professions or activities. These benefits are sometimes seen many years after the mentoring has taken place. Mentoring is a stunning example of our ability to minister to strangers, to turn unfamiliar people into friends, and to ameliorate the course of a life that could otherwise go wrong.

Our efforts to cherish and support Breastfriends may have felt alien to health professionals who were not part of the immediate Breastfriends network. Midwives and health visitors give care to women, but often feel they do not receive care themselves (Kirkham and Stapleton, 2001). Mentorship exists as a formal arrangement within midwifery, but is often found to be lacking in practice (Morgan and Kirkham, 2004). The contrast between the care Breastfriends received and their own working situation may even have been experienced as disempowering by some health professionals.

In the evaluation in 2001, only one professional respondent spoke of learning from peer supporters, and this was one of the midwives involved in the Breastfriends training (Curtis *et al.*, 2001, p. 29). This stands in contrast to Mary's conversations with health professional involved with later peer support projects. They talk about learning a lot from the peer supporters' 'complementary' ways of working with mothers, especially valuing their communication style of not using advice.

In the evaluation, there was no evidence of antenatal educational provision being reconsidered in the light of feedback from Breastfriends (Curtis *et al.*, 2001, p. 51). In other places, where Mary has worked with peer support schemes more recently, health professionals have listened carefully to the experiences of peer supporters. These professionals have often found it painful to hear justified criticism. Yet, they have tried and have sometimes been able to feed this back anonymously in meetings with their colleagues. This informal feedback aspect of peer support training is not, so far as we are aware, ever mentioned in research, where professional practice is seen as the model for peer supporters' work. In our experience, peer supporters will often have had enough good support to know already what is right, and have this confirmed in the training, and be taken aback by other health workers' lack of knowledge. Accustomed to support and constructive feedback themselves, volunteers may give what they see as constructive feedback to professionals, who interpret this as criticism and therefore as a threat.

Nevertheless, the presence of mothers with whom women can identify has been found to be helpful in antenatal education in general (Kirkham, 1991) and with regard to breastfeeding (Renfrew and Woolridge, 2003). So, as peer support finds its place in the evidence base of maternity care (see e.g. Protheroe *et al.*, 2003), midwives and health visitors are making uncomfortable adjustments.

Mary has begun to ask for preliminary meetings with health professionals in the local area before new peer support courses start. These have usually been happy occasions, but we do not know if those attending are somewhat self-selecting. We thought we had done this appropriately before we started Breastfriends Doncaster 2000, but Doncaster is a much bigger place than the area covered by projects based within the Sure Start areas.

Perhaps change is just a matter of time and of acceptance. As Breastfriends spreads, relationships with health professionals seem to improve. Angela and Daniella are now working to set up breastfeeding peer support projects in Barnsley. They have experienced no problems there with health professionals gatekeeping. We do not think that Barnsley is any different from Doncaster. Health professionals in South Yorkshire now know about Breastfriends and welcome them because of their positive reputation, whether in other towns or other parts of Doncaster. We appreciate, however, the need for ongoing support and feedback for all concerned and do not underestimate the time and diplomacy required.

We have learnt a lot from Breastfriends, some of which will be fed into future Breastfriends work in Doncaster and some of which is of wider relevance to peer support training, the training of health professionals and antenatal education.

There can be no doubt that Breastfriends has been an empowering project for the volunteers involved and for many women who have come into contact with them. The response from mothers has been overwhelmingly positive. Volunteers and mothers have gained in confidence and practised new skills. Babies and mothers have flourished and we have supported each other through crises in the project and in our own lives. Breastfriends have lost their shyness, found the support of peers, spoken at conferences, taught in schools and universities and got jobs that use their considerable talents. The enabling educational model has had a profound influence upon the thinking of all of those who have been involved with it. New volunteers come forward as others move on. The culture is slowly changing in Doncaster.

Acknowledgements

The authors are grateful for all the support and hard work of the other two members of the original Breastfriends team: Debbie Ellis and Rachael Hymans. We are also grateful to Vivienne Knight, Head of Midwifery, Doncaster and Bassetlaw Hospitals NHS Trust, who has supported the project throughout, facilitated it in many ways and always helped us when we needed her. Jane Flint has acted as administrator for our many endeavours from funding bids to conference planning; we thank her for her unfailing support.

We thank all the Breastfriends and the health professionals who have worked with them for their tremendous work, commitment and flexibility.

We thank the mothers and families of Doncaster, from whom we have learnt so much.

This work would not have been possible without two grants from the Department of Health Infant Feeding Initiative.

References

Battersby, S. (2004) Personal communication. University of Sheffield.

Brown, S. (1998) Peer support for breastfeeding: working with women in the community. *The Practising Midwife*, **1**, 7–8.

Bruner, J. (1996) *Towards a Theory of Instruction*. Harvard University Press, Cambridge, MA.

Curtis, P., Stapleton, S., Kirkham, M. and Smale, M. (2001) *Evaluation of the Breastfriends Doncaster 2000 Initiative*. University of Sheffield, School of Nursing and Midwifery, Sheffield.

Gready, M., Newburn, M., Dodds, R. and Guage, S. (1995) *Birth Choices – Women's Expectations and Experiences*. National Childbirth Trust, London.

Gregg, J. (1989) Attitudes of teenagers in Liverpool to breastfeeding. *British Medical Journal*, **299**, 147–8.

Gribble, J. (1996) An alternative approach. *New Generation*, **15**, 12–13.

Kirkham, M. (1991) Ante-natal learning. *Nursing Times*, **87**, 67.

Kirkham, M. and Stapleton, H. (2000) Midwives' support needs as childbirth changes. *Journal of Advanced Nursing*, **32**, 465–72.

Kirkham, M. and Stapleton, H. (eds.) (2001) *Informed Choice in Maternity Care*. NHS Centre for Reviews and Dissemination, University of York.

Morgan, R. and Kirkham, M. (2004) The experience of midwife returners. Research in progress, University of Sheffield.

Newman, P. and Peile, E. (2002) Valuing learners' experience and supporting further growth: educational models to help experienced adult learners in medicine. *British Medical Journal*, **325**, 200–2.

Protheroe, L., Dyson, L., Renfrew, M., Bull, J. and Mulvihill, C. (2003) *the Effectiveness of Public Health Interventions to Promote the Initiation of Breastfeeding*. Evidence Briefing, NHS Health Development Agency, London.

Ramcharan, P. and Borland, J. (1997) Preface. In: *Empowerment in Everyday Life* (eds. P. Ramcharam, G. Roberts, G. Grant and J. Borland). Jessica Kingsley, London.

Rogers, C. (1993) *Freedom to Learn*, 3rd edn. Merrill, New York.

Smale, M. (2004) *Training Breastfeeding Peer Supporters: An Enabling Approach*. University of Sheffield, Sheffield.

Stapleton, H., Kirkham, M., Curtis, P. and Thomas, G. (2002) Silence and time in antenatal care. *British Journal of Midwifery*, **10**, 393–6.

Taylor, S. E. (2002) *The Tending Instinct*. Henry Holt, New York.

Trewick, A., Ellis, D. and Kirkham, M. (2001) *Evaluation of the Breastfeeding Telephone Helpline at Doncaster Women's Hospital*. University of Sheffield, School of Nursing and Midwifery, Sheffield.

CHAPTER 9

Baby-led weaning

A developmental approach to the introduction of complementary foods

Gill Rapley

Introduction: what is weaning?

Taken literally, the term 'weaning' refers to the process by which an infant's total dependence on his mother for food (in the form of breast milk) is transformed into complete *in*dependence of any direct need for her, nutritionally speaking. This process begins when anything other than breast milk is introduced into the infant's diet and ends with the last breastfeed of that child's life. In the UK, the nation whose practices form the focus of this chapter, the word 'weaning' tends to have different meanings; some use the word to describe the cessation of breastfeeding, but more commonly it is used to describe the introduction of foods other than either breast milk or infant formula. These foods are usually semi-solid in consistency, although they are almost always referred to as 'solids'. It is worth noting here that, while the giving of supplementary drinks of water or juice to young breastfed infants is relatively common in the UK (55% by ten weeks; Hamlyn *et al.*, 2002), this is not generally referred to as weaning. Rather, the term 'weaning' is associated with the introduction of either solid or semi-solid foods.

The World Health Organization recommends exclusive breastfeeding for the first six months of life (WHO, 2002). Accordingly, foods and drinks given before this age are defined as 'breast milk substitutes' (WHO, 1981) (sometimes also referred to as 'supplementary foods'), and those given from six months onwards as 'complementary foods' (WHO, 2002). Since this distinction is blurred when 'complementary' foods are introduced earlier than the recommended age, these terms are not always helpful when studying the actual practices of parents. For this reason, the terms 'introduction of solid foods' and 'initiation of weaning' will be used throughout this chapter to describe the expansion of the predominantly breastfed infant's diet beyond breast milk alone towards both semi-solid and solid foods.

The move to the introduction of solid foods depends on the availability of suitable foods. One possible reason why the manner in which the initiation of weaning is managed has received little attention may be that much of the research on weaning has been conducted in countries where either food is scarce or families are living in extreme poverty and do not have ready access to it. In this case, close supervision and management may be required to ensure that the child receives adequate nourishment (WHO, 2001). It is reasonable to question, however, whether such measures are necessary in the context of the western world. In the UK, it appears that it is the mother rather than the baby who prompts and directs the move away from breastfeeding (Anderson *et al.*, 2001; Hamlyn *et al.*, 2002), but it is by no means clear that this practice is necessarily the most logical, the easiest nor the most effective.

For many years, researchers have sought to establish the right age for weaning to commence. From 1994 until 2003, the recommendation in the UK was that weaning foods should not be commenced before four months of age (Department of Health, 1994). In May 2003, the official recommendation was changed to six months (Department of Health, 2003), in line with the World Health Organization's recommendations published the previous year (WHO, 2002). This change has come about not only as a result of studies which have demonstrated the adequacy of breast milk for the first six months (e.g. Butte *et al.*, 2002; Kramer and Kakuma, 2002), but also because of the growing body of evidence of the detrimental effects, in terms of health and growth, of the early introduction of other foods (e.g. Howie *et al.*, 1990; Heinig *et al.*, 1996; Oddy *et al.*, 2003; Kramer *et al.*, 2004). At the same time, evidence has been collated showing that infants are not ready, in terms of their oral motor, gastro-intestinal and immunological abilities, to manage other foods before this age (Naylor, 2001). What has not been considered with the same degree of rigour is how this transition should be managed and who should initiate and control the process. Since the infant of six months behaves differently, and has different abilities, from the infant of four months it makes sense to re-evaluate the information parents receive about how to recognise an infant's readiness for other foods and how to go about introducing him to them.

The concept of developmental readiness

Throughout a baby's first year, many developmental milestones are achieved, but it is difficult to identify any whose timing is not initiated by the baby. Smiling, rolling over, sitting up, crawling – all may be stimulated by those around him but are ultimately controlled by the baby. A parent may hope that their son will walk before the baby next door, and thus appear 'advanced', but they have no direct control over the matter. While they await the momentous event, however, they regularly provide him with opportunities to walk; he is being given just such an opportunity even at one day old, when his mother puts him on the floor 'to have a kick'. The only constraining factor is his own ability to co-ordinate the necessary muscles.

It is, of course, possible to delay a child's development by *not* providing the necessary opportunities. This fact is explained in seminal work by Illingworth and Lister (1964), a paper which has had enormous consequences for the practice of weaning and to which we shall return later. Provision of opportunity is therefore crucial to ensuring that an infant walks as soon as he is able, but it is his own development which limits how young he is when it he takes his first step. Thus it appear that, given the right environment, infants will develop new skills when they are ready – no earlier and no later.

This approach, i.e. of letting the infant indicate his readiness, appears to be applied consistently to all aspects of an infant's early development, with one significant exception: the introduction of solid foods. This chapter sets out to explore why this should be and to establish a rationale which allows us to see baby-led weaning as a logical, realistic and safe approach to this significant milestone of development.

The historical perspective

It is probable that contemporary practices with regard to infant feeding in the UK have their roots in the early part of the 20th century. Since then there has been a gradual move away from breastfeeding as the accepted way to feed an infant, characterised by both the interest of the medical profession in infant feeding practices and the growth of the formula milk industry (Palmer, 1998). These same factors have probably also influenced the development of the prescriptive approach to weaning which currently prevails.

During the early 1900s, the nursery care practices of the upper classes and the long working hours of the working classes encouraged the practice of young children having their meals separately from their parents (O'Hara, 1989). Feeding was not seen as a learning process, except in the acquisition of table manners, and well-brought-up children were not encouraged to feed themselves until they were old enough to manage a spoon.

For most of the 20th century British infants have been subjected to the fashion of the age with regard to the introduction of foods other than milk, with recommendations ranging from one to nine months after birth and beyond. In 1934, mothers were advised that infants should not normally be given anything other than breast milk for the first eight months of life, when they should be started on an adapted cow's milk mixture (Liddiard, 1934). They were further cautioned that:

> for several months [after this] the milk mixture forms the chief part of baby's nourishment and must not be superseded by a large quantity of semi-solid starchy foods (Liddiard, 1934, p. 41).

In 1956, a professor of child health at the University of London advised that mixed feeding should commence at about five or six months of age (Moncrieff, 1956). The transition was to be a gradual process, taking one month to replace the first of the five (scheduled) breastfeeds with bone and vegetable soup, given by spoon. Weaning from the breast was to be completed by the age of nine months. The same procedure was recommended for infants fed with formula milk.

By the 1960s and 1970s, the acceptable age for moving beyond a milk-only diet (whether breast or formula) had been reduced to three months, but there were suggestions that a more appropriate age would be between four and six months (MAFF, 1976). In 1994, the UK Department of Health confirmed that weaning should be initiated between four and six months (Department of Health, 1994), while the World Health Assembly recommended that weaning should begin at 'about six months' (WHA, 1994, cited in WHO, 1998).

Six years later, in 2000, it was clear that this advice was not being followed by all. Figures for the UK show that 24% of infants had received some solid foods, i.e. foods not liquid in origin, by the age of three months, which rose to 85% by the age of four months. At six months of age, only 2% of British infants were being fed on milk alone, with 49% of infants having been introduced to solids during the recommended four to six months period (Hamlyn *et al.*, 2002).

Even as the report of the Committee on Medical Aspects of Food and Nutrition Policy (COMA) (Department of Health, 1994) was being published, writers such as Borresen (1995) were arguing in favour of a recommendation that foods other than breast milk should not be introduced before six months and, as the 21st century began, two key reviews – by Naylor and Morrow (2001) and Kramer and Kakuma (2002) – confirmed that there was sufficient evidence for exclusive breastfeeding to be recommended for the first six months. WHO and UNICEF accordingly published their Global Strategy, which states that (WHO/ UNICEF, 2002, Section 3.1):

> To achieve optimal growth, development and health, infants should be exclusively breastfed for the first 6 months of life. Thereafter, to meet

their evolving nutritional requirements, infants should begin to receive nutritionally adequate and safe complementary foods while breastfeeding continues for up to two years of age or beyond.

To date, however, there has been little recognition that the implementation of these guidelines is likely to be hampered by the prevailing language and assumptions related to weaning; for example defining an infant as 'ready' for solids, simply because he is four months old.

What prompts the move to solid feeding?

Mothers choose to initiate weaning for a variety of reasons (McCallion *et al.*, 1998; Anderson *et al.*, 2001; McDougall, 2003; Wright *et al.*, 2004). Many introduce solid foods because they are advised to do so, or believe they have been advised to do so, by health workers and child care manuals. It has been suggested, however, that the information that mothers receive from health professionals could be ambiguous or inconsistent. McDougall (2003) sampled 108 mothers and found that although 68% of them reported that they had had advice from a health visitor, only 10% were able to state correctly the currently recommended age for initiation of weaning. It seems that the WHO message regarding the appropriate age to introduce solid foods is often taken to mean that complementary foods should form a significant part of the diet by that age (WHO, 1998), rather than that a start should have been made.

Both Savage (1998) and Wright *et al.* (2004) found that the main reason given by mothers for introducing solids was the perception that their baby was hungry. A commonly accepted sign of hunger (among both mothers and health professionals) is the baby's 'return' to a pattern of waking at night, the underlying assumption being that the baby will already have started to sleep through the night. Since frequent feeding, by day and night, is physiologically fundamental to the success of breastfeeding (RCM, 1991) and should therefore be viewed as normal, this sign is clearly misleading for breastfeeding mothers. In any event, there is no evidence to suggest that solid feeding is associated with longer periods of sleep (Heinig *et al.* 1993).

Another sign often interpreted as hunger or as a readiness for tastes other than milk is the baby's apparent fascination with watching his parents eating. However, logic suggests that it is likely to be the activity itself, i.e. the handling of food and eating utensils, which interests the baby, since, as a means of satisfying hunger, what he sees his parents doing is not within his frame of reference.

Professionals often suggest that solid foods be started when an infant's rate of weight gain begins to lessen. Work by Dewey (1992, 1995) has shown that this happens naturally in breastfed infants from three months onwards and is not a sign of underfeeding or any cause for concern. By the same token, given what we now know about infants' digestive abilities (Walker, 2001), it is clear that infants who are in need of extra food would gain more from their mothers being given help to increase their breast milk supply (or, if this were not possible, from supplementation with donor breast milk or a suitable formula milk), than from the introduction of other foods.

Personal observations over 20 years of health visiting suggest that both mothers and professionals vary, over time and between individuals, in the markers they use to identify infants' readiness for solid feeding. These range from simple body weight – commonly used prior to 1974 and cited variously as 12 lb or 15 lb – to a variety of behavioural signs thought, but not proven, to be related to hunger. Since infants' developmental progress and their actual need for other foods do not vary from year to year or from one professional to another, it is clear that at least some of these markers are fortuitous rather than accurate.

Breastfeeding as the start of the self-feeding continuum

Reid and Adamson (1998) point out that, although the transition from milk to solid feeding is one process, the literature dealing with the nutritional intake of infants treats the two stages as if they were quite separate events. A study of the mechanics and features of breastfeeding shows that this method of feeding, at least, forms part of an ongoing continuum with more advanced feeding.

Breast milk is the ideal food for human infants. Not only does it contain everything needed for normal growth and development (Akre, 1991), but it varies from feed to feed. The flavour of breast milk changes with the mother's diet (Menella, 1994), so that the infant is introduced from birth to a variety of tastes and is thus prepared for the introduction of other foods. In addition, the breast-fed infant can control the fat content of his feed by the amount of time spent at the breast and the frequency of feeding (Woolridge and Fisher, 1988). He is thus able to accommodate all his fluid needs independently of the remainder of his diet. This adaptability means that breastfeeding is ideal both as a preparation for, and for combining with, complementary feeding.

In order to milk the breast effectively, the infant has to take a substantial amount of breast tissue, as well as the nipple, into his mouth in a process known as attachment. The jaw then moves up and down and the tongue undulates, exerting positive pressure against the hard palate to expel the milk from the breast (Woolridge, 1986). Infants are equipped to do this from about 37 weeks' gestation (Naylor, 2001). By contrast, bottle feeding works by lowering of the back of the tongue to create a vacuum, which draws the milk into the mouth. It is suggested that the movements associated with breastfeeding are more closely related to those required for the manipulation of solid foods than are those associated with bottle feeding. Sullivan and Birch (1994) found that breastfed infants accepted solid foods more readily than bottle-fed infants; it is not clear whether this is related to their experiences of different flavours or their ability to adjust their oral movements to manage a change in texture, but both are feasible explanations.

It is not possible to achieve effective breastfeeding without the baby taking an active part in the process; the mother offers the opportunity and the baby feeds (or not). By contrast, it is possible to manoeuvre a bottle teat into a baby's mouth and, by moving it against the palate, to trigger the sucking reflex. Thus the concept of feeding as something a mother does *to* her baby, i.e. with the baby in the passive role, would appear to be more closely related to bottle feeding than to breastfeeding. It follows that an approach to weaning which suggests that it is a natural, spontaneous progression on the *baby's* part, rather than something the mother imposes on the baby, fits within the breastfeeding rather than the bottle feeding paradigm.

This chapter therefore focuses on the provision of a model for the introduction of breastfed infants to solid foods, which may or may not be appropriate for bottle-fed infants.

The timing of first solids – physical development

Breast milk is best delivered by the infant feeding directly from the breast. Indeed, the action of breastfeeding itself has been shown to convey health benefits (e.g. Labbok, 1987; Neiva *et al.*, 2003), indicating that it is the biological norm for the infant to gain its nourishment in this way. The ability of the infant to cope with foods other than liquids relies on the development of the mouth and alimentary tract. Thus the ability to manoeuvre food around the mouth so as to bite, to chew, and to avoid gagging, all develop alongside the ability of the gut to produce the necessary enzymes for the digestion of complex foods. Naylor (2001) and Walker (2001) have compiled evidence to show that, firstly, the infant gut at birth is not equipped to digest foods other than breast milk (or, to a lesser extent, infant formula). The ability to produce the necessary enzymes for the digestion of more complex foods is acquired over several months. Secondly, the reflexes present in the mouth change over time. At birth, a reflex tongue thrust is apparent, which begins to fade at about three months and is usually absent soon after four months. At around the same time, the gag reflex moves from the middle to the posterior third of the tongue. Finally, at between four and seven months the ability to 'munch' develops. This is followed, between seven and twelve months, by the development of chewing movements, accompanied by the ability of the tongue to move laterally, so moving food to the cheek teeth. Rotary chewing movements are not generally achieved until after one year (Naylor, 2001; Walker, 2001).

While this internal maturation takes place, the infant develops other abilities with relevance to self-feeding. Sheridan (1973) describes the following sequence of infant behaviours. At birth, the rooting reflex enables the infant to locate the nipple and attach to the breast. At one month, the infant's fingers – normally held closed – fan out when his arms are extended. (It is possible that this movement may assist him to maintain his attachment at the breast). At around three months, the infant can wave his arms symmetrically and bring them together into the midline over his chest or chin. He watches the movements of his hands and is beginning to clasp and unclasp them. By six months the infant can sit with support and hold his head firmly erect. He fixates his gaze on small objects and stretches out both hands to grasp them. He uses his whole hand in a palmar grasp and takes everything to his mouth. Between six and twelve months, both the pincer grasp (using thumb and forefinger) and visual acuity develop to allow the infant to pick up progressively smaller objects. He also begins to release objects purposefully. He is thus able to transport small items to his mouth with increasing accuracy.

The sequence of events that Sheridan (1973) described is evident to anyone who observes infants and young children. Her work forms the basis of developmental surveillance to this day, and yet its fundamental importance to the initiation of weaning has been consistently overlooked. Indeed, we have sought to override and restrict infants' natural abilities with regard to feeding, presumably so that we could control the process according to the rules we have devised. Thus, while infants of eight to nine months, who have already demonstrated their ability to handle objects and transport them accurately to their mouth, are encouraged to feed themselves with their fingers, younger infants who are just beginning to develop these skills are rarely allowed to practise on the real thing.

The presentation of weaning foods – spoon feeding examined

Despite the move away from the very early introduction of solid foods, the advice given to British mothers about how weaning foods should be selected, prepared and presented has changed very little over the years. Puréeing is the method of choice, followed by a gradual progression towards more lumpy foods. Even the WHO, in the year that Naylor's review was published (confirming that an infant's ability to move food around the mouth develops considerably during the early months) and the move towards introducing solids at six months was under way, advised mothers to 'start with a few teaspoons' (WHO, 2001, p. 2) and to 'make the food soft [at first, then later to] mash it or cut it into small pieces' (p. 35). Whether these precautions are either appropriate or necessary at six months deserves to be questioned.

Since it is difficult to offer puréed foods other than from a spoon, spoon feeding has become the usual way for early solid foods to be given to infants. However, the briefest comparison of breast and bottle feeding shows that the use of a utensil to 'feed' an infant does not originate with breastfeeding. The representation of spoon feeding as the 'normal' way to introduce solid foods reinforces the interpretation of 'feeding' as something done by the mother, rather than something done by the infant.

Many advocates of the early (i.e. before six months) introduction of solid foods maintain that there is a 'window of opportunity' during which infants will readily accept a spoon and that this should be capitalised upon. Concern amongst health professionals about the consequences of missing the opportunity provided by this 'window' appear to stem from the paper by Illingworth and Lister (1964), who drew attention to the importance of the 'critical or sensitive period' in relation to the development of feeding skills.

Illingworth and Lister's work (1964) is based on the theory that there are critical periods for learning new skills; if the right stimuli are not provided at the right time, children will not achieve key developmental milestones. Thus, if they are not introduced to chewing at the appropriate stage of their development, they will not develop this skill. However, closer perusal of Illingworth and Lister's study (1964) reveals two key flaws in the extrapolation of their findings that has since taken place. Firstly, of the children they studied, only one was described as 'normal', while several were 'retarded' and others had anatomical problems such as oesophageal atresia. The 'normal' girl had, for reasons which are unclear, been fed exclusively on puréed foods until the age of two years. Secondly, they did not study the age at which *semi*-solids were introduced; their evidence relates to solid foods, which require biting and chewing. Their contention was that: 'if a baby is not given solid foods shortly after he has learned to chew, there may well be considerable difficulty in getting him to take solids later' (Illingworth and Lister, 1964, p. 843) and that: 'the average age at which [chewing] develops is 6 months' (p. 847). This suggests that children need to be introduced to food that requires chewing soon after six months. It is only the assumption that such foods *must* be preceded by semi-solids – irrespective of the age at which they are introduced – that leads to the conclusion that 'solids' should be introduced before six months.

More recent work by Northstone *et al.* (2001) found that infants who were introduced to lumpy foods after 10 months of age were significantly less likely to be eating family foods at 15 months. The reasons for late introduction of lumpy foods in each case were not made clear and several possibilities exist. The figures do, however, point to a difficulty in making the transition from puréed foods to those of a more solid consistency. Introduction of solid foods before infants can chew, which necessitates the use of purées, may therefore be a hindrance to the development of chewing skills.

Advocates of the early introduction of 'solids' point out that older infants who are not accustomed to spoon feeding will frequently turn their heads or use their hands to push away the spoon. What is rarely acknowledged is that spoon feeding provides a means whereby (semi-)solid food can be inserted into the mouth of an infant too immature to achieve this for himself. Seen in this light, the response of the older infant can be interpreted as the reasonable actions of an individual who is sufficiently physically mature to make his wishes plain, while the 'acceptance' of the younger infant becomes simply evidence of his inability to resist. Cohen *et al.* (1995) found no evidence that delaying the introduction of solid foods until six months increased the likelihood of children being fussy eaters.

The emphasis on the need to introduce spoon feeding when the infant is unlikely to show resistance appears to be based on the premise that acceptance by an infant of being fed in this manner is a necessary goal. Pridham (1990) makes this very clear; the ability to use the mouth to take food from a spoon is presented as one of four fundamental feeding skills and is expected to precede the skill of self feeding – with either fingers or a spoon. However, no evidence is presented to support this contention and the assumption does not appear to have been challenged elsewhere.

There is, in fact, no evidence to suggest that a child who has not been spoon fed as an infant will have difficulty acquiring the ability to use a spoon to feed himself. Indeed, if this were the case, few children would ever manage to use forks! Leaving aside a possibly genuine belief that infants require solid foods at an age when they are not capable of feeding themselves with them, the desire of adults to manage or control the feeding process could be a major reason (albeit unacknowledged) for the emphasis on spoon feeding.

The use of a spoon achieves control in two important ways; it makes eating less messy (something which is not a matter of concern to most infants) and it allows the carer to dictate not only the feeding process but also the amount eaten. This is not without risk, as Akre (1991) commented: 'Once a mother assumes responsibility for the amount of food her child receives, overfeeding becomes a possibility' (Akre, 1991, p. 64). Spoon feeding therefore has implications for the child's health as well as his enjoyment of food and the development of his self-feeding abilities.

My own personal observations suggest that the use of a spoon presents problems for many infants when they progress to 'second-stage dinners', with gagging and spitting out of lumps commonly reported by mothers. A closer look at

how infants manage spoons offers an explanation. Adults use different mechanisms when taking solid pieces of food from a spoon than when ingesting, for
example, soup. When young infants are first given puréed foods on a spoon they
use their existing oral skills to take the food, i.e. they suck (Wickendon, 2000).
When a suck-type mechanism is used to empty a spoon, any lumps will tend to
be transferred directly to the back of the throat, resulting in gagging.

Early chewing movements precede the development of the ability to form
a bolus of solid or semi-solid food and move it to the back of the mouth for
swallowing (Naylor, 2001). This explains why infants commonly 'lose' the first
foods they bite off for themselves. It also suggests that, provided the child is
in an upright position (so that gravity does not interfere), the risk of choking is
reduced if the child himself is in control of what goes into his mouth.

Examination of the processes of swallowing and choking therefore indicate
that, far from making feeding safer, spoon feeding may carry an inherent risk
of *causing* choking in young infants. This has been reflected in the author's
personal observation; that infants who are allowed to handle their food and
bite off pieces themselves appear to cope with lumps more effectively and at
a younger age than those who are either prevented from tackling them or have
them offered on a spoon.

It is interesting to note that the 'suck' response to food offered on a spoon
more closely resembles the mechanism used to extract milk from a bottle than
that used to milk the breast (as identified by Woolridge, 1986). It is possible that
bottle-fed infants adapt to spoon feeding more easily than breastfed infants and
this, along with the mother's familiarity with a feeding method which involves
the insertion of a utensil into the infant's mouth, may be a factor in the tendency,
as noted by Hamlyn *et al.* (2000), towards the earlier introduction of solid foods
in formula-fed infants.

All these observations appear to cast doubt on the assumption that spoon
feeding follows on – either naturally or logically – from breastfeeding and,
therefore, on the appropriateness of its use in early solid feeding. And yet,
although many authors have noted the importance of the environment and the
behaviour of the care-giver in determining the acceptance of food by the infant
(e.g. Southall and Schwartz, 2000; Parry and Jowett, 2001), none appear to have
examined the significance of how the food gets into the infant's mouth, except
in relation to the use of force.

Learning to chew

Infants do not 'learn' to chew, any more than they 'learn' to walk. They merely
become able, through a process of maturation, to perform new movements.

According to Naylor (2001), sucking (as opposed to suckling) develops between six and nine months, together with 'a new type of swallow ... which can be initiated without a preceding suckle' (Naylor, 2001, p. 23). Naylor further describes the development 'at or after six months' of the muscles of the tongue and mouth, which enables the infant to manipulate food that is more solid in nature in preparation for swallowing. This suggests that infants of this age are ready to deal with foods that require chewing.

If we return to the work of Illingworth and Lister (1964), we see that the best way to encourage the development of a new skill is to provide the opportunity for it to be practised. This would suggest that the best way for an infant to become skilled at chewing is to be given the opportunity to chew. If we further accept that he is not likely to choke as long as he is allowed to take the food to his mouth himself, food would seem to be the best material for him to practise on. There appears to be a process by which infants develop more volitional control and a new range of movements. As Wickendon (2000, p. 7) states: 'The perception of the differences between textures seems to stimulate the development of a broader range of motor skills'.

There are clearly limited opportunities for the infant to experience different textures when being fed puréed foods; self feeding with a variety of foods would seem to provide a better chance of helping the baby to develop new oral skills. This is supported by Arvedsen (2000, p. 39), who states that 'for most children, firm (solid) foods are more effective than viscous or puréed foods in the elicitation of chewing', also pointing out that 'the achievement of chewing is *not* dependent on the eruption of molar teeth'. Interestingly, Stevenson and Allaire (1991) noted that there was no evidence to support the use of transitional foods, such as soft purées, and that many cultures do not focus on them as a significant part of the weaning process.

Why infants spit out food

In the 2000 UK Infant Feeding survey (Hamlyn *et al.*, 2002), one in ten mothers reported problems with getting their infant to take solid foods: 52% reported that he or she would only take certain solids; 24% that he or she would not take solids and 22% that he or she was uninterested in food. However, the study does not explore the ages at which these infants were introduced to solid foods, nor how the mothers deduced food refusal or disinterest.

Mothers sometimes interpret spitting out of food as refusal. There are several probable reasons why infants spit out their food. One reason is the operation of the tongue thrust – an involuntary reflex action, present until around four months of age, which involves anything inserted into the mouth being spontaneously pushed forwards. This is presumably an evolutionary feature designed specifically to prevent anything getting into the infant's mouth which he has not actively scooped up for himself! Mothers who find difficulty in spoon feeding their three-month-old, and who later report that he has 'got used to the spoon' are merely observing the natural disappearance of the tongue thrust reflex.

Another possible reason for spitting out food is neophobia, the wish not to eat 'unseen' food, which is thought to be an important survival mechanism with evolutionary advantage (Wickendon, 2000). This suggests that being able to see one's food is an important part of ensuring one's safety; the fact that many infants are prevented from seeing what is being fed to them may go some way to explaining many older children's reluctance to try new foods.

A further factor may be the infant's simple desire to examine the food, both visually and by manipulation. Wickendon points out that feeling food with the fingers is an important experience which enables learning about the relationships between the sight and feel of objects and their size. She states that: 'links between manual and oral activity are regarded as part of the normal development of an integrated sensory system' (Wickendon, 2000, p. 7).

Certainly, observation of infants suggests that they enjoy the chance to manipulate food and it is reasonable to conclude that their experience of eating is enhanced if they are allowed to participate actively. Whatever the motivation for the infant, it has been noted anecdotally that many infants who have become 'fussy' eaters by about 7 or 8 months will accept a much greater variety of tastes and textures if they are allowed to feed themselves.

Infants learn by mimicking adult behaviour (Jessel, 1990). Thus, the infant who avidly watches his parents eating is probably motivated to copy the activity. It follows that perhaps the infant should first be given the opportunity to *handle* food. Allowing the infant to explore food with his hands as well as his mouth may fulfil his desire to join in and enhance his learning and skill development. Later, he may become skilled with cutlery through the same process of observation and imitation.

Infants who are enabled to handle food from an early age could learn how to relate size, shape and texture, using their eyes and hands, with the experience of taste being added to the mix when they first manage to get a piece of food successfully into their mouth. At this point they may also begin to equate the appearance of food and its feel on the skin with its feel in the mouth and its taste. They may begin to distinguish foods they like from those they dislike, and all of this could happen long before swallowing the food is possible. Indeed, far from being the reason for the infant's interest, ingestion could occur as a fortuitous by-product of following his inclination.

Naylor and Morrow's review (2001) showed a 'convergence of maturation', in terms of an infant's oral motor, digestive and immunological abilities, occurring at around six months of age. This, they said, pointed to an overall developmental readiness for foods other than breast milk at this age. However, Naylor and Morrow did not take into account the other skills relevant to feeding that might also form part of this convergence. Parkinson and Drewett (2001) studied feeding behaviour in the weaning period and suggested (p. 976) that an investigation of infants' other developing abilities was warranted:

> An obvious sequel to the present study would be to examine feeding behaviour developmentally, and to relate it to other developmental changes such as those in ... motor skills.

By broadening our view to incorporate the work of observers such as Sheridan we can see that hand–eye co-ordination and fine motor development also appear to reach a certain level at around six months. It is not unreasonable to suggest that nature has designed the 'biologically-driven processes' (Naylor, 2001) necessary for the move away from exclusive breastfeeding, to include the development of self feeding skills. This would mean that infants could be fully equipped to make the transition to solid feeding unaided provided that, as with walking, they are given the necessary opportunities. It is, indeed, possible that infants have evolved never to need to be fed actively by another person, but rather are pre-programmed to move on to solid feeding gradually, beginning at around six months.

Testing the self feeding theory

There are clearly persuasive arguments for an alternative approach to weaning that allows the infant to be the decision-maker regarding the timing and pace of the transition to solid feeding, and which relies on his innate abilities to guide the process. A recent observational study (Rapley, 2003), investigated whether such an approach might work in practice. The research involved presenting a small group of exclusively breastfed infants ($n = 5$) with the opportunity to handle a range of foods, of differing textures and sizes, from four months of age onwards, and observing their behaviour. Four months was chosen as the starting point because, at that time (2001–02), this was considered the earliest age at which a child might be considered 'ready' for solid foods. It should be noted, however, that the small sample size does not allow for generalisations to be made. The study does, however, provide valuable novel exploratory data on this under-researched and highly debatable area, which could inform the design of future research.

The infants in the study all showed an interest in food, or in others eating, from around four months. By six and a half months, they were capable of reaching out and grasping foods such as cooked 'sticks' of carrot or broccoli florets and of getting them to their mouth and chewing; most were also beginning to swallow what they had chewed. By nine months the infants were competent self-feeders and enjoyed a wide range of flavours and textures (fruits, vegetables, meat, fish, cheese, bread); some were already beginning to master spoons for themselves; most did not like to be spoon-fed. Overall, it appeared that the infants who displayed the greatest ability and the widest repertoire of accepted foods were those who had been allowed the greatest degree of autonomy by their parents.

The behaviour of the infants in this study showed a gradual move away from reliance on breast milk, apparently driven not by hunger but by curiosity. Individual progress was dictated by each infant's advancing developmental ability, while his safety was maintained by the same process. The infants' abilities with regard to self-feeding appeared to keep pace, not only with their ability to digest other foods, as described by Walker (2001), but with their need for a mixed diet, as outlined by writers such as Butte *et al.* (2002) and Kramer and Kakuma (2002).

An important element that was explored was the parents' reactions to the self-feeding programme, both beforehand and as it progressed (Rapley, 2003). All had volunteered to take part in the study because the idea sounded logical to them. Those who had older children commented either that it was more or less what they had done before anyway, or that they had previously followed the conventional method and found it unsatisfactory. By the end, all said they would follow a similar approach again. Several were pleasantly surprised at the range of foods their infant enjoyed and at how easy it was to eat as a family, especially when out of the home.

This small study showed that a focus on facilitating the self feeding continuum could provide a realistic way of initiating weaning in infants who are exclusively breasted. I now go on to consider what practical benefits such an approach may bring for both infants and parents in the longer term.

Possible implications of baby-led weaning for later health and well-being

It is known, from work such as that of Wilson *et al.* (1998), that the early introduction of other foods to the breastfed infant's diet results in a variety of adverse health outcomes, both in childhood and in later life. It is also becoming increasingly clear, in the light of research into gastro-intestinal development and the infant's ability to process and absorb nutrients, that giving solid foods to an infant who is too young to digest them will tend to lead to worse, not better, nutrition.

As infants get older, the differences between them in terms of development become more marked; while most infants will smile between five and seven weeks of age – a difference of two weeks – the normal variation in age for walking is of the order of six months. This suggests that a one-size-fits-all approach to solid feeding is likely to be even less appropriate at six months than it is at four months.

One of the difficulties in defining an age to initiate weaning (i.e. to introduce solid foods) for all children is the challenge of how to allow for the fact that not all infants will be ready at exactly the same age. Alimentary, oral and immunological readiness are difficult to detect. If, however, it is the case that hand–eye co-ordination and fine motor skills develop in parallel with the rest of the infant's abilities, perhaps it is possible to use them as indicators of readiness. In this way, providing infants with the opportunity to initiate their own weaning might be a way of ensuring that this happens at the optimal time for each infant.

At birth, an infant left in skin contact with his mother demonstrates his readiness to feed by locating the breast, attaching and feeding. In other words, he demonstrates by doing. In my study (Rapley, 2003), while all the infants moved towards solid feeding within a similar time frame, they did not all start at precisely the same age, nor progress at the same rate. It may be that exposing an infant to the opportunity to handle food may be the ideal way to determine the 'right' time for him, as an individual, to move on from exclusive breastfeeding.

Clearly, parents need information about how to enable their infant to eat healthily. However, giving them this information in advance and encouraging a method of weaning which means that the infant eats with his parents may do more to ensure a healthy diet for the whole family than insisting on the preparation of special foods for the infant. If baby-led weaning produces children who enjoy a range of foods and encourages families to eat together, then perhaps the western world's idea of a suitable restaurant menu for children will begin to change. Perhaps it will be the children themselves who complain when asked to choose between chicken nuggets and sausage-'n'-beans!

Preventing feeding and eating disorders

In their study of one-year-olds, Young and Drewett (2000) found that 'food refusal is a common feature of eating behaviour in normal children at this age' (Young and Drewett, 2000, p. 171). This is surely a regrettable situation. Eating, at best, is about more than simply staving off hunger. It is a pleasurable experience, with the appearance, temperature, texture and flavour of the food and the sociability of eating with others all playing a part in the enjoyment of food. For most adults, the idea of having all their meals spoon-fed to them, luke-warm, in homogenised format, at a pace decided by a carer, is the stuff of nightmares; of incapacity and old age. It is therefore reasonable to suggest that infants would not choose this either, and yet many are subjected to it.

When each meal varies little in texture and appearance, the only variable part of the feeding experience is the taste. It is therefore possible that, in such circumstances, the infant will pay more attention to taste than he would other-wise, and taste will play a greater part in determining what he will and won't accept. His parents will probably find that he will eat chocolate pudding with no problem but that they have to resort to games to distract him if they are to get him to eat anything else – tactics which, according to Carruth *et al.* (1998), may themselves lead to 'pickiness'. Occasionally, parents may even go so far as to pinch the infant's nose to force him to open his mouth. Experiences such as this, when observed through the infant's eyes, could explain the common anecdotal reports of infants who will eat a piece of apple but refuse to be fed with apple purée.

The standard advice to parents of young infants is to offer one food at a time at the beginning of the weaning period, moving on quite quickly to mini-meals of, for example, puréed chicken casserole. In these circumstances, the infant has the option of accepting or refusing (if he is able) what is offered, but is given no opportunity to compare tastes or to blend them for himself. If he doesn't like a food whose flavour pervades each mouthful he will likely refuse every mouth-ful. Thus, because he is unable to work out – far less to tell his parents – that he does not like parsnip, they could be driven to conclude that he will not eat chicken casserole.

It is suggested that, if denied the chance to recognise food, the infant who is fed conventionally will not know until the spoon is in his mouth what flavour to expect. (Smell may play some part but even this does not help the infant who is being fed from a jar while his nostrils are being assailed with the smells of the rest of the family's meal cooking!) We should therefore not be surprised if he shows a reluctance to try new foods, or regularly spits out the first mouth-ful of each meal. Can it be coincidence that a key element of the behavioural approach to helping children who refuse food is to allow the child the time and space to explore what he is being offered (Douglas, 2000) – an approach which gives him control over the situation and allows him to unlearn the fear he has developed?

Some parents experience great difficulty in persuading their infant to move on from spoon-feeding to coping with lumpy food. Gisel (1991) reported that, because children utilise the easiest motor skills possible for any food, if a child can manage a meal by sucking, it is likely that he will do so. Wickendon (2000, p. 11) suggests that children who have opted for sucking 'will not be precipi-tated into developing more mature oral movements required by more challeng-ing food textures'.

Many childhood feeding difficulties revolve around a child's unwillingness – or inability – to accept foods which require chewing. It has been suggested that, for some, there comes a point where true difficulties with chewing result because the 'critical period' (Illingworth and Lister, 1964) for the development of the necessary skills has been missed. If infants of six months can, in fact, manage lumpy food without having to experience puréed foods first and are, furthermore, capable of feeding themselves, it may be that puréed foods and spoon feeding are not necessary at all. If they were not introduced, then the problem of 'moving on' would not arise.

For practitioners who work with children with food phobias, a golden rule seems to be 'give the control back to the child'. Only when this has been established can real progress be made. The fact that this approach to food aversion works raises the question 'what if control had never been taken away from the child in the first place?'. Since breastfeeding is, from a physiological point of view, baby-led, this is suggestive of nature's starting position. Since it appears that infants may be capable of managing their own early experiences with solid foods, there seems no logical reason for an approach to weaning which takes away this control, only for it to be given back later.

Although small, my study (Rapley, 2003) suggests that allowing the infant to play an active part in the weaning process may lead to rapid acquisition of chewing skills, acceptance of a wide range of foods and a willingness to try new things. It is therefore possible that fussiness and food fads, as well as more serious feeding disorders, could be less likely in children weaned this way. In addition, since feeding and speech difficulties often co-exist, it is possible that early encouragement of self-feeding skills could have implications for speech development. Further studies are required to investigate these possibilities.

Moving on

At the time of writing, it appears that many health professionals have not yet modified their advice to parents in favour of a six-month start to weaning. Anecdotally, it appears that the reluctance of many health professionals to change the nature of their advice stems either from their uncertainty about how to move away from the 'old' markers of readiness for solid feeding, or from concern about how to progress from a liquid diet (via semi-solids) to foods that require chewing rapidly enough to ensure that the infant's development is not compromised.

A baby-led approach to the initiation of weaning may offer a more enjoyable experience for infants and a less fraught one for parents. It could permit individual infants to begin the transition to family meals at the right time and to progress at an optimal pace, and could result in greater acceptance of foods and enhanced self-feeding ability. Finally, it could enable professionals to concentrate on giving sound dietary advice for the whole family and could even encourage a return to the social occasion of a family meal.

Indications for further research

There are various opportunities for further research on the concept of baby-led weaning. One key question surrounds the appropriateness of this approach for bottle-fed infants; another is whether infants can be relied upon to choose a diet which will ensure adequate nutrition. Another point of interest is the role of other fluids in the diets of young children. WHO and UNICEF recommend that breastfeeding should continue alongside complementary foods for at least until the child is two years old (WHO/UNICEF, 2002). What is not clear is what quantity of breast milk is recommended. This may be important from a nutritional point of view; in countries where bottle feeding is prevalent it has become usual to introduce water or juice when an infant is receiving a recognisable amount of solid food. This is a necessary precaution for a formula-fed infant, who will otherwise be at risk either of an inadequate fluid intake or excessive consumption of calories. The introduction of other fluids is not necessary for breastfed infants, because breastfeeding enables an infant to accommodate his thirst independently of his hunger. Much has been written about infants' need for nutrients such as iron (e.g. Butte, 1987; Pisacane *et al.*, 1995; Griffin and Abrams, 2001; Domellof *et al.*, 2002). It is interesting to speculate that it may be the rush to introduce other *fluids* which puts babies' iron status at risk and that maintaining breast milk as the only source of fluid for, say, the first year, would change our perception of what young infants' additional vitamin and mineral requirements are.

Conclusion

Baby-led weaning cannot be seen as a new approach to feeding, if only because infants have clearly been capable of it all along. Further research is clearly needed, but there seem to be signs that infants have already known much of what science is only slowly establishing, namely that they are fully equipped to follow a path to family meals, without fuss and at the right time, which will enhance both their development and their nutrition.

There is now a wealth of information to support exclusive breastfeeding for the first six months as the best way to ensure optimal infant health. However, there exists also a huge and highly influential infant food industry which exerts pressure on both professionals and parents to conform to a carer-led model of infant feeding. While we battle to regain ground in support of breastfeeding as the best start an infant can have, perhaps the time has come to focus, too, on achieving a greater understanding of the relationship between breastfeeding and solid feeding – one which enables us to recognise babies' abilities, re-evaluate the role they can play and trust them to get it right.

References

Akre, J. (ed.) (1991) *Infant Feeding – The Physiological Basis*. WHO, Geneva.

Anderson, A. S., Guthrie, C. A., Alder, E. M., Forsyth, S., Howie, P. W. and Williams, F. L. (2001) Rattling the plate – reasons and rationales for early weaning. *Health Education Research: Theory and Practice*, **16**(4), 471–9.

Arvedsen, J. (2000) Evaluation of children with feeding and swallowing problems *Language, Speech and Hearing Services in Schools*, **31**, 28–41.

Borresen, H. C. (1995) Rethinking current recommendations to introduce solid food between four and six months to exclusively breastfeeding infants. *Journal of Human Lactation*, **11**(3), 201–4.

Butte, N. F., Garza, C., Smith, E. O., Wills, C. and Nichols, B. L. (1987) Macro- and trace mineral intakes of exclusively breast-fed infants. *American Journal of Clinical Nutrition*, **45**, 42–7.

Butte, N. F., Lopez-Alarcon, M. G. and Garza, C. (2002) *Nutrient Adequacy of Exclusive Breastfeeding for the Term Infant During the First Six Months of Life*. WHO, Geneva.

Carruth, B. R., Skinner, J., Houck, K., Moran, J., Coletta, F. and Ott, D. (1998) The phenomenon of 'picky eater': a behavioral marker in eating patterns of toddlers. *Journal of the American College of Nutrition*, **17**(2), 180–6.

Cohen, R. J., Rivera, L. L., Canahuati, J., Brown, K. H. and Dewey, K. G. (1995) Delaying the introduction of complementary food until 6 months does not affect appetite or mother's report of food acceptance of breast-fed infants from 6 to 12 months in a low income, Honduran population. *Journal of Nutrition*, **125**(11), 2787–92.

Department of Health Committee on the Medical Aspects of Food Policy (1994) *Weaning and the Weaning Diet* (Report on Health and Social Subjects No. 45). HMSO, London.

Department of Health (2003) National Breastfeeding Awareness Week press release, 12 May.

Dewey, K. G., Heinig, M. J., Nommsen, L. A., Peerson, J. M. and Lonnerdal, B. (1992) Growth of breast-fed and formula-fed infants from 0 to 18 months: The Darling Study. *Pediatrics*, **89**(6), 1035–41.

Dewey, K. G., Peerson, J. M., Brown, K. H., Krebs, N. F., Michaelsen, K. F., Persson, L. A., Salmenpera, L., Whitehead, R. G. and Yeung, D. L. (1995) Growth of breast-fed infants deviates from current reference data: a pooled analysis of US, Canadian, and European data sets. *Pediatrics*, **96**(3), 495–503.

Domellof, M., Lonnerdal, B., Abrams, S. A. and Hernell, O. (2002) Iron absorption in breast-fed infants: effects of age, iron status, iron supplements, and complementary foods. *American Journal of Clinical Nutrition*, **76**(1), 198–204.

Douglas, J. (2000) The management of selective eating in young children. In: *Feeding Problems in Children* (eds. A. Southall and A. Schwartz), pp. 141–52. Radcliffe Medical Press, Abingdon, Oxon.

Gisel, E. G. (1991) Effect of food texture on the development of chewing of children between six months and two years of age. *Developmental Medicine and Child Neurology*, **33**, 69–79.

Griffin, I. J. and Abrams, S. A. (2001) Iron and breastfeeding. *Pediatric Clinics of North America*, **48**(2), 401–13.

Hamlyn, B., Brooker, S., Oleinikova, K. and Wands, S. (2002) *Infant Feeding 2000*. The Stationery Office, London.

Heinig, M. J., Nommsen, L. A., Peerson, J. M., Lonnerdal, B. and Dewey, K. G. (1993) Intake and growth of breast-fed and formula-fed infants in relation to the timing of introduction of complementary foods: the DARLING study. *Acta Paediatrica*, **82**(12), 999–1006.

Heinig, M. J. and Dewey, K. G. (1996) Health advantages of breastfeeding for infants: a critical review. *Nutrition Research Reviews*, **9**, 89–110.

Howie, P. W., Forsyth, J. S., Ogston, S. A., Clark, A. and Florey, C. D. (1990) Protective effect of breast feeding against infection. *British Medical Journal*, **300**, 11–16.

Illingworth, R. S. and Lister, J. (1964) The critical or sensitive period, with special reference to certain feeding problems in infants and children. *Journal of Pediatrics*, **65**(6), 839–48.

Jessel, C. (1990) *Birth to Three*. Bloomsbury Publishing Ltd, London.

Kramer, M. S. and Kakuma, R. (2002) Optimal duration of exclusive breastfeeding. *The Cochrane Database of Systematic Reviews* 2002, Issue 1. Art. No.: CD003517. DOI: 10.1002/14651858.CD003517.

Kramer, M. S., Guo, T., Platt, R. W., Vanilovich, I., Sevkovskaya, Z., Dzikovich, I., Michaelsen, K. F. and Dewey, K. (2004) Feeding effects on growth during infancy. *Journal of Pediatrics*, **145**(5), 600–5.

Labbok, M. and Hendershot, G. (1987) Does breastfeeding protect against malocclusion? *American Journal of Preventive Medicine*, **3**, 227–32.

Liddiard, M. (1934) In: *The Hygiene of Life and Safer Motherhood* (ed. W. A. Lane), pp. 38–42. British Books Ltd, London.

Ministry of Agriculture, Fisheries and Food (1976) *Manual of Nutrition*. HMSO, London.

McCallion, C. R., Scott, E. M. and Doherty, M. (1998) Influences on weaning practices. *Journal of Social and Administrative Pharmacy*, **15**(2), 117–24.

McDougall, P. (2003) Weaning: parents' perceptions and practices. *Community Practitioner*, **76**(1), 25–8.

Mennella, J. (1994) A medium for flavor experiences. *Journal of Human Lactation*, **11**(1), 39–45.

Moncrieff, A. (1956) *Infant Feeding*. W & J Mackay & Co. Ltd, Chatham.

Naylor, A. J. and Morrow, A. (eds.) (2001) *Developmental Readiness of Normal Full Term Infants to Progress from Exclusive Breastfeeding to the Introduction of Complementary Foods: Reviews of the Relevant Literature Concerning Infant Immunologic, Gastrointestinal, Oral Motor and Maternal Reproductive and Lactational Development*. Wellstart International and the LINKAGES Project Academy for Educational Development, Washington, DC.

Naylor, A. J. (2001) Infant oral motor development in relation to the duration of exclusive breastfeeding In: *Developmental Readiness of Normal Full Term Infants to Progress from Exclusive Breastfeeding to the Introduction of Complementary Foods: Reviews of the Relevant Literature Concerning Infant Immunologic, Gastrointestinal, Oral Motor and Maternal Reproductive and Lactational Development* (eds. A. J. Naylor and A. Morrow). Wellstart International and the LINKAGES Project Academy for Educational Development, Washington, DC.

Neiva, F. C., Cattoni, D. M., Ramos, J. L. and Issler, H. (2003) Early weaning: implications to oral motor development. *Jornal de Pediatria*, **79**(1), 7–12.

Northstone, K., Emmett, P., Nethersole, F. and the ALSPAC Study Team (2001) The effect of age of introduction to lumpy solids on foods eaten and reported feeding difficulties at 6 and 15 months. *Journal of Human Nutrition and Dietetics*, **14**(1), 43–54.

Oddy, W. H., Sly, P. D., de Klerk, N. H., Landau, L. I., Kendall, G. E., Holt, P. G. and Stanley, F. J. (2003) Breast feeding and respiratory morbidity in infancy: a birth cohort study. *Archives of Disease in Childhood*, **88**, 224–8.

O'Hara, G. (1989) *The World of the Baby*. Doubleday, New York.

Palmer, G. (1988) *The Politics of Breastfeeding*. Pandora Press, London.

Parkinson, K. N. and Drewett, R. F. (2001) Feeding behaviour in the weaning period. *Journal of Child Psychology and Psychiatry*, **42**(7), 971–8.

Parry, A. and Jowett, S. (2001) The origin of early feeding problems. *Community Practitioner*, **74**(4), 143–5.

Pisacane, A., De Vizia, B., Valiante, A., Vaccaro, F., Russo, M., Grillo, G. and Giustardi, A. (1995) Iron status in breast-fed infants. *Journal of Pediatrics*, **127**, 429–31.

Pridham, K. F. (1990) Feeding behaviour of 6- to 12-month-old infants: assessment and sources of parental information. *Journal of Pediatrics*, **117**(2pt2), S174–80.

Rapley, G. (2003) *Can Babies Initiate and Direct the Weaning Process?* Unpublished MSc Interprofessional Health and Community Studies (Care of the Breastfeeding Mother and Child). Canterbury Christ Church University College, Kent.

Reid, M. and Adamson, H. (1998) *Opportunities for and Barriers to Good Nutritional Health in Women of Child-bearing Age, Pregnant Women, Infants Under 1 and Children Aged 1 to 5*. Health Education Authority, London.

Royal College of Midwives (2001) *Successful Breastfeeding* (3rd edn). Churchill Livingstone, London.

Savage, S. A. H., Reilly, J. J., Edwards, C. A. and Durnin, J. V. G. A. (1998) Weaning practice in the Glasgow longitudinal infant growth study. *Archives of Disease in Childhood*, **79**, 153–6.

Sheridan, M. (1973) *Children's Developmental Progress*. NFER Publishing Co. Ltd, Windsor, Berks.

Southall, A. and Schwartz, A. (eds.) (2000) *Feeding Problems in Children*. Radcliffe Medical Press, Abingdon, Oxon.

Stevenson, R. D. and Allaire, J. H. (1991) The development of normal feeding and swallowing. *Pediatric Clinics of North America*, **38**(6), 1439–53.

Sullivan, S. A. and Birch, L. L. (1994) Infant dietary experience and acceptance of solid foods. *Pediatrics*, **93**(2), 271–7.

Walker, W. A. (2001) Gastrointestinal development in relation to the duration of exclusive breastfeeding. In: *Developmental Readiness of Normal Full Term Infants to Progress from Exclusive Breastfeeding to the Introduction of Complementary Foods: Reviews of the Relevant Literature Concerning Infant Immunologic, Gastrointestinal, Oral Motor and Maternal Reproductive and Lactational Development* (eds: A. J. Naylor and A. Morrow). Wellstart International and the LINKAGES Project Academy for Educational Development, Washington, DC.

WHO/UNICEF (2002) *Global Strategy for Infant and Young Child Feeding*. WHO, Geneva.

Wickendon, M. (2000) The development and disruption of feeding skills: how speech and language therapists can help. In: *Feeding Problems in Children* (eds. A. Southall and A. Schwartz), pp. 3–23. Radcliffe Medical Press, Abingdon, Oxon.

Wilson, A. C., Forsyth, J. S., Greene, S. A., Irvine, L., Hau, C. and Howie, P. W. (1998) Relation of infant diet to childhood health: seven-year follow-up of cohort of children in Dundee infant feeding study. *British Medical Journal*, **316**(7124), 21–5.

Woolridge, M. (1986) The 'anatomy' of infant sucking. *Midwifery*, **2**, 164–71.

Woolridge, M. and Fisher, C. (1988) 'Colic', overfeeding, and symptoms of lactose malabsorption in the breast-fed baby: a possible artefact of feed management? *The Lancet*, **8605**, 382–4.

World Health Organization (1981) *International Code of Marketing of Breastmilk Substitutes*. WHO, Geneva.

World Health Organization (1998) *Complementary Feeding of Young Children in Developing Countries – A Review of Current Scientific Knowledge*. WHO, Geneva.

World Health Organization (2001) *Complementary Feeding: Report of the Global Consultation convened jointly by the Department of Child and Adolescent Health and Development and the Department of Nutrition for Health and Development*. WHO, Geneva.

Wright, C. M., Parkinson, K. N. and Drewett, R. F. (2004) Why are babies weaned early? Data from a prospective population based cohort study. *Archives of Disease in Childhood*, **89**, 813–16.

Young, B. and Drewett, R. (2000) Eating behaviour and its variability in 1-year-old children. *Appetite*, **35**, 171–7.

CHAPTER 10

Nutrition and nurture: dualisms and synergies

Fiona Dykes and Victoria Hall Moran

Introduction

This book has engaged with the synergistic and long-term effects of nutrition, and of the nature of the relationship that is engendered between mother and infant as a consequence of various types of nutritive and nurturing behaviour in the childbearing and infant period in general. It represents a positive move to disrupt disciplinary boundaries that have, in many cases, persisted with regard to maternal and infant nutrition, eating and feeding. In this chapter we summarise the ways in which the chapters have illustrated the synergies between perspectives to produce new ways of seeing within the field of maternal and infant nutrition and nurture. Before focusing upon the synergies it is useful to examine the ways in which some of the different perspectives have emerged.

Biomedical perspective

The traditional biomedical perspective on nutrition stemmed from an era commonly referred to as the 'Enlightenment'. This was a major turning point in human history – a 'self-proclaimed Age of Reason' that began in England in the 17th century and subsequently spread to Western Europe during the 18th century (Crotty, 1998, p. 18). The 'Enlightenment' was the era during which rationalistic science reached a supreme authoritative status, bringing with it an epistemology of objectivism. Objectivism was underpinned by reductionism and dualism. Reductionism refers to the philosophic view that complex phenomena are nothing more than the sum of their parts (Engel, 1977; Marston and Forster, 1999). Dualism, a concept developed by Descartes, a French philosopher, relates to the view that the mind is a separate entity from the body, thus paving the way for the objectification of the latter (Engel, 1977; Davis-Floyd, 1994). The notion of dualism extended to a distinction between the human mind and external objects and thus allowed the study of the universe as separate from any consideration of the mind (Crotty, 1998). The essence of objectivism, therefore, centred upon the view that 'things exist as meaningful entities independently of consciousness and experience, that they have truth and meaning residing in them as objects' (Crotty, 1998, p. 5). This objectivist epistemology enabled the viewing of the world through a positivistic lens so that it could be explained, described, codified and quantified in order to reveal its absolute laws and principles (Doyal and Pennell, 1979; Crotty, 1998; Marston and Forster, 1999).

The scientific assumptions of the Enlightenment came to powerfully influence the practice of biomedicine. The combination of reductionism and dualism when applied to medicine enabled the 'patient' to be conceptually separated into mind, body and soul, with the body seen, like a machine, as something which could be taken apart, examined and repaired (Davis-Floyd, 1994). The traditional biomedical perspective upon food and health focused upon the biochemical constituents of food and their transfer, absorption and influence upon body physiology and pathology. However, this approach, while yielding important insights, did not take into account the socio-cultural influences upon eating activities and behaviours.

Social constructionist perspective

As the 20th century progressed, a sociologically-based critique of the objectivist notions underpinning ways of seeing health developed. Kuhn (1970), for example, highlighted that for a given community or discipline there develops a specific way of 'seeing' the world by a specific discipline or community. He referred to this way of 'seeing' as a paradigm with a person's paradigmatic stance influencing what he or she attends to and what is ignored or taken for granted. The sociological critique enabled the legitimisation of other ways of seeing and understanding the world. Berger and Luckmann (1966), for example, are renowned for social constructionism – the ways in which meaning is constructed by people as they engage with the world. Culture and enculturation are important concepts in constructionism. These concepts are defined by Helman (1994, pp. 2–3), who states that:

Culture is a set of guidelines (both explicit and implicit) which individuals inherit as particular members of a society, and which tells them how to *view* the world, how to experience it emotionally, and how to *behave* in it in relation to other people, to supernatural forces or gods, and to the natural environment. It also provides them with a way of transmitting these guidelines to the next generation – by the use of symbols, language, art and ritual. To some extent, culture can be seen as an inherited 'lens' through which the individual perceives and understands the world that he inhabits, and learns how to live within it. Growing up within any society is a form of *enculturation*, whereby the individual slowly acquires the cultural lens of that society. Without such a shared perception of the world, both the cohesion and continuity of any human group would be impossible.

Thus, as Spradley (1980) argues, culture should be viewed as a cognitive map acting as a reference and guide. It should not be seen as constraining the person to adopt only one course of action, but culture does create in the person a taken for granted view of reality and in this sense individuals are *somewhat* culture bound (Spradley, 1980). In this way humans are able to exercise agency within their cultural parameters. Thus, from a constructionist perspective, eating and feeding practices within a given culture represent the ways in which people negotiate and incorporate cultural norms with their embodied experiences, personal circumstances and social support systems.

Political economy of health perspective

It is now clearly recognised that no aspect of food, eating and nutrition can be separated from its political context. The political economy of health perspective provides one way of incorporating this dimension, with its focus upon the relationships between capitalist modes of production, health, disease and health care practices (Frankenburg, 1980; Doyal and Pennell, 1981; Navarro, 1992; Gray, 1993; Illich, 1995). As Frankenberg (1980, p. 206) argues:

> The international political economy of medicine, dominated by great powers, themselves dominated by monopoly capitalist enterprise [have] an abiding interest in peddling pills and selling massive capital equipment, as well as changing the nutritional habits of the world's people's in order to sell their products.

Western capitalist modes of production appear to have both contributed towards, and indeed failed to alleviate, the high levels of morbidity and early mortality still borne by the mass of the population in socio-economically disadvantaged communities across the world (Doyal and Pennell, 1981; Gray, 1993). This is illustrated when therapies and medicines that could potentially make a dramatic difference are withheld because they are non-profit-making or they are costed at prices that place them out of reach of large sections of the population. The controversies regarding price-fixing of drugs to combat AIDS provide a recent example. The development, proliferation and multinational sales of breast milk substitutes constitute another powerful example of the ways in which capitalism and health are in tension (Dykes, 2002).

Creating synergies

The chapters in this book have offered a way forward by synergistically incorporating biochemical considerations with socio-cultural and political contexts and constraints. For example, Fiona Dykes (Chapter 1) and Victoria Hall Moran (Chapter 2) explored infant and maternal nutrition *in utero*, during infancy and during pregnancy and illustrated that the socio-economic and cultural conditions play a huge role in determining infant, child and adult diet. The social environment not only influences behaviour but also appears to act via sociobiological pathways to affect physiology (Tarlov, 1996; Braveman and Tarimo, 2002).

Darren Hart (Chapter 3), while focusing upon evidence related to eating in labour, also highlighted the issues related to cultures of practice and how they impact upon policies and actions of staff with regard to this issue. Sally Inch (Chapter 4) discussed the crucial components of breast milk for optimal infant feeding and then explored the ways in which breastfeeding has been fundamentally undermined by the multinational marketing of breast milk substitutes. These practices have contributed to a marginalisation of breastfeeding so that, in many communities across the world, it is no longer seen or experienced as the norm. Again the synergies between political activity and infant nutrition and nurture become alarmingly evident.

Magda Sachs (Chapter 5) highlighted the enormous challenges and controversies for women and health practitioners with regard to HIV and infant feeding. Nowhere is the complex interaction between physiology, pathology, culture and politics more evident than in relation to this issue. The resulting global, national and personal dilemmas with regard to HIV and infant feeding are indeed overwhelming. In Chapter 6, Sue Battersby highlighted the profound influence of the enculturation process upon midwives with regard to their attitudes to infant feeding. Further, she illuminated some of the reasons why providing health practitioners with evidence-based information on infant feeding is not enough to change practices, as personal and vicarious experience and embodied knowledge need to be reflected upon and incorporated. It becomes clear that developing synergies between ways of seeing and knowing becomes crucial.

Alison Spiro (Chapter 7) provided a striking illustration of the ways in which, for women from Gujarat, breastfeeding is described and experienced as highly relational and spoken about in terms of 'flow'. This contrasts with experiences in some western industrialised cultures in which breastfeeding is perceived as mechanistic and associated with production and supply. This illustrates the contrast between more dualistic notions of breastfeeding within a western industrialised setting and more synergistic ways of understanding and experiencing the embodied activity within a non-Western community.

Mavis Kirkham and colleagues (Chapter 8) provided an illuminating account of social capital and community capacity building with regard to infant feeding through development of a breastfeeding peer support programme. This places infant feeding firmly within a community-based model. However, within the training programme for peer supporters, the importance of integrating synergistically the biological, social and personal aspects of breastfeeding is strongly emphasised. Gill Rapley (Chapter 9) illustrated the ways in which doctrine and cultural beliefs have led to ways of 'managing' weaning and ignoring the developmental readiness and needs of babies. She highlighted that the best way in which to meet the WHO recommendations for exclusive breastfeeding to six months may be to enable the baby to go at his or her own pace in taking solid foods.

Integrating perspectives

Biomedical knowledge about maternal and infant nutrition generated through scientific methods is important. However, such knowledge should not be considered as more legitimate than women's embodied knowledge simply because it constitutes 'evidence-based' enquiry. Insights from biomedicine have a place, *but* their position must be alongside the knowledges generated through the experiences and accounts of women.

Understanding and reflecting upon the complexity of human situations, the indeterminacy of interpersonal issues and the individuality of people and situations (Schon, 1983) with regard to maternal and infant nutrition is crucial for practitioners. Reflection occurs at several levels (Freire, 1972; Schon, 1983; Peters and Lankshear, 1994; Brechin, 2000; Clarke and Wilcockson, 2001, 2002): upon personal and vicarious experiences; upon experiences in the practice settings and their links to theoretical knowledge; and upon the broader

socio-cultural issues. Firstly, it is crucial to reflect upon our own personal experiences, and this requires an acknowledgement that we are inevitably influenced by socio-cultural background, personal experiences, attitudes, values and
beliefs. Secondly, reflection upon our encounters and involvement in practice
settings is also essential to enable integration between formal theoretical knowledge and practice. This ensures that we do not simply partition knowledge and
remain unaware of the longer term and broader implications of our actions.
Thirdly, reflection should also relate to the broader socio-cultural and political issues that impinge upon self, others and the organisational culture (Freire,
1972; Peters and Lankshear, 1994; Brechin, 2000; Clarke and Wilcockson,
2001, 2002; Dykes, 2005). Such critical engagement with broader socio-political issues thus allows for collective understandings of situations and enables us
to move forwards in changing practices.

Political activity

The most powerful way in which improvements in maternal and infant nutrition may be made is through political activity and subsequent social policy.
As stated in Chapter 1, social inequality, both absolute and relative, within a
community or country, appears to be a key trigger to lowered health and well-
being. As Spencer (2003) argues, we need a long-term strategy to reduce levels
of poverty in children in order to optimise physical growth, cognitive development and psychosocial well-being. A redistribution of wealth to create a more
egalitarian situation in western countries requires enormous commitment from
governments to include a radical review and reconfiguration of the role of multinational corporations in determining the economic climate of a given country.
It would also necessitate implementation of comprehensive, co-ordinated community-based programmes to reduce social inequalities and social exclusion. As
health practitioners we must become more strategically engaged and influence
government agendas to bring about the fundamental changes required to ensure
that every woman across the globe has the resources to feed herself and her
infant in a way that optimises the health outcomes for both of them.

Conclusion

Understandings of maternal and infant nutrition need to take account of the
embodied, emotional and social nature of eating and feeding, the ways in which

women negotiate these in a range of cultural contexts *and* the macro-political influences upon women in relation to their dietary and infant feeding practices. When linked with biochemical nutritional considerations, a socio-biological synthesis of perspectives develops that has both informed and indeed further emerged from this book.

References

Berger, P. L. and Luckmann, T. (1966) *The Social Construction of Reality: A Treatise in the Sociology of Knowledge*. Penguin, Harmondsworth.

Braveman, P. and Tarimo, E. (2002) Social inequalities in health within countries: not only an issue for affluent nations. *Social Science & Medicine*, 54: 1621–35.

Brechin, A. (2000) Introducing critical practice. In: *Critical Practice in Health & Social Care* (eds. A. Brechin, H. Brown and M. A. Eby), pp. 25–47. Sage Publications, London.

Clarke, C. L. and Wilcockson, J. (2001) Professional and organizational learning: analysing the relationship with the development of practice. *Journal of Advanced Nursing*, **34**(2), 264–72.

Clarke, C. L. and Wilcockson, J. (2002) Seeing need and developing care: exploring knowledge for and from practice. *International Journal of Nursing Studies*, **39**, 397–406.

Crotty, M. (1998) *The Foundations of Social Research. Meaning and Perspective in the Research Process*. Sage Publications, London.

Davis-Floyd, R. (1994) The technocratic body: American childbirth as cultural expression. *Social Science and Medicine*, **38**(8), 1125–40.

Doyal, L. and Pennell, I. (1981) *The Political Economy of Health*. Pluto Press, London.

Dykes, F. (2002) Western marketing and medicine – construction of an insufficient milk syndrome. *Health Care for Women International*, **23**(5), 492–502.

Dykes, F. (2005) 'Supply' and 'Demand': breastfeeding as labour. *Social Science & Medicine*, **60**(10), 2283–93

Engel, G. L. (1977) The need for a new medical model: a challenge for biomedicine. *Science*, **196**, 129–36. (Accessed as a full reproduction in *Holistic Medicine* (1989) **4**, 37–53.)

Frankenberg, R. (1980) Medical anthropology and development: a theoretical perspective. *Social Science and Medicine*, **14B**, 197–207.

Freire, P. (1972) *Pedagogy of the Oppressed*. Penguin, Harmondsworth.

Gray, A. (ed.) (1993) *World Health and Disease*. Open University Press, Buckingham.

Helman, C. (1994) *Culture, Health and Illness* 3rd edn. Butterworth-Heinemann, Oxford.

Illich, I. (1995) *Limits to Medicine. Medical Nemesis: The Expropriation of Health*, 2nd edn. Marion Boyars Publishers, London.

Kuhn, T. S. (1970) *The Structure of Scientific Revolutions*. Chicago University Press, Chicago.

Peters, M. and Lankshear, C. (1994) Education and hermeneutics: A Freirean interpretation. In: *Politics of Liberation. Paths from Freire* (eds. P. L. McLaren and C. Lankshear), pp. 173–92. Routledge, London.

Marston, P. and Forster, R. (1999) *Reason, Science and Faith*. Monarch Books, East Sussex.

Navarro, V. (1992) Has socialism failed? An analysis of health indicators under socialism. *International Journal of Health Services*, **22** (4), 583–601.

Schon, D. (1983) *The Reflective Practitioner: How Professionals Think in Action*. Basic Books, New York.

Spradley, J. P. (1980) *Participant Observation*. Holt, Rinehart & Winston, USA.

Spencer, N. (2003) *Weighing the Evidence: How is Birthweight Determined?* Radcliffe Medical Press, Oxon.

Tarlov, A. R. (1996) Social determinants of health: the sociobiological translation. In: *Health and Social Organization, Towards a Health Policy for the 21st Century* (eds. D. Blane, E. Brunner and R. Wilkinson), pp. 71–93. Routledge, London.

Index